Religion and Belief Systems in WORLD HISTORY

宝库山精选：世界历史中的宗教和信仰体系

BERKSHIRE Essentials

Religion and Belief Systems in WORLD HISTORY

宝库山精选：世界历史中的宗教和信仰体系

William H. McNeill

Jerry H. Bentley, David Christian,
Ralph C. Croizier, J. R. McNeill,
Heidi Roupp, and Judith P. Zinsser

Editors

Brett Bowden

Associate Editor

Copyright © 2012 by Berkshire Publishing Group LLC

All rights reserved. Permission to copy articles for internal or personal noncommercial use is hereby granted on the condition that appropriate fees are paid to the Copyright Clearance Center, 222 Rosewood Drive, Danvers, MA 01923, U.S.A., telephone +1 978 750 8400, fax +1 978 646 8600, email info@copyright.com. Teachers at institutions that own a print copy or license a digital edition of *Religion and Belief Systems in World History* may use at no charge up to ten copies of no more than two articles (per course or program).

Digital editions
Religion and Belief Systems in World History is available through most major e-book and database services (please check with them for pricing).

For information, contact:
Berkshire Publishing Group LLC
122 Castle Street
Great Barrington, Massachusetts 01230
www.berkshirepublishing.com
Printed in the United States of America

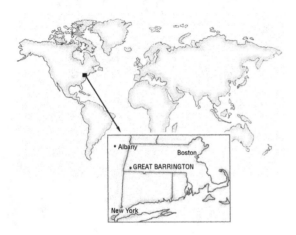

Library of Congress Cataloging-in-Publication Data

Religion and belief systems in world history / William H. McNeill ... [et al.], editors ; Brett Bowden, associate editor.
  p. cm. — (The Berkshire essentials series)
Selections from the Berkshire encyclopedia of world history, 2nd ed.
Includes bibliographical references and index.
ISBN 978-1-933782-93-5 (pbk. : alk. paper) — ISBN 978-1-61472-997-6 (e-book)
 1. Religions—Encyclopedias. I. McNeill, William Hardy, 1917- II. Bowden, Brett, 1968- III. Berkshire encyclopedia of world history.
BL80.3.R427 2012
200.3—dc23
                    2011037247

Top left: Sculptural representation of the Buddha, from the Gandharan region of northern Pakistan (first century CE). Musée Guimet, Paris.

Second row left: A photo of an icon of Saints Boris and Gleb. These two princes (sons of Price Vladimir) are known as the Passion-Bearers who accepted death rather than right in self-defense. A 13th century icon of the Moscow School. Courtesy of Allyne Smith.

Bottom left: Small shrines to commemorate the presence of a kami are symbolized by a torii, a gate-like structure composed of two support beams and a crossbeam. Photo by Mark McNally.

Center top: Independence Mural at Instituto Geografico Militar, Quito, Ecuador March 2000. Courtesy of Steve Donaldson.

Center: Painting of Mahavira (dated to 1900), whose teachings became the foundation of Jainism. Photo of painting by Jules Jain.

Center bottom: A carved stone guard at the Temple of Confucius at Qufu in Shandong Province, the legendary birthplace of Confucius. Photo by Joan Lebold Cohen.

Top right: Temple Mount, Dome of the Rock, Jerusalem, Israel November 1996. Photo by Steve Donaldson.

Second row right: Rock relief at Taq-e Bostan, Iran, depicting the Sasanian king of kings Ardeshir II (ruled 379-383 CE) standing (center) over the body of a slain foe, receiving a diadem of sovereignty from the Zoroastrian god Ahura Mazda (right) while the divinity Mithra (left) with sword in hand protects the king. Photograph courtesy of R. N. Frye

Bottom right: The central part of a floor mosaic (c. 200–250 CE) from a Roman villa depicts Aion, god of eternity, and the Earth mother Tellus (the Roman equivalent of Gaia).

THE **BERKSHIRE** *Essentials* SERIES

From the *Berkshire Encyclopedia of World History, 2nd Edition*:

- *Africa in World History*
- *Art in World History*
- *Big History*
- *Religion and Belief Systems in World History*
- *War, Diplomacy, and Peacemaking*
- *Women's and Gender History*
- *World Environmental History*

Distilled for
the classroom
from Berkshire's
award-winning
encyclopedias

BERKSHIRE ESSENTIALS from the *Berkshire Encyclopedia of China* and the *Berkshire Encyclopedia of Sustainability* also available.

Contents

About this "Berkshire Essentials" Volume IX

Introduction: Religion and Belief Systems in World History 1
Abraham 10
African American and Caribbean Religions 13
African Religions 21
Animism 26
Augustine, Saint 28
Baháʼí 31
Buddha 35
Buddhism 37
Chinese Traditional Religion 46
Christian Orthodoxy 53
Confucianism 60
Creation Myths 65
Daoism 71
Ecumenicism 78
Hinduism 82
Islam 90
Jainism 98
Jesus 101
Judaism 104

VIII · RELIGION AND BELIEF SYSTEMS IN WORLD HISTORY

Laozi 112
Latter-Day Saints 115
Law, Sacred... 119
Mahavira 122
Manichaeism... 124
Millennialism.. 127
Missionaries.. 132
Moses 142
Muhammad 145
Mysticism 148
Native American Religions 152
Paul, Saint 159
Pentecostalism 161
Pilgrimage 166
Protestantism.. 171
Religion and Government 178
Religion and War... 182
Religious Freedom 189
Religious Fundamentalism 195
Religious Syncretism 200
Roman Catholicism 205
Shamanism.. 213
Shinto.. 219
Sikhism.. 225
Thomas Aquinas, Saint 228
Zionism 231
Zoroastrianism 234

Index.. 237
Author Credits 248
Other Berkshire Titles 252

About this "Berkshire Essentials" Volume

For more than a decade Berkshire Publishing has collaborated with an extraordinary, worldwide network of scholars and editors to produce award-winning academic resources on popular, cutting-edge subjects for a wide-ranging audience. With our Berkshire Essentials series—inspired by requests from teachers, curriculum planners, and professors who praise the encyclopedic approach we often use, but who still crave single volumes for course use—we at Berkshire have designed a series that "concentrates" our content.

Each Essentials series draws from Berkshire publications on a wide-ranging topic—world history, Chinese studies, and environmental sustainability, for starters—to provide theme-related volumes that can be purchased alone, in any combination, or as a set. (For example, individual volumes of the Berkshire Essentials in World History series take a global approach to Africa; art; big history; war, diplomacy, and peacemaking; women's and gender studies; world environmental history; and, of course, with this volume, religion and belief systems.) Teachers will find the insightful, illustrated articles indispensable for jump-starting classroom discussion or independent study. Individuals—whether students, professionals, or general readers—will find the articles invaluable when exploring a line of research or an abiding interest.

The Oxford English Dictionary tells us that the word *religion* comes either from Middle English (as applied to "life under monastic vows") or from Old French and Latin (as a noun meaning "obligation, bond, or reverence," which is, perhaps, related to the Latin *religare*, "to bind"). Nevertheless, the concept behind the word and its significance is timeless: the human response to or belief in some supernatural or

Traditional Chinese households maintained a domestic altar for making offerings to deceased ancestors.

suprahuman force has given spiritual sustenance to individuals and communities for far longer than the earliest existing sacred texts would indicate. In fact, archaeologists have found gravesites in Europe and parts of Asia dating to over 70,000 years ago that suggest evidence of rituals performed by the living for the dead, in the care and concern for their well-being in the afterlife. So much evidence, Martin E. Marty writes in the introduction to this volume, "that many neuroscientists believe humans are 'hard-wired' to seek meaning through rites and ceremonies, myth and symbols, ideas and behaviors." All of these elements, singly or in some combination, contribute to what people today experience as religion—in the

IX

A Sikh family crosses a bridge over the Thames. Founded in India, Sikhism is now a world religion, with Sikhs living in many nations.

myriad languages they speak and by the names they chose to call it.

A number of articles in Berkshire Essentials' *Religions and Belief Systems* demonstrate the often-dual role of religion throughout history—as a private experience with an often-public presence, as both a catalyst for war and an agent of peace, as a supporter of empires and a consolation for victims. Others focus on how concepts and movements were perceived over time. Derek H. Davis provides an overview of how religious freedom, nonexistent during the ages when governments assumed a common religion necessary for social stability, came to be backed by international law and the constitutions of most states—even though religious freedom is still nonexistent in some parts of the world. In "Religious Fundamentalism" Martin Marty examines how the term *fundamentalism*, first applied in the early 1920s to Protestant sects devoted to biblical literalism, is today used contentiously (and often reflexively) to label different religious movements and sects around the globe—many of which have become political parties, such as the Muslim Brotherhood in Egypt, or militant groups, such as the Khomenei faction during the Iran revolution of 1979. With "Religious Syncretism" Steven D. Glazier explains why the also-contested term *syncretism*—the process of reconciling disparate beliefs and practices—can be seen as positive by those who seek underlying unity in the multiple and diverse facets of religion, as negative by those who find such "blending" as inauthentic or impure, and as universal inasmuch as syncretism takes place in many aspects of society and culture, through language, literature, music, the arts, technologies, economies, politics, and kinship.

From Abraham and his foundational role in the scriptures of three major monotheistic religions (Judaism, Christianity, and Islam), to Zoroaster (Zarathushtra), the prophet who reformed the ancient religion of the Indo-Iranian people by characterizing its two groups of deities as beneficent (the Ahuras) and maleficent (the Daivas)—and with nearly fifty articles (on millennialism, missionaries, Moses, and mysticism, for example) in between—this volume provides a solid grounding in the study of religions and belief systems worldwide.

We at Berkshire appreciate comments and questions from our readers. Please send suggestions for other Essential volumes you'd like to see in this world history–themed series. And do check our website for news about our other Essential volumes on China and environmental sustainability.

Karen Christensen
CEO and Publisher
Great Barrington, Massachusetts

Introduction: Religion and Belief Systems in World History

Religions are characteristically central in accountings of world history. While many people consider religion private, many are affected by its public presence. Religion supports empires and consoles victims. It inspires war and motivates warriors, but it can also be an agency of peace and the working of justice. The religious may be privileged as supporters of the state or hounded when they dissent.

Moderns have given the name "religion" to the many efforts through which people respond to what they experience or believe in as supernatural or suprahuman forces or beings. Exceptions in the form of purely humanistic religions are few. Most people in most cultures throughout most of history have given evidence that tending to religious matters is basic in their existence, and the energy they give to these has produced artifacts—temples and the like—and events, phenomena with which historians have consistently reckoned.

While religion may be what many modern people have come to call it—a private affair—it always has had a public presence. Individuals may be religious, but most of them form communities and these may collide with each other, attempt to exert power, and often turn out to be useful to civil authorities just as the religious communities find civil authorities useful.

Prehistory and Preliterate Cultures

Prehistoric and preliterate people could not and did not leave behind sacred texts of the sort that inform most study of religion throughout history. Yet archaeology reveals numberless grave sites whose contents show that the living engaged in ceremonies and left articles suggesting their care for the dead and their concern for their afterlife existence. Some of this evidence in Europe and parts of Asia dates back over 70,000 years. Lacking texts, scholars have to deduce the meanings of the relics, but these demonstrate that religion is a constant and profound dimension of human life, so much so that many neuroscientists hypothesize that humans are "hard-wired" to seek meaning through rites and ceremonies, myths and symbols, ideas and behaviors, that they associate with the word religion.

One of the most common and, to those who uncover the altars and bones, most unsettling set of practices, has to do with human sacrifice. Castes of people, usually priests, were assigned the task of pleasing deities, for example the gods of fertility or weather or war, by offering their fellows or their captives on altars. Especially when such killing occurred in northern climates, as in Scandinavia, some corpses were so well preserved that scholars can deduce much about the way of life of the sacrificed and the sacrificers. While human sacrifice has virtually disappeared in modern times, it was long a factor in societies. In Aztec cultures in South America just before Europeans arrived and conquered them, thousands of their people had been ceremoniously sacrificed. In many ancient religions animals were substituted for people by those who wanted to win the favor of their deities. Bloodless sacrificial offerings, for example, gifts of money, remain favored ways of being religious into our own times.

Not only beginnings and ends, birth and death, fertility and burial rites occupied the religious. From

The Dome of the Rock in Jerusalem is located on a site sacred to Islam (as the spot where Muhammad ascended to heaven), Judaism (as the place Abraham prepared to sacrifice his son Isaac), and Christianity (as the place during the Byzantine Empire where Constantine's mother had a small church built).

observing how great stones were placed, as in Stonehenge in England or throughout Maya and Aztec cultures in Central and South America, scholars deduce that people observed the heavens for signs of divine will. They paid attention to the seasons of the year and the movement of sun and moon and stars, calculating some of their bearings from these. Many ancients worshiped sun-gods or moon-gods. Such observance has lived on in moderated ways within literate cultures, where Judaism, Christianity, and Islam, among others, thrived. Their sacred texts prescribed certain ceremonial days in the light of the phases of the moon.

Just as they looked up to the heavens, these religious folks also looked backward and ahead, as their texts reveal: they wanted to account for how the world came into being and what its future, often a future ending in destruction, would be. Their stylized stories of beginnings (myths of origin) provided guidance for daily living. Their altars and relics also signal that they were concerned about weather and the gods or forces that control it, since it had so much impact on their survival and possible prosperity. They danced, prayed, and made offerings to deities associated with agriculture and hunting.

The Rise of "World Religions"

Knowledge of what religion meant in ancient lives becomes more sure when historians can deal with texts in which priests and scribes recorded their presumed transactions with the divine or in which they prescribed ceremonies. Many of those have left rich heritages where they appeared around the Mediterranean Sea and especially in the Middle East. In the fifth century BCE Athens was a bustling city, whose architects produced temples such as the Parthenon, where the statue of Athena by Phidias dominated. Readers of the literature of ancient Greece become familiar with large companies of gods, whom citizens always tried to understand, often to pacify, and sometimes to emulate.

While a thousand years before that, around 1500 BCE, Chinese peoples gave signs that they were preoccupied with the sacred, it was with the birth of Confucius in 551 BCE that texts appeared which provide access to the spiritual world of China. Whether Confucius should be thought of as a religious founder or a philosopher is a point of debate, but students of Chinese religion characteristically study his writings. These became influential in China and have remained so thousands of years later. He taught followers to be humble and generous, respectful of their ancestors, and devoted to civic life.

Even before Confucius died, China saw the emergence of another philosophy, a this-worldly faith, Daoism, which paid little attention to a life to come, as most other religions have done. Attractive especially to poor farmers, to peasant classes, it taught reverence for the natural world, the landscape, in the face of which people were to learn to be serene but never weak.

More vital and influential through the centuries have been religions that emerged in the subcontinent of Asia, especially in India. Less interested in science and invention than the Chinese, Indians can be said to have specialized in responses to the sacred. Settlers of Indo-European background planted the roots of Hinduism, a faith that called for respect, even awe, for priests and holy people called Brahmans. It is hard to grasp an essence of Hinduism, so diverse are the shoots and so manifold are the sacred writings that grew from those roots. It called for worship of many gods including one above the others, Brahma. A core belief of Hindus was that all living beings possessed an inner soul, one that outlasted the body but would then transmigrate to a new body. That belief led to regard for cows as sacred. But Hinduism is not only a set of beliefs: it stipulates complex practices, many of them related to the belief in transmigration.

Just as Daoism coexisted with and challenged Confucianism in China, so Buddhism emerged to rival Hinduism in India. In the case of this philosophy and religion it is possible to point to a single founder, Siddhartha Gautama (566–486 BCE), son of a prince from Nepal. Sheltered in childhood and assured a life of leisure and reasonable luxury, he left behind the way of life these permitted and rode off seeking enlightenment and salvation. Indeed, he did experience such, and became known as "The Enlightened," the Buddha. His journey led him and his followers to self-denial and the pursuit of sanctity. While Hinduism fostered a caste system in which the poor were destined to remain poor and the rich to enjoy riches, Buddhism was more spiritually democratic. But the wealthy were also attracted, and many of them contributed to the building of monasteries that were attractive to the most rigorous followers. Buddhist monasteries sprang up in city after city along the holy Ganges River.

Buddhism entered world history and was assured of a future when Asoka, a king of India, gained power and prestige often by the use of the sword but also with building and humanitarian concerns, around 265 BCE. Through his spreading empire Buddhism prospered, while Asoka built hospitals and educational centers to give it practical effect among the people he dominated. Hinduism, after early prosperity, languished but was periodically revivified. Buddhists meanwhile spread their self-disciplined ways of life into China and Japan, eventual and virtual home bases for one of what came to be called "the world religions."

Developments Called "Greco-Roman," Jewish, and Christian

Greek and Roman cultures survived in the centuries of great cultural productivity. Philosopher Karl Jaspers spoke of the centuries between 700 BCE to 200 BCE as an "axial period," a time of religious formation and creativity, and these dates are commonly accepted. This is often marked in Greek drama and Roman poetry as well as in the records of statecraft. While honor was shown the old Greek gods in the course of developments associated with Rome in the fourth century BCE, the Roman rulers increasingly came to be treated as divine agents worthy of worship. They, in turn, invoked some of the gods, offering them sacrifice of animals. Culturally open to other influences, they also welcomed Isis, the mother-god from Egypt, who ruled the universe, and Mithras, the sun-god from Persia. Much more complex was the arrival of Jews from Palestine and, from within their Judaism, a new sect that the Romans soon learned to name "Christian."

The Roman Republic came to be the Roman Empire in the centuries in which Judaism and Christianity came to be a presence. Together these two also became "world religions," dynamic inheritances from a five-hundred-year period in world history that saw special creativity and devotion. Webbed at the beginning and conflicted by the end of the first century CE, Judaism and Christianity also demand separate treatment by scholars of religion.

Hebrew people—their name refers to their having wandered—told themselves that they were people who came from slavery in Egypt. They had

4 · RELIGION AND BELIEF SYSTEMS IN WORLD HISTORY

To one who has faith, no explanation is necessary. To one without faith, no explanation is possible. • **Saint. Thomas Aquinas (1225–1274)**

seen glories, beginning with their conquest of many small ethnic groups in Palestine, and kingship beginning around 1000 BCE. They revered the memory of charismatic rulers such as David, who captured his capital city of Jerusalem, and then his son Solomon, a temple-builder there. The temple-goers and their priests and scribes recounted and lived by stories of their freedom from slavery, their wandering in a wilderness, and their conquest in Canaan, on the soil of Palestine.

Among their stories, one that inspired much of their moral concern and many of their religious rites was one about Moses, a leader who helped free them from slavery, often with apparently miraculous means. Among these was one that had to do with the deity they called Yahweh, revealed through ten "utterances" that came to be called the Ten Commandments. Followers of these commandments, in northern and southern kingdoms (the latter being called Judea, hence "Jewish"), considered to be the special chosen people of God, forbade the making of divine images. They often revered lesser gods whom they considered anti-Yahweh, but to whom they were frequently attracted. Their attraction quickened criticism by prophets, mainly in the eighth century BCE. These were men in a special calling that directed them to judge errant people and promise divine assurance to the righteous. God held Jews to an especially high standard, and, as they interpreted it, let them prosper or meet disaster, depending upon how well they kept divine laws, especially the Ten Commandments.

While most Jews, freed from captivity in Babylon after 586 BCE, lived in Palestine, they also saw the creation of the Diaspora, a dispersal of peoples, and they were strategically placed in much of what had become the Roman Empire. They built synagogues and worshiped in relative freedom so long as they did not give the rulers any troubles. It was Christianity, one of Judaism's offspring, originally a Jewish sect, that did give trouble and receive it.

This faith centered in a rabbi of Nazareth, Jesus, in the course of time believed by most of his followers to have been born of a virgin, Mary of Nazareth, who had been impregnated by the Holy Spirit, and without

a human father. He was one of many latter-day prophets, such as John the Baptist, who influenced his mission. In the sacred writings called the Gospels, which became part of a "New Testament," this Jesus was portrayed as a wonder-worker whose main task was healing and preaching the imminence of God's kingdom. Exactly what that meant depended upon who was writing about it or interpreting the writings, but it had to do with divine sovereignty exercised in "saving" people from their sins.

With Israel chafing under resented Roman rule, however, many wanted saving from the Romans. The Gospels picture Jesus teaching his disciples that he was to be executed. Meanwhile, a growing number of enemies among religious authorities targeted him for execution. The Gospels portray him as knowing that this form of execution, crucifixion, was to be his destiny, his means of saving people. In such portrayals his death was a sacrifice pleasing to the one he called Father. In the experience and belief of his followers, he was resurrected, raised from the dead, and after making appearances among them for forty days, ascended into heaven, thence to rule.

In the eyes of Greeks and Romans the sect that followed this resurrected one, called Christians, could have survived as one more strange movement. However, while some of them served in the Roman army and paid taxes, they refused to give signals of worship that would show they regarded the ruler, Caesar, as divine. Forty years after Jesus' death, around 70 CE, conflicts between these Christians and other Jews led to schism and growing enmity. More important for survival, however, was the attitude of Roman rulers and other elites, who scorned them and saw them as subversive. Before the year 70, persecution of Christians had begun in Jerusalem, Rome, and outposts along the way this fast-spreading faith was developing.

Divided Christendom and the Rise of Islam

In the course of three centuries as Rome declined, one of its emperors, Constantine, for a mixture of reasons, became a believer and directed his empire on a course that led Christianity by the end of the fourth century CE to be the official religion of Rome. The persecuted now became the persecutors in many instances. Christianity was official, legally established, and was to remain so for a millennium and more. When as the eastern half gained power and influence and Rome divided, the Christian movement also progressively divided, with headquarters in Rome and in Constantinople, Constantine's power became based in what is today's Turkey. The Christian story, including the account of the development of its creeds, doctrines, and practices, henceforth had western and eastern versions, and these split permanently in 1054 CE.

If Christianity sprang out of Judaism, still another world religion, second in size only to Christianity, developed out of and then over against those two. It developed in the small cities of the Arabian Peninsula, where Muhammad was born around 570 CE. Christians and Jews lived there, but old religions considered to be pagan thrived in the interior, where at Mecca, Muhammad's birthplace, people revered and made pilgrimages to a great black meteorite in a shrine they called Kaaba. In that city Muhammad experienced a profound religious revelation and claimed that he was recording the direct utterances of God, Allah, in the sacred book that became the Qur'an. Islam means "submission," and the religion that issued from the prophet Muhammad's revelation and transcription, stressing obedience to Allah, prescribed precise and simple ways in which one pursued Islamic faithfulness.

While the Qur'an included many passages advocating tolerance and peace, the text also included militant themes and the prophet's career included military ventures. The Arabian Peninsula, always dry, in the early years of the sixth century was experiencing drought, and many desperate Arabs joined Muhammad's conquering armies. By 635, Damascus in Syria fell, followed the year later by Jerusalem. The armies invaded Egypt and captured Alexandria in 641. Everywhere the victorious Muslims won converts and built mosques. Many of these moves were threatening and even devastating to Christians, who met defeat in northern Africa and parts of Europe, including Spain. There Muslims developed a sophisticated civilization,

A highly decorated Hindu processional cart in India. Photo by Klaus Klostermaier.

which it shared with Jews and Christians until 1492. Constantinople had fallen in 1453, and for much of the next century the Ottoman Turks spread Islam while assaulting Europe all the way into Hungary. The Christians earlier gained some selective victories as they tried to win back the holy places of Palestine in a series of bloody crusades, but outside Europe itself Islam held its own and became a permanent challenger.

Religious Expansion and Division

Meanwhile, for a thousand years Buddhists were on the move. They came from India into many parts of China, just as they had expanded into Sri Lanka. Mahayana, a new form of Buddhism, developed in northern India. It was a more aggressive and proselytizing faith than the passive Buddhism of earlier years. Shrines and giant statues of Buddha marked the path of their progress. Emperor Shomu in Japan embraced Buddhism in 737. Spared in an epidemic, he credited

This small Catholic chapel in New Mexico, El Santoria de Chimayo, was built by Spanish settlers and now is a pilgrimage site for people seeking cures.

Buddha and erected the Great Buddha at Nara. Like Christianity and Islam, Buddhism spread not only with armies but also through energetic missionaries and proselytizers. Each left in its trail and on its soil great houses of worship and thousands of smaller ones, places for pilgrimage and devotion, libraries for the encouragement of learning and piety—in short: civilizations.

While Western Catholic Christianity that was centered in Rome dominated Europe, with the Muslim present in the West, in Spain, and threatening in the East toward Vienna, and with Jews surviving as an often sequestered minority, one church system set the terms for religious and much of civil life. The Catholic Church was in position to enforce loyalty and persecute dissenters. The head of Catholicism, the pope, could not only field an army but also demand and frequently gain obedience from monarchs whose people would be denied access to heaven if their rulers did not acquiesce to Rome.

It was in that context that all over Europe restless reformers began to question the Catholic system and to subvert it. Their main instrument was the preached and taught Bible, a book of divine revelation that became available in the fifteenth century CE as Johannes Gutenberg's invention of movable type and new presses helped ordinary people gain access to it and its message. In German-speaking Saxony a monk, Martin Luther, after 1517 preached a gospel of liberation and came to storm the official church, which hounded him in turn. Joined by Swiss and other reforming scholars and with support of some princes in the Holy Roman Empire (much of today's Germany) and elsewhere, these questioners undercut the teachings and much of the edifice of Catholicism, though it continued to dominate in most of Europe. But as the new movements called Protestant after 1529 made their way, often in alliance with the state in Germany, England, Scandinavia, the Lowlands, and elsewhere, they helped assure that Europe would be divided religiously. This became doubly evident as Protestants themselves were divided, in no position to be attracted back to Rome as a unit or to be destroyed as one.

When the Western Hemisphere became a subject of knowledge in Europe, Catholic Christianity prevailed in the central and southern Americas. Meanwhile, Dutch, Swedish, and especially English churches had turned Protestant. Merchants and explorers from these countries dominated in that part of America that became the United States, as well as in all of Canada but Quebec.

Renaissance, Enlightenment, and Secularism

While the faith was spreading, Christianity and to a lesser extent all religions in the sixteenth century began to face fresh challenges from propagators of a new approach to the world. Sometimes it was called the Renaissance, because it involved a recovery in the thought world of the glories of Greece and Rome, just

The god of the cannibals will be a cannibal, of the crusaders a crusader, and of the merchants a merchant. • **Ralph Waldo Emerson (1803–1882)**

as it celebrated their arts and sciences. Sometimes the change came in what was called the Enlightenment. This was a movement in northwest Europe, one that celebrated reason, progress, and science, often at the expense of faith.

In Renaissance times some challengers such as Copernicus and Galileo, who presented new views of the physical universe, were harassed, the latter condemned by the pope. Sometimes they won converts from enlightened church leaders who fused rationalist or scientific thought with their faith and church. But in any case, the modern world saw an increase in tension between believers and nonbelievers. The emergent worldview of the latter came to be called "secular," from the Latin word *saeculum.* The implication or even overt claim was that whether or not God existed, one could live out a full life interpreting and changing the world without recourse to God, sacred texts, religious institutions, and the like.

In the nineteenth century, on the soil of secularism, there arose more pitiless and belligerent rivals to Judaism, Christianity, Islam, Buddhism, and Hinduism. Most of the twentieth-century forms ended in -ism: Fascism, Communism, Nazism, Maoism were typical. Many of these took on the trappings of the religions they set out to replace. They called for the sacrifice of millions of lives in war, and they took other lives. They generated myths of leadership and symbols such as the swastika, the hammer and sickle, and the star to rally or subjugate people. They invented ceremonies and rituals. In due course their creations imploded and they waned, while in most cases the religions they had set out to abolish returned and often prevailed in various areas.

Religious Survival and Revival

In the twenty-first century, religion without doubt plays as large a role as it had centuries earlier, despite many predictions that modernity, secularity, and science would sweep it away. The old heartland of Christianity, western Europe, did not experience the growth in the number of religious adherents, though

Christianity in its various forms survived there. Yet nearly 2 billion people around the world were numbered as Christian in 2009, about one billion of them Roman Catholic. Notably prosperous were new Christian movements, especially Pentecostalism, in the southern world, especially sub-Saharan Africa. Meanwhile Islam advanced by population growth, efforts to convert, and development of philosophies and movements attractive to many among the world's poor. Hinduism was also among the advancing religions.

Religion came wearing many guises. In a vast generalization that needs many qualifiers, it could be said that in the world of today, more people are being healed *and* more are being killed in the name of religion than of any other force. Healing here would mean not only physical and personal spiritual healing, but reconciliation, concord, works of justice and mercy. Killing here need not always mean literal murder; it could imply anything negative related to persons, including oppression, repression, suppression. But it can point directly to killing, since armies move against each other, or terrorists act in the name of their gods. Efforts at reconciling the religious do occur, and many people of good will in many cultures initiate and promote movements of interfaith dialogue and common action. These are dwarfed, however, by the massive, convulsive moments of tribe against tribe, people against people, and often nation against nation on the basis of mixed motives, but many of them being religious.

Religion in the Contemporary World

Any assessment of the role of religion has to begin with the place it plays in the life of individuals. This is as true in Jainism, Sikhism, Shinto, Babism, and other significant movements that one will find in atlases and encyclopedias of religion or in open encounters around the world. Historical change came because of Buddha realizing enlightenment, Jesus teaching and dying, monks like Francis of Assisi, Jewish scholars like Maimonides, and reformers like Martin Luther experiencing fire in their soul, acquiring a mission, and then spreading their message and changing the world. But there would be no religious movements were there not also stirrings and hungers in individual souls, and at least partial and often wholly enthusiastic responses to God or the gods.

At the other extreme, religions have to be appraised as mass movements. Millions of Muslims make pilgrimages to Kaaba in Mecca, as Christians went on crusades; they form armies in support of kings who they think rule by divine right, or they stimulate revivals, awakenings, and renewal movements. They can be attached to movements already existing: often nations are ready to war against nations, but they mobilize when they are convinced that God or the good is on their side, and that enemies of God—Satan, if you will, among others—are on the other side.

Religions often undertake revolutionary missions. While their main function may be conservative, urging respect as they often do for the wisdom and achievements of sacred ancestors and offering ballast and sanity in times of disturbance, they may also take it to be their mission to upset the world. Thus the Hebrew prophets of the eighth century BCE, acting on the basis of a covenant they claimed God had with Israel that was now being forgotten, called the people to repent, change their ways, and do works of justice and mercy. They may form resistance movements against modern dictators, or provide conscience for individuals who need courage and divine authorization. So religions make history both in their integrating roles and when they are prophetic and disruptive. Since they deal with invisibles, with soul and spirit and unseen forces, they may not be as easy to track and chronicle as are wars, earthquakes, famines, or catastrophes, but they do as much as such phenomena to alter the human landscape through history and into the present.

Martin E. MARTY
University of Chicago, Emeritus

See also Buddhism; Christian Orthodoxy; Daoism; Hinduism; Islam; Judaism; Roman Catholicism

Further Reading

Armstrong, K. (1993). *A history of God: The 4,000-year quest of Judaism, Christianity, and Islam.* New York: Ballantine.

Bianchi, U. (1975). *The history of religions.* Leiden, The Netherlands: E. J. Brill.

Bishop, P., & Darton, M. (Eds.). (1987). *The encyclopedia of world faiths: An illustrated survey of the world's religions.* New York: Facts on File Publications.

Braun, W., & McCutcheon, R. T. (2000). *Guide to the study of religion.* New York: Cassell.

Brown, P. R. L. (1971). *The world of late antiquity: From Marcus Aurelius to Mohammad.* London: Thames & Hudson.

Burkert, W. (1996). *Creation of the sacred: Tracks of biology in early religion.* Cambridge, MA: Harvard University Press.

Bush, R. C. (Ed.). (1993). *The religious world: Communities of faith.* New York: Macmillan.

Carmody, J. T., & Carmody, D. (1993). *Ways to the center: An introduction to world religions.* Belmont, CA: Wadsworth.

Denny, F. M. (1985). *An introduction to Islam.* New York: Macmillan.

Despland, M., & Vallée, G. (Eds.). (1992). *Religion in history: The word, the idea, the reality.* Waterloo, Ont, Canada: Wilfrid Laurier University Press.

Dowley, T. (1990). *The history of Christianity.* Oxford, U.K.: Lion.

Dumoulin, H. (1963). *A history of Zen Buddhism.* New York: Pantheon.

Durkheim, E. (1965). *The elementary forms of religious life.* New York: Free Press.

Earhart, H. B. (Ed.). (1993). *Religious traditions of the world.* San Francisco: Harper San Francisco.

Eastman, R. (Ed.). (1993). *The ways of religion: An introduction to the major traditions.* New York: Oxford.

Edwards, D. L. (1997). *Christianity: The first two thousand years.* Maryknoll, NY: Orbis.

Eliade, M. (Ed.). (1987). *The encyclopedia of religion.* New York: Macmillan.

Embree, A. T. (Ed.). (1966). *The Hindu tradition.* New York: Modern Library.

Esposito, J. (1998). *Islam: The straight path.* New York: Oxford.

Finegan, J. (1952). *The archaeology of world religions.* Princeton, NJ: Princeton University Press.

Frazer, J. G. (1963). *Golden bough: A study in magic and religion.* London: Macmillan.

Hastings, A. (Ed.). (1998). *A world history of Christianity.* Grand Rapids, MI: Wm. B. Eerdmans.

Hick, J. (1989). *An interpretation of religion: Human responses to the transcendent.* New Haven, CT: Yale University Press.

Hodgson, M. G. S. (1974). *The venture of Islam: Conscience and history in a world civilization.* Chicago: University of Chicago Press.

Holton, D. C. (1965). *The national faith of Japan: A study of modern Shinto.* New York: Dutton.

James, E. O. (1960). *The ancient gods: The history and diffusion of religion in the ancient Near East and the eastern Mediterranean.* London: Weidenfeld & Nicholson.

Jurji, E. G. (Ed.). (1946). *The great religions of the modern world.* Princeton, NJ: Princeton University Press.

Kitagawa, J. M. (1966). *Religion in Japanese history.* New York: Columbia.

Landis, B. Y. (1957). *World religions: A brief guide to the principal beliefs and teachings of the religions of the world, and to the statistics of organized religion.* New York: Dutton.

Rahman, F. (1968). *Islam.* New York: Doubleday Anchor

Ringgren, H. (1973). *Religions of the ancient Near East.* London: S.P.C.K.

Sachar, A. L. (1965). *A history of the Jews.* New York: Knopf.

Smart, N. (Ed.). (1999). *Atlas of the world's religions.* New York: Oxford.

Zaehner, R. C. (1961). *The dawn and twilight of Zoroastrianism.* London: Weidenfeld & Nicholson.

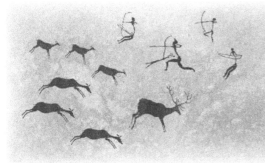

Abraham
(2ND MILLENNIUM BCE)
HEBREW PATRIARCH AND LEADER

Abraham plays a foundational role in the scriptures of the three major monotheistic religions (Judaism, Christianity, and Islam) as the first human to become aware of and act out divine will. Symbolic characteristics specific to each text—obedience in the Hebrew Bible, faithfulness in the New Testament, and submissiveness in the Qur'an—have resulted in conflicting theological positions with the potential to impact secular matters of the world.

According to the Hebrew Bible, New Testament, and Qur'an, as well as their respective interpretive literatures, Abraham is the first person to realize and act out the divine will. Although foundational figures appear in literatures (such as the Gilgamesh epic) that are more ancient than the Hebrew Bible (Old Testament), these have been forgotten to history and only rediscovered through archaeology and the deciphering of dead languages. Abraham first appears in the book of Genesis and serves as the original human to affirm monotheism and to act on that affirmation. The symbolic meaning and significance of Abraham differs among the three great monotheistic religious systems.

Abraham's symbolic importance is first established in Genesis, where in biblical religion he epitomizes obedience to the divine will. He obeys God's commands to leave his ancestral home for a foreign land (Genesis 12), circumcise himself and his male

Guercino, *Abraham Casting Out Hagar and Ishmael* (1657). Oil on canvas. An illustration of Genesis 21, in which Abraham exiles his eldest son. Pinacoteca di Brera, Milan.

10

offspring as part of God's covenant (Genesis 17), exile his eldest son Ishmael (Genesis 21), and finally, in his greatest act of obedience, raise up Isaac, his only remaining child, as a burnt offering (Genesis 22). In return for his obedience, God promises through the divine covenant to provide Abraham with a multitude of offspring and a land in which his progeny will live.

In the Christian Bible (New Testament), Abraham's significance lies in his unwavering faith. In Romans 4, Abraham's merit is associated less with obedience to the divine will than with his faith in God's ultimate grace. It is his faith that provides him the merit for God's having chosen him for the covenant in the first place, and the covenant becomes one of faith rather than obedience. Members of the divine covenant are, therefore, only those who demonstrate faith in the saving power of Christ (Galatians 4:21–5:1).

In the Qur'an, Abraham signifies human submission (the meaning of the word Islam) to God (2:127–128; 37:103). Abraham rebels against idolatry (37:83–99), fulfills God's commands (2:124), raises and purifies the foundations of God's "House" in Mecca (2:125–132), and establishes his offspring there (13:37). Although the ancient Israelites and Christians and Jews predate the emergence of Islamic monotheism, they did not remain true to the divine covenants (5:12–14) because they refused to submit themselves fully to God's absolute unity (9:30). Therefore, "Abraham

This sculpted goat, one of the most famous objects excavated from the royal cemetery in the ancient Sumerian city of Ur, is frequently referred to as the "Ram Caught in a Thicket" because the biblical image (from Gen. 22:13, in which Abraham finds a ram to sacrifice in lieu of his son) so aptly fits. The University Museum, Philadelphia, Pennsylvania.

was not a Jew nor a Christian, but was an early monotheist (hanif), one who submits to God's will (muslim), not an idolater" (3:67). Abraham's importance is so firmly established in the foundation narrative of the Hebrew Bible that he cannot be ignored in subsequent Scriptures. Each Scripture, however, imbues a special quality to the person of Abraham and the meaning of his character.

The nature of Abraham's leadership is also depicted with some variety among the three Scriptures. The Abraham of the Hebrew Bible is a literary character with foibles and weaknesses who struggles to realize his role of lonely monotheist in an uncertain and overwhelmingly idolatrous world. When he fears for his own life, he is willing to risk the wellbeing of Sarah (Genesis 12:12–13; 20:1–11), and he seems on occasion even to question God's promise (Genesis 17:15–18). By the time of the New Testament, however, religious figures have taken on a more consistently righteous character: "When hope seemed hopeless, his faith was such that he became 'father of many nations,' in agreement with the words which had been spoken to him: 'Thus shall your descendants be.'. . . And that is why Abraham's faith was 'counted to him for righteousness.' Those words were written, not for Abraham's sake alone, but for our sake too: it is to be 'counted' in the same way to us who have faith in the God who raised Jesus our Lord from the dead" (Romans 4:18–24, New English Bible). And by the period of the Qur'anic revelation, the biblical prophets (among whom was counted Abraham) were considered virtually free from error. Thus Abraham, as well as David and Solomon and a host of other characters, are free of all doubt and epitomize a somewhat different prophetic image in the Qur'an. The strength of Abraham's intellect proves the true unity of God (Qur'an 6:74–79), and Abraham never doubts the divine will or God's goodness (Qur'an 37:83–113).

While Abraham's role in world history is, therefore, as the mythic founder of monotheism, he symbolizes three different and often conflicting narratives. The competing and polemical narratives transcend the person of Abraham and bring in the other members of his family, including Sarah, Hagar, Isaac, and Ishmael as well as other scriptural characters and institutions. Not only does each narrative serve to justify a theological position, it also serves as a polemic to argue against the theological and institutional positions of the others. This, in turn, has served to justify and fuel ongoing intellectual, economic, political, and military competition and conflict among the three monotheistic religions in history.

Reuven FIRESTONE

Hebrew Union College

See also Judaism; Islam

Further Reading

Delaney, C. (1998). *Abraham on trial: The social legacy of biblical myth.* Princeton, NJ: Princeton University Press.

Feiler, B. (2002). *Abraham: A journey to the heart of three faiths.* New York: HarperCollins Publishers.

Firestone, R. (1990). *Journeys in holy lands: The evolution of the Abraham-Ishmael legends in Islamic exegesis.* Albany, NY: State University of New York Press.

Firestone, R. (1991). Abraham's association with the Meccan sanctuary and the pilgrimage in the pre-Islamic and early Islamic periods. *Le Museon Revue d'Etudes Orientales, 104,* 365–393.

Firestone, R. (2008). Patriarchy, primogeniture, and polemic in the exegetical traditions of Judaism and Islam. In D. Stern & N. Dohrmann (Eds.). *Jewish biblical interpretation in a comparative context.* Philadelphia: University of Pennsylvania Press.

Siker, J. (1991). *Disinheriting the Jews: Abraham in early Christian controversy.* Louisville, KY: Westminster/John Knox.

Van Seters, J. (1975). *Abraham in history and tradition.* New Haven, CT: Yale University Press.

African American and Caribbean Religions

The African slave trade had a huge impact on the transformation and spread of African religions worldwide. Numerous ethnic groups taken from Africa shared similar belief systems, which carried over to the New World. Though beliefs and practices often persevered within groups, forced migration and interaction with Europeans helped develop and change African American and Caribbean religions into what they are today.

African American and Caribbean religions are the products of one of the greatest forced migrations in human history. Historians estimate that between 1650 and 1900 more than 28 million Africans were taken from Central and West Africa as slaves. At least 12 million of these Africans crossed the Atlantic Ocean to be sold in the Caribbean, South America, and North America. While Africans from many parts of Africa were taken into slavery, West African groups were disproportionately represented. Beginning in the early sixteenth century and continuing, officially, until 1845 in Brazil, 1862 in the United States, and 1865 in Cuba, more than 11 million black Africans—Yoruba, Kongo, and other West Africans—were brought to the Americas to work sugar, tobacco, coffee, rice, and cotton plantations.

The African slave trade transformed economies around the world. In Africa, it stimulated the growth of powerful African kingdoms, while in the Islamic world, the African slave trade expanded commerce in the Indian Ocean and the Persian Gulf. In the Americas, it was a key component in the success of plantations established by Europeans. In addition, wealth generated by slavery transformed European economies dramatically, and the African slave trade also transformed African religions and fostered the spread of these religions around the world.

African Religions in the New World

In the Americas, the institution of slavery persisted much longer in some places than others. With the exception of African slaves in Haiti—who initiated a revolution in 1791 and in 1804 established the first black republic in the Americas—Africans became emancipated in the Americas in the following order: Jamaica and Trinidad in 1838; the United States in 1863; Puerto Rico in 1873; Cuba in 1886; and Brazil in 1888. These dates are highly significant. For example, the ethnologist Pierre Verger (1968) contends that the "purest" forms of African religion are to be found in northeastern Brazil primarily because the slave trade to Brazil continued illegally into the twentieth century.

Of the Africans taken to the Americas as slaves, 99 percent came from an area stretching from modern-day Senegal and Mali in the north to Zaire and Angola in the south. This corridor encompasses a number of ethnic groups belonging to the Niger-Kongo language family. A common language base and common cultural traditions facilitated the movement and exchange of people, goods, and ideas along this corridor.

These ethnic groups also shared similar concepts concerning deities, the universe, the social order, and the place of humans within that order. Unifying themes of African systems of belief and worship include the following: the idea that there is one god who created and controls the universe; a focus on blood

13

Religious and other culturally significant articles are on display at an Afro-Caribbean celebration.

sacrifices; and belief in the forces of nature, ancestral spirits, divination, the magical and medicinal powers of herbs, the existence of an afterlife, and the ability of humans to communicate with deities through trance-possession states.

Descendents of Kongo and Yoruba peoples account for about 17 percent of the African population in Jamaica, while the Akan and Kalabari account for, respectively, 25 percent and 30 percent of the Jamaican population. It is estimated that on Cuba and Hispaniola (the island that is home to Haiti and the Dominican Republic) Kongo ethnic groups constitute 40 percent of the African population, while the Yoruba and other related groups shipped from the Bight of Benin make up, respectively, 15 percent and 40 percent of the African populations of Haiti and Cuba. Among the descendants of slaves in the United States, it is estimated that one in four African Americans is of Kongo descent and that one in seven African Americans is of Yoruba descent. It should be noted that few slaves came to the United States directly from Africa. Most had worked plantations elsewhere before being sold in the United States.

These percentages are important for understanding African religions in the New World. Whenever a large number of slaves from a particular place in Africa were sold to a single New World location, they were better able to preserve selected aspects of their religions. Such religious retentions were never exact replicas of African religious practices. They represented a syncretism or blending. One reason for this is that African tribal religions were revealed over time. Only elders possessed extensive religious knowledge. During the early years of slavery, elders were seldom enslaved because older captives rarely survived the rigorous passage to the New World. Most first-generation slaves were under twenty years of age, and few were over thirty. Their knowledge of religious ritual was limited to what they had personally seen and/or experienced. On the other hand, later in the slave trade there were African religious specialists (like Robert Antoine, the nineteenth-century founder of the first Rada compound in Trinidad) who voluntarily migrated to the Caribbean specifically to establish African religious centers in the New World.

The relationship between African religions as practiced in Africa and these same religions in the New World is replete with examples of what Pierre Verger (1968, 31) has termed "flux and reflux." Building on a lifetime of fieldwork and archival research,

Verger documented extensive and continuous contact between religious specialists in Africa and religious organizations in the New World. He painstakingly demonstrated that the slave trade was not only "of" Africans (i.e., as objects of the trade itself), but "by" Africans as well, in the sense that Africans and African Americans were not only laborers but also producers and traders in the plantation system, and thus played an active role—not just a passive one—in the ongoing drama of slavery. But Verger also notes that such "flux and reflux" was rare during the early days of slavery, and most sixteenth- and seventeenth-century slaves were forced to improvise from a limited knowledge of African religious traditions.

On both sides of the Atlantic the meeting of religions among Africans and people of African descent involved more than Christianity and the traditional religions of Africa. It also involved Islam. Working its way from the Sahara long before Christianity began to touch the coast of West Africa, Islam—like Christianity—interacted in complex ways with the traditional religions of Africa. Brought to the Americas by enslaved African Muslims, Islam struggled to survive in an inhospitable, Christian-dominated environment.

African and African American religions have always been at the center of debates concerning the retention of African cultural traits in the New World. Some prominent scholars, most notably the sociologist E. Franklin Frazier (1964), have suggested that New World slavery was so disruptive that few African traits were able to survive. Other scholars, most notably the anthropologist Melville J. Herskovits (1941), have argued effectively for the survival of African traits in New World societies. Herskovits's view has predominated, but the issue remains complex (see Mintz and Price 1992).

The quest for African cultural traits in the New World continues, but with new and refined sensibilities. The question is no longer whether, but how much? As Stuart Hall (1990, 228)—commenting on the *presence africaine* in his native Jamaica—noted,

Africa was, in fact, present everywhere, in the everyday life and customs of the slave quarters, in the language and patois of the plantations, in names and words; often disconnected from their taxonomies, in the secret syntactical structure through which other languages were spoken, in the stories and tales told to children, in religious practices and belief in the spiritual life, the arts, crafts, music and rhythms of slave and post-emancipation society....Africa remained and remains the unspoken, unspeakable "presence" in Caribbean culture. It is "hiding" behind every verbal inflection, every narrative twist of Caribbean cultural life.

African American religious institutions in the United States and the Caribbean provide valuable insight into the inner workings of African American and Caribbean societies and cultures. Moreover, it is appropriate for social scientists to devote their attention to religion because—as C. Eric Lincoln and Lawrence Mamiya so effectively argued (1990, xi)— "religion, seriously considered, is perhaps the best prism to cultural understanding, not as a comparative index, but as a refractive element through which one social cosmos may look meaningfully at another and adjust its presuppositions accordingly."

Two erroneous assumptions have informed past studies of African and African American religions. The first is that the black experience of religion simply replicates white religious experience; the second is that it is totally dissimilar to it. Neither assumption is true because neither takes into account the complex interactions between African-based religions and other world religions. Correctly viewed, African American religious experience cannot be separated from North American religion. It is of one fabric. African religious experience is part and parcel of North American religious experience just as Christianity and Islam are now part and parcel of religious experience on the continent of Africa. Nevertheless, exact genealogies of African and African American religions are difficult to discern.

African Religions in the Caribbean

The best-documented religions—such as Haitian Vodun, Rastafarianism, Cuban Santeria, and the

Spiritual Baptists in Trinidad—serve as prime examples of creativity and change in this dynamic region, which has become a fertile ground for the development of new religious admixtures and syncretism. Almost everyone in the Caribbean is from someplace else, and Caribbean religions have been greatly affected by the presence of Europeans, Africans, and—to a lesser extent—by Asian people as well. A majority of these religions have either an African or Christian base, but Caribbean peoples have modified selected aspects of these traditions, added to them, and made them their own. While much attention has been given to African influences, one cannot completely understand religious developments in the region solely in terms of an African past. The African past is a piece—albeit a large piece—of a more complex whole. Syncretism of Hinduism and Christianity abounds, and one can never underestimate the potential impact of Islam.

Rastafarianism is perhaps the most widely known of Caribbean religions. It is difficult to estimate the exact number of Rastafarians, but the religion's influence vastly exceeds its numbers in Jamaica, elsewhere in the Caribbean, in Europe, Latin America, and the United States. The movement traces its history to a number of indigenous preacher-leaders in the 1930s, most notably Leonard Howell, Joseph Hibbert, Archibald Dunkley, Paul Earlington, Vernal Davis, Ferdinand Ricketts, and Robert Hinds. The influence of Marcus Garvey is also apparent. Each of these leaders—working in isolation from the others—came to the conclusion that Haile Selassie (1892–1975), then enthroned as Ethiopian emperor, was the "Lion of Judah" who would lead all peoples of African heritage back to the promised land of Africa. In the Amharic (Ethiopian language), Ras Tafari means "head ruler" or "emperor." It is one of the many formal titles belonging to Haile Selassie.

While Rastafarianism is by no means a homogeneous movement, Rastafarians share seven basic tenets: (1) black people were exiled to the West Indies because of their moral transgressions; (2) the wicked white man is inferior to black people; (3) the Caribbean situation is hopeless; (4) Ethiopia is heaven; (5) Haile Selassie is the living God; (6) the emperor of Ethiopia will arrange for all expatriated persons of African descent to return to their true homeland; and (7) black people will get revenge by compelling white people to serve them. Among contemporary Rastafarians different subgroups stress different elements of the original creed; for example, the alleged death of Haile Selassie (a large number of Rastafarians believe that Haile Selassie is still alive) has raised significant questions regarding Selassie's place in the movement.

Cuban Santeria combines European and African beliefs and practices. But unlike Vodun, the religion is inspired mainly by one African tradition—that of the Yoruba. In Santeria, the Yoruba influence is marked in music, chants, and foodstuffs, and by sacrifice. During major ceremonies, blood—the food of the deities—flows onto sacred stones belonging to the cult leader. These stones are believed to be the objects through which the gods are fed and in which their power resides. A significant religious development in North America has been the large-scale transfer of Cuban Santeria to urban centers, notably New York, Miami, Los Angeles, and Toronto. It is estimated that there are currently more than 100,000 Santeria devotees in New York City alone.

The Spiritual Baptists are an international religious movement with congregations in Saint Vincent (where some Baptists claim the faith originated), Trinidad and Tobago, Grenada, Guyana, Venezuela, Toronto, Los Angeles, and New York City. Membership is predominantly black, but in recent years congregations in Trinidad have attracted membership among wealthy East Indians and Chinese. A central ritual in the Spiritual Baptist faith is known as the mourning rite. This is an elaborate ceremony involving fasting, lying on a dirt floor, and other deprivations. A major component of the mourning rite is discovering one's true rank within the church hierarchy.

A critical issue in the study of Caribbean religions is the selection of a unit of analysis. Because syncretism plays such a prominent role in the development of religions in the region, it is often difficult to separate indigenous and foreign elements. Since there has been so much outreach, it is often difficult to discover the "true" origin of any single religious group.

Because most of the religions considered here lack a denominational chain of command, one cannot make statements about them as one might about the Roman Catholic Church or Presbyterianism. The most accurate assessments refer to individual congregations and their leaders. To examine movements such as Rastafarianism, Santeria, Vodun, and the Spiritual Baptists as if they were unified denominations on the European and North American model is to present an overly coherent picture of an incredibly fragmented and volatile religious situation.

African Religions in the United States

Scholarly studies on African American religion in the United States are often traced to W. E. B. Du Bois's classic *The Negro Church* (1903), "which constituted the first major book-length study of African American religion in the United States. Employing a wide range of research strategies (historical, survey, interview, and participant-observation) Du Bois explored multiple aspects of African American religious life including church finance, denominational structures, and beliefs. Du Bois characterized the Black Church as the first distinctly African American social institution" (Zuckermann 2000, 109). Subsequent studies of the Black Church were much more limited in scope. As noted, later scholars confined their attentions to the retention of African cultural traits in the New World, and scholars debated the extent to which African American religion draws from African religion in its diverse forms. Few slaves came directly to the United States from Africa, and the presence or absence of so-called Africanisms is more difficult to discern in American religions than in those of the Caribbean. Nevertheless, bits and pieces of African religious concepts and rituals are present in North America—but in greatly modified forms. These concepts and rituals include the call-and-response pattern in preaching, ancestor worship, initiation rites, spirit possession, healing and funeral rituals, magical rituals for obtaining spiritual power, and ecstatic spirit possession accompanied by rhythmic dancing, drumming, and singing.

Prior to the American Revolution, few American slaves were exposed to Christianity. Initially, planters did not promote the conversion of their slaves to Christianity because they feared that it might give slaves ideas about equality and freedom that were incompatible with slavery. Over time, however, slave owners became convinced that a highly selective interpretation of the Gospel message could be used to foster docility in their slaves. During the First Great Awakening (1720–1740), some free blacks and slaves joined Methodist, Baptist, and Presbyterian congregations. The Second Great Awakening (1790–1815), with its numerous camp meetings, attracted more slaves and free blacks to evangelical forms of Protestantism. In the eighteenth century, Methodists emerged as leaders in developing effective religious instruction among the slaves. Following its creation in 1845, the Southern Baptist Convention also undertook aggressive missionary work among slaves. Religion scholar Albert Raboteau (1978) has suggested that the Baptists were especially successful because baptism by immersion resembled West African initiation rites.

Throughout the United States, slaves worshiped in both mixed and segregated congregations. Masters often took house slaves with them to religious services at their own (predominantly white) churches, where blacks were required to sit in separate galleries. In addition to attending church services with their masters, slaves held secret religious meetings in their own quarters, in "praise houses," or away from the plantation in so-called hush arbors.

During the time of slavery, African Americans in the United States never experienced complete religious freedom, but a number of independent African American congregations and religious associations arose. Two early Baptist churches, the Joy Street Baptist Church in Boston (which was established in 1805) and the Abyssinian Baptist Church in New York City (which was established in 1808), were founded in response to discrimination in racially mixed congregations. Black Baptist congregations in the Midwest formed separate regional associations in the 1850s, and the first Baptist association, the National Baptist Convention, U.S.A., was formed in 1895. Black Methodists also established independent congregations and associations during the antebellum period. A group of blacks belonging to the Free African Society, a mutual aid society within St. George's Methodist Episcopal Church in Philadelphia, severed ties with its parent body in 1787 in response to what some black members saw as discriminatory practices. A majority of the dissidents united to form St. Thomas's African Episcopal Church in 1794, under the leadership of Absalom Jones. Richard Allen led a minority contingent to establish the Bethel African Methodist Episcopal Church. The Bethel Church became the founding congregation of the African Methodist Episcopal (AME) Church—the single largest black Methodist denomination. St. John's Street Church in New York City, with its racially mixed congregation, served as an organizational nexus for what became the second major black Methodist denomination, the African Methodist Episcopal Zion (AMEZ) Church.

African American religions became more diverse in the early twentieth century as blacks migrated from the rural South to northern cities. By this time, two National Baptist associations and three black Methodist denominations were already well established as the mainstream churches in black urban communities. Often these denominations cut across class lines. Conversely, black congregations affiliated with white-controlled Episcopalian, Presbyterian, and Congregational churches catered primarily to African American elites. Although mainstream churches attempted to address the social needs of recent migrants, their middle-class orientations often made migrants feel ill at ease. As a consequence, many migrants established and joined storefront churches. In addition, recent migrants became attracted to a wide array of Holiness-Pentecostal Churches, Sanctified Churches, and Spiritual Churches, as well as various Islamic and Jewish sects. Other independent groups, with such names as "Father Divine's Peace Mission" and "Daddy Grace's United House of Prayer for All People" also gained prominence. Today, approximately 90 percent of churchgoing African Americans belong to black-controlled religious bodies. The remaining 10 percent belong to white-controlled religious bodies. African Americans are also to be found within the memberships of liberal Protestant denominations, the Mormon church, the Southern Baptist Convention, and various groups such as the Jehovah's Witnesses, Unity, and the Seventh-day Adventists. There are more than 2 million black Roman Catholics in the United States, many of them recent migrants from the Caribbean.

A number of prominent African American religions in the United States are based on the teachings of Islam. Noble Drew Ali established the first of these, the Moorish Science Temple, in Newark, New Jersey, in the early twentieth century. The main teachings of the Moorish Science Temple were incorporated into the Nation of Islam, founded by Wallace D. Fard during the early 1930s in Detroit. Later, the Nation of Islam came under the leadership of the Honorable Elijah Muhammad. The Nation of Islam grew rapidly, in part due to the militant preaching of Malcolm X during the early 1960s. Rapid growth did not check schismatic tendencies that led to the appearance of numerous splinter groups, including the Ahmadiyya Muslim movement of Chicago, the Hanafis of Washington, D.C., and the Ansaru Allah community of Brooklyn. Following the assassination of Malcolm X and the death of Elijah Muhammad, Elijah's son, Wallace D. Muhammad, transformed the Nation of Islam into the more orthodox group known as the American Muslim Mission. To counter the Mission's shift to orthodox Islam, Louis Farrakhan established a reconstituted Nation of Islam.

Caribbean-based religions are among the fastest-growing religions in the United States. As noted above, Vodun, Rastafarianism, and the Spiritual Baptists have established large congregations in New York, Los Angeles, Miami, and other urban centers, attracting Caribbean migrants and American blacks, as well as a small number of white converts. Cuban Santeria is perhaps the most racially mixed and widespread of these religions.

I shall allow no man to belittle my soul by making me hate him • **Booker T. Washington (1856–1915)**

An African American Aesthetic

African and African American peoples do not conceptualize religion as something separate from the rest of their culture. Art, dance, and literature are understood as integral to the religious experience. This is aptly illustrated by the musician B. B. King's comment that he feels closest to God when he is singing the blues. Spirituals, the blues, gospel, rhythm and blues, bebop, Afro-Latin, and hip-hop are all rooted in West African sacred and secular music traditions. West Africans understand music as a means of propagating wisdom. In the Yoruba tradition, music stirs things up, it incites. West African music and art begin with God, the ideal. For example, Afro-Cuban music continues the African tradition of dispersing and expounding upon fixed and recurring God-generated themes that embody cultural ideals and values.

While African American music is derived from a variety of sources, religion has historically served as one of its major inspirations. As C. Eric Lincoln and Lawrence Mamiya (1990, 347) observe, "In the Black Church singing together is not so much an effort to find, or to establish, a transitory community as it is the affirmation of a common bond that, while inviolate, has suffered the pain of separation since the last occasion of physical togetherness."

Eileen Southern (1983) traced African American spirituals to the camp meetings of the Second Awakening, where blacks continued singing in their segregated quarters after the whites had retired for the night. According to Lincoln and Mamiya (1990, 348), black spirituals also appear to have had their roots in the preacher's chanted declamation and the intervening congregational responses.

The "ring shout," in which "shouters" danced in a circle to the accompaniment of a favorite spiritual sung by spectators standing on the sidelines, was a common practice in many nineteenth-century black churches. By 1830, many black urban congregations had introduced choral singing into their services. "Praying and singing bands" became a regular feature of religious life in many black urban churches.

Despite the opposition of African Methodists and other religious leaders to the intrusion of "cornfield ditties" into formal worship services, folk music became an integral part of African American sacred music.

According to Southern, black gospel music emerged as an urban phenomenon in revivals conducted in tents, football stadiums, and huge tabernacles. In 1927, Thomas A. Dorsey promoted what he called "gospel songs" in churches in Chicago, the Midwest, and the rural South. At a time when many Baptist and Methodist churches rejected gospel music, Sanctified churches (an aggregate of independent congregations stressing experience of the Holy Spirit and personal piety as keys to salvation) in both urban and rural areas embraced it wholeheartedly. The Church of God in Christ has been a strong supporter of contemporary gospel music. Spiritual churches (like the Israel Universal Divine Spiritual Churches of Christ, the Metropolitan Spiritual Churches of Christ, and the Universal Hagar's Spiritual Church) also accepted gospel music, and in New Orleans jazz is an integral feature of their worship services. In time, many mainstream congregations have incorporated gospel music into their musical repertoires.

African American religions in the Caribbean and the United States represent a coming together of African and European cultures in yet a third setting—that of the Americas. They are products of both voluntary and forced migrations, and represent a dynamic blending of Old World and New World faiths. E. Franklin Frazier (1964, 50–51) correctly argued that African American religion historically has functioned as a "refuge in a hostile white world." At another level, it has served as a form of cultural identity and resistance to a white-dominated society. In addition to serving as houses of worship, black churches were and are centers of social life, ethnic identity, and cultural expression in the African American and Caribbean communities.

Stephen D. GLAZIER
University of Nebraska, Lincoln

Further Reading

Baer, H. A., & Singer, M. (1992). *African American religion in the twentieth century: A religious response to racism.* Knoxville: University of Tennessee Press.

Brandon, G. F. (1993). *Santeria from Africa to the new world: The dead sell memories.* New Brunswick, NJ: Rutgers University Press.

Chavannes, B. (1994). *Rastafari—roots and ideology.* Syracuse, NY: Syracuse University Press.

Curtin, P. D. (1969). *The Atlantic slave trade: A census.* Madison: University of Wisconsin Press.

Desmangles, L. G. (1992). *The faces of the gods: Vodou and Roman Catholicism in Haiti.* Chapel Hill: University of North Carolina Press.

Du Bois, W. E. B. (1903). *The Negro church.* Atlanta, GA: Atlanta University Press.

Frazier, E. F. (1964). *The Negro church in America.* New York: Shocken Books.

Glazier, S. D. (1991). *Marchin' the pilgrims home: A study of the Spiritual Baptists of Trinidad.* Salem, WI: Sheffield.

Hall, S. (1990). *Cultural identity and diaspora.* In J. Rutherford (Ed.), *Identity: Community, culture, difference.* London: Lawrence and Wishart.

Herskovits, M. J. (1941). *The myth of the Negro past.* New York: Harper.

Lincoln, C. E., & Mamiya, L. (1990). *The black church in the African American experience.* Durham, NC: Duke University Press.

Mintz, S., & Price, R. (1992). *An anthropological approach to the Afro-American past. The birth of African American culture: An anthropological perspective.* Boston: Beacon Press.

Raboteau, A. J. (1978). *Slave religion: The "invisible" institution in the antebellum South.* New York: Oxford University Press.

Southern, E. (1983). *The music of black Americans.* New York: Norton.

Spencer, J. M. (1993). *Blues and evil.* Knoxville: University of Tennessee Press.

Verger, P. (1968). *Flux et reflux de la traite des negres entre le Golfe de Benin et Bahia de Todos los Santos, du XVIIe au XIXe siecle* [Flow and backward flow of the draft of the Negros between the Gulf of Benign and Bahia de Todos los Santos]. The Hague, The Netherlands: Mouton.

Zuckermann, P. (2000). *Du Bois on Religion.* Lanham, MD: AltaMira.

African Religions

Various traditional religions found in Africa are based on belief in one Supreme Being, while others embrace Earth deities, secret societies, and possession cults. Christianity and Islam, commonly practiced, came to Africa in the first centuries CE and the eighth century, respectively. Modern religion in Africa is a distinct blend and balance of traditional beliefs and new religious systems.

Africa is home to numerous "traditional" religions as well as various forms of Islam and Christianity and various more recent religious developments. There are certain religious characteristics that can be found in African spirituality that transcend any particular religion. Examining a sampling of traditional religions and Islamic and Christian denominations provides an insight into those overarching African spiritual characteristics.

Secret Societies

Secret societies, common among certain African peoples found mainly in West Africa, especially those among whom age-determined groups are not common, often have religious functions. They also unite people in different residence areas without kinship ties.

The religious or ritual knowledge of the secret society is not revealed to nonmembers. Allowing only members to know the secret—and, perhaps, only those members of a certain rank—adds to a secret society's mystery. Moreover, membership is limited to people of a given category. Categories can be as broad as all married women or all initiated men. There are categories for fishermen, hunters, craftsmen of all types, and market women, among others.

The Poro and Sande societies (for men and women, respectively) in Liberia have long interested anthropologists because these societies are major forces aiding government and facilitating social change. The Kpelle tribe opens a Sande bush school (which performs an initiation ceremony) every three or four years. Women of the Sande society are in complete control of the ceremony and school. Members of the initiation class are all girls between nine and fifteen years of age. They learn all they need to know to be Kpelle women from Sande members during the school session, which lasts from six weeks to three months.

During this period, Sande members perform cliterodectomy operations (cliterodectomies and circumcisions are common rites of passage in Africa), which are part of the transition from girlhood to womanhood. Sande members then perform rituals for those who have completed the bush school, marking their entrance into Kpelle society as women. Men of the Poro society dress in ritual regalia to welcome the women back into society.

A Supreme Deity

Most traditional African religions acknowledge one Supreme Being, though that creator god is often thought to have removed himself from the human sphere after creation, so that more focus is placed on lesser deities. In Sudan, for example, shrines exist in great numbers to lesser spirits but not to the creator god. The Yoruba of Nigeria acknowledge a Supreme Being, Olorun, but

A mosque in Capetown, South Afrcia. Mosques are focal points of communal worship for Muslims around the world. Photo by Frank Salamone.

it is the host of secondary deities, or *orisha*, that is the focus of Yoruba attention. Mulungu, the Supreme Being of the peoples of the great lakes region of East Africa, is only turned to in prayer after all other prayers have failed. But numerous African scholars and scholars of Africa dispute the interpretation that the creator god is viewed as remote. These scholars argue that the creator god is not remote, and rather that people can and do approach this god quite frequently. They indicate that there is a parallel with Christianity and its hierarchy of angels and saints.

In Sudanic religions, people are said to consult with the Creator before their birth, telling him what they want to do in life. The Creator gives each person what is needed to accomplish his or her fate. If a person fails, then he or she is said to be struggling against his or her chosen fate. Luck is focused in the head, so a person who has been lucky in life is said to have a good head.

In general, Africans deem that powers come from the Supreme Being. The Dogon of Mali, for instance, believe that the vital force of their Supreme Being, Amma, circulates throughout the universe. They name that vital force *nyama*. Other groups have similar beliefs. These forces control the weather and are associated with the forces of nature, directly or through the high god's servants.

Other Deities

There are Earth goddess cults in a number of societies. The Ibo of the lower Niger River area have the goddess Ala, and the goddess Asase Ya has devotees among the Ashante peoples of Ghana. The presence of a deity linked to a certain phenomenon or natural feature reflects the importance of that phenomenon or natural feature in daily life; hence the fact that the Yoruba worship Ogun, the god of iron, reflects the people's sense, from the days when iron first began to be used, of its importance.

Storm gods are in some way related to the Supreme Being. Storm gods generally command their own priests, temples, and ritual ceremonies. The Yoruba and Ibo have a full storm pantheon of gods of storm, lightning, and thunderbolt. Shango is the Yoruba lightning and thunder god; he is worshipped along with his wives, who are river gods, and the rainbow and thunderclap, which are his servants.

Islam and Christianity

Islam first came to the savanna areas of Africa through trade and peaceful teachings in the eighth through tenth centuries. The benefits of centralized government under Islamic law were obvious to various chiefs. Under Islamic law rulers were able to unite tribal elements into a coherent whole. The kingdoms of Wagadu (Ghana), Mali, Songhai, Kanem, and Bornu and the Hausa emirates were

A Shi'a Shrine in Capetown. South Africa's multicultural society embraces diverse religious expression and beliefs. Photo by Frank Salamone.

all centralized states that adopted Islam to their advantage.

The introduction of Islamic government and law also provided an excuse for religiously sanctioned rebellion against rulers who were not living up to the strict tenets of Islam, according to various religious military rulers. In the 1800s, militant Muslims objected to the halfhearted Islamic faith of their rulers and led holy wars against those whom they considered lax in the faith.

These nineteenth-century jihads were common among the Fulani peoples. They upset the balance that had prevailed since around the thirteenth century between local rulers, who adhered to Islam, and their subjects, who continued to practice traditional religions. Although the Fulani tend to be pastoralists, there were a number of settled Fulani who had intermarried with Hausa or other settled peoples. One result of these religious wars was that Fulani rulers replaced local rulers in the areas where the rebellions took place.

Christianity reached Africa in the first centuries CE, before it entered Europe. The Coptic Church (in Egypt), for example, go back to the first century of Christianity and still exists today. It, like the Ethiopian Orthodox Church, is a Monophysite church; that is, it teaches that Christ had a single nature rather than two distinct (human and divine) natures. The Ethiopian Orthodox Church has a large hierarchy of saints and angels, many monasteries and convents, and a strong worship of Mary, Gabriel, Michael, and Ethiopia's patron, St. George. There are many African saints, including Tekle Haimanot and Gabra Manfas Keddus. There is also belief in demons and other evil spirits, as well as in witchcraft and possession.

Possession Cults

Possession cults are one feature of traditional African religions that both African Christians and Muslims participate in, although often undercover. Although possession cults can be found in many regions, we will focus on the situation among the Hausa. In a 1975 study, the anthropologist Ralph Faulkingham notes that the Muslim and "pagan" Hausa in the southern Niger village he studied believed in the same spirits. Both believed in the same origin myth for these spirits as well. According to the myth, Allah called Adama ("the woman") and Adamu ("the man") to him and bade them to bring all their children. They hid some of their children. When Allah asked them where those children were, they denied that any were missing, whereupon Allah told them that the hidden children would belong to the spirit world. These spirits may, on occasion, take possession of those living in the everyday world.

Indigenous theology linked dead ancestors to the spirits of place in a union that protected claims and relationships to the land. Spirits of place included trees, rock outcroppings, a river, snakes, and other animals and objects. Rituals and prayers directed toward the spirits of family and place reinforced communal norms and the authority of the elders in defending ancient beliefs and practices. In return for these prayers and rituals, the spirits offered protection from misfortune, adjudication, and divination through seers or shamans, who worked with the spirits to ensure good and counteract evil. The Hausa incorporate those beliefs into their Islamic beliefs.

The majority of Muslim Hausa who participate in the spirit possession cult, called the Bori cult, are women and members of the lower classes; as one rises in social standing, one's practice of Islam tends to become stricter and more orthodox. The Bori rituals among the Hausa appear to be rituals of inversion; that is, traditional societal rules are turned on their heads. People who are possessed may behave in ways that would not be accepted in other circumstances. The Bori cult is widely understood as being a refuge from the strongly patriarchal ideal of Hausa Islam. Thus both women and effeminate males find some respite there. Indeed, the Bori cult provides a niche open to marginal people of all kinds, not simply women or homosexuals. Butchers, night soil workers, musicians, and poor farmers are welcome there. Mentally disturbed people of all classes similarly seek refuge among the Bori devotees.

African Religions Today

The peoples of Africa have been adept at accepting new religious systems while preserving essential features of traditional beliefs, and that approach to religion continues today, when New Age and Evangelical Christian denominations have become popular. An African base adapts new ideas and fits them to a basic pattern of kinship, personal spirits, ancestors, and age grades, seeking to fit all of these into personal networks of relationships.

Frank A. SALAMONE
Iona College and *University of Phoenix*

See also African American and Caribbean Religions

Further Reading

Anderson, D. M., & Johnson, D. H. (Eds.). (1995). *Revealing prophets: Prophecy in eastern African history.* London: Ohio University Press.

Beidelman, T. O. (1982). *Colonial evangelism: A socio-historical study of an east African mission at the grassroots.* Bloomington: Indiana University Press.

Besmer, F. E. (1983). *Horses, musicians & gods: The Hausa cult of possession-trance.* Westport, CT: Greenwood Press.

Chidester, D., & Petty, R. (1997). *African traditional religion in South Africa: An annotated bibliography.* Westport, CT: Greenwood Press.

Clarke, P. B. (Ed.). (1998). *New trends and developments in African religions.* Westport, CT: Greenwood Press.

Creevey, L., & Callaway, B. (1994). *The heritage of Islam: Women, religion, and politics in West Africa.* Boulder, CO: Lynne Rienner.

Echerd, N. (1991). Gender relationships and religion: Women in the Hausa Bori in Ader, Niger. In C. Coles & B. Mack (Eds.), *Hausa women in the twentieth century* (pp. 207–220). Madison: University of Wisconsin Press.

Evans-Pritchard, E. E. (1956). *Nuer religion.* New York: Oxford University Press.

Faulkingham, R. N. (1975). *The sprits and their cousins: Some aspects of belief, ritual, and social organization in a rural Hausa village in Niger* (Research Report No. 15). Amherst, MA: University of Massachusetts, Department of Anthropology.

Fortes, M. (1995). *Oedipus and Job in West African religion.* New York: Cambridge University Press.

Greenberg, J. (1947). *The influence of Islam on a Sudanese religion.* New York: J. J. Augustin Publisher.

Karp, I., & Bird, C. S. (Eds.). (1980). *Explorations in African systems of thought.* Bloomington: Indiana University Press.

Makinde, M. A. (1988). *African philosophy, culture, and traditional medicine.* Athens: Ohio University Center for International Studies.

Olupona, J. K. (Ed.). (1991). *African traditional religions in contemporary society.* St. Paul, MN: Paragon House.

Oppong, C. (Ed.). (1983). *Male and female in West Africa.* London: Allen & Unwin.

Parrinder, G. (1954). *African traditional religion.* London: Hutchinson's University Library.

Pittin, R. (1979). *Marriage and alternative strategies: Career patterns of Hausa women in Katsina City.* Unpublished doctoral dissertation, School of Oriental and African Studies, University of London.

Turner, E., Blodgett, W., Kahona, S., & Benwa, F. (1992). *Experiencing ritual: A new interpretation of African healing.* Philadelphia: University of Pennsylvania Press.

Walby, C. (1995). The African sacrificial kingship ritual and Johnson's "Middle Passage." *African American Review, 29*(4), 657–669.

Animism

Humans have long performed rituals for driving out, consulting, or appeasing the invisible spirits that they believe influence their own well-being and interact with the natural world of animals, plants, and objects. The concept today is known as *animism*, and its influences remain in modern language, habits, and ideas.

Animism is the name modern anthropologists gave to a very old set of ideas about how human beings and the natural world interact. The key concept is that animate and sometimes inanimate objects have a spiritual dimension that influences human well-being. The inhabitants of this invisible world of spirits behave much like ourselves, and interact with one another and with the visible world constantly. The spirits sometimes helped and sometimes defeated human purposes and hopes. Consequently, humans needed to maintain good relations with them, learn their wishes, and appease their anger whenever possible.

This idea probably dates back to the time when language developed fully among our ancestors, permitting them to create agreed-upon meanings to guide everyday behavior. And once they agreed on the importance of good relations with invisible spirits, human foraging bands probably came to rely on specialists who knew how to enter the spirit world at will and report back what the spirits wanted. Many anthropologists think that what Siberian shamans did among groups of hunters in the nineteenth century descended from and, at least loosely, resembled very ancient practices. At any rate, ritual singing and dancing allowed shamans to enter into trance at will; and when they returned to normal consciousness, they regularly explained what the spirits wished or intended. Ordinary people could then go about their daily tasks reassured, or, as the case might be, devote time and effort to rituals designed to appease or drive evil spirits away.

The idea of an invisible spirit world parallel to the material world of sense almost certainly spread with the wandering Paleolithic bands that occupied almost all the habitable lands of the Earth between about 100,000 and 10,000 years ago. At any rate, all the diverse and remote hunters and gatherers whom anthropologists began to study in the nineteenth century believed that invisible spirits surrounded them and had a lot to do with everything that happened.

What made animism plausible was the experience of dreaming. A sleeping person might remember strange sights and encounters, even with dead persons. It seemed obvious that when humans were asleep something invisible—their spirits—could and did travel about among other disembodied spirits. Moreover, breath offered a clear example of an invisible something—a spirit—essential to life, which departed from dying persons permanently, thus joining, or rejoining, other disembodied spirits.

Trance, too, was interpreted as arising when a person's spirit departed temporarily and returned with news from the spirit world. Illness could also be attributed to an evil spirit that, by invading the body, upset normal health. Rituals for driving out such spirits and for defeating other spirits that were interfering with particular human hopes and purposes became central to what may be called animistic religion.

What is life? It is the flash of a firefly in the night. It is the breath of a buffalo in the wintertime. It is the little shadow which runs across the grass and loses itself in the sunset. • **Crowfoot, Blackfoot warrior (1890)**

Surges of unusual excitement and extraordinary cooperative efforts were also interpreted as examples of how a single spirit might enter into the community as a whole or those persons who bore the brunt of common exertion, whether they were defending their home territory against an invading human band, stalking and killing a dangerous animal, or initiating young people into their adult roles by secret and solemn rituals. These and other occasions brought people together emotionally; and the excitement that sustained commonality could be attributed to a spirit shared, at least temporarily, by all.

Details of how different peoples attempted to control their interaction with the spirit world differed endlessly from place to place and must have altered across time too, so that we ought not to assume that recent practices accurately replicated ancient patterns even among Siberian hunters. But it is worth recognizing that animism in all its innumerable local variations endured far longer than successor religions have done. In fact, animism still pervades a great deal of common speech and thinking.

Athletes and businessmen often invoke "team spirit"; musicians and actors hope for an "inspired" performance. And we all admire a cheerful "spirit," whenever we meet such a person.

For millennia, management of relations with the spirit world in the light of animistic ideas and techniques sustained human communities in good times and bad. It made whatever happened intelligible and within limits curable as well. Every surprise and disappointment was believed to be the work of one or more spirits; and when matters were sufficiently critical, customary rituals could always be mobilized to find out exactly what kind of spirits were interfering and what sort of appeasement or change of human behavior might solve the problem.

A belief system that explained so much and served so many peoples across so many generations deserves serious respect. It was humankind's earliest effort to work out a worldview, uniting in an undifferentiated whole what later separated into science and religion. Everything later thinkers did to elaborate human knowledge took off from animism,

Animal spirits are featured in the carvings on these two totem poles in Portland, Oregon. Beinecke Rare Book and Manuscript Library. Yale University.

modifying and eventually abandoning it; and it is not really surprising that all of us still sometimes fall back on animistic phrases and habits of thought in everyday life.

William H. McNEILL
University of Chicago, Emeritus

See also Shamanism

Further Reading

Tylor, E. B. (1871). *Primitive culture.* New York: Harper.
Jensen, A. E. (1963). *Myth and cult among primitive peoples.* Chicago: University of Chicago Press.
Lowie, R. H. (1970). *Primitive religion.* New York: Liveright.
Eliade, M. (1964). *Shamanism: Archaic techniques of ecstasy.* New York: Bollingen Foundation.

Augustine, Saint
(354–430 CE)
EARLY CHRISTIAN THEOLOGIAN

Best known for his *Confessions* and *City of God*, the theologian Augustine of Hippo wrote numerous works after his conversion to Christianity in 386. His profound and lasting influence on Western Christianity and philosophy led to his canonization by popular acclaim, rather than by papal edict.

Augustine of Hippo (354–430 CE) was the dominant Christian theologian between Christian antiquity and the high Middle Ages. A prolific writer, he authored ninety-three books, hundreds of letters, and thousands of sermons. He was born in Tagaste (today Souk-Ahras, Algeria) in the Roman province of Numidia. Patricius, his father, belonged to the middle class and was a pagan. Monica, his mother, was a devout Christian who had him enrolled as a catechumen at an early age.

Augustine received his elementary and secondary education in Latin and Greek in Tagaste and Madaura. For higher studies, he was sent to Carthago, the half-pagan metropolis of Numidia. Here he formed a liaison with a woman (name unknown) with whom he lived for fifteen years and who bore him a son, Adeodatus.

Hitherto dissolute, Augustine came to a turning point about 373, when he was inspired by a reading of Cicero's *Hortensius* to seek "wisdom." Attracted by the cosmology and moral teachings of Manichaeism, he became a convert to that dualistic Gnostic religion. Nine years later, having become convinced that it lacked rationality, he abandoned it. In 384, after about ten years of teaching rhetoric in Tagaste, Carthago, and Rome, Augustine secured an appointment as professor of rhetoric and court orator in Milan, then the capital of the Western Roman Empire. Now a widow, Monica followed him to Milan and, concerned for his spiritual and economic welfare, arranged for his engagement to a Christian heiress. Augustine dismissed his concubine but retained their son. In his *Confessions* Augustine was to recall that separation from his mistress caused him excruciating pain.

As an imperial representative, Augustine met Ambrose, the scholarly bishop of Milan, whose sermons persuaded him that it was possible to be both a Christian and an intellectual. However, a close friendship with Ambrose did not develop, and Christian Neoplatonists in Milan were more influential in bringing Augustine to an acceptance of Christianity. In July 386, according to the dramatic account in the *Confessions*, Augustine surrendered to Christ. Resigning his professorship, and terminating his engagement with the Milanese heiress, he was baptized by Ambrose on Easter Sunday in 387. A new life dawned for Augustine, and he determined to return to Africa to establish a monastery. On their way back to Africa, Monica died and was buried in Ostia, Italy. In his *Confessions*, Augustine paid a very loving tribute to his mother.

Although Augustine loved and respected the two principal women in his life, his mother and his concubine, his writings were to reinforce early Christian antifeminism. Augustine wrote that only men were made in the true image of God; women were in the image of God only insofar as they were wives, engaged in procreation. Women were symbols of carnality, although they too with God's grace could attain salvation.

Sandro Botticelli, *St. Augustine in His Cell* (c. 1480). Fresco. Augustine of Hippo meditates under the Vespucci family coat of arms.

Augustine's fame as a preacher and theologian developed after his return to Africa. In 391, while on a visit to the port city of Hippo (or Hippo Regius; today Annaba, Algeria), he had the priesthood virtually thrust upon him by the local congregation. In 396 he became sole bishop (he had been co-bishop with Valerius) and remained such until his death.

As custom then dictated, he was both chief ecclesiastical officer and civil magistrate. Indefatigable, he found time to lead a semimonastic life, attend religious conferences, and write numerous theological tracts. Original sin, grace, predestination, freedom of the will, Scripture, heresy, philosophy, history, and sexuality were among the diverse topics that engaged his attention.

Two works became classics: the *Confessions* and *City of God*. Written in 397, the *Confessions* conveyed profound psychological and spiritual insight. Though relating some details of his childhood and adulthood, Augustine's intention was to glorify God, express repentance for his sins, and encourage others to seek God. The *City of God*, written between 414 and 427, was prompted by a shattering event, the sack of Rome in 410. In the first part of this work, Augustine set out to show that the disaster was not caused by desertion of pagan temples for Christian altars, as some Romans maintained, but by inner rot. In the second part, Augustine elucidated a philosophy of history that was linear, not cyclical. He argued that the result of the sin of Adam and Eve was the creation of two cities, two societies, the City of Man (the earthly city) and the City of God (the heavenly city). The two were not separate but intertwined, to be separated only at the Last Judgment.

In the early church Augustine was best known for combating heresy. His first fifteen years as bishop of Hippo were dominated by controversy with Donatism, a puritanical branch of Christianity that had a strong presence in Africa. In contrast with Donatist views, Augustine maintained that apostates who repented did not require rebaptism, and that the sacraments had a validity of their own, regardless of the state of grace of their administrators. After the issuance of an imperial edict, Augustine, who had sought a meeting ground with Donatist bishops, reluctantly acquiesced in the use of force against the Donatist churches. The concept of religious freedom was unknown at that time.

Other teachings that Augustine struggled against were Manichaeism, which he knew from personal experience, and Pelagianism. A recent arrival into Africa, Pelagianism denied that original sin had totally vitiated human nature. In opposition to this thesis, Augustine contended that the sin of Adam and Eve, passed on to all of posterity, had alienated human

Faith is to believe what you do not see; the reward of this faith is to see what you believe. • **Saint Augustine (354–430 CE)**

persons from God and therefore reconciliation could be achieved only by baptism.

Augustine died 28 August 430 during the Vandal siege of Hippo. A cult of Augustine spread quickly in Europe, and his canonization was not the result of any papal procedure (none existed at the time) but of popular acclaim. In 1295 Pope Boniface VIII proclaimed Augustine a doctor of the church.

Augustine's influence on western Christianity was unparalleled until Thomas Aquinas appeared in the thirteenth century. Augustinianism with its Platonic overtones gave way to Scholasticism with its Aristotelian underpinnings. During the Reformation era, Luther and Calvin revived Augustinian ideas regarding predestination. In more modern times Augustine's influence may be found in the works of Blaise Pascal, Jacques Maritain, and Joseph Ratzinger (elected as Pope Benedict XVI in 2005), among others, as well as in some of the documents of Vatican II. Though a man of his time in most matters, Augustine as a theologian and philosopher showed independence and originality.

Elisa A. CARRILLO
Marymount College of Fordham University

See also Religion—Roman Catholicism

Further Reading

Augustine. (1958). *City of God* (G. G. Walsh, et al., Trans.). New York: Doubleday Image.

Augustine. (2001). *The confessions* (R. Warner, Trans.). New York: Signet Classic.

Brown, P. (1967). *Augustine of Hippo*. Berkeley: University of California Press.

O'Donnell, J. J. (1985). *Augustine*. Boston: Twayne.

Wills, G. (1999). *Saint Augustine*. New York: Viking Penguin.

Wills, G. (2002). *Saint Augustine's memory*. New York: Viking Penguin.

Bahá'í

Founded by Baha'u'llah in the nineteenth century, the Bahá'í faith is a monotheistic religion that grew out of Islam. It recognizes Muhammad as a prophet, but not the last prophet. At the core of Bahá'í faith is the belief that all of humanity is spiritually unified and that Bahá'í will guide civilization toward an age of peace and prosperity.

The Bahá'í religion was founded and initially propagated toward the middle of the nineteenth century in the (then) Ottoman regions of Iraq, Turkey, and Palestine by a Persian-born messianic claimant named Mirza Hoseyn Ali Nuri (1817–1892), who adopted the title Baha'u'llah (Baha' Allah), meaning the "Splendor of God." Ranging across more than two hundred counties, his followers today number 5–6 million and are known as Bahá'ís (literally "radiant ones"). Given their range throughout the world, the modern Bahá'í religion can no longer be viewed as a purely Middle Eastern movement, an Islamic "sect," or a merely eclectic religious phenomenon.

Baha'u'llah was born a Shi'ite Muslim in a troubled Persian Islamic society. He called all humankind to a revolutionary and modernist post-Islamic religion, initially that of his predecessor the Bab (literally the "Gate") and subsequently to the Bahá'í religion, which he founded. To some, his message transcended and superseded Islamic legal and other religious norms as the new Bahá'í religion, not only for the contemporary world but also for times extending a millennium or more into the future. The developed Bahá'í religion is centered upon actualizing a spiritual unity in diversity of all humankind in a future world characterized by millennial justice and peace. Religion and science, Baha'u'llah and his successors indicated, should both harmoniously contribute to an advancing civilization in which racism, excessive nationalism, and materialistic capitalism are transcended.

The Religion of the Bab

Baha'u'llah became a follower of another young Persian messianic claimant, Mirza 'Ali Mohammad (1819/ 1820–1850), the Bab, at the outset of his religious mission in May 1844. He considered the Bab to be his divinely inspired forerunner. The Bab gradually established his own post-Islamic religious system and revealed new books in Arabic and Persian collectively known as the Bayan (Exposition). He was imprisoned for much of his six-year religious ministry, which ended with his execution for heresy in 1850. Several thousand of his followers were also martyred for apostasy and heresy. Though best known today as the Bab (gate to the messiah), this Persian Sayyid (descendant of Muhammad) actually claimed to be the awaited Islamic eschatological savior, the Qa'im (Ariser) or Mahdi (Rightly Guided One). He also subsequently claimed to be a divine "Manifestation of God" and underlined the eternally progressive continuity of religion, thereby transcending the Muslim concept of the finality of prophethood in Muhammad (Qur'an 33:40).

With his many revelations, the Bab claimed to disclose the deeper senses of the Qur'an and of pre-Islamic scripture, and to prepare the way for another messianic individual greater than himself. In claiming to supersede Islam, the

Modern-day view of the tomb of the Bab, who is considered the divinely inspired predecessor of Baha'u'llah.
Mount Carmel, Israel.
Photo by Tom Habibi.

Bab also spoke of endless future messiahs. These superhuman, divine figures were actually preexistent and theophanic manifestations of God, the next of whom might appear imminently or perhaps, for example, after 9, 19, 1,511, or 2,001 years.

In the Bahá'í religion the greatest name for god, Bahá', means "glory" or "splendor." The photo shows the name as it appears inside the Bahá'i House of Worship in Wilmette, Illinois. Photo by Sean M. Scully.

Baha'u'llah and Religion Renewed

Baha'u'llah followed and propagated the religion of the Bab from its inception in 1844 until the latter years of his exile from Iran to Iraq (1852–1863), when he began to gradually declare his own global mission. On announcing his mission on the outskirts of Baghdad in 1863, he outlawed the propagation of religion by the sword, indicated that his religion would continue for at least a millennium, and voiced doctrines indicative of the equality and oneness of all humanity.

Like the Bab, Baha'u'llah composed thousands of scriptural "tablets" in Arabic and Persian over a forty-year period (1852–1892). These 20,000 or so revelations vary in length from a few lines to weighty books and treatises such as his *Kitab-i iqan* (Book of Certitude, 1852), *Kitab-i badi'* (Innovative Book, 1867), and his major though slim book of laws, *al-Kitab al-Aqdas* (The Most Holy Book, 1873). Like his forerunner, he placed great emphasis upon the nonliteral interpretation of the Bible and the Quran and often gave figurative interpretations to messianic signs and latter-day prophecies. Apocalyptic upheavals and catastrophes, he explained, had been realized or would come to be fulfilled either literally or spiritually. Hopes of a new age and of the millennial future of humanity would, he predicted, definitely come to realization in a future Bahá'í-inspired new world order.

Despite being exiled and imprisoned for religious heresy for several decades of his life by Persian and Ottoman leaders, Baha'u'llah continued to address weighty and theologically authoritative epistles to various kings, rulers, and ecclesiastics of his day.

Among those he called to God and to righteous rule were the British queen Victoria (1819–1901), the French emperor Louis-Napoleon (Napoleon III; 1808–1873), the Russian czar Nicholas II (1868–1918), and the Italian pope, Giovanni Maria Mastai-Ferretti, Pope Pius IX (1792–1878).

It was clear from his *Kitab-i 'Ahdi* (Book of My Covenant) that on Baha'u'llah's passing in Palestine in 1892, his saintly and learned eldest son 'Abd ol-Baha' (1844–1921) would succeed him. His son wrote several books and many thousands of letters expounding his father's message and visited several western countries between 1911 and the outbreak of World War I in 1914. "The Master," as 'Abd ol-Baha' was respectfully known, was in turn succeeded in 1921 by an Oxford-educated great-grandson of Baha'u'llah named Shoghi Effendi Rabbani (1896–1957), the last single head or Guardian of the Bahá'í religion. In 1963, the globally elected Universal House of Justice came to direct and govern the Bahá'í world from its center in Haifa, Israel.

Baha'u'llah's oft-repeated statement that the Earth is but one country and all humankind are its citizens continues to underpin many activities of the Bahá'í faith today. Its adherents claim that its promotion of the spiritual dimensions of the oneness of humanity, the equality of the sexes, international justice, and world peace makes the Bahá'í religion a channel for the realization of a twenty-first-century religiosity that transcends contemporary secularism and exclusivism. The faith's continuing championing of a globally selected or newly-devised universal auxiliary language and its close relationship with the United Nations since the inception of the latter in 1945 in working towards a peaceful global society are proclaimed as some of the major contributions which the Bahá'í international community has made to world history. Under the direction of the Universal House of Justice, the Bahá'í International Community has consultative status with UN organizations including United Nations Economic and Social Council, United Nations Children's Fund, World Health Organization, United Nations Development Fund for Women, and the United Nations Environment Program.

In recent years, the Bahá'í international authority known as the Universal House of Justice has issued a statement entitled "The Promise of World Peace" (1985) addressed to the peoples of the world and another called "To the World's Religious Leaders" (2002) containing advice for the evolution towards a united humanity.

Stephen N. LAMBDEN

Ohio University

Further Reading

'Abdu'l-Baha. (1969). *Paris talks: Addresses given by 'Abdu'l-Baha in Paris in 1911–1912*. London: Baha'i Publishing Trust.

The Bab. (1978). *Selections from the writings of the Bab*. Haifa, Israel: Baha'i World Centre.

Baha'u'llah. (1978). *Tablets of Baha'u'llah*. Haifa, Israel: Baha'i World Centre.

Baha'u'llah. (1983). *The Kitab-i-iqan* (The book of certitude). Wilmette, IL: Baha'i Publishing Trust.

Baha'u'llah. (1992). *Kitab-i-aqdas* (The most holy book). Haifa, Israel: Baha'i World Centre.

Hatcher, W. S. and Martin, D. (1985). *The Bahá'í faith: The emerging global religion*. San Francisco: Harper and Row.

McMullen, M. (2000). *The Baha'i: The religious construction of a global identity*. New Brunswick, N.J.: Rutgers University Press.

Momen, M. (1997). *A short introduction to the Baha'i faith*. Oxford, U.K.: Oneworld.

Shoghi Effendi. (1960). *The dispensation of Baha'u'llah*. Wilmette, IL: Baha'i Publishing Trust.

Shoghi Effendi. (1991). *The world order of Baha'u'llah*. Wilmette, IL: Baha'i Publishing Trust.

Smith, P. (1987). *The Babi and Baha'i religions: From messianic Shi'ism to a world religion*. Cambridge, U.K., and New York: Cambridge University Press.

The Universal House of Justice. (1984). *The constitution of the Universal House of Justice*. Haifa, Israel: Baha'i World Centre.

The Universal House of Justice. (1985). *The promise of world peace*. Haifa, Israel: Baha'i World Centre.

Buddha

(TRADITIONALLY DATED C. 566–C. 486 BCE;
MORE PROBABLY C. 463–C. 383 BCE)
FOUNDER OF BUDDHISM

Buddha (Siddhartha Gautama) was born an Indian prince. His followers made him into a god, but in his lifetime he was much like other holy men of India. Buddha's influence increased as his devotees, seeking to live their lives in monasteries according to Buddha's example of wisdom and compassion, persuaded lay people to support them by donating land and other forms of wealth.

Siddhartha Gautama discovered and taught a path of liberation from suffering that has shaped the lives of Buddhists across the world for over two thousand years. He presented a vision of human existence that centers on wisdom and compassion, and he established monastic communities for both men and women in which intense meditation has been practiced for centuries. He advised kings and nobles on governing wisely and set forth precepts for lay people that continue to shape lives around the globe. For over two millennia, his life and teachings have had a profound impact on religion, culture, and history in central, eastern, and Southeast Asia; and since the nineteenth century many in Europe and the United States have been moved by his vision.

Siddhartha Gautama was born into a ruling family of the Sakya clan in present-day Nepal. The first written sources for his life, the texts of the Buddhist canon in the Pali language, come from long after his death and include legendary motifs, and so there is doubt about how reliable they are. At about the age of twenty-nine, he became dissatisfied with life at the court, saw that life as ordinarily lived is unsatisfactory, and embarked on a religious quest to find a way out of suffering. He studied with Hindu masters, but their wisdom and meditation practices did not provide the answer he was seeking. Meditating in solitude, he underwent a transforming enlightenment at age thirty-five, and his followers acclaimed him as the Buddha, "the awakened one." Because there are many Buddhas in the Buddhist tradition, Gautama is often referred to as Sakyamuni Buddha, the sage of the Sakya clan..

The Buddha expressed his insight in the Four Noble Truths, which are at the heart of Buddhist life and practice and are his central contribution. The First Noble Truth is that life as usually experienced is unsatisfactory because it is impermanent. All pleasures are transitory, leading to separation and suffering. The Second Noble Truth is that the unsatisfactory character of life arises from craving and grasping at impermanent objects and experiences, seeking lasting pleasure and security that these objects and experiences cannot provide. Ordinary life is marked by a fundamental illusion that there is a permanent, substantial self underlying our experiences. The Buddha taught that there is no such enduring self. All things, including humans, are composites of various factors that constantly change and that are profoundly interdependent. Whatever arises will cease to be.

The Third Noble Truth is the hopeful promise that there can be an end to the unsatisfactoriness of life through freedom from craving. This freedom is called *nibbana* in Pali or *nirvana* in Sanskrit. Nirvana, often translated as "extinction," is not complete annihilation. Nirvana is the extinction of craving; it is sometimes compared to the blowing out of a candle. Since craving causes the unsatisfactoriness of life, the extinction of craving brings peace and happiness. Nirvana is also the end of ignorance and thus is identified as unconditioned, absolute truth, which brings wisdom and compassion and ends the cycle of craving, grasping and

*We are shaped by our thoughts; we become what we think. When the mind is pure,
joy follows like a shadow that never leaves.* • **Buddha (c. 563–c. 483 BCE)**

Sculptural representations of the Buddha, such as this one from the Gandharan region of northern Pakistan (first century CE), varied as his iconic image moved from India to Central and East Asia.
Musée Guimet, Paris.

illusion. Nirvana cannot be defined or comprehended in concepts; it is a religious state that must be experienced to be fully understood. The Buddha described it in negative terms as not born, not produced, and not conditioned. Nirvana manifests itself in the Four Noble Dwelling Places: the virtues of loving kindness, compassion, appreciative joy, and equanimity. The Fourth Noble Truth is the Eightfold Path, which presents a way of life that leads to nirvana. It consists of three stages. The first stage, wisdom, comprises right understanding and right thought. The second stage is morality or ethical conduct and comprises right speech, right action, and right livelihood. The final stage is meditation and comprises right effort, right mindfulness, and right concentration.

Gautama challenged the social mores of his time by forming monastic communities in which all were equal, regardless of the class or caste they came from. Gautama may have been the first person in history to establish a monastic community for women. He taught a meditation practice that focuses on the direct experience of each moment, acknowledging sensations, emotions, and thoughts without grasping at pleasant moments or pushing away unpleasant experiences.

Gautama lived in northern India and Nepal. After his death, the Indian emperor Asoka (d. 232 BCE) promoted Buddhism throughout much of the Indian subcontinent and sent Buddhist missionaries to other parts of Asia, including present-day Sri Lanka, Kashmir, the Himalayas, present-day Myanmar (Burma), and the Greek kingdoms of Bactria in Central Asia. Through these efforts Buddhism began its growth as an international religion.

Leo LEFEBURE

Fordham University

See also Buddhism

Further Reading

Ling, T. (1973). *The Buddha: Buddhist civilization in India and Ceylon.* Harmondsworth, U.K.: Penguin Books.

Nakamura, H. (2000). *Gotama Buddha: A biography based on the most reliable texts* (G. Sekimori, Trans.). Tokyo, Japan: Kosei Publishing Company.

Nanamoli, B., & Bodhi, B. (Trans.). (1995). *The middle length discourses of the Buddha: A new translation of the Majjhima Nikaya.* Boston: Wisdom Publications.

Radhakrishnan, S. (Trans.). (1950). *The Dhammapada.* Oxford, U.K.: Oxford University Press.

Rahula, W. (1978). *What the Buddha taught* (Rev. ed.) London: G. Frasier.

Walshe, M. (Trans.). (1995). *The long discourses of the Buddha: A translation of the Digha Nikaya.* Boston: Wisdom Publications.

Buddhism

More than two millennia ago in India, Siddhartha Gautama became "the Buddha" and began to teach that one can only escape suffering and sorrow by living along a righteous path that ends with the extinction of desire and ignorance. The Buddha's teachings lie at the core of what has become one of the world's largest religions.

Buddhism is the world's fourth-largest religion after Christianity, Islam, and Hinduism. Buddhism is approximately twenty-five hundred years old and has influenced cultures, events, and thought for generations. It is devoted to the improvement and eventual enlightenment of people, primarily through their own efforts.

The Indian philosopher Siddhartha Gautama founded Buddhism. The traditional dates of his life are 566 to 486 BCE, although recent studies suggest that Gautama was born as much as a century later. Gautama became known as "the Buddha" (the Enlightened One) after achieving enlightenment. He was born a prince of the Sakya clan in a small Indian kingdom in what is now Nepal. He had every luxury of the day and on the surface an apparently satisfying life. He married, had a son, and was destined to inherit his father's kingdom. However, at the age of twenty-nine he became dissatisfied with his life of ease after being exposed to the true lot of humankind: suffering, old age, disease, and death. His father had protected him from these things because of a prophecy that Siddhartha would become either a great king or a great spiritual leader. His father's hopes for a powerful successor were dashed when Siddhartha walked away from this life of ease and became an ascetic, a wandering holy man.

For six years he studied and learned from various gurus and holy men while depriving himself of all but the most meager nourishment. Siddhartha discovered that the extremes of self-deprivation were no better than the extremes of luxury and self-indulgence, so he sought the "Middle Way," another name for Buddhism. Gautama found enlightenment while meditating under a *bodhi* tree. The Buddha achieved nirvana—the extinction of all desire and ignorance—and proceeded to teach others how to achieve the same state for the next forty-five years. Through discussions, parables, teaching, and living, the Buddha taught the "path of truth or righteousness" (Dhammapada). The scripture (*sutta*), "The Foundation of the Kingdom of Righteousness," contains a succinct exposition of the major points that the Buddha taught.

Basic Beliefs

The Buddha preached "the Four Noble Truths" that define the existence of humankind: (1) Life is sorrow or suffering, (2) this suffering is caused by our selfish craving and desires, (3) we can remove sorrow by removing our desires, and (4) the removal of our desires is achieved by following the Noble Eightfold Path. The Noble Eightfold Path defines the "correct" behavior as right conduct, right effort, right speech, right views, right purpose or aspiration, right livelihood, right mindfulness, and right contemplation or meditation. The Buddha had few prohibitions but listed "five precepts" that good Buddhists should generally adhere to: not to kill, not to steal, not to lie, not to imbibe intoxicants, and not to be unchaste or unfaithful.

A Buddhist cemetery in Kyoto, Japan, in the late 1880s includes open pavilion shrines and sculptural figures.

The Buddha taught that *skanda*s (experiential data) create our existence from moment to moment and that only karma (the law of cause and effect) operates through our experience and is never lost. However, everything is changeable and impermanent. The Buddha made few concrete statements about the afterlife or the nature of "god"—realizing that the Middle Way can be taught but that each person must experience dharma—the realization of nirvana. His final admonition to his followers was to "work out your salvation with diligence" (*Buddhist suttas* 2000, 114).

After the Buddha—Growth in India

The Buddha was a practical teacher who knew that people need instruction, and he established the *sangha* (community of Buddhist monks and nuns) to carry on his work and the work of their own salvation. The Buddha instructed the *sangha* that it could change or delete any of the lesser rules after his passing if the *sangha* saw fit. Ultimately, the Buddha urged his followers to be "a lamp unto themselves." Buddhism provides a system that demonstrates where we err and how to correct our errors not by miracles but rather by hard work and contemplation.

One of the most noted people who helped to expand Buddhism was the Mauryan ruler Asoka, who ruled from 272 to 231 BCE. The Maurya Empire (c. 324–200 BCE) grew from the state of Magadha after the time of the Buddha and rapidly expanded after Alexander of Macedon invaded India in the 320s BCE, creating the first really unified kingdom in India. Asoka became a convert to Buddhism and helped to expand it by providing for missionaries and monks, so that Buddhism became a world religion while Hinduism remained confined to India. He is often compared with Roman emperor Constantine in the West, whose conversion to Christianity in 312 CE helped that religion to grow. Inscriptions on pillars and rocks throughout Asoka's realm encouraged the citizens of the empire to follow the dharma, limit the killing and cruelty

Theravada, Mahayana, and Vajrayana Sects

The Maha-Parinibbana Sutta (Book of the Great Decease) concerns the final days and death of the Buddha and is important because the Buddha did not consider himself to be a deity. It illustrates the relationship between the Buddha and Ananda, a cousin of the Buddha who was a disciple and his personal servant. A warm, trusting relationship between the two shines through the text. The first Council of Buddhism met to organize and retain the teachings of the Buddha several months after his death. The Buddhist Suttas, probably recorded by the first or second century BCE, is the canon of the Buddhist faith.

However, by the second and first centuries BCE Buddhism had already begun to diverge into schools of thought that evolved into the major sects of Theravada, Mahayana, and Vajrayana. The Theravada claimed to adhere closely to the original teachings of the Buddha and evolved along more monastic lines to spread through Southeast Asia to Sri Lanka, Myanmar (Burma), Thailand, and Cambodia. Theravada is also known as "Hinayana," which means "lesser vehicle." Mahayana (greater vehicle) Buddhism became the more adaptive Buddhism. With an emphasis on compassion and flexibility, it meshed with the cultures it encountered to spread to China, Korea, Japan, and Vietnam. Mahayanists also developed the idea of the bodhisattva (a being who compassionately refrains from entering nirvana in order to save others and is worshipped as a deity). Vajrayana (diamond vehicle) Buddhism is also known as "tantric Buddhism" and spread to Central Asia, primarily Tibet.

The Silk Roads and the Spread of Buddhism in Asia

A network of trade routes called the Silk Roads made travel possible from China to the Mediterranean and to India from about the second century CE to approximately the fifteenth century, connecting the world in ways it had not been before. Religions in particular found their way to new lands and different cultures

The Great Mandala of Japanese Nichiren Buddhism. This hanging paper scroll includes inscriptions in Chinese characters and medieval Sanskrit, as well as images of protective Buddhist deities and elements that represent Buddha's enlightenment.

to animals, and live a righteous life. Like Christianity, Buddhism may also have provided Asoka and the Mauryans with a code of conduct and a way to help manage, enlarge, and consolidate the empire. Buddhism also benefited from the patronage of a king who helped it to reach beyond the borders of India.

Buddhist shrines originated as stupas (burial mounds for Buddha's ashes and relics). In China the dome form elongated to become a pagoda with layers of relief sculpture depicting the events of Buddha's life.

via the Silk Roads. Buddhism originated in India and spread to the Kushan areas, part of what is today Pakistan and Afghanistan, by the first century CE. Buddhism developed a number of sects, built many monasteries, and became a consumer of many of the luxuries of the day, especially silk. Buddhist monasteries often provided solace for weary travelers, and Buddhist monks, nuns, and their devotees acquired massive quantities of silk for ceremonial functions. A symbiotic relationship existed whereby the growth of Buddhist monasteries increased demand for silk while also supporting its trade and movement.

The earliest schools of Buddhism to spread along the Silk Roads were the Mahasanghikas, Dharmaguptakas, and Sarvastivadins, eventually to be subsumed by the Mahayana sect. As Buddhism spread to Central Asia and China, pilgrims began to seek the origins of Buddhism, visiting its holy sites and bringing home its sacred texts. The travels of fifty-four Buddhists, starting as early as 260 CE, are documented in Chinese sources.

Xuanzang, also known as Hsuan-tsang, was a Chinese Buddhist monk; like many others he sought a more in-depth understanding of his faith by seeking out original documents and visiting places where the faith began in India. Xuanzang began his 16,000-kilometer journey in 629 CE and returned in 645. As Xuanzang began his journey, the Tang dynasty (618–907 CE) emperor, Taizong, was beginning to restore China and make it a powerful force in Central Asia.

Xuanzang encountered Buddhist stupas (usually dome-shaped structures serving as Buddhist shrines) at Balkh and two large Buddhist figures at Bamian in Afghanistan. Although many areas of former Buddhist expansion were in decline, Xuanzang found in Kashmir one hundred Buddhist monasteries and five thousand monks. Welcomed in India at Nalanda by thousands, Xuanzang found a place of intellectual ferment. Cave paintings at Dunhuang record the triumphant passage of Xuanzang back to China; Xuanzang finished *The Record of the Western Regions* in 646 to document his journey. Gaozong, Taizong's son and successor, built the Big Wild Goose Pagoda at Xuanzang's urging to house relics and Buddhist scriptures.

A chaotic period of religious exchange and development began with the rise of the Mongols during the 1100s and 1200s. The Silk Roads' pivotal role in cultural and religious exchange eventually declined with the advent of the Age of Exploration during the fifteenth and sixteenth centuries. Additionally, Muslim control of long-distance trade routes helped to enhance the Islamization of Central Asia. Central Asian peoples apparently therefore accommodated themselves to those people who were the major participants in their trade connections. Trade led to cultural exchange; thus trade was an important factor in spreading the world's great religions.

Chinese emperors worshipped at this great Buddhist temple when they retreated to Beijing's Summer Palace during the hottest months.

Buddhism in China and Japan

Buddhism, Christianity, and Islam spread in various areas, but to truly make a home in foreign lands these faiths often accommodated themselves to the local culture and modified or even changed some of their values or traditions. In China Buddhists spreading the faith emphasized the compassionate aspects of the faith rather than the disciplined aspects of Theravada Buddhism, and Nestorian Christians used Daoist (relating to a religion developed from Daoist philosophy and folk and Buddhist religion) or Buddhist terms, calling the books of the Bible "sutras" (precepts summarizing Vedic teaching).

Buddhism reached China by the first century CE, and a number of Mahayana sects developed there, including Tiantai, Huayan, Pure Land, and Chan.

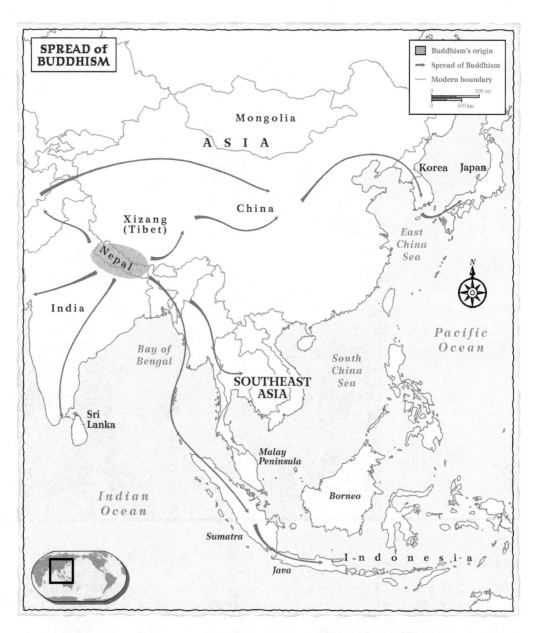

Pure Land developed as a way to reach the general population without its members having to grasp all the intricate philosophical teachings of Buddhism. Followers of Pure Land simply were to call or chant the name of Amitabha Buddha for salvation in paradise or the Pure Land.

The Indian monk Bodhidharma is reputed to have brought Chan Buddhism to China during the sixth

Religion is to mysticism what popularization is to science.
• Henri Bergson (1859–1941)

century CE. The word *Chan* (*Zen* in Japanese) derives from the Sanskrit word *dhyana* and means "meditation," so Chan is meditation Buddhism. Towering figures such as Huineng (638–713) and Zhaozhou (778–897) strengthened Chan so that by the ninth century major schools of Chan called "Linji" and "Caodong" had developed and would later be exported to Japan as the Zen sects of Rinzai and Soto.

Buddhism had already arrived in Japan from China and Korea during the 500s CE. During the Kamakura period of Japanese history, from 1185 to 1333, Buddhism experienced dramatic growth and reinvigoration. Energetic and charismatic figures such as Nichiren (1222–1282) founded new sects. The medieval period has been characterized as one of the most religious times in Japanese history.

Buddhism had evolved in China to the point that, during the Southern Song dynasty (1127–1279), Chan or Zen dominated Buddhist teachings. Scholars usually credit Myozen Eisai (1141–1215) for introducing Rinzai Zen and Dogen Kigen (1200–1253) for introducing Soto Zen. The Rinzai sect emphasizes *koan* (spiritual exercise) as its prime tool for achieving understanding and enlightenment, whereas the Soto sect emphasizes *zazen* (sitting meditation). Both Eisai and Dogen studied in China under Chan masters, receiving recognition of their enlightenment— an official document of lineage is important in Zen and helps to provide credentials to teach upon one's return home. During the twentieth century, appreciation of Dogen's work grew, and today Dogen is perceived as one of Japan's greatest geniuses and the most noted Zen figure in Japan.

With the influx of Chinese masters during the 1200s and 1300s, Japanese Zen more closely resembled its Chinese Chan counterpart. In fact, the Five Mountains system of temple organization, which arose during the late 1300s, was based on the Chinese model. The ironic aspect of Zen growth is that Zen had few real practitioners. Its primary role initially was transmitting Chinese culture to Japan. The Japanese and Chinese masters achieved influence and success because of their access to Chinese culture during the Song dynasty (960–1279).

Buddhism and the West

Much of the early Western exposure to Buddhism came through the Japanese. Eight people, including three Buddhist priests, represented Japanese Buddhism at the World Parliament of Religions in 1893, held in Chicago. The writings of D. T. Suzuki helped to open Western eyes to Buddhism and began to popularize Zen Buddhism. During the last half of the twentieth century, new patterns of immigration and many U.S. and European citizens who turned to non-Western faiths helped Islam, Buddhism, Hinduism, Confucianism, and Daoism have an impact on Western culture. Older and recent emigrants from Asia—Chinese, Koreans, Vietnamese, and Tibetans—have played a large role in establishing a Buddhist foothold in the West and exposing Westerners (Euro-Americans) to the traditions of Asia.

Buddhism's rise in the United States can be attributed to people's search for answers and the rapid changes brought about by a modern and consumer-driven society. Buddhism's rise is also because of dedicated teachers, such as Sylvia Boorstein, Chogyam Trungpa, and Jon Kabat-Zinn, who have helped to popularize the faith. The Vietnamese monk Thich Nhat Hanh has had an important influence on U.S. Buddhism. The Dalai Lama (the spiritual head of Tibetan Buddhism) also has promoted a more engaged Buddhism with his pleas for Tibetan freedom from China. The Tibetan diaspora (scattering) has opened up access to teachers and lamas (monks) who, until the Chinese occupied Tibet in 1959, were little known outside their own country. The Dalai Lama himself has come to symbolize for many the face of Buddhism shown to the world. His character and compassion in the face of difficulties for his own people exemplify for many the best attributes of the Buddhist life.

Shunryu Suzuki was a Japanese Zen priest who came to the United States in 1959 and settled at a small temple in San Francisco. He is credited with establishing the first Zen monastery in the United States at Tassajara, California, in 1967. *The Three Pillars of Zen* (1965) by Philip Kapleau was one of the first books in English that discussed the practice of Zen Buddhism. The book has had an impact far beyond the students of Kapleau because many people in the United States lacked access to a Buddhist teacher but were shown how to begin meditating and practice on their own by Kapleau's book. Much of the Buddhist faith in Asia is centered on the *sangha*, whereas in the United States no real *sangha* exists.

Buddhism and Change

Buddhism flowered in the West during the last three decades of the twentieth century, and Zen became a cottage industry. What attracted Westerners, particularly well-educated and professional people, to the faith? The beliefs of Buddhism "are more compatible with a secular scientific worldview than those of the more established Western religions" (Coleman 2001, 205).

In a world that grows smaller each day, the Internet has provided a link to the Buddhist communities of the world and has begun to house the vast amount of Buddhist scriptural writing. The Internet may hold hope for many who practice alone or who are in ill health to have access to qualified teachers. Nonetheless, Buddhism is uniquely suited to isolated practice and meditation. Whether Buddhism will continue to broaden its appeal in the West is difficult to say. Even in Asia monasteries and monkhood are difficult choices in an ever-broadening world consumer culture. Buddhism, like many of the great faiths of the world, has found ways to adapt and survive for centuries. Buddhism continues as a way, the Middle Way, to work toward peace, compassion, and enlightenment. Yet, we have only to look back to the Buddha's own words to find the future of Buddhism. The Buddha said that the only really permanent thing in this world is change.

Phillip WHIGHAM

Georgia Military College

See also Buddha

Further Reading

Adler, J. (2002). *Chinese religious traditions.* Upper Saddle River, NJ: Prentice Hall.

Bentley, J. (1993). *Old World encounters. Cross-cultural contacts and exchanges in pre-modern times.* New York: Oxford University Press.

Broughton, J. (1990). *The Bodhidharma anthology: The earliest records of Zen.* Berkeley and Los Angeles: University of California Press.

Buddhist suttas: Major scriptural writings from early Buddhism (T. W. Rhys Davids, Trans.). (2000). Escondido, CA: Book Tree. (Original work published 1881)

Burt, E. A. (Ed.). (1982). *The teachings of the compassionate Buddha.* New York: Penguin Books.

Chadwick, D. (1999). *Crooked cucumber: The life and Zen teaching of Shunryu Suzuki.* New York: Broadway Books.

Coleman, J. W. (2001). *The new Buddhism: The Western transformation of an ancient tradition.* New York: Oxford University Press.

Dhammapada: The sayings of the Buddha (T. Byrom, Trans.). (1993). Boston: Shambhala.

Dumoulin, H. (1976). *Buddhism in the modern world.* New York: Macmillan.

Dumoulin, H. (1994). *Zen Buddhism: A History: Vol. 1. India and China* (J. Heisig & P. Knitter, Trans.). New York: Macmillan.

Foltz, R. (1999). *Religions of the Silk Road. Overland trade and cultural exchange from antiquity to the fifteenth century.* New York: St. Martin's Press.

Goddard, D. (Ed.). (1966). *A Buddhist bible.* Boston: Beacon Press.

Hakuin. (1999). *Wild ivy: The spiritual autobiography of Zen master Hakuin* (N. Waddell, Trans.). Boston: Shambhala.

Huang Po. (1958). *The Zen teaching of Huang Po: On the transmission of mind* (J. Blofeld, Trans.). New York: Grove Press.

Hui-neng. (1998). *The sutra of Hui-neng* (T. Cleary, Trans.). Boston: Shambhala.

Joshu. (1998). *The recorded sayings of Zen master Joshu* (J. Green, Trans.). Boston: Shambhala.

Kapleau, P. (1989). *The three pillars of Zen: Teaching, practice, and enlightenment.* New York: Anchor.

Keizan. (1990). *Transmission of light (Denkoroku): Zen in the art of enlightenment* (T. Cleary, Trans.). San Francisco: North Point Press.

Lin-chi. (1993). *The Zen teachings of master Lin-chi: A translation of the Lin-chi lu* (B. Watson, Trans.). New York: Columbia University Press.

Liu, X. (1998). *The Silk Road: Overland trade and cultural interactions in Eurasia.* Washington, DC: American Historical Association.

Nagarjuna. (1995). *The fundamental wisdom of the Middle Way: Nagarjuna's Mulamadhyamakakarika* (J. L. Garfield, Trans.). New York: Oxford University Press.

Nukariya, K. (1973). *The religion of the samurai: A study of Zen philosophy and discipline in China and Japan.* London: Luzac.

Prebish, C., & Baumann, M. (Eds.). (2002). *Westward dharma: Buddhism beyond Asia.* Berkeley and Los Angeles: University of California Press.

Rahula, W. S. (1974). *What the Buddha taught.* New York: Grove Press.

Shantideva. (1997). *The way of the bodhisattva: A translation of the Bodhicharyavatara* (Padmakara Translation Group, Trans.). Boston: Shambhala.

Skilton, A. (1994). *A concise history of Buddhism.* New York: Barnes & Noble.

Suzuki, D. T. (1956). *Zen Buddhism: Selected writings of D. T. Suzuki.* New York: Image Books.

Suzuki, S. (1996). *Zen mind, beginner's mind: Informal talks on Zen meditation and practice.* New York: Weatherhill.

Tanabe, G., Jr. (1999). *Religions of Japan in practice.* Princeton, NJ: Princeton University Press.

Threefold lotus sutra (B. Kato, Y. Tamura, & K. Miyasaka, Trans.). (1997). Tokyo: Kosei Publishing.

Vimalakirti sutra (B. Watson, Trans.). (1997). New York: Columbia University Press.

Wriggins, S. (1996). *Xuanzang: A Buddhist pilgrim on the Silk Road.* Boulder, CO: Westview Press.

Wumen, H. (1997). *Unlocking the Zen koan: A new translation of the Zen classic Wumenguan* (T. Cleary, Trans.). Berkeley, CA: North Atlantic Books.

Yoshinori, T. (Ed.). (1999). *Buddhist spirituality in later China, Korea, and Japan.* New York: Crossroad.

Chinese Traditional Religion

Chinese traditional religion borrows elements from Daoism, Buddhism, and Confucianism, blending them into a system of beliefs centering upon the gods and spirits who are said to rule the physical world. The pantheon of the popular religion includes the spirits of the deceased and has a hierarchy similar to that of an empire.

The customary beliefs and practices of Chinese popular religion have constituted an integral part of Chinese civilization throughout the course of its five-thousand-year history. Even today, popular religion remains a vital force in many Chinese ethnic communities, thriving particularly in Taiwan, Hong Kong, and Southeast Asia, where it has never been actively suppressed by the political authorities. In general, the ideas and customs associated with this form of religious expression represent a syncretic popularization of the more literary and institutionalized traditions of Confucianism, Daoism, and Buddhism. Existing in relative harmony with these more established systems of belief, popular religion in China has evolved and flourished much more freely than similar folk traditions in the West, where the established religions, such as Christianity and Islam, are exclusivist and have historically suppressed heterodox religious movements.

The belief in the existence of gods and spirits (*shen*) that have power over the affairs of this world constitutes the essential feature of the differing forms of popular religion in China. These spirits are variously conceived of as the deceased members of one's family or community, as deified figures from history or literature, or as the spiritualized embodiments of natural and geographical forces. The most common form of religious practice involves the maintenance of private shrines and community temples, where the prayers and supplications of the believer are frequently accompanied by ritual offerings of food or the ceremonial burning of incense. Various forms of shamanism and divination are practiced in an effort to attain a more sympathetic union between the human and the divine and thereby discern or influence the course of one's personal or community destiny. In short, the values and aspirations that have sustained popular religion throughout the ages are those related to the survival and preservation of the family and community, along with the desire to maintain the delicate harmony and reciprocity conceived to exist between the human and spiritual realms.

Household Rituals

Ancestor worship is one of the most common rituals associated with Chinese popular religion. Dating back to the ceremonial practices of China's ancient kings, it has evolved to constitute a popular expression of the deeply rooted Confucian ethic of filial piety. Traditional Chinese households maintained a domestic altar where ancestral tablets of stone, wood, or paper were inscribed with the names of the deceased to serve as the focus of offerings made to their spirits. Today, photographs often take the place of the more traditional tablets, but the desire for blessings, along with the family's obligation to ensure its deceased members a comfortable existence in the next world, remain the primary motivation of such practices. Those that died with no descendents to maintain their ancestral rites, or who perished

Traditional Chinese households maintained a domestic altar for making offerings to deceased ancestors.

under particularly violent or evil circumstances, were of great concern to the community in traditional times. These "hungry ghosts," as they were known in popular legend, could resort to frightening forms of spiritual mischief if they were not properly propitiated. Many communities therefore established shrines specifically devoted to the ritual commemoration of these orphan spirits.

Another common expression of popular religion at the household level was the worship of the stove god (Zao Jun). Also dating back to very ancient times, this practice represents one of the most enduring cults associated with the Chinese folk tradition and shares many similarities to the worship of fire or kitchen gods in other traditional societies. As the benevolent preserver of the family hearth, the stove god was believed to oversee the moral conduct and ritual propriety of the family unit and to issue a yearly report on such matters to Heaven around the time of the traditional lunar new year. In this respect, the stove god was conceived of as a sort of policeman in a hierarchy of divine officials that ruled the spiritual realm just as the earthly authorities governed the affairs of this world. Worship of the stove god thus reflected the pervasive belief in Chinese popular religion that the spiritual world was organized in a bureaucratic fashion that paralleled the centralized imperial administration of China's dynastic rulers.

Public Rituals

Many other activities associated with Chinese popular religion served as civic ritual intended to preserve social harmony, reinforce local identity, or ensure the good favor of the gods and spirits in meeting the various challenges of community survival. One particularly prevalent cult associated with this sort of community ritual was the worship of the local earth god (Tudi Gong). A small shrine for this deity was maintained in virtually every neighborhood or rural locality in China, bolstering the sense of regional solidarity so characteristic of traditional society. The earth god was believed to protect the community from the potentially evil influences of wandering ghosts or malevolent spirits (*gui*), along with overseeing and reporting the activities of those inhabiting his precinct to higher deities. Thus, like the stove god, the earth god was seen as another component of the spiritual hierarchy that constituted what one modern scholar has described as the "imperial metaphor" of popular religion.

The city god (Cheng Huang) was next highest in the rank of divine officials accorded the task of supervising the spiritual affairs of the local community. Enshrined in a temple near the center of his jurisdiction, the city god was normally depicted in the traditional robes of a Confucian scholar-official. Indeed, the various city gods were frequently associated with a deceased notable honored in local history for his righteousness and efficacy as an official of the imperial government. The city god was even believed to be in command of soldiers that could be used to enforce his divine edicts and preserve the moral integrity of the community. These soldiers were themselves the recipients of ritual offerings by the local residents, who occasionally placed small portions of simple food on the thresholds of their homes to reward them for their service and to assuage their ferocity. On key holidays or anniversaries, it was customary to physically convey the statue of the

Making sacrifices at ancestral gravesites to honor deceased relatives was a basic part of religious ritual beginning in the Zhou dynasty (1045–256 BCE).

city god on an inspection tour of the region under his command. These ritual processions were often accompanied by great celebration and fanfare as the local residents reconfirmed their sense of community by organizing various festivities.

The Supreme Deity and the Influence of Daoism

The origin and essential nature of the Chinese belief in a supreme deity remains one of the most obscure and debated topics in the study of Chinese philosophy and religion. From the investigation of Shang dynasty (1766–1045 BCE) oracle bone inscriptions dating back to the second millennium BCE, it is clear that the Chinese considered Shangdi ("Ruler on High") to be the supreme god of the spiritual realm. Because of its awesome and overwhelming powers, this deity could not be supplicated directly, and the divinatory practices of the Shang kings normally consisted of calling upon the spirits of deceased royal ancestors to intercede with Shangdi on their behalf. In the centuries that followed, this supreme deity became increasingly referred to as Tian ("Heaven") and was regarded somewhat more abstractly, and in a less personified manner, than in earlier times. During the Zhou dynasty (1045–256 BCE), the Chinese ruler became formally regarded as the Son of Heaven (Tianzi), a development that permanently linked the imperial institution with the chief deity of the spirit world. Thus, throughout most of Chinese history, the ruler was regarded as the primary intermediary between Heaven and Earth, and only he was permitted to worship or implore Heaven directly.

From the time of the Northern Song dynasty (960–1126 CE), the supreme deity of the Chinese has been popularly conceived of as the Jade Emperor (Yu Huang Shangdi), the supreme ruler of the heavens and the underworld and the protector of mankind. According to Daoist legend, the Song emperor Zhen Zong (968–1022; reigned 997–1022) experienced a visitation from the Jade Emperor in a dream, afterwards proclaiming himself the deity's incarnate descendant. This official acknowledgement of the Jade Emperor placed the god at the pinnacle of the Chinese pantheon and formally sanctioned the popular conception of an elaborate bureaucratic order in the spiritual world that paralleled the imperial institutions of the world below. In Chinese popular religion, the Jade Emperor reigned supreme over all the Daoist, Buddhist, and other popular deities of traditional lore in addition to commanding the various spiritual forces of the natural world. Approached primarily through intermediaries, the

At the New Year, calligraphy hanging on homes in South China honors kitchen gods and other auspicious guardians who will keep the evil spirits away from the door. Photo by Joan Lebold Cohen.

Jade Emperor was often implored by the common people for good harvests and protection against natural calamities. He was also turned to for the remission of sins, in the hope that his pardon, as the ruler of the underworld, would secure a more favorable afterlife. This popularized conception of the supreme deity was, therefore, less abstract and more accessible to the masses than the Tian associated with classical Confucianism.

Many of the deities associated with Chinese popular religion, including the Jade Emperor, are derived from the various sects of folk (or religious) Daoism that emerged during and following the Han dynasty (206 BCE–220 CE). Differing significantly from the philosophical Daoism of the earlier classical tradition, folk Daoism placed great emphasis upon mastering the sublime forces of the natural and spiritual worlds with the ultimate goal of attaining everlasting felicity and physical immortality. Daoist immortals (*xian*) therefore became the primary subjects of religious veneration, and their individual stories provided the legendary basis for an elaborate pantheon of divine beings. These Daoist "saints," who collectively symbolized happiness and prosperity, included allegedly historical figures from a variety of social and occupational backgrounds, both male and female. The members of an especially noteworthy group, the Eight Immortals, were often venerated as the patron deities of various professions in a fashion quite similar to the veneration of patron saints in Western Catholicism. Daoist deities also included spiritual beings associated with the forces of nature or the agricultural cycle, such as the Lei Gong (the god of thunder), Yu Shen (the god of rain), and Feng Shen (the wind god). Daoist priests trained in the esoteric traditions of their sect were often called upon in times of drought or other natural calamities to perform rituals of exorcism to rid a region of malevolent spirits or to conduct magical ceremonies to restore harmony to the natural forces.

When joss sticks (incense) are burned as offerings, the aroma reaches gods and ancestors for their pleasure in the afterlife. Photo by Joan Lebold Cohen.

Buddhist Influences

Folk Buddhism was another source of many of the deities and ideas incorporated into Chinese popular religion. The most popular among these are drawn from the Mahayana Buddhist belief in bodhisattvas, supremely compassionate beings that have postponed their attainment of nirvana for the sake of assisting all others in the quest for spiritual salvation. The female bodhisattva Guanyin (called the goddess of mercy) was by far the most widely worshipped of these spiritual beings. Often supplicated in times of personal loss or tragedy, Guanyin was regarded as a benevolent savior for the masses, who in her infinite compassion would never fail to rescue or console her sincere devotees. Statues of Guanyin could be found in many Buddhist shrines and temples throughout China, and households frequently maintained her image on their domestic altar. The spiritual comfort of turning toward the loving goddess Guanyin has many parallels to the deep devotion directed toward the Virgin Mary in Western Catholicism.

Folk Buddhism also influenced popular beliefs pertaining to life after death. One of the mostessential features of popular religion in China is belief in a divine system of rewards and punishments, in which departed individuals are judged according to their merits in this life and sent either to a blissful abode in heaven or a tormenting corner in hell. These visions of heaven and hell, along with other notions regarding ghosts and the afterlife, have served for centuries as one of the most creative subjects in Chinese art and storytelling. In short, popular religion in China has

A supplicant puts fake paper money into a burning vat, believing that the "cash" will be delivered to ancestors who will have use for it in the afterlife.
Photo by Joan Lebold Cohen.

assimilated many of the concepts and deities central to both the Buddhist and Daoist traditions, informally combining and transforming them in a manner that has stimulated and inspired the popular imagination throughout Chinese history.

Tradition of Syncretism

The enduring appeal of popular religion among many ethnic Chinese communities around the world testifies to its lasting importance as a conveyor of China's accumulated cultural traditions. By incorporating, in syncretic fashion, key elements of the country's diverse religious and philosophical traditions, it has consistently served to bring a measure of cultural harmony to potentially conflicting systems of belief. Popular religion in China thus illustrates the inherent tolerance and flexibility of Chinese civilization at the level of folk culture. Thus, while sharing some notable similarities with the veneration of saints and other aspects of popular religion in the West, Chinese popular religion has enjoyed a freer course of evolutionary development and has, therefore, more readily assimilated and preserved the diverse influences that have contributed to Chinese civilization throughout its long history.

Michael C. LAZICH
Buffalo State College

See also Buddhism; Confucianism; Daoism

Further Reading

Boltz, J. (1987). *A survey of Taoist literature: Tenth to seventeenth centuries.* Berkeley and Los Angeles: University of California Press.

Bosco, J., & Ho, P.-P. (1999). *Temples of the Empress of Heaven.* Cambridge, U.K.: Oxford University Press.

Chard, R. (1990). Folktales on the god of the stove. *Chinese Studies, 12*(1), 149–182.

Dean, K. (1995). *Taoist ritual and popular cults of southeast China.* Princeton, NJ: Princeton University Press.

Dell'Orto, A. (2002). *Place and spirit in Taiwan: Tudi Gong in the stories, strategies and memories of everyday life.* London: RoutledgeCurzon.

Feuchtwang, S. (2001). *Popular religion in China: The imperial metaphor.* Richmond, Surrey, U.K.: Curzon Press.

Fowler, J. & Fowler, M. (2008). *Chinese religions: Beliefs and practices.* Portland, OR: Sussex Academic Press

Henderson J. (1984). *The development and decline of Chinese cosmology.* New York: Columbia University Press.

Johnson, D. (Ed.). (1995). *Ritual and scripture in Chinese popular religion: Five studies.* Berkeley, CA: The Chinese Popular Culture Project.

Kieckhefer, R., & Bond, G. D. (1990). *Sainthood: Its manifestations in world religions.* Berkeley and Los Angeles: University of California Press.

Lagerwey, J. (1987). *Taoist ritual in Chinese society and history.* London: Collier Macmillan.

Ma, X., & Seiwert, H. M. (2003). *Popular religious movements and heterodox sects in Chinese history.* Leiden, Netherlands: Brill Academic Publishers.

Sangren, P. S. (1987). *History and magical power in a Chinese community.* Stanford, CA: Stanford University Press.

Saso, M. (1985). Vernacular and classical ritual in Taoism. *Journal of Asian Studies, 45*(1), 21–57.

Shahar, M., & Weller, R. (1996). *Unruly gods: Divinity and society in China.* Honolulu: University of Hawaii Press.

Shahar, M. (1998). *Crazy Ji: Chinese religion and popular literature.* Cambridge, MA: Harvard University Press.

Stevens, K. G (2001). *Chinese mythological gods* (Images of Asia Series). Oxford, U.K.: Oxford University Press.

Teiser, S. F. (1996). *The ghost festival in medieval China.* Princeton, NJ: Princeton University Press.

Weisgrau, M. K., & Klass, M. (Eds.). (1999). *Across the boundaries of belief: Contemporary issues in the anthropology of religion.* Boulder, CO: Westview Press.

Weller, R. (1987). *Unities and diversities in Chinese religion.* London: Macmillan.

Christian Orthodoxy

Although it has no central authority, the doctrine of Orthodox Christianity is based on holy tradition, especially the tradition established by the seven ecumenical councils that were held during the fourth through eighth centuries CE. The Eastern Orthodox Church initiated its separation from the Roman Catholic Church of the West in the ninth century, and its theology differs from that of the Western denominations.

The Orthodox Church is a communion of independent Eastern churches organized geographically, usually by country. Together they constitute the second-largest Christian denomination after the Roman Catholic Church. Orthodoxy sees itself as the one holy, catholic, and apostolic Church founded by Jesus Christ.

Eastern and Oriental Orthodox Churches

Most Orthodox churches belong to the Eastern Orthodox family of churches, with a smaller number belonging to the Oriental Orthodox family. In Eastern Orthodoxy, the churches are classified as either autocephalous (completely self-governing) or autonomous (mostly self-governing, but dependent upon a mother church). First among the autocephalous churches are the four ancient patriarchates that remain Orthodox; they are, in order of seniority, the churches of Constantinople, Alexandria, Antioch, and Jerusalem. These are joined by the eleven autocephalous churches of Russia, Serbia, Romania, Bulgaria, Georgia, Cyprus, Greece, Poland, Albania, the Czech Republic, and Slovakia, and the Orthodox Church in America. The autonomous churches are those of the Sinai, Finland, Japan, China, and Ukraine.

The Oriental Orthodox churches are those that may be traced to disputes over the Third and Fourth Ecumenical Councils. The Assyrian Church of the East, sometimes erroneously referred to as "Nestorian," is generally regarded as having not recognized the Third Council. Those churches generally regarded as having rejected the Fourth Council are the Armenian, Coptic (Egyptian), and Ethiopian churches, and the Syrian churches of Antioch and India.

Theological Authority

While Western Christians dispute whether the proper sources of theological authority are the Bible alone or the Bible together with the tradition of the church, Orthodox Christianity understands there to be one source, holy tradition. This tradition is rooted first of all in the Bible, and then in the seven ecumenical councils (including what is commonly called the Nicene-Constantinopolitan Creed, or Symbol of Faith, completed in 381 CE), and in later councils, the writings of the church fathers, the liturgy, the canons of ecumenical and local councils, and the holy icons.

When it comes to the formulation of church dogma, however, the Eastern Orthodox churches accept the validity of the first seven ecumenical councils. These meetings of bishops in the first eight centuries of the church's history, all convened to settle theological disputes within the Church, are considered the most authoritative expressions of Christian doctrine. The First Council of Nicaea (325 CE) affirmed the humanity and divinity of Christ and composed the first

A page from Miroslav's Gospel (c. 1180) an illuminated manuscript resulting from the fusion of Western (Italian) and Eastern (Byzantine) elements. The text is now housed at the National Museum of Serbia in Belgrade.

two-thirds of the Nicene-Constantinopolitan Creed. The First Council of Constantinople (381 CE) affirmed the divinity of the Holy Spirit and added the final third of the Creed. The Council of Ephesus (431 CE) affirmed the unity of Christ and declared his mother, the Virgin Mary, to be Theotokos ("birthgiver of God"). The Council of Chalcedon (451 CE) defined the human and divine natures of Christ, as opposed to the "one nature" doctrine of the Monophysites. The Second Council of Constantinople (553 CE) continued the work of Chalcedon. The Third Council of Constantinople (680–681 CE) condemned the Monothelite ("one-will") heresy, affirming that Christ has two wills (divine and human). The Second Council of Nicaea (787 CE) condemned the iconoclasts ("icon breakers") and upheld the proper veneration of icons.

The Great Schism

The break between East and West, between the Eastern Orthodox Church and the Roman Catholic Church, is often dated to 1054 CE, but the history is more complex. The Great Schism was the result of an estrangement between the East and the West that developed over several centuries due to differences in culture, politics, and language, as well as theology. The chief theological controversies that exacerbated the estrangement and led ultimately to a break in communion had to do with the authority of the Roman pope and a change in the Nicene-Constantinopolitan Creed. Both issues led to the so-called Photian Schism of the ninth century and to the mutual excommunications that occurred in 1054.

The five centers of the church in the first millennium CE, the so-called Pentarchy, were Rome, Constantinople, Alexandria, Antioch, and Jerusalem. Rome, as the first capital of the empire and as the traditional location of the death of two Apostles, Peter and Paul, was honored by being accorded primacy. In the East, the proximity of the patriarchal sees to one another functioned like a system of checks and balances, allowing the East to maintain the polity of autocephalous churches in communion with one another. But Rome was alone in the West, and over time the office of the pope began asserting more and more authority, even to the point of claiming jurisdiction over the Eastern churches. The proclamation of papal infallibility in the nineteenth century added a further obstacle to reunification.

The Nicene-Constantinopolitan Creed declares that the Holy Spirit "proceeds from the Father." Beginning in Spain in the sixth century, however, some Western Christians began adding a word (*Filioque*) to the Latin translation of the Creed that results in the declaration that the Spirit proceeds "from the Father *and the Son*." Despite efforts to add this word to the creed at Rome, it was not officially added to the text until 1054 CE. The *Filioque* issue is really twofold. On the one hand, there is a possible dogmatic dispute. If by *Filioque* the West means that the existence of the Holy Spirit has two sources (the

Clergymen of the Eastern Orthodox Church. From *Costumes of All Nations: 123 Plates, Containing over 1500 Coloured Costume Pictures by the First Munich Artists.* London: Grevel and Co., 1913.

Father and the Son), then the East sees the resulting subordination of the Spirit to the Son as heresy. If the West means something else, however, such as the position of St. Maximos the Confessor (580–662 CE) that the Spirit proceeds from the Father and through (*dia*) the Son, then a resolution of the theological difference is possible. On the other hand, the East clearly believes that no one autocephalous church has the authority to change the Creed, which was the product of two ecumenical councils. So even if there is a dogmatic resolution, the Orthodox position would still require the elimination of *Filioque* from the Creed.

A Liturgical Theology

The etymology of the term *Orthodox* is twofold, having the meaning of either "right belief," "right glory," or both. This is suggestive of Orthodoxy's fundamental assumption that worship is the primary theological transaction. Thus it is the Church's worship, especially its eucharistic liturgy, that is the locus of theology, and not the classroom or the library. The theologian is not the academic but the one "who prays truly," in the words of Evagrios of Pontus (c. 346–399 CE). Orthodox theology is therefore best understood as doxological in character.

The Orthodox Church celebrates at least seven mysteries or sacraments: baptism, chrismation (confirmation), Eucharist, repentance (confession), marriage, anointing of the sick (unction), and ordination. The principal forms for celebrating the Eucharist are the Divine Liturgy of St. John Chrysostom (used most of the year), the Divine Liturgy of St. Basil (used ten times annually), the Liturgy of the Presanctified Gifts (used on weekdays during Lent and the first part of Holy Week), and the Divine Liturgy of St. James (traditionally used on the feast of St. James of Jerusalem, but there is a growing use of this liturgy on other days during the year). While refraining from speculation as to the metaphysics of eucharistic presence, Orthodoxy believes strongly in the real presence of Christ's body and blood.

The Church year begins 1 September and includes the pre-Nativity fast (Advent); Nativity (Christmas); Theophany (Epiphany); Great Lent; Pascha (Easter); Pentecost; and the additional fasts preceding the feast of the Apostles Peter and Paul (29 June) and the Dormition (Assumption) of the Theotokos (15 August). The Twelve Great Feasts of the Church are the Nativity of the Theotokos (8 September); the Exaltation of the Cross (14 September); the Nativity of Christ (25 December); Theophany (6 January); the Meeting of Our Lord (2 February); the Annunciation (25 March); the Entry of Our Lord into Jerusalem (Palm Sunday); the Ascension; the Day of Pentecost; the Transfiguration (6 August); and the Dormition (Assumption) of the Theotokos (15 August). Most Orthodox churches reckon these dates according to the Julian calendar, although since the beginning of the early twentieth century, a number have adopted the secular Gregorian calendar for fixed dates. The Paschal cycle of movable feasts is still reckoned according to the Julian calendar.

Vstriecha krestnago khoda na prazdnik Vsiekh Sviatykh (Procession for the Feast of All Saints) 1945.

In addition to the mysteries, the Church observes the canonical hours of prayer: vespers, compline, the midnight office, matins, the third hour, the sixth hour, and the ninth hour. As in the West, these are rarely celebrated fully outside of monasteries. However, most parishes celebrate Saturday night vespers and/or Sunday morning matins.

Theological Positions

In addition to differences from Western Christianity as to the sources of theological authority, the theology of the Orthodox East is characterized by numerous theological positions, also known as theological distinctives, that greatly affect its understanding of God, humankind, and the economy of salvation. Because Orthodoxy did not undergo Roman Catholic scholasticism or the Protestant Reformation that resulted, the East has avoided many of the theological polarities associated with the internecine struggles of the West.

Mystical Theology

For the Christian East, theology—dogmatic, moral, or otherwise—must be lived. "Mystical theology" is the term that identifies the inextricable relationship between dogma and life, between the teaching of the Church and one's personal experience. In the Orthodox view, theology that is not experienced is useless, and mysticism without theology is mere subjectivity. It is noteworthy that the East has given only three of its saints the title of "theologian"—St. John the Evangelist in the first century, St. Gregory of Nazianzus (329–389 CE), and St. Symeon the New Theologian (c. 949–1022 CE).

Apophatic Theology

The Orthodox tradition distinguishes between apophatic (negative) theology, and kataphatic (positive) theology. While each has a role within the Orthodox theological tradition, the apophatic is clearly preeminent. Following the lead of (Pseudo) Denys the Areopagite (fifth or sixth century CE), the East emphasizes the radical inability of human thought and language to describe God and "utterly excludes all abstract and purely intellectual theology which would adapt the mysteries of the wisdom of God to human ways of thought" (Lossky 2002). The theological ascent to God must be apophatic. Kataphatic theology, on the other hand, is a kind

CHRISTIAN ORTHODOXY · 57

Greek Orthodox churches, like this one in Warsaw in the early twentieth century, share distinctive elements of architecture, especially onion-shaped domes topped by crosses. New York Public Library.

of descent in which God manifests himself within the created order.

The Trinity

At the heart of all Orthodox worship, theology, spirituality, and life is the Holy Trinity—the Father, the Son, and the Holy Spirit. It is commonplace tosay that Eastern theology begins with the three Persons and goes on to affirm the one Being, while Western theology generally begins with the one Being and then proceeds to a consideration of the three Persons. The value of this generalization is limited, but it is accurate to say that the East has emphasized the three Persons of the Trinity more radically than the West. Perhaps the most famous Orthodox icon of all is the Old Testament Trinity painted by the Russian iconographer St. Andrei Rublev, c. 1410. It is a depiction of the three angels who appeared to Abraham in Genesis 18, an appearance understood by the East to be a Theophany ("manifestation") of the Trinity.

Original Sin

Western Christianity's understanding of many subjects, not least of them the question of Adam's sin in the Garden of Eden, has been greatly shaped by the thinking of St. Augustine of Hippo (354–430 CE). Unfortunately, Augustine's view of original sin was predicated on St. Jerome's Latin (mis-) translation of Romans 5:12, which Jerome misunderstood to say that all humans bear the guilt of Adam's sin, and not merely the consequence of that sin, which is death. To avoid association with Augustine's view, Orthodox Christians generally prefer to refer to Adam's sin as "ancestral sin." Christian Orthodoxy also rejects the Calvinist notion that humankind is utterly depraved as a result of the Fall and the resulting denial of human freedom.

The Atonement

Western Christians since the eleventh century have largely understood the reconciliation between God and humankind in terms associated with St. Anselm of Canterbury (1033–1109). His "satisfaction theory" of the Atonement seems to portray God as requiring satisfaction for the sins of humankind, with Christ undergoing the required vengeance. In contrast, the Orthodox or "classical" theory sees the Cross as the victory of Christ over the forces of evil. More than that, however, the Christian East understands the salvific work of Christ as considerably wider and more far ranging than the Crucifixion alone. Humankind was separated from God by our nature, by sin, and by death; Christ overcame these obstacles through his Incarnation (by which he assumed and therefore healed human nature), his Crucifixion (by which he overcame sin), and his Resurrection (by which he destroyed death and made all of humankind immortal).

Soteriology

Orthodoxy has been largely untouched by the Western disputes concerning justification and sanctification, instead understanding salvation as a mater of *theosis*, or deification. Tracing the idea from biblical texts such as 2 Peter 1.4, the Gospel of John, and the epistles of St. Paul, through the texts of patristic witnesses such as St. Irenaeus of Lyons (c. 120–203 CE), St. Athanasius of Alexandria (298–373), and St. Gregory Palamas (1296–1359), the Orthodox understand salvation as our becoming by grace what God is by nature.

Grace versus Free Will

A great part of the Reformation debate with Roman Catholicism centered on the relative roles of grace and free will in human salvation. Some Protestants, concerned to safeguard the efficacy of God's grace, went too far and denied human freedom. Orthodoxy overcomes this opposition with its understanding of synergy, the biblical idea (as in 1 Corinthians 3:9) that we are cooperators with God.

Moral Theology

Western moral theology, utilizing the insights of philosophical ethics, usually portrays the nature of morality as a function of nature (natural law), utility (various consequentialist theories), the character of the moral agent (virtue ethics), or simply as a matter of God's command or prohibition (voluntarism). While these elements play a role in the work of some Orthodox moral theologians, the patristic understanding characteristic of the tradition as a whole sees the moral life as a function of *theosis*.

Spiritual Theology

The classic text of Orthodox spirituality is *The Philokalia of the Neptic Fathers,* a five-volume Greek work edited by St. Nicodemus of the Holy Mountain (1748–1809) and St. Makarios of Corinth (1731–1805), published in 1782. The *Philokalia* ("love of the beautiful") is a collection of writings on the life of prayer ranging from the fourth to the fourteenth centuries. It is associated with hesychastic (from the Greek *hesychia,* meaning "stillness") spirituality and gives special attention to the Jesus Prayer ("Lord Jesus Christ, Son of God, have mercy on me").

Science and Religion

Because Orthodoxy has emphasized a spiritual epistemology, or gnosiology, aimed at the deification of the creature rather than a totalizing narrative subjugated to biblical accounts, it has not been concerned with either the astronomical debates sparked by Galileo in the seventeenth century or the creation–evolution debate that began with the work of Charles Darwin in the nineteenth century but which was more characteristic of the twentieth century.

Allyne L. SMITH Jr.
St. Joseph Center

See also Roman Catholicism

Further Reading

Baum, W., & Winkler, D. W. (2003). *The Church of the East: A concise history.* London: RoutledgeCurzon.

Cunningham, M. (2002). *Faith in the Byzantine world.* Downers Grove, IL: InterVarsity Press.

Lossky, V. (2002). *The mystical theology of the Eastern Church.* Crestwood, NY: St. Vladimir's Seminary Press.

Meyendorff, J. (1981). *The Orthodox Church: Its past and its role in the world today* (4th rev. ed.). Crestwood, NY: St. Vladimir's Seminary Press.

Meyendorff, J. (1996). *Rome, Constantinople, Moscow: Historical and theological studies.* Crestwood, NY: St. Vladimir's Seminary Press.

Papadakis, A. (1994). *The Christian East and the rise of the papacy: The Church, 1071–1453 ad.* Crestwood, NY: St. Vladimir's Seminary Press.

Sherrard, P. (1995). *The Greek East and the Latin West: A study in the Christian tradition.* Limni, Greece: Denise Harvey.

Sherrard, P. (1996). *Church, papacy, schism: A theological inquiry.* Limni, Greece: Denise Harvey.

Smith, A. (1998). Divine liturgy. In P. Steeves (Ed.), *Modern encyclopedia of religions in Russia and Eurasia* (Vol. 7). Gulf Breeze, FL: Academic International Press.

Smith, A. (2004). Eastern Orthodoxy (pacifism in). In G. Palmer-Fernandez (Ed.), *The encyclopedia of religion and war.* New York: Routledge.

Smith, A., et al. (2000). Orthodoxy. In G. Ferngren (Ed.), *The history of science and religion in the Western tradition.* New York: Garland Publishing.

Ware, T. (1993). *The Orthodox church* (rev. ed.). New York: Penguin Books.

Watson, J. H. (2000). *Among the Copts.* Brighton, U.K.: Sussex Academic Press.

Confucianism

Confucianism, based on teachings of the Chinese philosopher Confucius (551–479 BCE), has inspired philosophers and statesmen for more than 2,500 years. It stresses the importance of education for moral development—humane relationships, good intentions, and decorum, as well as loyalty and trustworthiness—so that rulers can govern the state according to virtue rather than coercive laws.

Confucianism, a social and ethical philosophy rather than a religion, originated with Confucius (551–479 BCE), whose name represents a Latinized version of the title Kong Fuzi (Kong the Grand Master). With Daoism and Buddhism, it was one of the three ways of thought in traditional China. The era in which Confucius lived was one in which other major philosophers and founders of religious traditions also lived, including Siddhartha Gautama (the Buddha, c. 563–c. 483 BCE) in India, Zoroaster (c. 628–c. 551 BCE) in Iran, the Hebrew prophets in Palestine, and Thales (627?–547 BCE.) in Greece. He shares with these figures the role of defining the classical heritage of the subsequent civilizations in those regions. In response to conditions of large-scale warfare, diasporas, and rapid social change, all five eras produced humankind's first conscious responses to factors of global impact. The responses were ethical in nature and shared a human-centered belief in the human ability to forge new answers. The parallelism of developments in these five areas, constituting as it does a distinctive world epoch (which the philosopher Karl Jaspers called the Axial Age) intrigues the historical imagination to this day.

Early Confucianism

Confucius first sought ministerial rank in Lu, one of numerous states constituting a not-yet-unified China. Failure at that turned him toward teaching. It is as a teacher that he was remembered, and a philosophy of statehood (sponsored by the state) formed around his teachings. He initiated three traditions: teaching any who would learn (the democratic temper), being a private teacher (education for its own sake), and valuing the transforming influences of history, arts, letters, and music (liberal education).

Confucius wrote no books, but his teachings are gathered in the *Analects* (*Lunyu*), a collection of 479 sections of sayings attributed to him by three generations of students and disciples. Disparate in subject, timeframe, and personal nuance, the work is unified by the fact that all its utterances have to do with Confucius. This work stands at the center of the Confucian tradition, not only in China but in the entire eastern Asian context. The seventeenth-century Japanese Confucian thinker Ito Jinsai called it the most profound book in the universe.

Basic Principles

The three principal ideas in the *Analects* are *ren, yi,* and *li*. *Ren* means interpersonal humane regard, from which flows the entire Confucian social philosophy, in which a person sees his or her own humanity in another person. *Yi* is the impulse to do the right thing, to be *ren*. *Li* (social ritual) is the composite of all decorum and manners from the mundane to the loftiest of rites, the outward manifestations of *ren* and *yi*. These qualities underlie the Confucian interpersonal

A carved stone guard at the Temple of Confucius at Qufu in Shandong Province, the legendary birthplace of Confucius. Photo by Joan Lebold Cohen.

philosophy, and, along with the important qualities of trustworthiness (*xin*) and loyalty (*zhong*), give life to his view of state and society as consisting of the five cardinal relationships: ruler-ruled, father-son, husband-wife, elder brother-younger brother, and friend-friend. Confucius viewed the family as the microcosm of the state and the state as the macrocosm of the family. His philosophy is this-worldly. When queried about his view of religion and the spirits, he said, "Not yet serving humans, how can one speak of serving the spirits" (*Lunyu* [analects], *xianjin* [chapter]).

Mencius and Xunzi

Early Confucianism depended on the thinking of two other philosophers: Mencius (385–303/302 BCE) and Xunzi c. 298–c. 230 BCE), disciples of Confucius who lived some two hundred years after the master. Each with a work carrying his name, the two propounded the idealistic and realistic tendencies, respectively, inherent in the master's teachings. Both works are examples of elegant Chinese prose. Mencius argued philosophically that human nature was innately good. From this premise, the Mencian program for humanity valued persuasion over coercion, exemplary action over dictated rules, and moral factors over utilitarian motives. Mencius appreciated the people as arbiter of moral rule, and in a three-tier order of importance, ranked them above the agrarian economy and the ruler. From this ordering, subsequent generations derived justification for a right of the people to rebel.

Mencius's contemporary, Xunzi, on the other hand, argued that human nature was rapacious and untrustworthy and that morality was acquired by imposing the strictest rules of decorum and control. Good action was to be ritually coerced. Xunzi's teachings encouraged a view of Confucius as a transmitter of ancient norms rather than as a moral exemplar. This realistic strain of Confucianism lends encouragement to Legalism, another philosophy that flourished in China at this time. Legalism, however, demanded strict laws and harsh punishments without hesitation.

State Confucianism

With the Qin dynasty (221–206 BCE), China went from a multi-state arrangement of power based on private and personal loyalties to centralized, bureaucratic rule based on public law. With the changeover from the Qin dynasty to the Han dynasty (206 BCE–220 CE), early Han rulers looked for change from the brutal legalism on which the Qin was based. The first Han emperor (Han Gaozu, reigned 206–195 BCE), a powerful and illiterate wielder of power, had the acuity to ask the Confucian scholar Lu Jia (d. 170 BCE) to discourse on why the Qin failed and Gaozu had succeeded. Lu Jia presented him with twelve lectures (*Xin yu*, or New Discourses), the burden of which was that the Qin ruled with inhumanity and that

Gaozu could enjoy a long rule by observing moral scruples. In 195 BCE, Gaozu paid a ceremonial visit to the grave of Confucius, a symbolic union of brute power and Confucian reasoning. Another Confucian scholar, Jia Yi (201–168? BCE), was asked by the Han emperor Wen (Han Wendi, reigned 179–157 BCE) to propound on the same theme. Jia Yi's efforts (*Xin shu*, or New Writings) brilliantly discussed the faults of the Qin and a vast range of topics on the art of ruling. Thus Confucian ethics and moral behavior entered Chinese politics of state. The grand fusion of moral and political power came when Emperor Wu (or Han Wudi, reigned 140–87 BCE), listening to Dong Zhongshu (179–104 BCE), fully instituted Confucianism as a state religion. Dong's work (*Chunqiu fanlu*, or Luxuriant Dew of the Spring and Autumn Annals) expounded on the role of the scholar in government, whom he claimed was the only appropriate person—not the priest and not the people—to know the ways of heaven, earth, and man. Dong envisaged the ruler, advised by the scholar, as the link between those three realms. He incorporated ancient yin–yang thought (a system based on complementary opposites, as in positive-negative or male-female) into the emerging Han intellectual universe, giving Confucianism properties of a secular religion. The Chinese son of heaven (the emperor), as the first scholar of the land, from then on performed solemn Confucian rites of state. For the next two millennia, by virtue of such institutions as the civil-service examination system, censorial admonition, and imperial universities, the Chinese government fully deserved the adjective *Confucian*.

China after the Han was divided, politically and geographically. The north supported Buddhism, and the Confucian state could only survive in the south, and there only intermittently. China was reunited under the short-lived Sui dynasty (581–618 CE), which favored Buddhism. The Sui, which reunified China in the name of Confucianism, exhibited strong Buddhist features in its ideological outlook. For six hundred years, from the late Han to the Tang dynasty (618–907 CE), Buddhism and Daoism permeated Chinese life. Intellectual, aesthetic, and religious impulses were greatly stirred by these two outlooks, which competed robustly with Confucianism. In those centuries, these three persuasions together shaped the eventual Chinese cultural outlook: Confucianism supporting a successful public life, Buddhism supporting a religious life of compassion, and Daoism satisfying a psyche freed for imaginative excursions. But in the late ninth century, with the success of the Tang state and government, attention was focused once again on Confucianism.

Neo-Confucianism

Beginning with such late Tang thinkers as Han Yu (d. 824) and Li Ao (d. 844), philosophical attention turned to human nature. Centuries of Buddhist and Daoist influences awakened within Confucianists an interest in the languages of metaphysics and metempsychosis (the movement of the soul after death into a new body). A series of thinkers appeared during the Song dynasty (960–1279) to take up the task of explaining the universe, a task that had hitherto been the province of Buddhism and Daoism. Song thinkers like Zhou Dunyi (1017–1073), Shao Yong (1011–1077), Zhang Zai (1021–1073), the brothers Cheng Yi (1033–1107) and Cheng Hao (1032–1085), Lu Jiuyuan (1139–1193), and finally Zhu Xi (1130–1200) excited their age with intellectual vigor and perspicacity. Two schools emerged in Neo-Confucianism. One, the Cheng-Zhu named for Cheng Yi and Zhu Xi, who did the most for it, saw a phenomenal world of disparate objects and appearances, which they labeled *qi* and a noumenal world of ultimate organizing principles (*li*) behind the *qi*. The other school (*xin*), led by Cheng Hao and Lu Jiuyuan, viewed the universe as a organism, whole in itself, with the organizing principle of *qi* (matter-energy or mind; a different word from the previous *qi*) explaining micro- and macrolevels of human existence. The first school propounded a dualism that explained the seeming disparities between phenomena and their ultimate principles; the latter dispenses with the dualism and offers the mind, or matter-energy, as the means of uniting the knower and the known, thereby stressing human intuitive

Hold faithfulness and sincerity as first principles. • **Confucius (551–479 BCE)**

faculties. The two schools are known also as the *li* (principle) and *xin* (mind) schools.

Song philosophical efforts imbued Confucianism with metaphysics and a way to explore one's mind and psyche. Buddhist and Daoist influences ebbed, and Neo-Confucianism supported Chinese state and society for the next seven hundred years. Metaphysics and metempsychosis, however, were not the real goal of this Confucian revival, which aimed primarily at appropriating elements of Buddhism and Daoism to buttress its emphasis on human ethics. Using the new dualism, Neo-Confucianism could now point to individual human nature (*qi*) and ideal human nature (*li*), thus exhorting moral action throughout Chinese society toward higher ideals. Chinese society at all levels—whether manifested in village rules or in the imperial civil-service examinations, and in all intellectual endeavors, whether literary composition or historical inquiry—now emulated a Confucian norm. Thus, while Neo-Confucianism was dynamic in the making, it produced subsequent centuries of intellectual, ideological, and pedagogical formalism in China, and its influences were pervasive in Korea, Vietnam, and Japan.

Modern Fate and New Confucianism

As China met the onrush of modern civilization from mid-nineteenth century on, Confucianism came under attack for having supported the entire Chinese body politic and social hierarchy. Intellectuals such as Hu Shi (1891–1962), Chen Duxiu (1879–1942), Wu Yu (1872–1949), and Lu Xun (1881–1936) called for its abolition, chanting "Crush the Confucian Establishment (*Dadao Kongjiadian*)!" and hailing "Science" and "Democracy." This iconoclasm produced in reaction a twentieth-century neo-traditionalism, nurtured by the call of Zhang Zhidong (1837–1909) in 1898, when China was at the nadir of national strength in face of foreign encroachments, to preserve Chinese culture for substance (*ti*) and exploit Western culture for application (*yong*). While the logic of this saying is faulty in reserving for one culture only morality and for another only instrumentality, it was

eminently satisfying emotionally. Chinese who feared and bewailed the passing of Confucian efficacy embraced the sentiment. Thinkers in the twentieth century such as Liang Soumin (1893–1988) and Xiong Shili (1884–1968) constituted the first generation of the New Confucianism (*Xin rujia*).

After 1950, a second generation of New Confucianists arose in Hong Kong in contradistinction to intellectuals both on the Communist mainland and in Nationalist Taiwan. Amidst manifestos and educational endeavors, scholars such as Tang Junyi, Xu Fuguan, and Mou Zongsan envisaged a new Confucian synthesis combining Confucian moral life with Western modes of living. Their message brought forth a third generation of intellectuals, mostly university professors who wrote in the public sphere from the 1970s. This trend coincided and sometimes coalesced with the rise of an enthusiastic belief that Confucianism was compatible with capitalism. Economic leaps in Korea, Taiwan, Singapore, Hong Kong, and Japan—all nations historically touched by Confucianism—gave them the sobriquet of tigers or dragons of capitalist success. The position was that they were successful capitalist economies *because* of Confucianism. Whether mainland China for two millennia did not develop capitalism *in spite* or *because* of Confucianism has not been satisfactorily answered by the claimants. The bursting of the economic bubble in the late 1990s somewhat shook their faith in this belief.

As modern society's rampant individualism has taken its toll on the collective conscience, New Confucianism has gained adherents who defend its collective ethic against individualism and debate its merits with proponents of individualistic human rights. The debate continues.

Daniel W. Y. KWOK
University of Hawaii

Further Reading

Chan, W. (1963). *Source book in Chinese philosophy*. Princeton, NJ: Princeton University Press.

Chang, C. (1957). *The development of Neo-Confucian thought.* New York: Bookman Associates.

de Bary, W. T., & Bloom, I. (Ed.). (1999). *Sources of Chinese tradition: Vol. 1* (2nd ed). New York: Columbia University Press.

de Bary, W. T., & Lufrano, R. (Ed.). (2000). *Sources of Chinese tradition: Vol. 2* (2nd ed). New York: Columbia University Press.

de Bary, W. T., & Weimin, T. (Ed.). (1998). *Confucianism and human rights.* New York: Columbia University Press.

Fingarette, H. (1972). *Confucius: The secular as sacred.* New York: Harper & Row.

Fung, Y. (1952–53). *A history of Chinese philosophy* (D. Bodde, Trans.). Princeton, NJ: Princeton University Press.

Legge, J. (1960). *The Chinese classics: Vol. 1. Confucian Analects, the great learning, the doctrine of the mean.* Hong Kong: Hong Kong University Press. (Original work 1893–1895)

Legge, J. (1960). *The Chinese Classics: Vol. 2. The works of Mencius.* Hong Kong: Hong Kong University Press. (Original work 1893–1895)

Mote, F. (1971). *The intellectual foundations of China.* New York: Knopf.

Nivison, D. S., & Wright, A. F. (Eds.). (1959). *Confucianism in action.* Stanford, CA: Stanford University Press.

Schrecker, J. (1991). The Chinese revolution in historical perspective. New York: Praeger.

Shryock, J. (1932). *The origin of the state cult of Confucius: An introductory study.* New York and London: The Century Co.

Weber, M. (1951). *The religion of China* (H. H. Gerth, Trans.). Glencoe, IL: Free Press.

Wright, A. F. (Ed.). (1960). *The Confucian persuasion.* Stanford, CA: Stanford University Press.

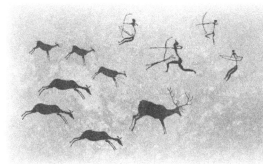

Creation Myths

Almost every human society has had a set of stories that explain the origins of the cosmos; these creation stories (never "myths" to those who believe them) attempt to give meaning to all of existence and often reflect the cultures from which they derive. Modern creation stories, although based on scientific observation and research, still strive to answer the same basic questions as earlier myths.

Creation myths are stories, or collections of stories, that tell of the origins of all things: of communities and landscapes, of the Earth, its animals and plants, of the stars, and of everything that exists. They represent what "history" has meant for most human communities. Creation myths appear to have existed in all human societies and they are deeply embedded within all the major world religions. By offering answers to questions about origins, creation myths provide maps of reality within which people can learn about their place in the cosmos and the roles they are expected to play. As Barbara Sproul states in her book *Primal Myths* (1991, 2–3): "[C]reation myths are the most comprehensive of mythic statements, addressing themselves to the widest range of questions of meaning, but they are also the most profound. They deal with first causes, the essences of what their cultures perceive reality to be. In them people set forth their primary understanding of man and the world, time and space." Marie-Louise von Franz, in *Creation Myths* (1972, 5), writes that they "refer to the most basic problems of human life, for they are concerned with the ultimate meaning, not only of *our* existence, but of the existence of the whole cosmos."

Many striking parallels exist between traditional creation myths and the foundation stories of modern societies, which are embedded within modern science and historiography. Are modern accounts of origins fundamentally different from those of traditional societies? Or can they, too, be regarded as "creation myths"? Such questions are worth pursuing because they raise important questions about the nature of the truths that can be attained within modern historiography, particularly when, like world history, it aspires to a coherent account of the past on many scales.

A Creation Myth Example

Creation myths have taken many different forms. The Genesis story within the Judeo-Christian-Islamic religious tradition counts as a creation myth. So do the origin stories found in the oral traditions of societies without written histories. Appreciating the full significance of creation myths is difficult because, like so many cultural traits, their meaning is obvious to those brought up with them, but opaque to outsiders. So the creation myths of others are almost invariably experienced as strange, exotic, and *wrong*. As the definition of "myth" in the *Encyclopaedia Americana* points out, "a myth is understood in its own society as a true story. (It is only when it is seen from outside its society that it has come to acquire the popular meaning of a story that is untrue)" (Long 1996, 699). The difficulties of understanding a creation myth from outside can be appreciated from the following extract. It comes from the account of a French anthropologist, Marcel Griaule, who is summarizing his conversations with Ogotemmeli, a wise man of the Dogon people of Mali. Ogotemmeli had been authorized to

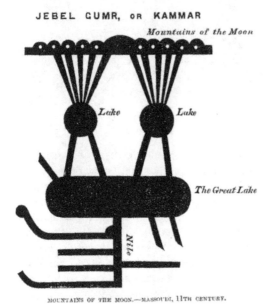

MOUNTAINS OF THE MOON.—MASSOU'DI, 11TH CENTURY.

This diagram, combining myth and reality, depicts an eleventh-century African Muslim belief about the origin of the Nile.

reveal something of his society's cosmology, but it is clear from the conversation that he was aware of speaking to an outsider, who might not understand or fully appreciate all he said, and Griaule himself was acutely aware of the difficulties of this complex process of translation.

> The stars came from pellets of earth flung out into space by the God Amma, the one God. He had created the sun and the moon by a more complicated process, which was not the first known to man but is the first attested invention of God: the art of pottery. The sun is, in a sense, a pot raised once for all to white heat and surrounded by a spiral of red copper with eight turns. The moon is in the same shape, but its copper is white. It was heated only one quarter at a time. Ogotemmeli said he would explain later the movements of these bodies. For the moment he was concerned only to indicate the main lines of the design, and from that to pass to its actors. He was anxious . . . to give an idea of the size of the sun. "Some," he said, "think it is as large as this encampment, which would mean thirty cubits. But it is really bigger. Its surface area is bigger than the whole of Sanga Canton." And after some hesitation he added: "It is perhaps even bigger than that." . . .
>
> The moon's function was not important, and he would speak of it later. He said however that, while Africans were creatures of light emanating from the fullness of the sun, Europeans were creatures of the moonlight: hence their immature appearance. . . .
>
> The god Amma . . . took a lump of clay, squeezed it in his hand and flung it from him, as he had done with the stars. The clay spread and fell on the north, which is the top, and from there stretched out to the south, which is the bottom of the world, although the whole movement was horizontal. The earth lies flat, but the north is at the top. It extends east and west with separate members like a foetus in the womb. It is a body, that is to say, a thing with members branching out from a central mass. This body, lying flat, face upwards, in a line from north to south, is feminine. Its sexual organ is an anthill, and its clitoris a termite hill. Amma, being lonely and desirous of intercourse with this creature, approached it. That was the first occasion of the first breach of the order of the universe.
>
> Ogotemmeli ceased speaking. . . . He had reached the point of the origin of troubles and of the primordial blunder of God. "If they overheard me, I should be fined an ox!"
>
> At God's approach the termite hill rose up, barring the passage and displaying its masculinity. It was as strong as the organ of the stranger, and intercourse could not take place. But God is all-powerful. He cut down the termite hill, and had intercourse with the excised earth. But the original incident was destined to affect the course of things for ever; from this defective union there was born, instead of the intended twins, a single being, the *Thos aureus* or jackal, symbol of the difficulties of God. . . . God had further intercourse with his earth-wife, and this time without mishaps of any kind, the excision of the offending member having removed the cause of the former disorder. Water, which is the divine seed, was thus able to enter the womb of the earth and the normal reproductive cycle resulted in the birth of twins. Two beings were thus formed. God created them like water. They were green in color, half human beings

and half serpents. From the head to the loins they were human: below that they were serpents. Their red eyes were wide open like human eyes, and their tongues were forked like the tongues of reptiles. Their arms were flexible and without joints. Their bodies were green and sleek all over, shining like the surface of water, and covered with short green hairs, a presage of vegetation and germination. These figures were the Nummo twins, water gods who later play a crucial role in the creation of the earth. (Sproul 1991, 50–51, citing Griaule 1975, 16–40)

Features of Creation Myths

These brief extracts, from the start of a long and complex story, illustrate several features of creation myths in general. First, Ogotemmeli's account is told as a story. This may be simply because narrative is the most powerful and memorable way of explaining and transmitting complex, important truths. "Like myth, memory requires a radical simplification of its subject matter. All recollections are told from a standpoint in the present. In telling, they need to make sense of the past. That demands a selecting, ordering, and simplifying, a construction of coherent narrative whose logic works to draw the life story towards the fable" (Samuel and Thompson 1990, 8).

Second, origins are explained as the result of conscious actions by spirits or gods. That spiritual entities created the basic structures of the world is a default hypothesis in many traditional cosmologies. But it is not universal. Many origin stories rely on metaphors of birth, positing the existence of a primordial egg or a primordial sexual act, whose meaning can be understood more or less literally. Some origin stories explain creation as an awakening from sleep, a reminder that our own personal origin stories all have the quality of awakening from preconsciousness. Some creation myths face the paradoxes of origins squarely, positing a realm preceding that of the gods, which was balanced precariously between existence and nonexistence. According to the Rig Veda, the ancient sacred hymns of northern India, "There was

The central part of a floor mosaic (c. 200–250 CE) from a Roman villa depicts Aion, god of eternity, and the Earth mother Tellus (the Roman equivalent of Gaia). The children might possibly personify the four seasons.

neither non-existence nor existence then; there was neither the realm of space nor the sky which is beyond. What stirred? Where? In whose protection? Was there water, bottomlessly deep? There was neither death nor immortality then. There was no distinguishing sign of night nor of day. That one breathed, windless, by its own impulse" (O'Flaherty 1981, 25). Such language hints at the paradox present in all stories of ultimate origins—how can something (whether a god or an entire universe) come out of nothing?

Third, all creation myths are more complex than they may seem at first sight. Because they deal with ultimate realities, with truths so complex that they can only be referred to using richly metaphorical or poetic language, their tellers are usually well aware of their paradoxical, even provisional nature. At one point, Marcel Griaule was puzzled by a detail in Ogotemmeli's story, according to which large numbers of creatures appeared to be standing on a single step, only one cubit deep and one cubit high. How was that possible? Ogotemmeli replied: "All this had to be said in words, but everything on the steps is a symbol, symbolic antelopes, symbolic vultures, symbolic hyenas. Any number of symbols could find room on a one-cubit step." Griaule adds that the word Ogotemmeli used for symbol literally meant "word of this (lower) world" (Sproul 1991, 64).

Fourth, embedded within cycles of creation myths there is generally much hard empirical information about the real world, information about animal migrations, about technologies of hunting and farming, information that younger members of society needed to learn. Such information is often of little interest to outsiders, who may thereby miss the practical, empirical nature of most cycles of myth, but it helps explain their fundamental role in informal systems of education. Ogotemmeli's story, for example, contains a long list of important animals, much lore about procreation and sexuality, details of the major grains farmed in his region, and symbolic accounts of human anatomy and the world's geography.

Finally, partly because they contain so much familiar information, creation stories have the feeling of truth for insiders, just as modern science does

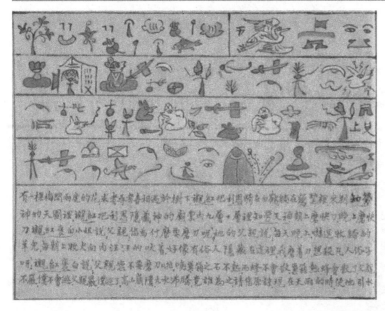

Page from the Translation of the Entire Text of the "Yao Annals of Creation," a bilingual document recording the origins of the Naxi peoples living near the Li River in Yunnan, China. The Dongba glyphs (top) characters were developed circa the seventh century; here they vividly portray the story of Chaozeng Lien, the founder of the Naxi, and his wife, Chenhong Baobai.
National Library of China.

for those educated in the early twenty-first century. To those brought up with them, particular creation myths represent the best available guide to reality and much of what they say fits in well with commonsense experience. This does not mean that creation stories are necessarily treated uncritically by insiders—it is always possible to argue about details of a creation story or express skepticism or even confusion about certain aspects of the story. As Griaule comments of Ogotemmeli, "Ogotemmeli had no very clear idea of what happened in Heaven after the transformation of the eight ancestors into Nummo" (Sproul 1991, 59). But it does mean that familiar creation myths are felt to be the best available guides to reality and therefore to conduct; in some sense, they hold society together. And this makes them extremely important, not to be told lightly or carelessly, and to be treasured and passed on with care by those who keep the knowledge they contain. Creation myths contain potent information, which is why Ogotemmeli lowers his voice when discussing the first blunder of the God Amma.

Similarities and Differences

This partial list of the features of traditional creation stories suggests some of the main similarities and differences between creation myths and modern, "scientific," accounts of the past. Both modern and traditional accounts of origins play an important educational role because traditional creation stories also contain much carefully tested information about the real world. Like creation myths, modern accounts of the past can also be passed on best in narrative form, which is still the dominant form for history writing and much popular science. Modern accounts of origins also struggle with the problem of ultimate origins, something that is clear in the case of modern big bang cosmology, which can say nothing precise until just after the moment of creation. Indeed, like many traditional creation myths, modern physics sees non-being (the vacuum) as a state of potentiality, a realm of emptiness out of which things can appear. Further, when the epistemological going gets tough, even modern science has to fall back on complex and

paradoxical concepts whose full significance may remain somewhat obscure. In this sense, concepts such as gravity or black holes or quantum uncertainty play roles similar to those of gods or other mythic creatures in traditional creation stories. Finally, to an educated person today, modern origin stories have the same feeling of truth that traditional creation myths had for those brought up within them. Because of these many similarities, it seems reasonable to suggest that modern "scientific" historiography, particularly in the form of world history, can play many of the roles that creation myths played in the past.

Yet there are also important differences. It is tempting to claim that modern scientific accounts of the past are truer than those of traditional creation stories. Such claims may be true, but they need to be made with care. Even modern origin stories are anchored in time and place, so in the future they will undoubtedly seem naive and primitive in some respects, as traditional creation stories do today. Furthermore, all creation stories have something to teach outsiders insofar as they offer different ways of thinking about reality. For example, many environmentalists have argued that modern societies need to recapture the sense of being a part of the natural world that is so pervasive in the creation stories of foraging societies. A clearer difference is that scientific origin stories (like modern science in general) aim at universality. They expect to be believed not by just a single culture, but by all educated people on Earth. To earn such universal respect, they require a flexibility and openness that was lacking in many creation stories, for they have to appeal to intelligent people from many different cultural backgrounds, and they have to be able to incorporate new information. This requires a constant testing of hypotheses and details to avoid the parochialism of most traditional creation myths. Because modern scientific historiography (like science in general) appeals to a global audience, the tests to which it is subjected are numerous and thorough. (Unlike Ogotemmeli, we now know from direct experience what the moon is made of and how large it is.) Modern creation stories can claim to be truer than traditional creation myths insofar as the information

70 · RELIGION AND BELIEF SYSTEMS IN WORLD HISTORY

The day will come when the mystical generation of Jesus by the Supreme Being in the womb of a virgin, will be classed with the fable of the generation of Minerva in the brain of Jupiter. • **Thomas Jefferson (1743–1826)**

they contain has been more carefully tested, and as a result they feel true to a much wider audience. The universality and openness to testing of modern scientific accounts of the past explain a final, crucial difference: their unwillingness to invoke anthropomorphic or spiritual explanations for origins. Such explanations are ruled out by modern science because they are too flexible to provide rigorous, refutable explanations, and therefore cannot be subjected to the strict rules of testing that underpin modern science.

As this discussion suggests, world history is perhaps not so different from traditional creation myths. It, too, represents an attempt to tell the story of origins. But its audience is global, and to generate the feeling of "truthfulness" that all creation myths aspire to from a worldwide audience it must try to tell its origin stories without any taint of cultural bias, and with careful testing for rigor and objectivity.

David CHRISTIAN

Macquarie University, Sydney
Ewha Womans University, Seoul

Further Reading

Berry, T. (1988). *The dream of the Earth.* San Francisco: Sierra Club Books.

Brockway, R. W. (1993). *Myth from the Ice Age to Mickey Mouse.* New York: State University of New York Press.

Christian, D. (2004). *Maps of time: An introduction to big history.* Berkeley: University of California Press.

Griaule, M. (1975). *Conversations with Ogotemmeli.* Oxford, U.K.: Oxford University Press.

McNeill, W. H. (1985). *Mythistory and other essays.* Chicago: University of Chicago Press.

O'Flaherty, W. D. (Trans.). (1981). *The Rig Veda.* Harmondsworth, U.K.: Penguin.

Samuel, R., & Thompson, P. (Eds.). (1990). *The myths we live by.* London: Routledge.

Sproul, B. (1991). *Primal myths: Creation myths around the world.* San Francisco: HarperCollins.

von Franz, M.-L. (1972). *Creation myths.* Dallas, TX: Spring Publications.

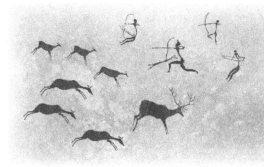

Daoism

Daoism is a philosophy that focuses on self-cultivation and finding value and purpose in this life. It developed into a philosophy of nature, a political philosophy, and a religion that has had a profound impact on cultural, social, and religious life in China. While Daoism changed and developed from its early days before the common era and throughout the centuries—and spread worldwide—it maintained its original position as the Way (*dao*) of conducting human life.

One of the Three Teachings (*sanjiao*) of China (the others being Confucianism and Buddhism), Daoism is perhaps the most difficult to define. Strictly, Daoism is a religio-philosophical system developed during the Warring States period (475–221 BCE); broadly characterized, it is simultaneously an attitude toward life and a soteriological (salvation-oriented) tradition based on harmony with the *dao* (the Way), the immanent source of all existence and the path it lays for humans to follow. Daoism encompasses often-contradictory beliefs and practices, such as shamanism, alchemy, and martial arts. Traditionally, scholars distinguish between an original Daoist philosophy and a later Daoist religion, the former given greater legitimacy than the "superstitions" of the latter. More recently, this division has been challenged, and the development of Daoism is now described as a cumulative process integrating commonly held teachings and fundamental notions, particularly the unity of man and the natural order. The integrative character of Daoism and the unofficial nature of many of its sects make current estimates of its worldwide membership range widely, from 20 million to 55 million.

Most Daoist concepts come from Daoism's foundational book, the *Daodejing* (Classic of the Way and Its Power). Although more likely a compilation developed over centuries and only finalized in the third century BCE, it has traditionally been attributed to Laozi (sixth century BCE), an archivist at the Zhou court. According to China's first universal history (second century BCE), after observing the dynasty's decline, Laozi headed west. Before leaving the empire, he was convinced to record his precepts. Only five thousand characters in length and divided into two parts, the *Daodejing* lays out Laozi's definition of *dao* and his prescription for a "right" society in accord with it. It is a series of cryptic, short teachings, meant as a handbook for rulers in the art of governing in harmony with the universal order. Laozi's teachings were expanded by Zhuangzi in an eponymously titled book (c. 330 BCE) that first presents Daoism as a philosophy for ordinary individuals. Using parables to demonstrate the relativity of all knowledge and values, the *Zhuangzi* levels social difference and, in contrast to Laozi's writings, rejects all participation in society. It harks to a primitivist society where, free from the ethical dangers of the world, ultimate harmony with nature can be achieved. Together, the *Daodejing* and *Zhuangzi* outline Daoism as a metaphysical rather than human-centered philosophy, in which the ultimate end is *wu* (nonbeing), an emptiness through which *dao* can work unimpeded.

As a philosophy of life, Daoism is ingrained in Chinese culture, bridging the more rational Confucianism and the more metaphysical Buddhism. Daoism's influence is clear in Chinese science and medical knowledge, which draw on its emphasis on

71

I realized that Eastern thought had somewhat more compassion for all living things. Man was a form of life that in another reincarnation might possibly be a horsefly or a bird of paradise or a deer. So a man of such a faith, looking at animals, might be looking at old friends or ancestors. In the East the wilderness has no evil connotation; it is thought of as an expression of the unity and harmony of the universe. • **William O. Douglas (1898–1980)**

harmony with nature and its practitioners' belief that to understand nature is to glean insight into the universal order. Daoism has also shaped Chinese literary and aesthetic sensibilities. Its ideas have been acculturated into other Asian cultures, particularly those of Japan, Korea, and Taiwan, where they have influenced autochthonous traditions. It has also become influential in the West, offering an alternative spirituality through practices like *taijiquan* (tai chi) and feng shui.

Daoism and Chinese Syncretism

Though the division into the Three Teachings is practical for appreciating the differences between Confucianism, Buddhism, and Daoism, the boundaries between them have never been sharply drawn. Rather, they are seen as complementary, pointing to the same goals: humankind's full possession of its humanness and its immortality through harmony with *dao*. The Chinese share singular conceptions, most clearly that of *dao*, which means "road" or "way," though it is also understood as "way to follow" or "rule of conduct." The fluidity of the term allows for each of the Three Teachings to nuance its definition. The concept, however, shares a common cosmology, which describes the universe as a hierarchically organized mechanism in which the parts correspond to the whole. The world is divided into three spheres (heaven, Earth, and human), each with its own *dao*, mirroring one another in a macrocosm–microcosm relationship. Communication and harmony between these spheres is crucial to maintain a universal order constantly under threat. Chinese thinkers also see the natural order as manifested in simultaneously antithetical and complementary aspects, known as yin and yang, each of which cannot be defined without the other. Yin and yang encapsulate

the relativity of all things, because any one thing can be either yin or yang in relation to another.

The complementarity of the Three Teachings' foundational concepts is made apparent by efforts throughout Chinese history to integrate the Teachings into a single movement. But this complementarity must not be overstated; deep-seated rivalries for influence at court and over the masses existed among Confucians, Daoists, and Buddhists. Their differences were more than political; while sharing basic concepts, each adopted a distinct attitude toward life, society, and nature. Confucianism, for example, concentrates on creating an ethico-political system to shape a "right" society through propriety. Buddhism abjures Confucian social values, while espousing beliefs, like the illusory nature of the physical world, diametrically opposed to Daoist doctrine. For its part, Daoism represents a more personal and spontaneous approach to life than Confucianism, and a metaphysics more firmly grounded in nature than Buddhism. It builds upon collective concepts, elaborating them into a distinct "way."

Basic Concepts of Daoism

Dao, as defined by Laozi, is a metaphysical principle, both the ultimate order of the cosmos and the source from which everything emanates. The term itself is a mere approximation, as Laozi admits: "I do not know its name; I call it the Way. If forced to define it, I shall call it supreme" (*Daodejing* chapter 25; these and subsequent quotations are from the Beck translation). Although the term was originally used to convey an object's place in a hierarchical order, *dao* itself is outside that order. Not a creator, it is nonetheless the origin of all things in the hierarchy. For example, *dao* is not God (*ti*), but God originates in *dao*. One of its essential attributes is spontaneity. Although it is the ordering principle of the universe, "the Way never interferes, yet through it everything is done" (chapter 37).

Closely related to *dao* is the concept of *de*. Usually translated as "power," *de* refers to the Way's efficacy in the realm of the tangible. *De* is also "virtue," not moral action but the power that the Daoist acquires by living in harmony with the universal order. Daoists approach *de* in three distinct ways: one aims, through meditation, at the conservation of the *dao*'s power as it flows through the body; the second, in contrast, seeks to increase *de* through various programs of movement, such as *taiqijuan* or kung fu exercises, which unblock the *qi* (life force or breath) and rejuvenate the body; the last offers the help of priests in managing *de*, because Daoist practices are efficacious only if consistently performed. Thus, Daoist priests, who understand the flow of *qi*, help the untrained to unblock its flow.

In the concept of *de* we see the interaction between *dao* and man. As a microcosm of the universal order, the body mirrors the plan of the cosmos; and the same forces flow through both. To Daoists, the metaphysics of *dao* and *de* explain and shape human ethics. The ethical ideal of Daoism is self-suppression—*wu*, or inner emptiness. As there is no thing other than emptiness at the core of the Way, so it should be in the human mind. One should be moved by instinct, not rational thought, like a child, embracing the spontaneity inherent in *dao*. *Wu* is outwardly manifested in *wu wei*, or nonaction, a concept that refers not to absolute inaction but to the absence of self-determined action for particular ends. Daoists use the metaphor of a river, malleable yet powerful enough to erode rocks, to explain the above. *Wu wei* is intrinsically tied to the concept of yin and yang, which makes it intelligible: since each action inevitably leads to its opposite, every deliberate intervention ends in failure. In contrast, nonaction leads to success. Even in following the Way, people should not consciously endeavor to do so, for striving results in straying from *dao*.

Daoists seek a return to a past prior to the corruption of civilization, advocating a primitivist society that follows the rhythms of nature. According to

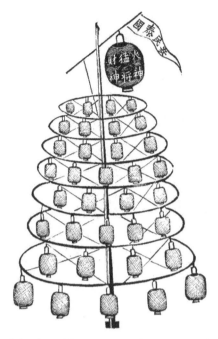

In celebration of the New Year, Chinese display the Lantern Pagoda. Hung with fifty individual lanterns it honors various gods and brings light, a symbol of prosperity.

Daoists, the unity of the universal order has declined since the golden age, a fact elucidated by the short life span of man, who in the past supposedly lived hundreds of years. Zhuangzi explains that, attempting to stem the decline, rulers unsuccessfully interfered with the flow of *dao*, resulting in defiled purity and a useless search for knowledge. Two main doctrines follow: the espousal of laissez-faire government and the rejection of education. Laozi most clearly elucidates Daoist social ideals: "the more restrictions there are, the poorer the people; . . . the more clever cunning, the more contrivances. . . . Do not interfere, and people transform themselves. . . . Do not intervene, and people prosper" (chapter 57). The king's *wu wei* must extend to the rejection of education. Laozi condemns even the desire for knowledge, because it leads to competition over status and profit. The ideal society has neither schools nor books; its people are simple in their true nature. Zhuangzi goes further: law and virtue must be excised, since good and evil, inevitably reverting to each other, are relative concepts. This relativity points to an emerging Daoist skepticism and leveling of moral distinction.

Historical Development

Daoism originated from the shamanic practices of the third millennium BCE. Exhibiting themes such as the search for harmony and immortality, in the first millennium BCE shamanism became associated with the *fangshi*, respected healers and diviners. During this period, Laozi's mystical politics and anarchic ideals also developed, together with Zhuangzi's emphasis on subjectivity and disregard for external behaviors. During the Qin and Han dynasties (221–206 BCE; 206 BCE–220 CE), the Huang-Lao masters, adherents of Laozi's precepts and his ideal government, gained influence at court. Although the emperor Han Wudi (156–87/86 BCE) established Confucianism as the state's official doctrine, rulers privately practiced Daoism, seeking to emulate the semimythical Yellow Emperor.

Emergence of Religious Daoism

During the first century BCE, a messianic Daoism developed that was utopian in outlook and aimed at establishing an era of "great peace." It inspired the Rebellion of the Yellow Turbans (184 CE), who sought to overthrow the Han dynasty. Although the rebellion was defeated, messianic tendencies remained within Daoism. The second century CE saw the emergence of religious Daoism in a new organization that brought temporal and spiritual powers together under the control of the Tianshi (Celestial Masters). In 142 CE, the now-deified Laozi is said to have given Zhang Daoling the definitive, "orthodox" doctrine to replace people's contemporary religious practices. The doctrine sought, through rituals like confession, to expiate sins that resulted in disease. In 215 the Celestial Masters sect was constrained to submit to Cao Cao, founder of the Wei dynasty during the Three Kingdoms period (220–265 CE). The result was the official recognition of the Celestial Masters, who helped legitimize both the Wei and the succeeding Western Qin dynasty (265–316 CE).

The fall of the Western Qin to northern barbarians led to a migration southward, where the Wu dynasty (222–280 CE) arose. In the period of the Southern Dynasties, Daoism was influenced by the traditions of the lower Yangzi (Chang) River, particularly the belief in *zhenren*, pure immortals immune to the world's decay. The immortals became models of attained agelessness, the realization of which was seen as possible through alchemy and magic. By the fourth century CE, this synthesis of the Daoism of the Celestial Masters and preoccupation with immortality led to the development of a competing sect, the Mao Shan school. In general, Daoism gained official support but not sole recognition in the South, while in the North it became the official religion of the Northern Wei dynasty (386–534), whose rulers claimed to be deputies of Lord Lao.

Daoism from the Seventh Century

Daoism's greatest success came with the reunification of China under the Tang dynasty (618–907 CE), as it spread throughout the empire. The founder of the dynasty was believed to be Laozi's messianic descendant, a notion which became part of official state ideology. Numerous temples and monasteries were built, and the *Daodejing* joined the Confucian classics as part of the civil-service exam. During this time, Daoist scriptures also attracted the attention of foreign rulers and were translated into other languages. During the Song dynasty (960–1279), the Daoist canon was expanded and printed for the first time. However, with the decline of the first (Northern) portion of Song dynasty (1126), Daoism lost its place as the official religion. In the fray, several new sects developed. Of these, the Zhuangzhen (Complete Perfection) sect, noted for its ethical teachings, gained the favor of the Mongols and was thus able to challenge the Celestial Masters' preeminence. The sect's emphasis on asceticism and hygienic techniques to prolong life became one of the most important and prevailing currents in Daoism.

During the Yuan dynasty (1279–1368), Daoists used their prominence in the north to lead a persecution against Buddhism, hoping to diminish its growing influence. However, the tide turned, culminating in the state-sanctioned burning of Daoist apocrypha in 1281. In the south, meanwhile, the Celestial Masters' influence continued unabated, although challenged by newly developing currents in Daoism. These new currents embraced Neo-Confucian beliefs, which gained them the support of conservative officials and intellectuals.

During the Ming dynasty (1368–1644), the elite became estranged from Daoism, and Daoism's social status dwindled. The Ming elite held double standards in respect to Daoism: they still drew on its notions to justify their rule, but they put the religion under strict control, inhibiting its independent development. Stifled by the ruling class, Daoism flourished among underground religious sects. The rulers of the Qing dynasty (1644–1911/12) saw Daoism as potentially seditious and started to suppress it, withdrawing most of its privileges. The religion continued to develop among minorities and the lower classes however.

Spread and Influence

With the exception of Taiwan, which saw an influx of Daoists in the seventeenth and eighteenth centuries as part of mass migrations from Fujian Province in the southern mainland, Daoism has not spread systematically to other areas of the world. Its doctrines and practices, however, were absorbed into local traditions across East Asia and are now making inroads in the West. The seeming lack of an exclusive mythology, historical contexts, and personal references in Daoist scriptures has helped give them universal appeal.

Korea and Japan

Daoism arrived in the Korean Peninsula in 624 CE, when it was at its height at the Tang court. The emperor sent emissaries bearing the *Daodejing* and *Zhuangzi* to the three Korean kingdoms, two of which fully welcomed their teachings. In the kingdom of Koguryo, Daoist priests' influence was such that many local Buddhist temples were made Daoist. The kingdom of Shilla sent scholars to China to learn more about the religion and included the *Daodejing* in the Shilla civil-service exam. Although a Daoism stressing self-discipline was popularized at all levels of Korean society, by the fourteenth century Daoism was in decline as Buddhism resurged. Further suppression came with the Japanese invasion of 1592, after which the vitality of Daoism as an independent religion faded. Yet Daoism's influence in Korea is evident in traditional gardening and in the country's flag, the central symbol of which is the Taeguk, representing the correspondence between heaven and Earth.

The Japanese first encountered Daoism in the seventh century CE. Early on, Daoism's affinities with the animism of Japanese Shinto eased an acculturation of Daoist doctrines into Shinto traditions. The introduction of specific Daoist practices dates to the Heian period (794–1185), when Masters of Yin and Yang—diviners learned in the occult—gained influence at court. In the eighth and ninth centuries, practitioners of Shingon Buddhism adopted Daoist physiological practices and the belief in the immortals. Tendai Buddhists embraced Daoist magical arts and techniques for prolonging life. Daoist mysticism made its strongest inroads in Japan through its influence on the Zen schools of Rinzai and Soto, which were introduced from China in the twelfth and thirteenth centuries and are still active today.

Daoism in the West

Western opinions of Daoism have changed from the days when the Italian Jesuit Matteo Ricci first visited China in 1582. Seeing Daoism as an obstacle to the spread of Christianity, Ricci allied himself with court Confucianism and decried Daoism as perverted paganism. This negative attitude persisted into the nineteenth century, when philosophers such as G. W. F. Hegel deemed it a throwback to philosophy's infancy. However, popular nineteenth- and early twentieth-century writers such as Leo Tolstoy and

Franz Kafka brought it to a broader audience, while thinkers such as the philosopher Martin Heidegger and the psychologist Karl Jung embraced its tenets as confirmation of their own subjective philosophies.

The Western interest in comparative studies has brought Daoism to the forefront. Daoist theories have infiltrated discussions of scientific subjects, while its doctrines serve environmentalists as an alternative philosophy with which to criticize Western attitudes toward nature. Daoism's questioning of traditional authority and the substantial presence of women in institutionalized practice have also made it appealing to certain strands of feminism, which see in the interdependence of yin and yang a less divisive way to conceptualize gender. Daoism has also attracted attention at the popular level, its prescription for a simplified life appealing to those who seek to lessen the effects of technological dependence. For example, feng shui is used as a means to harmonize urban living with the energies of nature.

Daoism Today

With over eighty-six sects worldwide, Daoism is one of five sanctioned religions in the People's Republic of China—the others being Buddhism, Islam, Protestantism, and Catholicism. However, its relationship with the government is uncertain at best, since only two sects are officially recognized: the school of Complete Perfection and that of the Celestial Masters. Although the greatest number of Daoists live in China, Taiwan is the center of official modern Daoism and has been since 1949, when the sixty-third Celestial Master, Zhang En Pu, took refuge there. With millions of adherents practicing *taijiquan*, visiting Daoist temples, and studying Daoist healing methods both on Taiwan and on the mainland, the ultimate influence of Daoism in modern Chinese culture is unmistakable.

Maritere LOPEZ
California State University, Fresno

See also Laozi

Further Reading

Allinson, R. E. (Ed.). (1989). *Understanding the Chinese mind: The philosophical roots.* Hong Kong: Oxford University Press.

Beck, S. (1996). *dao de jing way power book, by Lao-zi.* Retrieved July 29, 2004, from http://www.san.beck.org/Laotzu.html

Bell, C. (1983). In search of the Tao in Taoism: New questions of unity and multiplicity. *History of Religions, 33*(2), 187–201.

Bloom, I., & Fogel, J. A. (Eds.). (1997). *Meeting of minds: Intellectual and religious interaction in East Asian traditions of thought.* New York: Columbia University Press.

Cahill, S. (1990). Practice makes perfect: Paths to transcendence for women in medieval China. *Taoist Resources, 2*(2), 23–42.

Clarke, J. J. (2000). *The Tao of the West: Western transformations of Taoist thought.* London: Routledge.

Cleary, T. (Ed. & Trans.). (1989). *Immortal sisters: Secrets of Taoist women.* Boston: Shambhala.

Creel, L. G. (1970). *What is Taoism? and other studies in Chinese cultural history.* Chicago: University of Chicago Press.

Dean, K. (1993). *Taoist ritual and popular cults of South-East Asia.* Princeton, NJ: Princeton University Press.

Kirkland, R. (1997). The historical contours of Taoism in China: Thoughts on issues of classification and terminology. *Journal of Chinese Religions, 25*, 57–82.

Kohn, K., & Roth, H. D. (2002). *Daoist identity: History, lineage, and ritual.* Honolulu: University of Hawaii Press.

Lau, D. C. (Trans.). (1963). *Lao Tzu: Tao Te Ching.* New York: Penguin Books.

Lin, T. (1995). Chinese philosophy: A philosophical essay on the "state-of-the-art." *The Journal of Asian Studies, 54*(3), 717–758.

Maspero, H. (1981). *Taoism and Chinese religion.* Amherst: University of Massachusetts Press.

Moore, N., & Lower, L. (Eds.). (1992). *Translation East and West: A cross-cultural approach.* Honolulu: University of Hawaii Press.

Olstone-Moore, J. (2003). *Taoism: Origins, beliefs, practices, holy texts, sacred places.* Oxford, U.K.: Oxford University Press.

Park, O. (1974). *Oriental ideas in recent religious thought.* Lakemont, GA: CSA Press.

Reid, D. (1989). *The Tao of health, sex, and longevity: A Modern practical approach to the ancient Way.* London: Simon & Schuster.

Tucker, M. E., & Grim, J. A. (Eds.). (1994). *Worldviews and ecology: Religion, philosophy, and the environment.* Maryknoll, NY: Orbis.

Watson, B. (Trans.). (1968). *The complete works of Chuang Tzu.* New York: Columbia University Press.

Wong, E. (Trans.). (1995). *Feng-shui: The ancient wisdom of harmonious living for modern times.* Boston: Shambhala.

Ecumenicism

Generally, ecumenicism is associated with the Christian tendency to promote religious unity, but the term more loosely refers to a desire for global cooperation among all religions. Ecumenicism dates back as far as the split between Rome and Byzantium in 1054. In modern times, ecumenicism was seen during European colonial expansion and again as those colonies gained independence and began their search for religious freedom.

Ecumenicism refers to the striving for reconciliation and unity across the diversity of Christian denominations. To a lesser extent, it can also mean a looser goal of harmony among religions, both Christian and non-Christian. The term *ecumenicism* comes from the Greek word *oikoumene*, designating the entirety of the inhabited Earth (in the scope of Greek knowledge, roughly the lands from the western Mediterranean to India). It is one among many modes of universalistic thinking in world history.

Premodern Ecumenicism

The first wave of Christian ecumenicism occurred in the centuries after the split between Rome and Byzantium. The fairly short-lived unity of early Christendom had rested on the success of the Council of Nicaea (325 CE) and Constantinople (381 CE) in stamping out heretical sects, and of the far-reaching rule of the Roman Empire, which had adopted Christianity as its official religion in the fourth century. The division between the Latin West, centered on Rome, and the Orthodox East, centered on Byzantium, came to involve differences deeper than mere politics: a divergence of ideas about state–church relations, the relative strength of Roman and Greek cultural legacies, and so on. When the crusades brought more intense contact between western and eastern Christendom, the greater visibility of contrasts only worsened the state of ill will. Ecumenical thinking in these centuries revolved around the perceived need to restore the unity of Christendom as one expanding community of believers defined by correct doctrine and loyalty to one organized church (in practice, given the greater Western interest in ecumenicism, the Catholic Church with its pontiff at Rome).

To a lesser extent, the same kind of thinking appeared in sixteenth- and seventeenth-century western Europe. The Protestant Reformation had put an end even to the unity of western Christendom, which had rested on the cultural-religious-intellectual syntheses of Aquinas, Dante, and the like. Despite these multiplying political and doctrinal divisions, the ideal of a single universe of believers lingered throughout Christianity's second millennium. Much as in the other major Eurasian civilizations, a fragmented reality was being measured against the standard of a unified golden age. It was believed that cleavages of nation, race, and class should properly yield to the ultimate solidarity of the faithful.

Of course, broader ecumenical patterns of thinking had long allowed intellectuals to imagine unity, or at least convergence, across the boundaries of sect and rite. Mystics within the world religions have often believed that ultimate spiritual truth, being higher than any doctrine or practice, cuts across the world religions. The most ecumenically

The Indian religious leader Swami Vivekananda played a leading role in bringing Hinduism to the attention of the Western world in the early 1900s.

minded groups have included world renouncers like the gnostics, the Sufis, and the Upanishadic forest dwellers. But even more mainstream theologians in each of the world religions have found ways to justify interreligious openness. For medieval Catholics, there was the idea that other religions, even if they lacked the crucial centrality of Jesus as savior, at least reflected natural law and an innate human tendency to seek the divine. Islam had a framework of respecting other religions, such as Judaism, Christianity, and Zoroastrianism, as legacies of earlier divine revelations that had become distorted over time. And the various branches of Hinduism tended to imagine all religions as alternative paths to the same goal. This kind of ecumenical openness has been a recurring theme in those world-historical encounters that go beyond trade and migration into the more challenging realm of intellectual dialogue. Religious cosmopolitans have always tried to step back from superficial differences of practice and symbolism, to find common ground in divine or human nature. Examples include the interreligious councils of Akbar and Abu'l Fazl in Mughal India, and the entry of Jesuit missionaries to Confucian China in the 1500s.

Ecumenicism in Modernity

The twentieth century saw a second major wave of Christian ecumenicism. At first the need for a common front in European colonial missionary activity drove the search for unity, especially across the Protestant denominations. The 1910 World Missionary Conference at Edinburgh is often seen as the start of this ecumenicism. Later, the broadening of ecumenicism to encompass Protestant, Catholic, and Orthodox branches of Christianity responded to other pressures, like the crisis of secularization in the West. Many Christians saw fragmentation as due to petty squabbles, and as an obstacle in counteracting the broader decline of religious belief among the peoples of the developed world. Social and geographic mobility also increased many believers' desire to cross-denominational boundaries and do such things as take communion together.

In the later twentieth century, ecumenicism often took on a more leftist cast. The rise of national Christian churches in newly independent African and Asian countries broadened the base of transnational ecumenical bodies like the World Council of Churches. Issues of human rights, nuclear disarmament, and social equality figured more prominently in ecumenical circles from the 1960s onward. Efforts have aimed mainly at enhancing practical cooperation, moving toward mutual recognition of baptisms and marriages, and overcoming thorny debates over the historical roots of priestly authority. Ecumenicism has tended to draw support mainly from high-culture establishment versions of Christianity like Anglicanism and Catholicism, and from the more liberal currents like Unitarianism. Opposition has remained strong among Evangelicals and others who consider it misguided to downplay core doctrinal commitments, or who for

Thomas S. Sinclair, *Christian Union* (c. 1845). Lithograph. Protestant clergymen officiate at the altar of the New World flanked by the lion and lamb, iconic symbols of Christianity, while a Native American man and an African slave gesture toward a dove, symbol of peace.

various reasons dislike the political agendas that ecumenicism has embraced. Often the strongest voices of present-day religious resurgence, such as born-again Christians, have affirmed their identities in a way that leaves little room for ecumenical bridge-building.

Broadening Horizons in World Religions

In the last few decades, the scope of ecumenicism has also expanded to include openness to non-Christian religions. Theological dialogues with Jews and Muslims, who share many of the same historical and metaphysical reference points, are one example. The broadening of ecumenicism also reflects a growing Western interest, especially since midcentury, in Asian religious traditions such as Buddhism. Ecumenically minded clergy and laypersons alike often look beyond Christianity for sources of meaning in a disenchanted modern world, and for potential allies in an era of growing secularization. This interest in the non-Christian traditions is loosely analogous to the way the study of world history itself has been broadened, and the effort to overcome earlier Eurocentrism

I love you when you bow in your mosque, kneel in your temple, pray in your church. For you and I are sons of one religion, and it is the spirit. • **Kahlil Gibran (1883–1931)**

in how Westerners made sense of their place in the world.

Adam K. WEBB
Princeton University

See also Religious Freedom; Religious Syncretism

Further Reading

Kryanev, Y. (1980). *Christian ecumenism.* Moscow: Progress Publishers.

Panikkar, R. (1964). *The unknown Christ of Hinduism.* London: Darton, Longman, and Todd.

Rizvi, S. A. A. (1975). *Religious and intellectual history of the Muslims in Akbar's reign, with special reference to Abu'l Fazl.* New Delhi, India: Munshiram Manoharlal Publishers.

Ronan, C. E., & Oh, B. B. C. (Eds.). (1988). *East meets West: The Jesuits in China, 1582–1773.* Chicago: Loyola University Press.

Rouse, R., Neill, S. C., & Fey, H. E. (Eds.). (1970). *A history of the ecumenical movement, 1517–1968.* London: Society for Promoting Christian Knowledge.

Sagovsky, N. (2000). *Ecumenism, Christian origins and the practice of communion.* New York: Cambridge University Press.

Schuon, F. (1975). *The transcendent unity of religions* (P. Townsend, Trans.). New York: Harper and Row.

Till, B. (1972). *The Church's search for unity.* Baltimore: Penguin Books.

Hinduism

Hindu culture began about 4000 BCE on the Indian subcontinent; today some 900 million followers worldwide practice Hindu traditions, or the "Vedic dispensation." Early Vedic culture was founded on the premise that humans are not born equal, and it considered domestic and public rituals indispensable to the well-being of society and the individual. Pluralism was a hallmark of its religion, with many gods and goddesses invoked in Vedic hymns.

English scholars in the early nineteenth century coined the term *Hinduism* as a collective name for the indigenous religions of India. They added *-ism* to the designation *Hindu*, which goes back several thousand years to the Persians and the Greeks, who had so named the people living beyond the Indus River. It may be impossible to define Hinduism as one religion, but it makes perfect sense to speak of a Hindu culture and Hindu civilization. Over thousands of years there grew on the Indian subcontinent a distinctive culture embracing all spheres of human activity. From India it was carried to large parts of Southeast Asia, including Sri Lanka, Myanmar (Burma), Indonesia, and the Philippines. Ships coming from India via the Philippines may well have reached Central America centuries before Columbus. Today the various streams comprising Hinduism claim more than 900 million followers worldwide.

Origins

Hindus call their own tradition *Vaidika dharma*, "the Vedic dispensation." Its original heartland was the Sapta Sindhava—the area watered by the seven great rivers flowing into the Indus. Later this region came to be called the Punjab, the Five-River Country, after one river had dried out and another had changed its course. *Itihasa Purana*, a vast ancient narrative literature that is the repository for ancient Indian history, contains tales of the beginnings of humankind and of Hindu civilization, including long lists of dynasties going back several thousand years.

To account for the close affinity of many European and Indian languages, around 1860 British scholars invented the Aryan invasion theory. Not supported by literary or archaeological evidence but based purely on linguistic speculation, they asserted that a warrior people, coming from the West, invaded India and imposed their culture, their language, and their social structure on the indigenous population. The supporters of this theory equated this invading people with the Aryans mentioned in the Vedas, India's ancient liturgical literature (c. 1500–1200 BCE). Such an invasion would have been quite a feat, considering that the indigenous population of India at that time is estimated to have been around 23 million. When in the 1920s the first major remnants of the Indus Valley civilizations were unearthed—ruins of large, ancient, well laid-out cities—these were first identified with the fortified places described in the Vedas as having been destroyed by the Aryans' warrior-god Indra. It later emerged that these cities were not destroyed by foreign invaders but abandoned by 1750 BCE, probably because of drastic climate changes. The Sarasvati River, described in the Rig Veda as a mighty river, had completely dried out by 1900 BCE.

There is growing agreement today that the Vedic civilization originated around 4000 BCE or earlier in northern India itself (and not in the west) and that

HINDUISM · 83

the Indus civilization (c. 2500–1750 BCE, now called by some scholars the Sindhu-Sarasvati civilization), was part of it. When the settlements in Sapta Sindhava had to be abandoned, most of the inhabitants moved east into the densely wooded region of the land between the Yamuna and Ganges Rivers (called the Yamuna-Ganges Doab), which became the new center of Vedic civilization. Archaeologists affirm that there is no cultural break between the earlier and the later civilizations in North India.

The Hindu Holy Land

Hindu civilization was from the very beginning closely tied to the land that is present-day India. "The Motherland" has a unique emotional appeal for Indians: the physical features of the country are associated with the gods and goddesses, the religious practices, and the eschatological expectations of the Hindus. The Ganges (or, in Sanskrit and Hindi, Ganga), the Yamuna, the Narmada, the Kaveri are not only reservoirs of water and transportation ways, but also sources of inspiration and ritual purification: they are divinities to be worshipped. The towns and cities along their banks—Varanasi, Mathura, Nasik, Prayaga (Allahabad), and so on—are places where pilgrims congregate to obtain supernatural blessings and from which one can reach liberation. The Himalayas, the Vindhyas, the Ghats, and the Nilgiri Hills are the abodes of gods, sanctified by thousands of *rishis* (visionaries or sages) and *sannyasins* (renunciates) since ages immemorial. Ancient and medieval India was dotted with numerous sacred groves—large uninhabited areas in which the gods dwelled and where nobody could harm an animal or a tree with impunity. Countless temples embellish India's landscape, visibly transforming the country into a holy land, where gods dwell among humans.

Scriptures

Hindu scriptures have come down through the ages in two major streams: the Vedas and the Agamas. The Vedas are the literature of the religious professionals, to be memorized and recited by Brahmans only. They comprise the four Samhitas (collections of hymns: Rig Veda, Sama Veda, Yajur Veda, and Atharva Veda), a large number of Brahmanas (ritual texts), the Aranyakas (forest treatises) and Upanishads (mystical writings). The Agamas are the sacred literature of the people at large. The great epics—the *Ramayana* and the *Mahabharata*—are also important sources of Hindu religion: many Hindus consider the *Bhagavad Gita*, a section of the *Mahabharata*, to be an epitome of their religion. The Puranas, which are Bible-like sacred books, are widely read by Hindus from all classes. Texts such as the Vaisnava Samhitas, Saiva Agamas, and Shakta Tantras are considered to be divinely revealed by the followers of specific worship traditions. They contain creation narratives, genealogies of kings and patriarchs, myths of gods and goddesses, edifying stories, and eschatological lore. Based on these texts, poets and playwrights such as Kalidasa (flourished fifth century CE) and Bana (seventh century CE) produced dramatic literature of a high order in Sanskrit. Poet-saints such as Tulasidasaand Kambha (sixteenth century) created popular vernacular versions

Puja, the worship of great Hindu gods like Lord Siva, still involves old Vedic rituals.

84 • RELIGION AND BELIEF SYSTEMS IN WORLD HISTORY

Hindu Sadhus (Holy Men) walking in a procession. Photo by Klaus Klostermaier.

of the classics, performed in plays and (since the advent of film) dramatized on screen to this very day.

The language of the most ancient literary documents of Hinduism, Vedic, is an archaic form of Sanskrit, the refined language standardized around 400 BCE by Panini. Sanskrit was called *deva vani*, the "language of the gods," a sacred language. It became the language of Hindu scholarship as well as Hindu religious literature.

Rituals

Domestic and public rituals were a prominent feature of early Vedic culture, considered indispensable for the well-being of society and individuals. The praxis and the theory of *yajna* (sacrifice) can justly be called a science: hundreds of intricate and interrelated rules had to be memorized and observed. The construction of the altars required the solution of difficult arithmetic and geometric problems. The altars were built with special bricks arranged in a prescribed geometric pattern, and were conceived of as symbols of the human body as well as of the universe: the 360 bricks of an altar represented the 360 days of the year and the 360 bones in the human body. Additionally, astronomical knowledge of a fairly high order was required to determine the right time for the performance of Vedic sacrifices, and ancient text explained how to determine the positions of celestial bodies at different times of the year.

The routine of fixed, or obligatory, rituals structured the course of the year and the lifecycle, creating a framework supporting communities and families. Rituals accompanied the change of seasons, as well as the stages in the development of persons: public offerings ensured the fertility of fields and domestic animals, while home rituals accompanied birth, adolescence, marriage, and death. Occasional, nonobligatory, rituals were available to give spiritual support in special circumstances and additional comfort to individuals. In later centuries, when *puja*, the worship of great gods like Vishnu and Siva associated with images and temples, became the predominant form of religion, the old Vedic rituals were not given up. Besides the *pujas* the performance of Vedic rites continues to this very day: Brahmans recite Vedic hymns at initiations, marriages, and last rites.

Many Hindus participate in daily temple *pujas* and partake of consecrated food. Major temple festivals are great public events for every village and town. The performance of numerous domestic rituals, such as offering food to the image of a deity or, in the evening, rotating a plate with burning pieces of camphor before the image, is still very widespread in India.

Music is an important part of Hindu rituals. Vedic hymns are recited according to a definite pattern of pitches. Instrumental and vocal music, together with ritual dance, are indispensable ingredient in temple worship.

Societal Hierarchy and Government

Traditional Hindu society functioned on the assumption that humans are not born equal and that their

Flowers serve as offerings in the *puja* (worship) of Ganesh, one of the best-known Hindu gods. Also called the Remover of Obstacles, Ganesh is usually portrayed as having the head of an elephant.

birth in different *varnas* (classes) defines their specific rights and duties. Brahmans, born from the Great Being's mouth, were the custodians of the Veda, the highest in rank. Kshatriyas, born from the chest, were rulers and warriors. Vaishyas, born from the belly—businesspeople, artisans, farmers, and clerks—had to provide the necessities of life for society at large. Sudras, originating from the feet, were to serve the upper three classes. Ati-sudras, the people below the Sudras, are known in English as "untouchables." They were outside the pale of Hindu society proper and were relegated to work that was considered ritually polluting, such as skinning carcasses, cleaning latrines, and disposing of the dead. They were not allowed to dwell in the village proper and were not entitled to using amenities reserved for caste people. Today, in spite of legislation forbidding discrimination, they are still often exposed to disadvantage and mistreatment. Each of the four classes comprise of hundreds of *jatis* (subcastes) that also observe ranking among each other.

Duties varied not only according to *varnas*, but also with respect to one's stage in life. Men of the upper three *varnas* were to spend the first twelve years after their initiation with a reputable teacher. They then had to marry and to produce children. After the children had grown up they were to live lives of simplicity and meditation, and finally they were to become renunciates and as homeless pilgrims were to visit holy places till death relieved them of the burden of their bodies. In reality, relatively few men actually ended their lives as homeless pilgrims.

An important element of the Hindu tradition was the theory and practice of government. Kings were usually Kshatriyas, but Brahmans had great influence as advisers and ministers. One of the aims of the Hindu awakening that began in the early twentieth

God has made different religions to suit different aspirations, times and countries . . . one can reach God if one follows any of the paths with wholehearted devotion. • **Ramakrishna (1836–1886)**

century was to reestablish Hindu dominion after centuries of rule by non-Hindus. The Hindu Mahasabha, the first modern Hindu political party, proclaimed in its manifesto: "Hindus have a right to live in peace as Hindus, to legislate, to rule themselves in accordance with Hindu genius and ideals and establish by all lawful and legal means a Hindu State, based on Hindu culture and tradition, so that Hindu ideology and way of life would have a homeland of its own" (Pattabhiram 1967, 217).

The Indian struggle for independence from the British in the twentieth century was fought by many for the purpose of reviving Hindu civilization. Jawaharlal Nehru (1889–1964), the first prime minister of India (1947–1964), advocated secular socialism and state-promoted industrialization, calling steel mills and hydroelectric dams the "temples of the new India," but under his successors the revitalization of Hindu culture became a major issue.

In former centuries Hindu rulers built temples and supported religious endowments. Today government-appointed temple boards oversee the activities and budgets of most large temples. Businesspeople and industrialists, together with the followers of famous gurus, found new temples all over India. Since independence in 1947, more new Hindu temples have been built in India than in the five hundred years before, amongst them the well-known Birla Temple in New Delhi. Today more than 25 million Hindus live outside India. In Southeast Asia, Europe, North America, Africa, Australia, and Oceania hundreds of Hindu temples have been built, often replicas of famous Indian temples, with Hindu priests performing Hindu ceremonies. The Vishva Hindu Parishad, or World Association of Hindus, founded in 1964 in Mumbai, is active in India and among overseas Hindus protecting and promoting Hindu culture.

The Transmission of Tradition

Vedic religion was family based: specific branches of the Veda were preserved in individual families. The home was also a center for religious practices. The sacred hearth fire was not allowed to die out. Husband and wife together had to perform the domestic rituals. Families were responsible for the lifecycle rituals. Young boys moved into the families of gurus, to be taught. The role of the guru reached great prominence when specific worship communities developed under the leadership of charismatic personalities, who often claimed to be the embodiment of a deity. These religious leaders helped to shape mainstream Hinduism and still exercise great influence on Hindus at large. They regulate the lives of their followers and reinterpret scriptures and traditional teachings. Their writings—especially the commentaries on the Upanishads, *Bhagavad Gita*, and the Brahma sutras—are the main texts for students of Hindu theology. In some circles Vedic tradition has remained intact—in others, it has not. Instead of leaving home with a guru, many boys in big cities receive the sacred thread at the appropriate age and begin being taught traditional ethics and lore by a senior relative or a Brahmin who is a family friend.

Pluralism was a hallmark of Hindu religion from its very beginning. Many gods and goddesses are invoked in Vedic hymns, and Hindus continue to worship a great variety of deities in their temples. There is no creed to which all Hindus subscribe and no one doctrine or practice that is common to all Hindus, except perhaps the nominal acceptance of the Vedas as revealed scripture and the belief in karma and rebirth.

Education

The initiation ceremony at which the sacred thread was given to a young boy (now increasingly again to young girls) was the "second birth" which entitled someone to receiving instruction. It was given to the three higher *varnas*: Brahmans, Kshatriyas, and Vaishyas. Sudras and Ati-sudras were excluded. Traditionally, education was a high priority for Brahmans, whose early life was devoted to study and for whom life-long education was a duty. In addition to learning from a guru in his home, a student could attend a school attached to an ashram or temple. The well-organized, publicly and privately sponsored ancient Indian universities, such as Taksasila (now

Taxila, established c. 700 BCE) in the Punjab, and Nalanda (traditionally dated to the sixth or fifth century BCE, though archaeological evidence points to establishment around the fifth century CE) and Vikramasila (established c. 800 CE) in Bihar, had thousands of teachers and tens of thousands of students. They taught not only the Vedas, but also the "eighteen sciences," later supplemented by the "sixty-four arts." The basic curriculum included linguistics, arts and crafts, medicine, logic and dialectics, and spirituality.

High ethical standards were expected both from students and teachers. Students not only had to pass stringent examinations to prove their aptitude, they also had to live an austere and pure life. Hindus believed in a balance of values, however, as expressed in the four "aims of life." It was legitimate to acquire wealth and to enjoy life, but one also had to practice morality and religion and to seek final emancipation from the bonds of this existence in order to lead a fulfilled life.

Ayurvedic Medicine

Ayurvedic medicine, whose principles derive from the Vedas, was cultivated systematically from early on. It was mainly oriented towards preventing diseases and healing through herbal remedies. Good health was not only considered generally desirable, but also a precondition for reaching spiritual fulfillment. The practice of medicine as a form of charity was widely recommended and supported by Hindu rulers. It was considered a charitable act to provide medicine to the sick free of charge, and it was one of the activities in which monks were encouraged to participate. Two Indian medical handbooks, the result of centuries of development, became famous in the ancient world far beyond India: the *Caraka samhita* (dating from 200 BCE to 300 CE) and the *Sushruta samhita*. Ayurveda was also applied to animals and plants; there is an ancient handbook for professional gardeners and a text for cattle-veterinarians. Other texts deal with veterinary medicine relating to horses and elephants. Ancient India also had veterinary hospitals as well as animal clinics. *Goshalas*, places in which elderly cattle are provided for, are still popular in some parts of India. The scientific value of Ayurvedic pharmacology is being recognized today by major Western pharmaceutical companies, who apply for worldwide patents on medicinal plants discovered and described in ancient Indian texts.

Philosophy

India does not know the division between philosophy and theology that characterizes much of modern Western intellectual history. It is natural for Hindus with an enquiring mind to analyze and investigate the teachings of their traditions, and professional philosophers with a Hindu background deal also with religious issues in a philosophically meaningful way. Hindu philosophical systems are not mere abstract constructs, but paths for the realization of the highest purpose of life. Among the qualifications required for beginning philosophical study is the earnest desire to find liberation from the sufferings of the cycles of rebirth and death, which are caused by ignorance of the true nature of reality.

Among the six orthodox systems of philosophy (*darsanas*) is Samkhya, which teaches a general theory of evolution based on the interactive polarity of nature and matter on the one hand with spirit and soul on the other. All reality is subsumed under five-times-five principles that originate from one substratum. The twenty-five categories to which Samkhya reduces the manifold world became widely accepted in Hindu thought. A second *darsana*, the Yoga system of Patanjali, which dates to around 200 BCE, is wholly based on it.

Vaisesika, the third of the six *darsanas*, offers a theory of atomism that is possibly more ancient than that of the Greek philosopher Democritus (c. 460–c. 370 BCE), as well as a detailed analysis of qualities and differences. It also developed the notion of impetus.

Adhyatma vidya (the term refers to spirituality in general—not a specific system), the spiritual or inner sciences, which relate to Brahma, the supreme reality, was considered the highest: it employed personal experience, a coherent epistemology, and the exegesis of revealed utterances. The Upanishads mention thirty-two *vidyas*, paths leading to the goal of all science. The knowledge aimed at through these was of a particular kind, involving a transformation of the student. The ideas of the Upanishads were further developed into the system of Vedanta philosophy laid down mainly in commentaries on the Brahma sutras ascribed to Badarayana (first centuries CE). Beginning with Shankara (eighth century CE) and continuing with Ramanuja (c. 1017–1137) and Madhava (1296?–1386?), the greatest spiritual minds of India have endeavored to cultivate that science of the eternal reality of the spirit.

Hinduism in World History

Membership in the Hindu community was for many centuries restricted to those who were born from Hindu parents and who had undergone the various sacraments that made a Hindu a full member of the Hindu community both here and in the beyond. Hinduism was always a "world religion" due to the fact that India has always been a densely populated, large country and thus home of a considerable part of humankind. In its heyday (prior to the Muslim invasion which began in the eighth century CE) India attracted students and pilgrims from all over Asia who studied at the large indigenous universities or visited holy places associated with such figures as the Buddha.

During the first half of the first millennium Hinduism also spread into most of Southeast Asia, as mentioned earlier. This period was followed by a prohibition to cross "the black seas" under threat of loss of caste. This prohibition was most likely a move to protect the Hindu community from erosion after the Muslims had invaded India and pressured Hindus to convert to Islam. Hindu thought and culture, however, were adopted by many foreigners who came into contact with India during this time. With the establishment of British rule in India in the eighteenth century and the advent of Christian

missions, Hindus' interest in spreading their religion abroad was awakened: the much-celebrated presentations of Swami Vivekananda (1863–1902) at the World Parliament of Religions in Chicago 1893 and his subsequent journey through the United States and Great Britain resulted in the establishment of Vedanta centers in many places and a fairly widespread interest in Hinduism. The coming of ever more Hindu swamis and gurus to the West since the 1960s familiarized thousands with sectarian Hinduism and attracted many Westerners to Hindu religious communities. It was no longer deemed necessary to have been born Hindu, one could become a Hindu by accepting Hindu doctrines and ritual practices and by receiving initiation from a qualified Hindu guru.

By now millions of Hindus have settled all over the world and have brought Hinduism as their inherited faith to the places where they now live. Scientists with a Hindu background often endeavor to integrate their scientific specialties with Hindu traditional thought and thus consciously promote Hinduism as a modern faith. New Age literature, popular among the educated all over the Western world, is replete with Hindu ideas and images, which it presents as having anticipated modern scientific discoveries and insights. Both by virtue of the large number of adherents and the sophistication of its culture and philosophy, Hinduism is bound to be a major influence on the global civilization of the future.

Klaus K. KLOSTERMAIER
University of Manitoba

Further Reading

Basham, A. L. (1959). *The wonder that was India*. New York: Grove Press.

Dasgupta, S. N. (1925–1955). *A history of Indian philosophy*. Cambridge, U.K.: Cambridge University Press.

Fuller, C. J. (1992). *The camphor flame: Popular Hinduism and society in India*. Princeton, NJ: Princeton University Press.

Halbfass, W. (1988). *India and Europe: An essay in understanding*. Albany: State University of New York Press.

Heimann, B. (1964). *Facets of Indian thought*. London: Allen & Unwin.

Kane, P. V. (1933–1975). *History of Dhamasastra*. Pune, India: Bhandarkar Oriental Reseacrh Institute.

Klostermaier, K. K. (1984). *Mythologies and philosophies of salvation in the theistic traditions of India*. Waterloo, Canada: Wilfrid Laurier University Press.

Klostermaier, K. K. (1994). *A Survey of Hinduism* (2nd ed). Albany: State University of New York Press.

Klostermaier, K. K. (1998). *A concise encyclopedia of Hinduism*. Oxford, U.K.: Oneword.

Klostermaier, K. K. (2000). *Hinduism: A short history*. Oxford, U.K.: Oneword.

Klostermaier, K. K. (2000). *Hindu writings: A short introduction to the major sources*. Oxford, U.K.: Oneword.

Kramrisch, S. (1981). *The presence of Siva*. Princeton, NJ: Princeton University Press.

Lannoy, R. (1971). *The speaking tree: A study of Indian culture and society*. Oxford, U.K.: Oxford University Press.

Lipner, J. (1994). *Hindus: Their religious beliefs and practices*. London: Routledge.

Majumdar, R. C. (Ed.). (1951–1969). *The history and culture of the Indian people*. Mumbai (Bombay): Bharatiya Vidya Bhavan.

Pattabhiram, M. (1967). *General Election in India 1967*. New York: Allied Publishers

Prabhu, P. H. (1961). *Hindu social organisation* (5th ed). Mumbai (Bombay): Popular Prakashan.

Ramakrishna Institute of Culture. (1958–1972). *The cultural heritage of India* (2nd ed). Calcutta, India: Author.

Singhal, D. P. (1969). *India and world civilization*. East Lansing: Michigan State University Press.

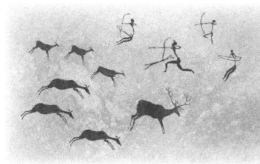

Islam

Islam is both a worldwide community of believers and a major world belief system based on submission to one God, Allah. In the twenty-first century there are almost a billion and a half Muslims (people who accept Islam as their faith) in more than two hundred countries.

Although Islam was initially historically identified with Arabs, today only around 15 percent of the world's Muslims (the people who accept Islam as their faith) are Arabs, with the largest national communities of Muslims being in southern and southeastern Asia. The historic Islamic community began in the seventh century CE in the western part of the Arabian Peninsula; within two centuries the Muslim world stretched from Central Asia to northern Africa and Spain. The term *Islam* refers to a worldwide community of believers and to one of the major belief systems in the world.

The core of the belief system of Islam is the affirmation that one God (Allah) exists. The word *Allah* means in Arabic "the divinity." The word *islam* means "submission," and the belief system is based on submission to the one God, with the person engaging in submission being called a "Muslim." Muslims understand their faith to be a continuation of the message of God presented to humanity through a series of messengers and prophets, including Abraham and Jesus. In the Islamic belief system the final presentation of the message of God was made through the Prophet Muhammad, who lived in Mecca and then Medina in modern Saudi Arabia at the beginning of the seventh century CE. The revelation was recorded and preserved in the Qur'an, the holy book of Islamic faith.

The basic requirements of the Islamic belief system are frequently called the Five Pillars of Islam. The first pillar (*shihadah*) is bearing witness publicly to the belief that "There is no divinity but Allah and Muhammad is the messenger of Allah." Praying (*salat*) is the second pillar. Praying involves performing five prescribed prayers daily. The third pillar (*zakat*) is taking the responsibility to contribute alms to provide assistance to the poor in the community. Undertaking the fast during the month of Ramadan is the fourth pillar. The fifth pillar is performing the pilgrimage (hajj) to Mecca at least one time during the believer's lifetime, if possible. Each of the pillars is a responsibility for the individual believer, and no priesthood or clergy is required to fulfill any obligation. Although "striving in the path of God" (jihad) is an expected part of the life of faith for Muslims, jihad defined as "holy war" is not one of the Five Pillars of Islam.

The Formation of Community and Faith

Muhammad was born in Mecca around 570 CE. He was part of an active merchant community that was involved in trade between the Indian Ocean and the Mediterranean Sea. In addition to being a commercial center, Mecca was a religious center with a shrine that housed important religious relics from many of the tribes in the region. Muhammad's own family was influential in both religious and commercial activities, but his father died before he was born, and his mother died when he was still young. As a young man he gained a reputation for reliability and married a prosperous widow, Khadijah, whose affairs he managed. His life was transformed when he experienced his first revelations around 610 CE.

The Meccan belief system at that time was basically polytheistic, but Meccans were familiar with Christianity and Judaism. Muhammad preached a message of strict monotheism and soon aroused the opposition of the Meccan merchant elite. After many struggles he and his small community of followers moved to Yathrib, a neighboring oasis community whose leaders invited Muhammad to come and be the arbitrator and judge in its disputes. The oasis became known as Medina, or "the city [Medina] of the Prophet." This migration in 622 CE is called the Hijra and marks the beginning of the Islamic community as a distinct entity. Muslims date the years of the Islamic era from the Hijra, with 622 CE being year 1 in the Islamic calendar. This calendar is based on a lunar year of approximately 354 days or twelve lunar months.

During the next ten years most of the people in the Arabian Peninsula became Muslims or were allied in some way with the new Islamic community. The defeat and conversion of Mecca was an important step in this process. The shrine of the Kaaba, a cube-shaped structure at the center of Mecca, was purified of polytheistic relics and recognized as the altar of Abraham. In the prescribed prayers Muslims were to face the Kaaba (for a short time they faced Jerusalem), and the building became the center of pilgrimage rites. The basic foundations of the Islamic belief system and the Islamic community were laid.

The Era of the Caliphs

The Islamic community was dynamic by the time of Muhammad's death in 632 CE. Some confusion existed about the transition to a community without Muhammad. The majority of the community accepted the idea that the successor (*khalifah* or caliph) to Muhammad as leader would be one of his close companions, Abu Bakr. A minority within the community came to believe that the idea was an error and argued that the first successor should

have been the son-in-law and cousin of Muhammad, Ali. In later tradition this minority group came to be identified as the faction (Shiah) of Ali (Shi'as), whereas the majority were called "Sunni" (those who follow the Sunnah or precedents of the community).

The first four caliphs were all close associates of Muhammad (two were the fathers of wives he married after Khadijah died), and their rule is identified by Sunni Muslims as the era of "the Rightly-Guided Caliphs" (632–661 CE). Under their leadership Islamic armies conquered all of the Sasanid Empire and most of the Middle Eastern territories of the Byzantine Empire. Through these conquests the Islamic community became the heir of the great imperial traditions of Persia and Rome as well as the Middle Eastern monotheistic traditions. In structure and administrative practices the emerging caliphate resembled the older empires that had been conquered.

The political history of the Islamic community during the early centuries involves the rise and fall of dynasties controlling the caliphal state, and the political experiences of the community shaped the belief systems that developed. Civil war brought an end to the era of the Rightly-Guided Caliphs, and the new political community was ruled by the Umayyad dynasty (661–750 CE) and then by the Abbasid dynasty (749/750–1258).

Early Abbasid caliphs built a new capital at Baghdad, not far from the location of ancient imperial capitals. Although the Abbasid state was strong, it never established control over all of the territories of the Islamic world. Umayyad princes continued to rule in the Iberian Peninsula, and gradually independent Islamic states were established across North Africa. By the end of the tenth century CE three caliphs claimed authority in parts of the Islamic world—an Umayyad ruler in Spain, a Shi'i ruler in Egypt, and the Abbasid caliph in Baghdad. Local military rulers, who came to take the title of "sultan," increasingly dominated political affairs. The Mongol conquest of Baghdad in 1258 CE brought an end to the Abbasid caliphate. Although the concept of the caliphate as a symbol of Islamic unity continued, basic Islamic

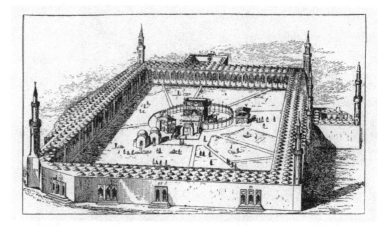

A mosque in Mecca in the early twentieth century.

political organization took the form of sultanates, representing rule by military commanders. This transformation was possible because of the evolution of the nature of the Islamic community itself.

The Faith-Based Community

During the early centuries of Islamic history the caliphate was the most visible aspect of the new Islamic community. However, the development of the Islamic belief system provided the basis for a faith-based community that involved more than an allegiance to a particular ruler or political system. The definition of a legal and normative framework that shaped politics but that was independent of the state helped to create a sense of community identity. The development of popular devotional organizations associated with the growing importance of Sufi (Islamic mystic) brotherhoods strengthened this identity.

The Islamic belief system initially developed within the framework of the caliphate but was not tied to the specifics of the political system. Scholars, not political leaders, undertook the important functions of interpreting the Qur'an and organizing the traditions (hadith) of Muhammad as basic sources for law and guidance. These scholars, literally the "learned people" (*ulama*), never became an ordained clergy and maintained independence from rulers. However, the political and legal dimensions of the Islamic faith were an important part of the belief system. These dimensions were the primary area of disagreement among Sunnis and Shi'as. The Sunnis believed that the historic caliphate was Islamically legitimate, whereas the Shi'as insisted that the only legitimate ruler would be the divinely designated imam (an Islamic leader) who would be a descendant of Muhammad. Most Shi'as are called "Ithna Ashari" or "Twelvers" because they believe that the twelfth imam in the series was taken into divine seclusion and will return at some future time to establish God's rule.

The *ulama* during Abbasid times developed a framework of legal concepts and precedents that provides the foundation for the legal and normative structures of the sharia (Islamic law). No single system of canon law developed. Instead, among the Sunni majority, four schools of legal thought, each identified with a major early scholar—Hanafi (Abu Hanifa, d. 767), Maliki (Malik ibn Anas, d. 796), Shafi'i (Muhammad Shafi'i, d. 819), and Hanbali (Ahmad ibn Hanbal, d. 855)—were accepted as authoritative. Among the Shi'as most recognized the legal thought of Jafar al-Sadiq (d. 765), the sixth imam. In these schools the fundamental sources of the sharia were agreed to be the Qur'an and the traditions or Sunnah of Muhammad. Although theology was important, the core intellectual disciplines for Muslims became legal analysis (*fiqh*) and collection and analysis of the hadith (reports of the words and actions of Muhammad). Differences arose regarding analogical reasoning and consensus of the community. Use of independent informed judgment in analysis was called *ijtihad*. In later centuries Sunnis limited its scope more than did Shi'as.

The content of this legal structure emphasized the universality of law based on God's revelation and the equality of all believers. It was not strictly speaking a code of law; it was rather a framework for a just and virtuous society. The sharia defined both the duties to God and social responsibilities. It covered commercial practices, family life, and criminal behavior. This vision of society did not depend upon a particular state structure and could be presented by scholars rather than rulers and soldiers.

The faith of the majority of the population was also shaped by popular preachers and teachers whose devotional life was an inspiration. The development of special devotional paths or *tariqah*s is associated with what came to be called "Sufism," the mystical piety of early inspirational teachers. By the eleventh and twelfth centuries CE social organizations associated with these devotional paths became an increasingly important part of Islamic societies. The devotional paths emerged as brotherhood organizations that were instrumental in the Islamization of societies in central and southeastern Asia and sub-Saharan Africa.

Expanding Community and the Great Sultans

The Islamic world virtually doubled in size between the tenth and the eighteenth centuries. Great trade networks brought Islamic merchants to most regions of the Eastern Hemisphere. Islamic scholars and Sufi teachers followed, and dynamically growing communities of believers developed as interactions with local people set in motion activities that resulted in the gradual Islamization of societies.

By the sixteenth century the great central states of the Islamic world represented a commanding dynamism. In the eastern Mediterranean the Ottoman Empire began during the thirteenth century in the Aegean area, conquered Constantinople (modern Istanbul, Turkey) in 1453, and, by the eighteenth century, controlled much of the Balkan Peninsula, the Arab world, and North Africa. In southern Asia the smaller Islamic sultanates of medieval times were replaced by the Mughal Empire, which dominated virtually the entire Indian subcontinent by the seventeenth century. In western Africa a series of increasingly Islamized states beginning with medieval Ghana and Mali and ending during the sixteenth century with the Songhai Empire established Islam as a major historic force in the region. Similar developments took place in southeastern and Central Asia.

A dramatic change occurred in the Persian-Iranian heartland. Iran had long been an important part of the Sunni world, with some Shi'a minority groups. However, around 1500 a militant popular religious group called the "Safavids" conquered much of modern-day Iran and beyond. During the next century the Safavid rulers declared Ithna Ashari Shi'ism to be the religion of the state, and most Iranians converted. Shi'i scholars came to the Safavid Empire, especially from the Arab world, and received privileges that gave the *ulama* in Shi'i Iran a special influence that has continued to the present.

Challenges of the Modern Era

This powerful and expanding Islamic world had long interacted with western European and Christian-majority societies. These interactions entered a major new phase during the eighteenth century with the transformation of western European societies, especially through the Industrial Revolution, and the beginnings of European imperialist expansion. Throughout the Islamic world Europeans came to dominate Islamic lands, and Muslims responded in many ways. Muslims mounted major efforts to fight European expansion, as in the wars led by the emir (ruler) Abd al-Qadir in Algeria after the French invasion of 1830. Most military opposition failed.

Leaders in major Islamic countries introduced programs of reform to reshape their societies and states using Western models. Early reformers included Muhammad Ali in Egypt (reigned 1805–1849) and the Ottoman sultan Mahmud II (reigned 1808–1839), whose programs laid the foundations for the emergence of modern-style secular states. Later other

A leaflet in Arabic and Chinese used by Muslims in China in the nineteenth century.

reformers emphasized intellectual and religious dimensions. By the end of the nineteenth century efforts to create an effective synthesis of Islam and modernity resulted in the movement of Islamic modernism. Major figures are Muhammad Abduh (1849–1905) and Jamal al-Din al-Afghani (1839–1897), whose ideas influenced groups as diverse as the Muhammadiyya movement established in Java in 1912 and intellectuals in India and North Africa. A different emphasis in reform is provided by more puritanical movements that seek a "return" to a more strict adherence to Islamic norms interpreted in a relatively literalist manner. This mode of reform has deep roots in Islamic history and can be seen in the premodern movement of Muhammad ibn Abd al-Wahhab (1703–1792), whose ideas have been an important part of modern Islamic revivalist movements.

The broad spectrum of responses to the challenges of modernity in the nineteenth century extended from the Westernizing programs of state reform to the explicitly Islamic modernists and fundamentalists. The work of all of these people set the framework for the developments of states and societies in the Muslim world during the twentieth century. By the end of the nineteenth century few groups could be considered purely non-modern (or, in the terminology of twentieth-century social scientists, "traditional"), since even the most conservative were interacting with the modernity of the time. That era was still largely defined by Western European experiences, so that modernization tended to be viewed as a process of Europeanization or Westernization. But by the end of the nineteenth century, distinctive non-European modes of modernity were beginning to be visible, and the emergence of these different styles of modernity would play an important role in shaping the history of Muslim societies and thought in the twentieth century.

Twentieth-Century Modernity

Global Muslim communities experienced important transformations during the twentieth century. At the beginning of the century, most of the Muslim world was under direct or indirect European imperialist control, and the emerging political systems were primarily conceived as Western-style nation states. Explicitly Islamic movements and organizations were often viewed, even by "modern" Muslims, as anachronisms and obstacles to modernization. By the end of the twentieth century, however, virtually every Muslim majority society was politically independent, and classical European imperialism was an image from a seemingly distant past. An explicitly Islamic republic was created by a revolution that overthrew a Westernizing autocracy in Iran in 1979, and the new Islamic republic was sufficiently strong at the beginning of the twenty-first century to be viewed as a potential nuclear power and as an important major regional power. Muslims and Islamic movements became major influential agents in global affairs.

Prayer carries us half way to God, fasting brings us to the door of His palace, and almsgiving procures us admission. • **Qur'an**

This transformation involved three broad historical phases, which can be defined in terms of the evolution of modernity itself during the twentieth century. In the era of domination by European imperial powers during the first half of the century, most new movements followed European-style patterns of political development. Resistance to European rule took the form of nationalist movements, and social and political reforms were generally secular in orientation. Modernity was defined in Western European terms. The most successful of these movements was led by Mustafa Kemal Ataturk, who built a secular nationalist state in Turkey after the collapse of the Ottoman Empire in World War I.

In the middle of the century, following World War II, the second phase was shaped by the experience of newly-achieved political independence. Most Muslim states became politically independent, and various forms of secular and radical nationalism dominated the intellectual and political scene. Leaders such as Gamal Abd al-Nasir in Egypt and Ben Bella in Algeria incorporated Islamic themes into their radical nationalist programs, but these programs were not primarily Islamic in orientation or identification. By the 1960s, it appeared that the most important political developments and reform movements in the Muslim world represented radical programs of modernity that competed with older visions of modernity. Competing definitions of modernity—or multiple modernities—shaped Muslim policies and visions. An important culmination of this development was the Islamic Revolution in Iran in 1979, when radicalism was defined in explicitly Islamic terms, and the older more secular forms of radicalism became marginalized.

By the final quarter of the twentieth century, distinctively Islamic modernities were articulated as the bases for social visions and political programs. The new movements in the third era of twentieth-century Muslim history had some roots in earlier organizations that were modern in organization but more puritanical in terms of intellectual content. The most important of these groups are the Muslim Brotherhood, established in Egypt by Hasan al-Banna in 1928, and the Jamaat-i Islam, established in 1941 in India by Abu al-Ala Mawdudi.

In the final decades of the century, the major signal that the radical and the secularist nationalist movements had failed to bring the expected prosperity and freedom to Islamic peoples was the Iranian Revolution of 1979, which brought to power a regime dedicated to a full implementation of Islamic rules and norms. During the early 1980s many other movements with strongly defined Islamic goals and agendas came to prominence. These movements represent the emergence of what came to be called "political Islam" because the primary focus of the programs was the control of the state. Some movements, such as the Islamic Salvation Front in Algeria, contested elections, whereas others, such as the Mujahidin in Soviet-occupied Afghanistan, engaged in violent opposition defined in its terms as jihad. These movements of jihad became a significant part of the Islamic experience of the 1990s. In the context of globalization, militant global networks such as al-Qaeda represented an important part of Islamic interaction with the world. However, such movements remained only a small part of Islamic life and often were in conflict with the mainstream Islamic organizations and sentiments that reflected the views of the majority of Muslims.

Although the movements of political Islam attracted the most attention, other important trends also developed during the 1980s. Intellectuals gave increasing attention to the definition of the place of women in Islamic society, and by the beginning of the twenty-first century, an "Islamic feminism" had emerged. This feminism involved a reexamination of the Qur'an, noting the Qur'an's emphasis on the equality of all believers and then noting the influence of more patriarchal perspectives in the way that the Islamic tradition was historically defined. Similarly, some intellectuals have emphasized pluralistic dimensions of the Islamic worldview and tradition and have also drawn back from the emphasis on political activism as a means for imposing Islamic norms.

Some of the impetus for these developments has come from the emergence of minority Islamic communities in western Europe and North America as important parts of the broader Islamic world. In those regions issues of gender equality and religious pluralism have great importance for Islamic community life.

New Twenty-First Century Realities

The continuing significance of religion at the beginning of the twenty-first century confirms the development of forms of modernities that are different from the definitions of modernity popular during the nineteenth and much of the twentieth century. Contrary to the expectations of theories of modernization in those periods, modernization did not mean the inevitable nonreligious secularization of state and society. In the Muslim world, new movements develop that are not simply continuations of old-style movements from premodern times or even twentieth century modern movements in some slightly different form.

The new movements that get the most attention are the militant movements like al-Qaeda. These are clearly different from the early Sufi movements of resistance to European imperialist expansion in the nineteenth century, and from the activist radical nationalist movements of the twentieth century. Globalization and the new electronic media of communication transform the nature of organization and shape the way that the messages of the movements are framed.

The largest of the new movements are not, however, the terrorist organizations. Throughout the Muslim world, new popular preachers and teachers have millions of followers in many countries. Islamic television ministries like that built by the Egyptian Amr Khaled are reshaping the ways that many Muslims participate in the sense of belonging to a global community of believers. Analysts speak of "iMuslims" and "e-jihad" in ways that illustrate the new modernities of Muslims in the world of the twenty-first century. The long history of the flexible adaptations of the Islamic community and belief system to changing historic conditions suggests that new forms of Islamic institutions and perspectives will continue to be defined by believers.

John O. VOLL
Georgetown University

Further Reading

Ahmed, A. S. (1999). *Islam today: A short introduction to the Muslim world*. London: I. B. Tauris.

Ali, A. (Trans.). (1988). *Al-Qur'an: A contemporary translation by Ahmed Ali*. Princeton, NJ: Princeton University Press.

Al-Tabari, A. J. M. b. J. (1985–1999). *The history of al-Tabari* (E. Yar-Shater, Ed.). Albany: State University of New York Press.

Barlas, A. (2002). *"Believing women" in Islam: Unreading patriarchal interpretations of the Qur'an*. Austin: University of Texas Press.

Eaton, R. M. (1990). *Islamic history as global history*. Washington, DC: American Historical Association.

Esack, F. (2002). *The Qur'an: A short introduction*. Oxford, U.K.: Oneworld.

Esposito, J. L. (1998). *Islam, the straight path* (3rd ed.). New York: Oxford University Press.

Esposito, J. L. (Ed.). (2000). *The Oxford history of Islam*. New York: Oxford University Press.

Hodgson, M. G. S. (1977). *The venture of Islam: Conscience and history in a world civilization*. Chicago: University of Chicago Press.

Knysh, A. (2000). *Islamic mysticism: A short history*. Leiden, The Netherlands: Brill.

Kurzman, C. (Ed.). (2002). *Modernist Islam, 1840–1940: A sourcebook*. New York: Oxford University Press.

Lapidus, I. (2002). *A history of Islamic societies* (2nd ed.). Cambridge, U.K.: Cambridge University Press.

Lewis, B. (2001). *The emergence of modern Turkey* (3rd ed.). New York: Oxford University Press.

McCarthy, J. (1997). *The Ottoman Turks: An introductory history*. London: Longman.

Nasr, S. H. (2004). *The heart of Islam.* San Francisco: Harper San Francisco.

Peters, F. E. (1994). *A reader on classical Islam.* Princeton, NJ: Princeton University Press.

Rahman, F. (1984). *Islam and modernity.* Chicago: University of Chicago Press.

Ramadan, T. (2003). *Western Muslims and the future of Islam.* New York: Oxford University Press.

Schulze, R. (2002). *A modern history of the Islamic world.* New York: New York University Press.

Sonn, T. (2004). *A brief history of Islam.* Oxford, U.K.: Blackwell Publishing.

Voll, J. O. (2000). Islam as a special world system. *Journal of World History, 5,* 213–226.

Watt, W. M. (1974). *Muhammad: Prophet and statesman.* London: Oxford University Press.

Jainism

The cosmology of Jainism, originating in India as early as the sixth century BCE, asserts that karmic particles adhere to the soul and obstruct its true nature. Through acts of benevolence, and by adopting a strict moral code of nonviolence (ahimsa), some 4 to 6 million practitioners of Jainism today—mainly in India, eastern Africa, Britain, and North America—seek to shed their karmic burden.

The Jaina tradition arose in India more than 2,500 years ago. The great Jaina teacher Mahavira Vardhamana (c. 500 BCE) was a contemporary of the Buddha, and both taught a doctrine grounded in renunciation of worldly concerns. Starting around 300 BCE, two strands of Jainism arose: the Digambara group, found mainly in south and central India, and the Svetambara group, found mainly in western and northern India. The Digambara require total nudity for their most advanced monks and claim that women must be reborn as men to achieve liberation (kevala). The Svetambara allow their monks and nuns to remain clothed in white and allow for the possibility of women's ascent to the highest spiritual realms. Most Jaina follow a lay life and have excelled in business, particularly in publishing, pharmaceuticals, the diamond trade, marble, and textiles. Although many Jaina self-identify with the larger Hindu tradition, census figures place the Jaina population at between 4 and 6 million.

Jainism emphasizes the teaching of nonviolence (ahimsa). According to the tradition, karmic particles adhere to the soul, obscuring its true nature. By the progressive application of five ethical vows, one is able to diminish and eventually expel the influence of karma, resulting in spiritual liberation. Twenty-four great teachers (tirthankara) are said to have attained this goal and set an example for others through their teachings; the first is known as Adinath, or Rishibha, who is said to have established agriculture, kingship, marriage, and the spiritual path. Mahavira is the most recent; his immediate predecessor was Parshvanatha (c. 800 BCE).

The earliest extant Jaina text is the Acaranga Sutra (c. 400 BCE), written in the Prakrti language and revered by the Svetambara community. It provides detailed instructions on how to practice the five great vows: nonviolence (ahimsa), truthfulness (satya), not stealing (asteya), celibacy (brahmacarya), and nonpossession (aparigraha). Both traditions agree on the intricate Jain theory of karma and cosmology outlined by the scholar Umasvati in his Tattvartha Sutra, a Sanskrit text written in the fifth century BCE.

Umasvati's Tattvartha Sutra proclaims that countless individual life forces (jiva) have existed since the beginning of time. They take many interchangeable forms and are found in the four elements of earth, water, fire, and air, as well as in microorganisms (nigodha), plants, and animals. At the point of death, the life force moves from one body to the next, depending on its karmic constitution. The goal of Jainism entails an elevation of consciousness about one's karma, leading to birth in a human body, and the adoption of a nonviolent lifestyle that will ultimately free a person from all karmic entanglements. At this final stage of blessedness, one ascends to the realm of perfection (siddha-loka) wherein one dwells eternally observing the machinations of the world but never again succumbing to its allurement. All twenty-four great teachers of Jainism are said to have attained this state, along with an undetermined number of saints.

I adore so greatly the principles of the Jain religion that I would like to be reborn in a Jain community. • **George Bernard Shaw (1856–1960)**

Umasvati categorized forms of life hierarchically according to the number of senses they possess. The lowest realm, Earth organisms and microorganisms, as well as plants, possess only the sense of touch. Earthworms and mollusks have as well the senses of taste and touch. Crawling insects have, in addition, a fourth sense: smell. Moths, bees, and flies add a fifth: sight. The Jaina place animals that can hear—and those that can hear and think, including reptiles, birds, and mammals—at the highest realm. As such, these life forms develop moral agency, and can make clear decisions about their behavior. Jaina cosmology imbues all aspects of the world that surrounds us with feelings and consciousness. The earth we tread upon, the water we drink, the air we inhale, the chair that supports us, the light that illumines our day—all these entities feel us through the sense of touch, though we might seldom acknowledge their presence. Humans, as living, sensate, sentient beings, have been given the special task and responsibility of growing in awareness and appreciation of these other life forms, and acting accordingly. Humans have the opportunity to cultivate ethical behavior that engenders respect toward the living, breathing, conscious beings that suffuse the universe. Consequently, the Jaina community maintains thousands of animal shelters (*pinjrapole*), particularly in western India.

The Jaina tradition emphasizes in great detail the perils of karma and urges people to avoid all forms of harm. A traditional tale warns against the wanton destruction of trees, while simultaneously explaining the mechanics of karma:

A hungry person with the most negative black lesya karma uproots and kills an entire tree to obtain a few mangoes. The person of blue karma fells the tree by chopping the trunk, again merely to gain a handful of fruits. Fraught with gray karma, a third person spares the trunk but cuts off the major limbs of the tree. The one with orangish-red karma carelessly and needlessly lops off several branches to reach the mangoes. The fifth, exhibiting white or virtuous karma, "merely picks up ripe fruit that has dropped to the foot of the tree." (Jaini 1916, 47)

Trees were not to be regarded covetously for their fruits, but like all life forms were to be given respect and treated without inflicting harm. This ethic of care was to be extended to the entire biotic community, engendering awareness of and sensitivity to the precious nature of life.

During the period of the Islamic incursion into India, the Jaina community was often in retreat, with some of its temples taken over and converted into mosques. Some Jaina monks, however, helped exert nonviolent influence within the Islamic world. In 1591, Jinacandrasuri II (1531–1613), a leader of the Khartar Gacch of the Svetambaras, traveled to Lahore, where he greatly influenced the Mughal emperor Akbar the Great. He gained protection for Jaina pilgrimage sites, as well as legal protection ensuring that Jain ceremonies would not be hindered. He even lent support to Jaina advocacy for animals, and forbade the slaughter of animals for one week each year.

Mohandas Gandhi (1869–1948), who liberated India from British colonialism through the enactment of nonviolent principles, was deeply influenced by the Jaina tradition. He eschewed all forms of violence and even titled his lengthy autobiography after the second Jaina vow: *Satyagraha or My Experiments with Truth*. He learned of Jainism during his childhood in Gujarat, an Indian state with a large Jaina presence, and from Raichandra, a prominent Jaina lay-teacher.

Another modern-day example of Jaina activism can be found in the work of Acharya Tulsi (1914–1997) and his successor, Acarya Mahaprajna, both leaders of the Svetambara Therpanthi movement. In June of 1945, deeply disturbed by World War II, he issued a nine-point declaration of the basic principles of nonviolence including guidelines for both individuals and governments.

The Jaina community remained almost exclusively within India until the twentieth century, when many Jaina migrated to eastern Africa, Britain, and North America. Today, this diaspora community tends to identify readily with values centered on environmental protection. The classics and religion professor Anne Vallely notes that "rather than through the idiom of self-realization or the purification of the soul, ethics are being expressed through a discourse of environmentalism and animal rights" (2000, 193). These values are expressed through such journals as *Resurgence*, edited by the former Jaina monk Satish Kumar, and *Jain Spirit: Sharing Jain Values Globally*, edited by a Jaina lay-scholar, Atul Shah. Extensive websites buttress the new global reach of the Jaina community, which continues to espouse vegetarianism and animal activism as key components of its ethical expression.

Jaina cosmology asserts that the world consists of myriad souls all seeking their own way. Through mistakes of karma, their karma becomes thick and entrenched. Through acts of benevolence, their karmic burden becomes lighter. By the adoption of a strict moral code grounded in nonviolence, the Jaina seek to shed their karmic cloak. This practice requires a clear understanding of what constitutes life, and how one can cultivate care and concern in one's encounters with all forms of life. By careful dietary observance and restriction of acquisitiveness, the soul gradually detaches itself from the clutches of karma. This process also benefits others, in that through the abatement of one's greed, others can live more freely. As age-old problems of human conflict and more contemporary problems of environmental mismanagement become more pressing, the abstemious lifestyle offered by the Jaina may become increasingly instructive to those seeking peace and environmental protection.

Christopher Key CHAPPLE
Loyola Marymount University

See also Mahavira

Further Reading

Chapple, C. K. (Ed.). (2002). *Jainism and ecology: Nonviolence in the web of life*. Cambridge, MA: Harvard Divinity School.

Dundas, P. (2002). *The Jains* (2nd ed.). London: Routledge.

Jaini, J. (1916). *The outlines of Jainism*. Cambridge, U.K.: Cambridge University Press.

Jaini, P. S. (1979). *The Jaina path of purification*. Berkeley: University of California Press.

Vallely, A. (2000). From liberation to ecology: Ethical discourses among orthodox and diaspora Jains. In Chapple, C. K. (Ed.). *Jainism and Ecology: Nonviolence in the web of life*. Cambridge, MA: Harvard University Press.

Jesus
(c. 6 BCE–c. 30 CE)
RELIGIOUS LEADER AND FOUNDER OF CHRISTIANITY

Jesus, who began his ministry in small towns around Galilee, was a Jew. After the Romans crucified him as rebel, his followers deemed him the Son of God, believing he would soon return to end wickedness in the world and judge the living and the dead. Most Jews rejected this idea, but missionaries made converts among pagans, founding a church that eventually divided into the rival Christian churches of today.

Although Jesus (of Nazareth) is one of the most important historical figures who ever lived, very little historical information is actually known about him. The principal sources for his life and ministry are the four canonical gospels of the Christian Bible: Matthew, Mark, Luke, and John. While these documents contain actual sayings of Jesus, they are products of a developed tradition and themselves use established sources. Alongside information of undoubted historical value, then, there are later stories and sayings inserted for their theological value.

Jesus was born into a milieu of vigorous political activism and religious speculation. Within the context of first-century Judaism, these were interlinked as a result of widespread apocalyptic speculation. In the years when Judaea had been ruled by Hellenistic kings, many of its people began to concentrate their hopes for political change upon a direct intervention by God. The apocalyptic literature, most famously, for example, the Book Of Daniel, that they developed expressed the view that God would act by sending a leader to free the people ("Messiah") and restore the cult based in the Temple at Jerusalem to its proper function. At the time of Jesus' birth, the long rule of the region by the Roman client-king Herod the Great had come to an end. His immediate successors were proving inadequate and so the Romans were undertaking a more direct role in administration and policing.

Jesus came from Nazareth, a village in the hills of Galilee, under the direct authority of one of Herod's sons, Herod Antipas. Galilee itself was geographically and intellectually peripheral to the Temple cult operating in Jerusalem. Instead, the central religious

Peter Paul Rubens, *Christ on the Cross* (1627). Oil on panel. Rockox House, Antwerp.

Franz von Rohden, *Gerburt Christi [The Nativity]* (1853). Oil on canvas. In this biblical scene three wise men bear gifts.

institution in Galilean life was the synagogue. The religious community of the synagogue met weekly to be led in formal devotions by a teacher (rabbi). The focus of the synagogue was upon the reading and interpretation of Scripture, and it was in this context that religious reform groups like the Pharisees, who placed particular emphasis upon personal religious devotion, flourished.

Jesus' public ministry, when it began, was mostly amongst the small villages and towns of Galilee. Although there were several cities nearby (Scythopolis [Bet She'an], Tiberias, and Sepphoris [Zippori]—itself only a few kilometers from Nazareth), the gospel accounts make it clear that he preferred to concentrate his activities within the small fishing communities of the Galilee region, and Capernaum in particular. He seems to have followed on from the earlier ministry of his cousin, John the Baptist. John, an ascetic and itinerant preacher, had demanded a revival of personal piety, to be expressed through a ritual cleansing in water (baptism). At the beginning of his own ministry, Jesus had been baptized by John and, while he did not himself baptize, many of his followers baptized in his name.

Jesus' principal message was an assertion of the need for a personal piety as a response to the love of God. He stressed the need for personal compassion, and many of the miracles associated with him are miracles of healing, which emphasize Jesus' own compassion. In focusing upon personal integrity as

I believe there is no one deeper, lovelier, more sympathetic and more perfect than Jesus—not only is there no one else like him, there never could be anyone like him. • **Fyodor Dostoevsky (1821–1881)**

a measure of piety, Jesus came into conflict with another religious reform movement, the Pharisees, who also laid heavy emphasis upon religious authenticity, although through devoted obedience to Jewish religious law. Jesus' most colorful language was reserved for Pharisees, whom he depicted as liars and hypocrites who were slavishly devoted to the letter of the law.

Jesus' principal notoriety was not so much for his words, however, as for his deeds. He swiftly gained a reputation as a miracle worker through miraculous healings, exorcisms, and even the restoration of life.

When Jesus sought to remove his ministry to Jerusalem, he immediately came into conflict with Temple authorities, whom he accused of profiteering. They in turn sought help from the Roman administrators. Depicting Jesus as a revolutionary and a messianic troublemaker, they secured his conviction and execution by the Romans as a rebel. It is certainly clear that his visit was accompanied by considerable speculation that he would proclaim himself as the Messiah and lead a revolt. While he encouraged this speculation by his entry into Jerusalem in deliberate fulfillment of a messianic prophecy, he stopped short of ever actually claiming to be the Messiah.

Within weeks of his death, a significant number of his followers began to claim that he had risen from the dead. That belief in Jesus' resurrection empowered communities of his followers to survive and grow, forming the kernel of the Christian church. This community expected his imminent return from heaven to complete his messianic task. When that did not occur, Jesus' words and deeds, along with stories about him, were written down as gospels and other documents. Jesus himself wrote nothing except, once when asked to judge a woman caught in adultery, he scribbled some words in the dust (John 8:1–6).

Bill LEADBETTER
Edith Cowan University

See also Christian Orthodoxy; Paul, Saint; Pentecostalism; Protestantism; Roman Catholicism

Further Reading

Sanders, E. P. (1993). *The historical figure of Jesus.* Harmondsworth, U.K.: Allen Lane.

Vermes, G. (1983). *Jesus and the world of Judaism.* London: SCM Press.

Judaism

Judaism's greatest legacy to world history is its success as the earliest entire community to adopt monotheism. The religion's impact on world history is therefore both direct and felt through its relationships with the conquering religious civilizations that followed it, first Christianity and then Islam.

Starting from the Hellenistic period, when outside observers first attempted to write about the "other" in a dispassionate manner, Greek writers observed the unique monotheism of Judaism, noting how this aspect of their religion singled out Jews from all other peoples that the Greeks had encountered. The reports that reached philosophers such as Theophrastus and Megasthenes (c. 300 BCE) led them to consider the Jews a nation of philosophers. The Jews, they wrote, were stubborn believers in a singular god who was both the god of Israel and the god of the world. Other writers noted that the Jews insisted on certain practices that were strange to the Greeks: circumcision, abhorrence at consuming pork, and a kind of insular culture that was at odds with what the Greeks believed to be their own open-mindedness. Such traits were considered by some observers as both peculiar and the reason for what they called—perhaps unconsciously describing their own elitism—Jewish misanthropy, lack of patriotism (toward Greek culture), and general disregard for humankind outside of their own nation.

The Greeks thus articulated both a kind of attraction and repulsion toward Judaism. Despite such ambivalence, however, many Romans (to the dismay of their ruling classes) were fascinated by this religious civilization. Large numbers either converted or "Judaized," meaning that they adopted Jewish customs such as holiday observance and food habits without enduring the circumcision that was required for full conversion. Roman writers noted that Judaism's popularity was based on its great antiquity, its written scriptures, its deep sense of morality, and its monotheism. Judaism's engagement with Western civilization was thus deep and enduring but not without controversy.

Judaism had an overwhelming influence on the premodern history of the world west of the Indus River, and an enduring impact on the entire world in the modern period. The impact of Judaism on world history is both direct and felt through its relationships with the conquering religious civilizations that followed, first Christianity and then Islam.

Impact of Origins

Judaism emerged out of a religious civilization based on what is often referred to by scholars as "biblical" or "Israelite" religion. As such, what we today call Judaism must be distinguished from its older forms. In fact, Judaism is only one of the heirs of biblical religion, as are all the faiths in the family of religions referred to as Christianity. Biblical religion itself is multifaceted, since it evolved for centuries during the historical period represented in the Hebrew Bible (Old Testament). It has become evident to scholars that biblical religion was not always purely monotheistic, for it reflects periods of tension between those who would allow rituals associated with figurines representing other powers or deities and those who would accept nothing other than the one god, the God of Israel (1 Sam. 26:19, 1 Kings 11, 2 Kings 23).

An illustration by Jean Fouquet from *Jewish Antiquities*, a manuscript written by Flavius Josephus (38?–100?) that recounts Jewish history from the Creation to the revolt against the Romans in 66 CE. The text was read by early Christians and remained popular with both Christians and Jews. This manuscript, copied and illustrated in the fifteenth century, belonged to French royalty. National Library of France.

It is clear, however, that the people that called itself Israel (the name derives from the biblical figure Jacob, who was also called Israel—Gen. 32:29) was the first community to take on the doctrine of monotheism successfully. It is likely that the concept of monotheism existed among individuals before the emergence of the people of Israel. Even powerful and influential individuals such as the pharaoh Akhenaton (mid-fourteenth century BCE) may have been monotheists or proto-monotheists, but no entire community succeeded in adopting monotheism prior to ancient Judaism. This is perhaps Judaism's greatest legacy to world history. It established a theological paradigm that would have a profound impact on the nature of all subsequent religions, whether monotheistic or not.

Election

Ancient Israel saw itself as a small and beleaguered monotheistic people living in a world of countless foreign nations, all sharing the temptation of

worshipping multiple deities (Deut. 7:7). Out of this awkward and precarious social and political situation, coupled with a feeling of obvious theological uniqueness, emerged an impression, and then a doctrine, of election, of being chosen by the one and only true god to represent and worship him unreservedly and unconditionally (Deut. 7:6–8). Throughout the Hebrew Bible we find the message that all the nations of the Earth worship their sets of gods, but only Israel worships the One God, the God of the entire world. Election, therefore, became deeply ingrained into the Israelite consciousness. Ironically, despite or perhaps because of Israel's beleaguered position in relation to the mighty idolatrous nations and empires of the ancient world, its unique community commitment to monotheism engendered the feeling that only it was uniquely elected to carry out the will of the true God. Israel was God's royal nation (Exod.19:5, Deut. 7:6, 14:2, 26:18), and a holy nation (Exod.19:6, Deut. 14:2, 21). Israel was God's chosen people (Deut. 7:6, Isa. 43:20, 45:4, Pss. 33:12, 132:13, 135:4).

Covenant

The special relationship of election is symbolized by an institution called "covenant" (*b'rit* in Hebrew). The term actually refers to a host of formal or legal relationships in the Hebrew Bible ranging from agreements between two individuals (Gen. 21:22–33, 1 Sam. 18:3) to pacts between nations (1 Kings 5:26, 20:34). But one special type of biblical covenant agreement came to define the relationship between the only community of monotheists and the only true God. Forged between God and Israel, this is the "covenant par excellence," an institution found throughout the Hebrew Bible and a unique contribution of Israelite religion. The covenant was first rendered between God and Abraham's family (Gen. 17). It was reaffirmed with the biblical patriarchs (Gen. 26:23–24, 28:10–15) and then at Mount Sinai (Exod. 19, 24) between God and all the extended families and clans of Israel that were redeemed from Egyptian bondage. This divine covenant was extended also to non-Israelite peoples who escaped along with Israel in the redemption from Egypt (Exod. 12:38).

The concepts of election and covenantal relationship with God originated with ancient Israel and its religion, but these traits became intimately associated with monotheism in general. Election and covenant, therefore, are not only essential to Judaism, but are intimately associated with Christianity and Islam. Early Christians came to articulate their religion as representing a "new covenant" between God and a "new Israel," namely, those who accept the particular self-definition of Christianity. Christians, therefore, become the new "chosen," with only those who had chosen Christ as savior able to achieve their own salvation (1 Cor. 11:23–32, Heb. 8–9). Although less prominent in Islam, covenant (*'ahd* or *mithaq*) also defines the relationship between God and a newer community of believers. But Islam is less exclusionary in that it accepts, in theory, the salvation of prior communities of righteous believers (Qur'an 2:62, 5:72). Nevertheless, Muslims are defined in the Qur'an as a kind of elect, the most moderate or a "middle community," chosen to be witnesses (Qur'an 2:143), and "the best community brought forth for humankind" (Qur'an 3:110).

Election and covenant, closely associated with Israel and Judaism (and an integral part of all expressions of monotheism), can be viewed as divisive traits. The legacy of Israelite religion is not, however, all exclusion and division. The inclusive and compassionate aspects of the universal religious imperative in Western religions also seem to have originated in ancient Israel.

Compassion For the "Other" and Repairing the World

The exclusivist aspects of monotheism in Israelite religion were always in tension with inclusionism, as defined by care for the stranger and a sense of responsibility toward others. Thus, although Israelites may have considered themselves to be the only people in the ancient world that truly respected the one God of the universe, God was nevertheless the God of all, including those who did not recognize him. Israelite monotheism thus required care and concern even for those outside of Israel, and this responsibility was articulated through the concept of *imitateo dei*, emulating God, because the creator of all the world must be good: "For the Lord your God is God supreme, who shows no favor and takes no bribe, but upholds the cause of the fatherless and the widow, and befriends the stranger, providing him with food and clothing. You too must befriend the stranger, for you were strangers in the land of Egypt" (Jewish Publication Society, Deut. 10:17–19).

Social Justice

Codes or lists of formalized social precedents (customs) and formulaic duties existed before the emergence of ancient Judaism. These are similar to what today would be called law (obligations to state, society, and private individuals). The ancient Mesopotamian "codes" of Ur-Nammu (twenty-first century BCE), Eshnunna (c. 1800 BCE), and Hammurabi (mid-eighteenth century BCE) existed long before the legal and social requirements enumerated in the biblical parallel, the Book of the Covenant (Exod. 20–23). This pre-Israelite material was as closely associated with a sense of societal justice as that found in the Hebrew Bible. That is, offences would be termed criminal when they were considered inimical to the well-being of society as a whole, and sanctions were imposed by the public authority rather than the injured party or a powerful private individual (the latter might be termed "family justice" and was not law).

On the other hand, the prebiblical codes maintained a sharp tripartite division of society into an upper level of free men, a class of state dependents, and a slave caste. There was no expectation of social mobility between these classes, and the rights, responsibilities, and sanctions in the codes reflected this rigid division. In contrast to the previous systems, the biblical codes extend the rights of the elites to all layers of society: "You shall appoint magistrates and officials for your tribes, in all the settlements that the Lord your God is giving you, and they shall govern the people with due justice. You shall not judge unfairly: you shall show no partiality; you shall not take bribes, for bribes blind the eyes of the discerning and upset the plea of the just. Justice, justice shall you pursue, that you may thrive and occupy the land that the Lord your God is giving you (Deut. 16:18–20)" and "You shall have one standard for the stranger and citizen alike: for I the Lord am your God" (Lev. 24:22).

Civic Duty and Responsible Behavior

Another of Judaism's most important legacies, found not only in its sister expressions of monotheism but also in democracies and all forms of responsible government, is the idea that people are responsible to one another. Individuals are accountable, not only for themselves but also for others. This is represented by the term, and the concept, *Torah* (meaning "teaching"), which has sometimes been misunderstood as a rigid code of Israelite law. It should be likened more to a set of behavioral expectations for ritual and social behavior, centered around the idea that the individual is responsible to the group and the group to the individual. That the entire nation is punished by God for the misbehavior of the few is a foundation of Israelite law and referenced throughout the Hebrew Bible. One is accountable for both the behavior and the welfare of one's fellow. All the people were witnesses at the giving of the Torah at Mount Sinai, and all are therefore responsible to ensure that the Torah teaching is upheld. This is the essence of the Israelite system, which is based upon a balance between individual and community and between freedom and responsibility (Deut. 29–30).

From Israelites to Jews

The true origin of the Israelites remains uncertain. While some have suggested that it lies in Mesopotamia or Egypt, recent scholarship places it within Canaanite society, suggesting that Israel symbolizes a monotheistic trend in Canaanite culture originating perhaps as early as the second millennium BCE that eventuated in an independent identity. The danger of assimilation back into the old and familiar idolatrous

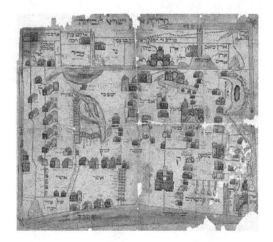

This drawing, which shows the division of Israel among the twelve tribes, is a copy of a work by Rabbi Elijah ben Shlomo Zalman (1720–1797), better known as the Vilna Gaon or Elijah of Vilna (Vilnius, in present-day Lithuania).

ways of local Canaanite culture is a constant theme of biblical literature, and the nations "here at hand" (Deut. 20:15) in the land of Canaan always represent the most dangerous threat to Israel's distinctive identity and existence.

But the tribes of Israel were not always purely monotheistic, and the journey into the kind of theology we would recognize today as monotheism did not end until the exilic or post-exilic periods after the destruction of the first Temple in Jerusalem in 586 BCE. Prior to that time, such seminal statements as "Who is like you among the gods" (Exod. 15:11) suggest that while ancient Israelite theology required unconditional obedience to the God of Israel, it did not deny the possibility of other gods existing as well. It may have been the realization that the God of Israel could be worshipped even in Babylonian exile that solidified the tendency toward monotheism and convinced the exilic community that there was one God who created the universe, and that the same one God maintained it.

Israel had divided into two separate nations with independent monarchies and centers of worship shortly after the reigns of kings David and Solomon (c. 900 BCE). The northern kingdom, composed of ten of the twelve tribes of Israel, was destroyed by the Assyrian empire in 721 BCE and never recovered. The southern kingdom, formally made up of the large tribe of Judah and the small tribe of Benjamin (but including parts of other tribes and peoples as well), was destroyed a century and a half later by the Babylonian empire. But the Babylonians were soon overtaken by the Persians, who were friendly to the exiles from the tribal areas of Judah and Benjamin. The Persians invited the exiles to return from their banishment to the east and reestablish themselves in the ancient land. The overwhelming majority of survivors were from the large tribe of Judah, so the returnees joined with those who remained and were soon known as Judeans, or Jews (biblical books of Ezra and Nehemiah), though Jews throughout history have also referred to themselves as Israel, Israelites, or the people or nation of Israel (Hebrew: *b'ney yisra'el* or *'am yisra'el*).

The Judean community, like its parent, the intertribal community of Israel, remained small in numbers relative to the great empires of Mesopotamia and Egypt. But as a result of the conquests by the Mesopotamian powers and the dispersion of the Israelite tribes, Jewish communities began to establish themselves in many parts of the Mediterranean basin. The largest communities remained in Mesopotamia and Judea, but significant communities grew up also in Egypt, Anatolia, Greece, and North Africa.

These communities did not look like Jewish communities of today, for they practiced a kind of ancient Judaism that was still oriented toward temple worship with sacrifices and burnt offerings. In some places such as Elephantine, an Egyptian island community in the Nile, they established their own temples independent of the Temple in Jerusalem. In others closer in proximity to Jerusalem, the communities joined in the annual pilgrimage festivals to the Jerusalem Temple and worshipped according to the systems described in the Bible.

The Hebrew Bible conveys the message that monotheism always survived precariously and, aside from the Persians, was resented by the nations of the world. The Assyrians, Babylonians, Egyptians, Canaanites, Midianites, and Aramaeans—all opposed the Israelites' stubborn worship of one god only. The reason for Israel's isolation in this regard appears quite simple. When traveling, for example, it was a common

Our Jewish experience leads us to be more aware of dangers than of opportunities. This tendency has to be transcended if we are to emerge into a future different from the recent past. • **Abba Eban (1915–2002)**

practice among polytheists to make offerings to the gods of the local area or people. It was considered a common courtesy and expected polite behavior, and to peoples who worshipped multiple deities, it created no theological problem to make a token offering to foreign gods. Not so Israel, which was commanded to worship only the one God of Israel, the God of the universe. The Hebrew Bible indicates that it was quite expected that other peoples worship their national gods or even other people's gods (Judg. 11:23–24), but Israel was allowed to worship only the one God (Jer. 44:1–10).

This situation continued into the Hellenistic period that began with the invasion of Alexander in the 330s BCE, and into the Roman occupation of Judea that began three centuries later. The Judeans remained a small community and largely without power aside from a few generations under the rule of the Jewish Hasmonean dynasty of kings. Finally, in 70 CE, after a major Judean revolt against Roman imperial rule, the Jerusalem Temple was destroyed a second and final time, never to be rebuilt.

By this time, Jews had been dispersed throughout the Mediterranean and Middle Eastern worlds and brought their religion with them. Monotheism, the theological core of ancient Judaism, survived the vicissitudes of history, but the religious rituals and worship that articulated that basic theology evolved and changed over the centuries. The repeated destructions of the Jerusalem Temple put an end to the sacrificial system, but the core idea of a singular god endured. However, the geographical dispersion, influence of multiple cultures, and internal cultural change brought new ideas into biblical Judaism. This eventuated in a synthesis that gave birth to factions or parties, sects, and eventually new religious movements. One of these was the Jesus Movement that began in Judaism and became the starting point out of which the family of Christian religions emerged.

Judaism of the Rabbis

Another was a movement that emerged around a core group of leaders steeped in an oral tradition of Judaism that existed parallel to the sacrificial system and written scripture of the Bible. Those leaders we know of were almost all men, though it is clear that women were also instrumental in the transmission of oral lore. They could be described as traditionists, and included the Pharisees as well as others. Later, they were known as rabbis. When the long process of recording the oral tradition ended in the sixth century CE, it became known as the Talmud.

This form of Judaism is called Rabbinic Judaism, and all expressions of Judaism today, aside from one tiny group known as Kara'ites, derive from the Judaism of the rabbis and their great source of authority, the Talmud. This Judaism existed in exile for close to two millennia, even in the core land of Judea, which was governed by non-Jews. Rabbinic Judaism always represented the stranger in the lands of others. It is quietist and highly intellectual, relying more on the survivability of its adherents and the wits of its leaders than directly on the biblical God acting in history. Unlike Christianity, Rabbinic Judaism requires little dogmatic theological belief beyond that in the unity of God, and salvation is presumed for all who live a pious life of good deeds.

One of Rabbinic Judaism's great contributions to world history has been its unique ability to adapt to multiple environments within a world hardly tolerant of diversity, religious or otherwise. Its stubborn existence in both Christian and Muslim worlds required all religious leaders, thinkers, and politicians to consider and respond to the Jews, the quintessential "other" in their midst. This required repeated reevaluation of the meaning of self in relation to the other of Judaism, and resulted in the growth of theologies, laws, and various religious and secular sciences in both Jewish and non-Jewish civilizations.

At the same time, the Jews' lack of political power throughout this period required that their religion consider a larger range of possible doctrine than the religions of political powers who could enforce their will by the sword. Judaism therefore contains many ideas but little absolute dogma. The customary argumentation found in Jewish literatures rarely arrives at any final conclusions. Every

Gravestones broken during the Holocaust were set into a wall in the Jewish cemetery in Worms, Germany, where the Jewish community dates back more than a thousand years.

issue and point can and should be revisited and reexamined, and new meanings are always possible. The huge written compendium of the Talmud and its interpretation contain complex discussion and argument over topics that range from folk medicine to legal theory, property law, family law, business ethics, and theologies. The literatures that epitomize Rabbinic Judaism stress the need for a deep and universal intellectual engagement with the divine word in Bible and Talmud, and this foundation of Judaism encouraged a very high per capita involvement in reading and education.

In the Modern World

In the modern period, when Jews were eventually released from their restricted status in the West and were allowed to enter the universities and engage in the professions and sciences, their religious culture provided the intellectual training that would result in contributions far above their per capita representation. To provide one striking example, Jews make up less than one-hundredth of 1 percent of the world population, yet they account for some 18 percent of the Nobel Prizes awarded in the twentieth century. There is no need to list the many contributions of Jews to the arts, science, literature, and music. Some of the ideas that were incubated in premodern Judaism have come to the fore in contemporary postmodern thought. These include aspects of literary deconstruction and concepts of exile, both of which have had a major impact on current intellectual discourse.

Judaism, like all religions, encompasses more than a theological system of beliefs. It is best described as a religious civilization, and this civilization has had a foundational influence on world civilizations west of the Indus River for two millennia. Its influence comes not only from its own direct contribution, but also through the contribution of the religious civilizations that emerged from or associated themselves with it. Monotheism, the belief in the universality and unity of the divinity, is the very core of Judaism, and religions that preach monotheistic theologies have not only encompassed the Western and Mediterranean worlds, but now reach deeply beyond into Africa and Eastern Asia. Although representing a tiny fraction of the human population, Jewish religious civilization has remained of great significance in world history.

Reuven FIRESTONE
Hebrew Union College

See also Abraham; Moses; Zionism

Further Reading

Alon, G. (1977). *Jews, Judaism and the classical world.* Jerusalem: Magnes.

Ben-Sasson (Ed.). (1976). *A history of the Jewish people.* Cambridge, MA: Harvard University Press.

Cohen, M. (1994). *Under crescent and cross: The Jews in the Middle Ages.* Princeton, NJ: Princeton University.

Cohen, S. (1987). *From the Maccabees to the Mishnah.* Philadelphia, PA: Westminster.

Finkelstein, J. (1970). Cuneiform law. *Encyclopedia Judaica, 16,* 1505f–1505k.

Firestone, R. (2008). *Who are the real Chosen People: The meaning of chosenness in Judaism, Christianity and Islam.* Woodstock, VT: Skylight Paths Publishing.

Goldenberg, R. (1997). *The nations that know thee not: Ancient Jewish attitudes toward other religions.* Sheffield, U.K.: Sheffield Academic Press.

Holtz, B. (1984). *Back to the sources: Reading the classic Jewish texts.* New York: Summit Books.

Killebrew, A. (2005). *Biblical peoples and ethnicity: An archeological study of Egyptians, Canaanites, Philistines, and early Israel 1300–1100 BCE.* Atlanta: Society of Biblical Literature.

Mendez-Flohr, P., & Reinharz, J. (1980). *The Jew in the modern world: A documentary history.* New York: Oxford University Press.

Orlinsky, H. (1960). *Ancient Israel.* Ithaca, NY: Cornell University Press.

Sacher, H. M. (1977). *The course of modern Jewish history.* New York: Delta.

Schiffman, L. (1991). *From text to tradition: A history of the second temple and Rabbinic Judaism.* New York: Ktav.

Stow, K. (1992). *Alienated minority: The Jews of medieval Latin Europe.* Cambridge, MA: Harvard University Press.

Laozi

(SIXTH CENTURY BCE)
LEGENDARY CHINESE PHILOSOPHER

Laozi, a book also known as *Daodejing (The Way and Its Power)* or *The Book of Five-Thousand Characters* (because it contains just about that number of Chinese characters), refers to the text that set forth in eighty-one poems the principles of Daoist philosophy and religion; its alleged author is also known as Laozi.

Laozi (Lao-tzu), who is commonly credited with writing the Daoist classic, the *Daodejing (The Way and Its Power)*, was among the most influential figures in Chinese history, second to, if not equal to, the philosopher Confucius (551–479 BCE). Ideas in the *Daodejing*, although seemingly mysterious and paradoxical, are subtle and profound and have influenced every aspect of Chinese civilization (government, philosophy, religions, sciences, medicine, arts, and martial arts).

The name "Laozi" means "old master." Little information about the man exists. The earliest record of Laozi is in *Shiji* (Records of the Grand Historian), written during the Han dynasty (206 BCE–220 CE) by Sima Qian (145–87? BCE). In his biography of Laozi, Qian gave Laozi's birth name as Li Er, also known as Li Dan, the name of a staff official at the imperial library of the Zhou dynasty (1045–256 BCE). Laozi cultivated learning but did not reveal his knowledge or ability. As the Zhou dynasty declined, Laozi decided to leave. At the city gate, at the request of the gatekeeper, he wrote two books, *Dao* and *De*, with a total of about five thousand characters (words). No one knew where he went then, and Qian wrote that some people said Laozi lived to the age of 160 or 200 and attributed his longevity to the cultivation of *dao* (the Way).

Qian's account of Laozi's life includes a visit Confucius made to Laozi. Using Confucius as a medium, Qian referred to Laozi as a dragon, the most auspicious and grand symbol in Chinese civilization to illustrate the breadth, depth, and versatility of his words. Qian also mentioned another person, Lao Laizi, who also wrote Daoist text and who also was the contemporary of Confucius, but Qian did not identify Laozi as Lao Laizi. Some modern scholars question whether Laozi was the contemporary of Confucius and date him in the third century BCE, during the Warring States period (475–221 BCE). Other scholars support Sima Qian's dating.

During the second century BCE, at the end of the Han dynasty, folk beliefs blended with Daoist ideas and developed the religion of Daoism. After that Laozi was venerated as the founder, and the *Daodejing* became a text with magical and protective power for followers of several schools of religious Daoism. When Buddhism became popular in China, legend claimed that Laozi went to the West and was reincarnated as Buddha. During the Tang dynasty (618–907 CE) Laozi was honored as an imperial ancestor to enhance the prestige of the imperial family, who had the same last name. Temples were built for Laozi, and Daoist monasteries were popular throughout the Tang dynasty. Moreover, the *Daodejing*, as a book about philosophy and governance, was adopted as a text in the imperial government's civil service examination for sixty-six years, along with Confucian classics. From the third through the tenth centuries "Laozi" was a common name for Chinese intellectuals as well as religious people.

The *Daodejing* consists of eighty-one short chapters of philosophical prose, which often are paradoxical;

I have three treasures. Guard and keep them: / The first is deep love, / The second is frugality, / And the third is not to dare to be ahead of the world. / Because of deep love, one is courageous. / Because of frugality, one is generous. / Because of not daring to be ahead of the world, one becomes the leader of the world. • **Laozi (c. sixth century** BCE**)**

therefore, commentaries on the text became important. Ho-shang Gong's commentary of the Han dynasty and Wang Bi's commentary of the fifth century became the standard version. Recent tomb excavation unearthed an earlier version of this text that has slight variations. Some scholars believe that the *Daodejing* is an anthology by more than one author. The thought in the book, however, is consistent.

The *Daodejing* states that a metaphysical, all-encompassing, and organic *dao* (Way) is the originator and sustainer of all things in the universe. It can't be described. As the *Daodejing* states, "the *Dao* that can be told is not the constant *Dao*," yet this *dao* is modeled after naturalness or spontaneity and can also be discerned in ordinary or even lowly things.

The *Daodejing* draws its inspiration from the observation of nature, for which it has a profound preference. It exhorts frugality, contentment, and tranquility and promotes few desires. Moreover, contrary to common assumptions, it claims that the weak overcome the strong and that the soft overcome the hard. The *Daodejing* states, "Of all things in the world, nothing is more soft and weak than water, yet none could rival water in dissolving the hard and the strong." Some scholars believe that the *Daodejing* teaches people means of self-preservation during troubled times. The *Daodejing* also proposes ways for a sage ruler to govern. Its ideal society is a simple and primal society where people are content. Moreover, its best government has only a shadowy existence: it interferes little with people's lives either in taxation or labor conscription. The *Daodejing* states, "I [the ruler] practice *wu-wei* [nonactions] and the people were self-transformed; I love tranquility, and the people became pure and good . . ." But the *Daodejing* is not just a creed for simplicity and contentment, it also embraces and understands changes, making it a seemingly simple but profound text.

Ideas in the *Daodejing* have been applied in Chinese government, notably during the early Han dynasty under the emperors Wen and Jing (180–141 BCE). Under the name of "Huang-Lao" (combining the name of the legendary Yellow Emperor with "Laozi"), the early Han government was frugal and nonactive and levied light taxes to allow citizens to recover from the heavy taxation and wars of the previous Qin dynasty (221–206 BCE). Near the end of the Han dynasty and for the next several centuries, religious Daoism thrived. People revered Laozi as a deity; philosophers adopted ideas from the *Daodejing* and eventually wrote a large collection of Daoist scriptures. Daoism also influenced Chinese arts. Along with *Zhuang Zi* (Master Zhuang), another Daoist classic written during the Warring States period, the *Daodejing* inspired literati landscape painting, most notably during the Song dynasty (960–1279). The scene was usually of one or two scholars strolling among mountains and trees. Daoist ideas also inspired many of China's most treasured poems. People often consider Li Bai (701–762 CE), a Daoist of the Tang dynasty, to be China's greatest poet.

During the early Qin dynasty Daoism also inspired Chinese primitive sciences and martial arts and influenced Chinese medical theories and practices. Daoists' search for a longevity elixir promoted the development of alchemy (a chemical science and speculative philosophy that aimed at, among other goals, the discovery of a means of indefinitely prolonging life).

Laozi's *Daodejing* fundamentally changed Chinese civilization. It balanced goal-oriented, ethically motivated, and duty-bound Confucianism with a sense of individual freedom in its tranquil appreciation of the beauty of nature and understanding of changing and unpredictable fortunes. Since the late eighteenth century the *Daodejing* has also attracted many Western minds. Today it is one of the books most translated into English. Scholars and laypersons explore and perceive its ideas from different angles, comparing it with Christianity, appreciating its tranquility and love of nature, seeking an individual's freedom from highly structured modern society, or simply studying the ritual and practices of the religion of Daoism. Western intellectuals have freely interpreted and explored the text in their own search for a space in a highly standardized and bureaucratic world. Regardless of whether Laozi or more than one author wrote the *Daodejing*, it has significantly influenced Chinese civilization, and its influence has spread beyond the Chinese horizon and into world history.

Lily HWA
University of St. Thomas, Minnesota

See also Confucianism; Daoism

Further Reading

Ames, R., & Hall, D. (2003). *Dao De Jing: A philosophical translation*. New York: Ballantine Books.

Chan, A. (1991). *Two visions of the way: A study of the Wang Pi and the Ho Shang-kung commentaries on the Lao-tzu*. Albany: State University of New York Press.

Chan, W. (1963). The natural way of Lao Tzu. In W. Chan (Ed.), *A source book in Chinese philosophy* (pp. 136–176). Princeton, NJ: Princeton University Press.

Fung, Y. (1966). *A short history of Chinese philosophy*. New York: Free Press.

Graham, A. (1989). *Disputers of the Tao: Philosophical argument in ancient China*. LaSalle, IL: Open Court.

Kohn, L., & LaFargue, M. (Eds.). (1998). *Lao Tzu and the Tao-te-ching*. Albany: State University of New York Press.

Lau, D. (1963). *Lao Tzu: Tao Te Ching*. New York: Penguin Books.

Needham, J. (1956). *Science and civilization in China: Vol. II. History of scientific thought*. Cambridge, U.K.: Cambridge University Press.

Nienhauser, W., et al. (2002). *The Grand Scribe's Records: Vol II.* (Ssu-ma Ch'ien, Trans.). Bloomington: Indiana University Press.

Schwartz, B. (1985). *The world of thought in ancient China*. Cambridge, MA: Harvard University Press.

Latter-Day Saints

The Church of Jesus Christ of Latter-Day Saints (LDS), also called the Church of Jesus Christ, is the fifth-largest Christian denomination in the United States. The church is often called the "Mormon" church because of members' adherence to *The Book of Mormon: Another Testament of Jesus Christ* as scripture in addition to the Bible.

Headquartered in Salt Lake City, Utah, but with members in more than 160 countries in 2010, the Church of Jesus Christ of Latter-day Saints has quickly established itself as a significant world denomination. Scholars have referred to it as "a new religious tradition" (Shipps 1985, 149) and have seen in its growth "the rise of a new world faith" (Stark 1984, 18).

Founding and Membership

The Church of Jesus Christ was founded on 6 April 1830, in Fayette, New York, by Joseph Smith Jr. (1805–1844), who, as a fourteen-year-old boy, sought an answer to which of the many competing Christian denominations he should join. He testified that he was visited by God and Jesus Christ and was instructed to join none of the denominations. Church members believe that Joseph Smith Jr. was called as a prophet and received divine revelations, many of which were published in the *Doctrine and Covenants*, a book that details Smith's received revelations. It is now part of the Latter-day Saint canon of scriptures.

Since the time of Joseph Smith Jr., the Church of Jesus Christ has experienced dramatic growth. By the end of 2009 the church had a worldwide membership of about 13.8 million. Less than half of Latter-day Saints live in the United States and Canada. Some countries in the South Pacific and many Latin American countries and regions have comparatively large Latter-day Saint populations, including Mexico, the Caribbean, Central America, and South America. The church is still a small minority but has experienced substantial growth in Asia, Africa, and Europe.

Basic Beliefs and Practices

Core teachings of the church include beliefs in Joseph Smith Jr.'s call as a modern-day prophet, the church as a restoration of the original pure Christianity established by Jesus Christ during his mortal ministry, acceptance of *The Book of Mormon: Another Testament of Jesus Christ* as a translation of records of ancient prophets in the Americas and, with the Bible, as divine scripture. Church members believe in Christ and see him as the head of their church, but the church does not belong to the Catholic, Protestant, nor Eastern Orthodox families of churches. Many of the basic beliefs of the church are stated in the *Articles of Faith*. Key doctrines include the restoration of divine priesthood authority; continuing revelation to church members and modern prophets; high moral standards of honesty, chastity before marriage, and fidelity after marriage; and a health code that prohibits the consumption of alcohol, tea, and coffee and any form of substance abuse. Church members pay one-tenth of their incomes to the church as a tithe and are encouraged to fast monthly and give the money they would have

Stipple drawing of the prophet Joseph Smith.
Courtesy of L. Tom Perry Special Collections, Harold B. Lee Library, Brigham Young University.

spent on food, or more, to a fund to help the needy. The church also has an extensive welfare program, designed to meet the temporal needs of church members who are unable to provide for themselves or their families.

The Church of Jesus Christ had 130 operating temples throughout the world as of 2009, which are used to conduct ordinances such as marriage ceremonies, but are not used for ordinary weekly worship services. Latter-day Saint doctrine teaches that marriages solemnized ("sealed") in Latter-day Saint temples do not dissolve at death and that the family is the core unit of the church and society. The church also encourages education and offers a subsidized loan fund for members seeking higher education in developing countries. The church also has an extensive educational system, including Brigham Young University in Utah, one of the largest private universities in the United States.

Many university-age single men and women, as well as retired married couples, serve as full-time missionaries for the church around the world for one to two years. At the end of 2009 more than fifty thousand missionaries were serving at their own expense in the region of the world they were assigned to by church headquarters; in many cases they learn a foreign language to serve. Local leaders of the church are not salaried ministers. They, along with most members who serve as part-time teachers, leaders, and youth leaders in local congregations, are lay volunteers who give of their time for a few years in an assigned church position while continuing normal employment.

Historical Development

The early years of the Church of Jesus Christ were marked by persecution and movement westward. During the first two decades of the church, members were driven to Ohio; to Independence, Missouri; to Far West, Missouri; and, after being the subject of an extermination order by the governor of Missouri, to Nauvoo, Illinois. After the martyrdom of Joseph Smith Jr. at the hands of an angry mob in 1844, the Latter-day Saints eventually migrated 2,000 kilometers west to Salt Lake Valley, now part of Utah, under the leadership of the second president of the church, Brigham Young (1801–1877). After moving to Utah the Latter-day Saints faced an occupying army from 1857 to 1860, sent by U.S. President James Buchanan, who acted on false rumors of a Latter-day Saint rebellion.

Early official persecution and mob violence against Latter-day Saints constitute one of the harshest examples of religious persecution in U.S. history. Friction arose from religious, cultural, and political differences with their fellow frontier people, particularly over issues of slavery, which was legal in Missouri, and fears of Latter-day Saint political domination.

Another point of contention was the Latter-day Saint practice of polygamy (plural marriage), which was publicly taught from 1843 until it was discontinued in 1890, and efforts by the Latter-day Saints to establish economically self-sufficient

Mormon Temple, Salt Lake City. Courtesy of L. Tom Perry Special Collections, Harold B. Lee Library, Brigham Young University.

communities. Fears of Latter-day Saint practices led to federal U.S. legislation from 1849 to 1896 attacking polygamy, denying civil rights to polygamists and nonpolygamous members of the church, and dissolving the Corporation of the Church of Jesus Christ of Latter-day Saints. Legal challenges by Latter-day Saints to antipolygamy legislation resulted in the first U.S. Supreme Court cases interpreting the free exercise clause of the U.S. Constitution: *Reynolds v. United States* (1878) and *Davis v. Beason* (1890), which upheld federal legislation against both polygamy and the Church of Jesus Christ.

Despite the persecutions of the early years of the church, missionary work continued to fuel its growth. During the 1840s thousands of people joined the Church of Jesus Christ from missionary efforts, particularly in Great Britain, and immigrated to the Americas. As early as the 1850s, missions were opened in Chile, France, Germany, Gibraltar, Hawaii, India, Italy, Malta, Scandinavia, South Africa, the South Pacific, and Switzerland. Since that time international missionary efforts have increased, but by the 1920s church policy no longer encouraged members to gather at a central geographical region.

During recent years the international growth of the church has been increasingly reflected in LDS demographics. By 1996 more church members lived outside the United States than inside, only 30 percent of members lived in the western United States, and fewer than 20 percent lived in Utah. As of 2009 church members belonged to 28,424 local units; church materials are available 166 languages. Since the late 1960s the church has had a growth rate of about 50 percent per decade. Based on this growth rate, the sociologist Rodney Stark has argued that Latter-day Saints "will soon achieve a worldwide following comparable to that of Islam, Buddhism, Christianity, Hinduism, and the other dominant world faiths" (Stark 1984, 18).

Elizabeth A. SEWELL
Brigham Young University

See also Religious Freedom

Further Reading

Allen, J. B., & Leonard, G. M. (1976). *The story of the Latter-day Saints.* Salt Lake City, UT: Deseret Books.

Arrington, L. J., & Bitton, D. (1992). *The Mormon experience: A history of the Latter-day Saints* (2nd ed.). Chicago: University of Illinois Press.

Bushman, C. L., & Bushman, R. L. (1999). *Building the kingdom: A history of Mormons in America.* Oxford, U.K.: Oxford University Press.

Bushman, R. L. (1984). *Joseph Smith and the beginnings of Mormonism.* Urbana: University of Illinois Press.

Daynes, K. M. (2001). *More wives than one: The transformation of the Mormon marriage system.* Urbana: University of Illinois Press.

Gaustad, E. S., & Barlow, P. L. (2001). *New historical atlas of religion in America.* Oxford, U.K.: Oxford University Press.

Givens, T. (2002). *By the hand of Mormon: The ancient scripture that launched a new world religion.* New York: Oxford University Press.

Ludlow, V. H. (Ed.). (1992). *The encyclopedia of Mormonism.* New York: Macmillan.

Shipps, J. (1985). *Mormonism: The story of a new religious tradition.* Urbana: University of Illinois Press.

Smith, J. (1908). *History of the church.* Salt Lake City, UT: Deseret News.

Stark, R. (1984). The rise of a new world faith. *Review of Religious Research, 26*(1), 18–27.

Law, Sacred

The term "sacred law" generally denotes a body of laws that is understood by a group of believers to have been divinely revealed. Most, but not all religions, have such legal aspects: Hinduism, for example, traces the origins of its sacred laws to the oral traditions recorded in the Vedas, while for Judaism the earliest source of sacred law is in the Torah.

Divine law usually refers to a divinely created natural law or to the unwritten and universal rules of morality, but sacred law is intended to govern human actions in the temporal sphere in accordance with the sacred, and often takes the form of positive written laws and oral or customary laws. Sacred law, therefore, leaves room for human interpretation and adjudication of conduct and transgressions of sacred law, usually by a priestly class. Although most, if not all, religions have legal aspects, this article will focus on the sacred laws of the major religions: Hinduism (and by extension Buddhism), Judaism, Islam, and Christianity—religions in which the law is believed to be divinely inspired or revealed, organized in a discernable collection of written or oral codes, and binding over human activities in the temporal sphere.

Hindu and Buddhist Law

Hinduism, the oldest of the major world religions, traces the origins of its sacred law to the earliest written texts, the Vedas, a collection of oral traditions written down in the period around 2000 BCE. Although the Vedas concentrated primarily on rituals devoted to a pantheon of gods, and not on law, the concept of dharmas, moral principles which guide human action in conjunction with *karma* (the force generated by a person's actions to bring about transmigration and to determine the nature of the person's next existence), is discernable throughout. The dharmas also contributed to the development of the caste system of Hinduism, and thus formed a customary code of social obligations in ancient India.

Toward the end of the Vedic period, around 500 BCE, many of the rituals and rules that had developed from oral tradition were collected in texts known as sutras. The *Dharmasutras*, the rules of daily life, became the first codes of Hindu law. Living according to dharma became one of the "jewels" of Buddhism as well, and therefore, in terms of sacred law, Buddhism and Hinduism share a common origin. In Buddhism, however, the concept of dharma evolved aesthetically, with individuals seeking to achieve an inner tranquility, and it achieved its fullest expression in the Japanese cult of the Buddhist monk Nichiren (1222–1282 CE) and the Lotus school. In India, the Hindu law of dharma became a comprehensive code of personal law, governing marriage and the family, inheritance, and social obligations. In 1772, the British ordered that the *Dharmasutras* be considered binding as personal law in the Anglo-Indian courts, and thus the Hindu law, in conjunction with English rules of criminal and civil law, remained an effective code in a secularized form in the modern age.

Jewish Law

The Torah, also known as the Pentateuch, is the first source of sacred law for the Jewish tradition; it is a written, substantive law governing Jewish religious, social, and familial obligations believed to have been

119

120 · RELIGION AND BELIEF SYSTEMS IN WORLD HISTORY

divinely revealed to Moses during the Exodus from Egypt. During the fifth century BCE, after the Persian emperor Cyrus the Great (c. 550–529 BCE) permitted Jews to return to Palestine following the Babylonian conquest, a number of Jewish scribes provided commentaries on the Torah; some of the most significant are found in the Book of Ezra, and they created the foundations of a comprehensive Jewish jurisprudence. In addition to the Torah, Jewish tradition holds that the sacred law also included a divinely revealed oral law (halakha). Halakha, which was comprised of the statements of oral positive law (Mishna), commentaries on these laws (Gemara) and a number of moral and ethical precepts (Haggadah), were put into written form in the third through sixth centuries CE in the Palestinian and Babylonian Talmuds. The Mishnas are organized categorically and they cover legal matters ranging from religious observances to dietary laws, contracts and torts, criminal law, family law, and property and legal procedure. In the last few centuries BCE, legal questions turned into sectarian rivalries between the high priests, the Sadducees, who regarded only the Torah as authoritative, and the scribes and laity, the Pharisees, who regarded the oral law as an equal part of divine law. The activities of the Pharisees proved vitally important in Jewish history, as they developed a method of legal study of the law centered on a rabbinic tradition and scholarly communities that became a permanent feature of Judaism. Still, later movements in Jewish history, such as the Hasidic movement of the eighteenth century and the Jewish Enlightenment (*haskalah*) and secularizing reform movements of the late eighteenth and nineteenth centuries, have significantly challenged the binding authority of Jewish law to regulate the private and public lives of Jews.

Islamic Law

Islamic law (sharia) originated with divine revelation. The Qur'an, which Muslim tradition holds was divinely inspired, and which is generally believed to have been written by Muhammad (c. 570–632 CE), contains the founding principles of Islamic law,

principally, definitions of the holy obligations of believers. The Qur'an has few direct legal statements, and these are limited to modifications of Arabic customary law. However, once Muhammad had established an Islamic community at Medina in 622, he began to apply the general ethical and moral principles of Islam to matters of secular jurisprudence, thus forming a basis for a specifically Islamic customary law. The application of Qur'anic ethics to secular affairs developed into an Islamic jurisprudence, by which the juridical goal was the discovery of the exact meaning and application (*fiqh*) of Allah's law in secular matters. The founding of the first Islamic dynastic state, the Umayyad dynasty, in Damascus in 661 broadened the focus of Islamic law into areas of civil, commercial, and administrative law. The ninth-century Shafi'i school created a comprehensive Islamic jurisprudence that integrated elements of positive, customary, and natural law. Jurists were first obligated to consult the Qur'an and the precedents set by Muhammad on matters of law. In cases to which the positive law of the Qur'an did not directly apply, judges were then to compare elements of the case at hand with established precedent (customary law), and finally to take into consideration matters of public interest and equity (natural law). The Shafi'i school of Islamic jurisprudence became the dominant school of Islamic law, especially within the Sunni communities, and it generally fixed the available sources of law and juridical procedure. However, the Shi'a tradition, which became especially influential in modern-day Iran, held that secular rulers were divinely inspired descendants of Muhammad, and therefore their legal decisions established a much wider set of case law that jurists might examine for relevant precedents.

Christian Law

The early development of Christianity entailed a break with Judaism and Jewish law. Christian belief considered Jesus Christ the fulfillment of the Jewish prophets' prediction that a messiah would arrive. The mission of Paul (first century CE) to non-Jewish communities within the Roman world, and Paul's insistence that converts to Christianity were not obligated to follow Jewish law, entailed a decisive break between Christianity and Judaism. Intermittent Roman persecution of Christianity in the first three centuries CE made the religion essentially a private cult, one which developed little in the way of laws that governed public life. The conversion of the Roman emperor Constantine (c. 274–337 CE) to Christianity, and the subsequent adoption of the religion as the official cult of the Roman Empire, meant that in secular legal matters, the Christian church deferred to the secular powers. The collapse of the Roman Empire in the West left the Christian church as one of the only central authorities in western Europe, yet it remained under the dominance of secular kings in legal and jurisdictional matters. The Investiture Controversy (1075–1122 CE) between the Holy Roman emperors Henry IV and Henry V and Pope Gregory VII, which started as a conflict over lay nomination of bishops, was as much a conflict about whether or not the state had jurisdiction over the affairs of the Church. The outcome decidedly favored the Church, and it emerged as an independent institution, a virtual state, with its own hierarchy and rules of governance. The Church created a system of canon law, the *jus novum*, which drew heavily from the Roman Code of the Byzantine emperor Justinian, which was newly discovered in the West. The monk Johannes Gratian (d. c. 1160 CE) drew up the full code of canon law, *A Concordance of Discordant Canons*, in 1140; although not formally a sacred law since it was not held to be divinely revealed, Christian canon law was the first widely used code of law in the West following the collapse of the Roman Empire.

Sacred Law and Integrative Jurisprudence

The modern trend by which in some societies the law is viewed as a fixed body of rules set by lawmakers acting out of secular and rational concerns, while in other societies the law continues to be understood as a function of the sacred, has led to what Samuel P. Huntington (1996) called a "clash of civilizations." Nonetheless, even various sacred law traditions contain elements of jurisprudence that would be recognizable to modern secular legal traditions. In other words, despite the fact that sacred law is held by believers to be divinely revealed, these sacred law traditions all contain elements of what the legal scholar Harold J. Berman (1993) called an integrative jurisprudence of positive law (the rules established by the law maker), customary law (the law in a historical and social dimension), and natural law (moral and ethical principles). Thus, the seeming dissonance between the various religious legal traditions, or between religious and secular law, may very well be overstated when considered in terms of common elements of integrative jurisprudence.

Douglas PALMER
Emory University

See also Christian Orthodoxy; Judaism; Religion and Government

Further Reading

Berman, H. J. (1993). *Faith and order: The reconciliation of law and religion.* Grand Rapids, MI: William B. Eerdmans.

Derret, J. D. M. (1963). *Introduction to modern Hindu law.* Oxford, U.K.: Oxford University Press.

Edge, I. (1996). *Islamic law and legal theory.* New York: New York University Press.

Hecht, N. S. et al. (Eds.). (1996). *An introduction to the history and sources of Jewish law.* Oxford, U.K.: Clarendon Press.

Helmholz, R. H. (1996). *The spirit of classical canon law.* Athens: University of Georgia Press.

Huntington, S. P. (1996). *The clash of civilizations and the remaking of the world order.* New York: Simon and Schuster.

Kamali, M. (1989). *Principles of Islamic jurisprudence.* Cambridge, U.K.: Islamic Texts Society.

Nanda, V., & Sinha, S. (1996). *Hindu law and legal theory.* New York: New York University Press.

Neusner, J. (2002). *The Halakah: Historical and religious perspectives.* Leiden, The Netherlands: Brill.

Winroth, A. (2000). *The making of Gratian's Decretum.* Cambridge, U.K.: Cambridge University Press.

Mahavira
(c. 599–527 BCE)
INDIAN RELIGIOUS LEADER

The historical significance of the Indian religious leader Mahavira—who lived in the sixth-century BCE, a time when India society was rooted in the inequity of its caste system and relied for its well-being on the widespread use of slavery and the large-scale sacrifice of animals—lies in his revolutionary worldview of amity and harmony with all living beings. His teachings became the foundation of one of the world's oldest religions, Jainism.

The Indian religious leader Mahivira lived in the sixth century BCE. Two of his core teachings—the principle of ahimsa (nonviolence) and the philosophy of *anekanta* (many-sided reality)—have universal significance and are relevant to contemporary inquiries in peace building, ecology, bioethics, and animal rights. His teachings are also the basis of the canonical literature (*Agama*) of Jainism, which not only plays a significant role within the religion but also is regarded as a primary source for understanding the history of ancient India.

Jainism regards Mahavira as the twenty-fourth *tirthankara* (ford maker) or *jina* (spiritual

Painting of Mahavira (dated to 1900), whose teachings became the foundation of Jainism. Photo of painting by Jules Jain.

conqueror). Having overcome attachment and aversion he attained omniscience and preached the way to overcome worldly suffering and attain *moksa* (liberation from the cycle of rebirth). Jainas (the followers of the *jina*) use the epithet "Mahavira" (great hero) instead of his given name, Vardhamana, and follow his adherence to ahimsa in thought, word, and deed amid adverse circumstances.

Vardhamana was born to mother Trishala and father Siddhartha, members of a royal clan, at Kundagrama in the ancient kingdom of Vaishali near the modern city of Patna in eastern India. His parents were followers of Parshvanatha, the twenty-third *tirthankara*, who is said to have lived during the ninth century BCE. At age thirty Vardhamana renounced his kingdom and became a mendicant practicing austerity in search of enlightenment for thirteen years. Throughout this period he frequently fasted, sometimes for long periods of time and often without even water. During the thirteenth year Mahavira attained *kevalajnana* (infinite knowledge) and became omniscient. For the next thirty years Mahavira taught about ahimsa and compassion and attained nirvana (liberation) in 527 BCE.

Although ahimsa was recognized as a virtue in the Vedas (Hindu sacred writings), such recognition remained a mere scriptural knowledge. In reality Vedic society during

Kill not. Cause no pain. • **Mahavira (c. 599–527 BCE)**

Mahavira's time operated on a fundamental inequity rooted in the caste system and relied for its well-being on the widespread use of slavery and the large-scale sacrifice of animals (*yajna*). In this context Mahavira's teachings were revolutionary. He taught the true meaning of ahimsa and compassion. A precondition of the practice of ahimsa, according to him, is knowledge of the various forms of life: earth, water, fire, wind, vegetation, and mobile beings with two or more senses. Equally important is the awareness that in essence all living beings, regardless of their life form, are equal; all experience pleasure and pain; and all desire to live. Violence against others, in his view, is violence against oneself. This sense of our being the same as other beings, explained Mahavira, is at the core of compassion and nonviolence. Therefore, he preached the principle of universal amity and friendship. Salvation of the self, according to Mahavira, is deeply connected with one's concern for universal well-being. Every thought, word, and deed has a result and creates happiness or suffering for oneself and for others.

In addition to the virtue of being nonviolent, Mahavira emphasized the virtues of telling the truth, not stealing, being celibate, and not being possessive. He prescribed these as the *mahavrata* (great vows) for mendicants; lay Jainas may observe these vows in a limited manner as *anuvrata* (small vows).

Mahavira's philosophy of understanding reality with respect to a given context (*naya*) became the basis for the Jain philosophy of *anekanta*. Jainas not only evolved their own theory of knowledge (*anekantavada*) in the context of their metaphysics and ontology (a branch of metaphysics concerned with the nature of being), but also, more importantly, were concerned about questions such as, "What constitutes valid knowledge, and how is such knowledge acquired?" In the latter sense the philosophy of *anekantavada* allows room for multiple views of reality and reduces conflict often arising from absolutist views of reality. Based on Mahavira's teachings of ahimsa and *anekanta*, Jainas observe vegetarianism, reject the slaughter of animals for human consumption, and, in the context of world religions, advocate harmony and peace, acknowledging the equality of all spiritual traditions. Many people see Mahavira's emphasis on simplicity and *aparigraha* (nonpossession, nonattachment) as a valuable antidote to the rising culture of consumerism at a global scale.

Tara SETHIA
California State Polytechnic University

See also Jainism

Further Reading

Dundas, P. (2002). *The Jains*. New York: Routledge.

Jaini, P. S. (1979). *The Jaina path of purification*. Berkeley and Los Angeles: University of California Press.

Mahapragya, A. (1974). *Sramana Mahavira*. Ladnun, India: Jain Vishva Bharti.

Schubring, W. (2004). *Mahavira's words by Walther Schubring* (W. Bollee & J. Soni, Trans.). Ahmadabad, India: L. D. Institute of Indology.

Sethia, T. (Ed.). (2004). *Ahimsa, anekanta and Jainism*. Delhi, India: Motilal Banarsidass.

Soni, J. (2000). Basic Jaina epistemology. *Philosophy East and West, 50*, 367–377.

Manichaeism

Manichaeism was a religion founded in Mesopotamia during the first half of the third century CE; it incorporated aspects of Zoroastrianism, Judaism, Christianity, and Buddhism. While almost universally attacked by the mainstream religions of the West, the teachings of Manichaeism came to shape debates within the Abrahamic traditions concerning the nature of good, evil, humans, and the world.

Manichaeism was founded by Mani (or Manes; 216–276 or 277 CE), a Persian prophet who proclaimed himself "the messenger of God come to Babel" and the Paraclete (Holy Spirit). He held that God had revealed himself at various times and places in human history: as the Buddha in India, Zoroaster in Persia, and Jesus in Palestine. Mani believed that each of these figures taught that the path to salvation came through gnosis (spiritual knowledge) rather than through faith or acts. In 242 Mani set out to disseminate his message publicly, traveling extensively in Central Asia and, according to some sources, visiting India and China. While only fragments of his written works survive today, they reveal that Mani certainly had familiarity with the Christian synoptic Gospels and the epistles of Paul, Jewish Orthodox and noncanonical texts, Zoroastrianism, and Mahayana Buddhism. He reportedly said: "As a river is joined to another to form a powerful current, just so are the ancient books joined in my writings; and they form one great wisdom, such as has not existed in preceding generations" (BeDuhn 2000, 6). Mani's challenges to the Zoroastrian priesthood, the Magi, led to his execution in 276 or 277.

Mani's teachings, however, spread rapidly. By 370 Manichaean churches could be found throughout much of the Roman Empire, from southern France to North Africa. Augustine of Hippo (354–430), the profoundly influential Christian bishop and theologian, served for nine years as a Manichaean novice before his conversion to orthodox Christianity in 386. While violently suppressed in the old Roman provinces in the sixth century, Manichaeism continued to flourish in Persia and Chinese Turkestan for centuries, even becoming the state religion of the (Chinese) Uighur Empire (eighth century to mid-ninth century CE) in 762. In western Europe, especially France, a significant revival of Manichaeism occurred in the eleventh to thirteen centuries. It was labeled the Albigensian heresy and its challenge to the Roman Catholic Church was perceived as so great that Pope Innocent III (reigned 1198–1216) ordered a crusade against the "scourge of God," bringing a violent end to the movement in the West. In China, Manichaeism persisted until 1600.

Beliefs and Cosmology

Like the Zoroastrian and Gnostic belief systems that influenced it, Manichaeism portrays the universe in radically dualistic terms. The universe is constituted by two oppositional forces: light and darkness. Light corresponds to the spiritual realm, the realm of goodness. Darkness corresponds to the material and bodily realm, which is evil. History is to be played out in three stages: a golden age when the realms of darkness and light are distinct and separate; a middle age in which light and darkness battle for control of the universe; and a final age in which the realms again will be separated, with the spiritual returning to the realm of light and the material being relegated to the realm of darkness. We presently are in the middle age, the time of the great cosmic battle between the forces of good and evil.

The realm of light is ruled by and equated with God, who is known as the King of Light or the Father of Light. The material realm is ruled by an independent and powerful Archon (God) of Darkness, or Hyle (matter), who uses the process of creation to trap light in a fleshly cell. The two gods are in cosmic battle, with the universe as their battlefield. Christ, the Buddha, and other prophets came to earth to impart to humans knowledge of how to release the light imprisoned within the material realm by the God of Darkness. In some Manichaean depictions, the creator God of Genesis *is* the Archon of Darkness, and Christ is the serpent in the garden, imparting good knowledge to Adam and Eve as a path to liberating the light. In China, Mani himself became known as the Buddha of Light.

Manichaean dualism and its resulting cosmic war are used to account for the existence of evil in the world: evil emerges in this realm when the Archon of Darkness wins a battle over the good, but not omnipotent, King of Light. All material creation is evil in its very conception. Humans, being spirit incarnate, are in a tragic and flawed state, subject to evil and ignorance through the imprisonment of their spiritual essences in fleshly bodies.

Prescriptions and Practices

Because during this life humans live in the corrupt, material realm, Manichaeism attempted to separate them from the actions of the Archon of Darkness as much as possible. Manichaean clergy (the Elect) were held to the highest standards of purity: sexual abstinence (since each new birth constituted another spirit imprisoned in the flesh and hence a victory for the forces of Darkness), vegetarianism (since meat was judged to be more highly impure than vegetables),

This Manichaean icon incorporates aspects of Zoroastrianism, Judaism, Christianity, and Buddhism.

refusal to participate in food preparation (since the chopping of even vegetables harmed the light trapped within them), and abstinence from all forms of violence against human or animal (for the spiritual light could be liberated properly from living entities only by knowledge, not by slaughter).

Of these priestly prohibitions (likely a reflection of the influence of Buddhism), only the dictate against all forms of killing was required equally of the Manichaean laity, making Manichaeism a completely pacifistic religion in theory. The actual practice was somewhat different, with Manichees who fell short of the ascetic ideals often attributing their failings to a determinism resulting from their role as pawns in the cosmic battle between the forces of light and darkness.

Manichaeism Today

In contemporary intellectual discussions, Manichaeism is most often used as a pejorative term, describing a radical dichotomy between good and evil that allegedly misconstrues the nature of reality. The U.S. Conference of Catholic Bishops, for example, writes that it is "a Manichean heresy to assert that war is intrinsically evil and contrary to Christian charity" (National Conference of Catholic Bishops 1983, 162). The historian Bernard Lewis claims that the tendency of some forms of modern-day Islam to demonize Christians and Jews as "enemies of God" is attributable to Manichaeism's influence on Islam. Whether such accusations are fair or not, the Manichaean depiction of the world as a place of cosmic conflict between the forces of the spirit and those of the flesh doubtless has had a profound influence on modern Jewish, Christian, and Muslim discussions of humans and the world.

Timothy M. RENICK
Georgia State University

Further Reading

Asmussen, J. (1975). *Manichaean literature: Representative texts.* Delmar, NY: Scholars Facsimiles and Reprints.

Augustine. (1984). *City of God.* New York: Penguin Books.

Barnstone, W. (1984). *The other Bible.* San Francisco: Harper San Francisco.

BeDuhn, J. (2000). *The Manichaean body in discipline and ritual.* Baltimore: Johns Hopkins University Press.

Brown, P. (1967). *Augustine of Hippo: A biography.* Berkeley & Los Angeles: University of California Press.

Burkitt, F. (1925). *The religion of the Manichees.* Cambridge, UK: Cambridge University Press.

Greenless, D. (2007). *The Gospel of the Prophet Mani.* San Diego, CA: Book Tree.

Haloun, G., & Henning, W. (1952). The compendium of the doctrines and styles of the teaching of Mani, the Buddha of Light. *Asia Major, 3,* 184–212.

Lewis, B. (1990, September). The roots of Muslim rage. *Atlantic Monthly, 266*(3), 47–60.

Lieu, S. (1994). *Manichaeism in Mesopotamia and the Roman East.* Leiden, The Netherlands: E. J. Brill.

National Conference of Catholic Bishops. (1983). The challenge of peace: God's promise and our response (the pastoral letter on war and peace). In J. Elshtain (Ed.), *Just war theory* (pp. 77–168). New York: New York University Press.

Robinson, J. (1977). *The Nag Hammadi library.* San Francisco: Harper Collins.

Tardieu, M. (2008). *Manichaeism* (M.B. DeBevoise, Trans.). Urbana: University of Illinois Press. (Original work published 1981)

Millennialism

Millennialism is the belief in an imminent transition to a collective salvation, either earthly or heavenly, accomplished according to a superhuman or supernatural plan. The term (based on *millennium*, meaning "one thousand years") is drawn from the New Testament book of Revelation (Apocalypse), which predicts a thousand-year reign of Christ on Earth.

Religious and political movements inspired by millennialism, the belief that collective salvation (either earthly or heavenly) is imminent—and based on and carried out by a superhuman or supernatural plan—have had a major impact on world history; these include the theological revolutions associated with Christianity, Islam, and Chinese combinations of Daoism and Buddhism, and secular movements such as Communism and Nazism. The human hope for a perfect world has been perennial, at least since the founding of the Zoroastrian religion, which possibly dates from as early as about 1000 BCE. Millennial groups oriented toward a heavenly salvation have occasionally startled the world by opting to leave earthly life via group suicide, as was seen in the 1990s with the Solar Temple in Switzerland, Quebec, and France, and Heaven's Gate in the United States. If earthly salvation for an elect group of people in a millennial kingdom is demonstrated to be impossible, then believers can shift easily to expecting a heavenly salvation, which may have been the case as early Christianity was institutionalized and became more accommodated to mainstream culture in the Roman Empire.

The millennial belief in an imminent transition to a new realm of existence has had a great impact on world history in many times and places, and has been associated with a range of behaviors. Millennial beliefs can motivate people to convert to entirely new religions, as with early Christianity and Islam, or strengthen their existing faith as they await divine intervention to destroy the old order and create the new. Millennialism can motivate people to engage in social action to improve the world and in spiritual disciplines to transform themselves, but it can also motivate them to commit revolutionary violence in attempts to eradicate an evil society and create the millennial kingdom. Millennialism does not necessarily have to result in violence, and when millennialists are caught up in violent episodes, they are not necessarily the ones who initiate the violence. Numerous millennial prophets and messiahs and their followers have been assaulted or executed because of the threat they pose to the established order.

Millennial Leaders

Millennial movements are often stimulated by someone claiming to have received a new revelation. In the study of religions, the term *charisma* refers to the belief that an individual has access to an unseen, superhuman source of authority. It is impossible objectively to validate the person's claim: people either accept it on faith or reject it. If others do not believe the individual's claim to revelation or empowerment, then the person does not have this kind of socially constructed charisma.

Both prophets and messiahs have charisma in this sense. A prophet is someone who is believed to receive revelations, perhaps about the imminent transition to the millennial kingdom. Although also

The Millennium Wheel in London, England, was built to commemorate the beginning of the third millennium CE.

a prophet, a messiah is, in addition, believed to have the superhuman power to create the millennial kingdom. There can be religious apocalyptic prophets, such as Muhammad, and religious messiahs, such as Jesus Christ, who according to the gospels was also an apocalyptic prophet. There can also be secular messiahs, such as Adolf Hitler, who claimed to be empowered by "nature" to create the Third Reich as the millennial kingdom for the German *völk* (folk).

Millennial movements do not necessarily have to have prophets and messiahs. They may arise from the widespread anticipation and/or fears of a number of people, such as the diffuse Euro-American (white supremacist) movement in the United States at the end of the twentieth century and the beginning of the twenty-first, which includes Identity Christians, racist Neopagans, neo-Nazis, and secular survivalists and warriors expecting an apocalyptic conflict with the federal government.

Main Patterns of Millennialism

Scholars now use the term *millennialism* (or *millenarianism*) to refer to two common patterns, which are not mutually exclusive; millennialists may shift from one pattern to another in reaction to different circumstances. Both types of movements may or may not have prophets and/or messiahs.

Catastrophic Millennialism

Catastrophic millennialism, often termed apocalypticism, anticipates a catastrophic transition to the millennial kingdom, either earthly or heavenly. Human nature and society are so evil that society has to be destroyed and created anew. Christians who have these expectations are often categorized by scholars as "pre-millennialists," because they expect Jesus Christ to return *first*, defeat evil powers, destroy the

This Mexican broadside from 1899 shows skeletons in pandemonium as they anticipate the end of the world.

current world, resurrect the dead, judge all people, and then create the millennial kingdom (either earthly or heavenly).

Most catastrophic millennialists wait for divine intervention to carry out the catastrophic events. Some, such as the Branch Davidians and some Identity Christian communities, may arm themselves for self-protection during the tribulation period believed to lead to the end-time events; if they are attacked they will fight back. Some, such as a succession of violent movements in Christian medieval Europe, become actively revolutionary. If the revolutionaries do not have a critical mass they become terrorists.

Progressive Millennialism

Progressive millennialists believe very strongly in progress, and are typically concerned with creating a millennial kingdom on Earth. They believe that humans acting according to a divine or superhuman plan can progressively create the millennial kingdom. Christian progressive millennialists are often termed "post-millennialists" by scholars to indicate that they believe they must do God's will by creating the conditions for God's kingdom on Earth, and *then* Christ will return.

Progressive millennialists include Protestants working peacefully to improve society by carrying out the Social Gospel, as well as post–Vatican II Catholics with a "special option for the poor" working for social justice. Logically, however, progressive millennialists could arm themselves if they felt their community was threatened and fight back if attacked, but this possibility has not received much study. And some progressive millennialists, wishing to speed progress up "to an apocalyptic rate" (Ellwood 2000, 253), become revolutionaries. They are willing to kill others and to carry out massive violence to accomplish their vision of the millennial kingdom. Scholars have identified Nazism, the Marxist Khmer Rouge regime, and Mao Zedong's Communist Revolution and Great Leap Forward as examples of revolutionary progressive millennialism.

On the revolutionary end of the spectrum, there appears to be little difference between catastrophic and progressive millennialists, other than the latter having a strong belief in progress. Both types possess a rigid dualistic outlook, seeing situations and people in terms of good versus evil, us versus them, and they kill to accomplish their millennial dreams.

Nativist Millennial Movements

Nativist millennial movements, sometimes called "revitalization movements," result when a people feels colonized and oppressed by a dominant power and its accompanying bureaucracy. Their traditional way of life is being destroyed and they often are losing their land and means of livelihood. They wish for a return to an idealized earlier time for their people, which they imagine to have been perfect. They are millennialists in that they expect an imminent transition to a collective salvation, which will eliminate their oppressors. These movements have been found in every part of the world in response to colonialism.

In the United States nativist millennialism can be seen in the nineteenth-century Ghost Dance movement, a response by Native Americans to removal from their lands and destruction of their traditional way of life. Beginning in the late twentieth century, nativist millennialism could be discerned also among certain white people in the United States, who imagined themselves to be the "natives" of America. Living in the countryside and towns, and also in cities, they felt oppressed by federal agencies, and believed that their traditional way of life was being destroyed by increasing ethnic diversity, changing gender roles, and greater acceptance of diversity in sexual lifestyles. This unnamed but influential movement could be called the Euro-American nativist movement.

Some nativist millennialists, like the Native American Ghost Dancers, may expect divine intervention to remove the hated oppressors in response to a magic or sacrificial ritual such as the Ghost Dance, which was intended to bring the return of the ancestors. Some, like the Pai Marire movements among the Maori in nineteenth-century New Zealand, may alternate between expecting divine intervention, committing active revolutionary violence, and progressively building their own separate communities. Nativists' actions

I worry that, especially as the Millennium edges nearer, pseudo-science and superstition will seem year by year more tempting, the siren song of unreason more sonorous and attractive. • **Carl Sagan (1934–1996)**

depend on a variety of factors, including whether they are left alone to build their perfect societies or they are attacked.

Millennialism in the Twenty-First Century

Millennialism will remain an important factor in world history. It might be stimulated by significant dates, such as 2000, but the hope for the collective salvation has existed for thousands of years and will not disappear. In the new temporal millennium, Christian Dispensationalists, for instance, interpret events in the Middle East as fulfilling prophecies leading to Christ's Second Coming; they expect that the faithful will be "raptured" into heaven and thus escape the catastrophic end-time events. With the terrorists attacks of September 11, 2001, al-Qaeda became the most visible segment of a diffuse and widespread revolutionary Islamist movement that aims to destroy what is seen as a confederation of "unbeliever" nations, including the United States and "hypocrite" Muslim nations aligned with the West, to create the perfect Islamic state enforcing sharia (Islamic law)—a Muslim vision of the collective earthly salvation. Those revolutionary Islamists who die for the cause are assured that they will receive immediate rewards in heaven —a very dangerous combination of expectations concerning earthly and heavenly salvations.

While people in all parts of the world continue to interpret catastrophic tragedies and oppression through an apocalyptic lens, many progressive millennialists, from Jews, Christians, and Muslims to Hindus, Buddhists, and New Agers, still hope and work for a peaceful world.

Catherine WESSINGER
Loyola University

Further Reading

Adas, M. (1979). *Prophets of rebellion: Millennarian protest movements against the European colonial order.* Chapel Hill: University of North Carolina Press.

Barkun, M. (1997). *Religion and the racist right: The origins of the Christian Identity Movement* (rev. ed.). Chapel Hill: University of North Carolina Press.

Boyer, P. (1992). *When time shall be no more: Prophecy belief in American culture.* Cambridge, MA: Harvard University Press.

Burridge, K. (1969). *New heaven, new Earth: A study of millenarian activities.* Oxford, U.K.: Basil Blackwell.

Cohn, N. (1970). *The pursuit of the millennium: Revolutionary millenarians and mystical anarchists of the Middle Ages* (rev. ed.). New York: Oxford University Press.

Cohn, N. (1993). *Cosmos, chaos and the world to come: The ancient roots of apocalyptic faith.* New Haven, CT: Yale University Press.

Cook, D. (2002). Suicide attacks or "martyrdom operations" in contemporary Jihad literature. *Nova Religio: The Journal of Alternative and Emergent Religions, 6*(1), 7–44.

Ellwood, R. (2000). Nazism as a millennial movement. In C. Wessinger (Ed.), *Millennialism, persecution and violence: Historical cases* (pp. 241–260). Syracuse, NY: Syracuse University Press.

Hunt, S. (Ed.). (2001). *Christian millenarianism: From the early church to Waco.* Bloomington: Indiana University Press.

Lanternari, V. (1963). *The religions of the oppressed: A study of modern messianic cults.* L. Sergio (Trans.). New York: Knopf.

Rhodes, J. M. (1980). *The Hitler movement: A modern millenarian revolution.* Stanford, CA: Hoover Institution Press.

Rosenfeld, J. E. (1995). Pai Marire: Peace and violence in a New Zealand millenarian tradition. *Terrorism and Political Violence, 7*(3), 83–108.

Wessinger, C. (2000a). *How the millennium comes violently: From Jonestown to Heaven's Gate.* New York: Seven Bridges Press.

Wessinger, C. (2000b). *Millennialism, persecution, and violence: Historical cases.* Syracuse, NY: Syracuse University Press.

Wessinger, C. (2003). New religious movements and conflicts with law enforcement. In D. Davis & B. Hankins (Eds.), *New religious movements and religious liberty in America* (pp. 89–106, 201–204). Waco, TX: Baylor University Press.

Wojcik, D. (1997). The end of the world as we know it: Faith, fatalism, and apocalypse in America. New York: New York University Press.

Missionaries

For centuries, believers committed to a particular religion have endeavored to convert those with differing beliefs, and thus have affected great change throughout the world. The three main "missionizing" religions in history have been Buddhism, Christianity, and Islam.

Missionaries are men and women who propagate a particular religious belief, attempt to convert those holding a different belief, and found new communities of people to practice their belief. For at least 2,500 years, missionaries have been some of the most important agents of change in world history. In innumerable ways, missionaries have significantly shaped, and continue to shape, the world we live in today.

The definition of missionaries given above presupposes several conditions. First, the missionary's religion is not associated with a particular village or region. That is, the religion must be transportable and not bounded geographically. It cannot be associated solely with, for example, an oracle residing in a sacred grove near an African village. Second, there is some higher authority that sends the missionary out "on mission." Christian missionaries, for example, might receive their authority from a particular missionary society, but ultimately they believe their authority comes from God. Third, missionaries intentionally set out to try to convert others to their faith. Fourth, the missionary must believe that his or her religious belief is universally "true" and that all other beliefs are in error. This revelation needs to be shared with all nonbelievers so that they may be "liberated" from evil and falsehood. Finally, the missionary feels uniquely "called" to mission, believing that he or she has received a special commission or mandate to bring the religious vision and its benefits to the nonbeliever.

It is also important to distinguish between "home" and "foreign" missions, although the distinctions are becoming increasingly blurred. Examples of home missionary work would include youth programs, shelters and food kitchens, door-to-door evangelizing, distribution of religious literature, public witness, and protests or pressure directed toward religious and political leaders to come more in line with specific doctrinal beliefs, such as antiabortion. Obviously, many such activities are also carried out by missionaries in "foreign" missions, which carry the religion beyond its land of origin. But foreign lands that were considered "pagan" a century ago, such as parts of Africa, are now sending Christian missionaries to the United States and Europe to convert Europeans or bring apostates back to their faith. Major world missionizing religions for at least the last two or three centuries have focused their activities not only on nonbelievers who practice local religions, such as among the Native Americans in the United States, but also on each other, such as Christians and Muslims trying to convert each other's members. The Christian evangelical movement has targeted Central and South America for much of its missionary efforts, not toward non-Christians, but to convert the majority Roman Catholic Christian populations to Protestant versions of Christianity. While recognizing these increasingly fuzzy distinctions between home and abroad and "us" and "them," this essay will focus primarily on missionaries working in "foreign" missions for the major world missionizing religions.

Through the notion of universality, missionaries consider their religious beliefs to be transcultural and transcendent. The supreme power or truth that these beliefs possess overrides the nonbeliever's personal bonds with his or her immediate family, clan, ethnic identity, political organization, and local religious belief. Missionaries themselves, however, are seldom able to fully separate themselves from their own social and cultural heritage and traditions. There are some core beliefs that are essential to the faith, and therefore required of all believers in all cultures. There are other religious practices that are unique to a missionary's own national or regional (as Scotland, the Middle East) culture and heritage, and these should be modified and adapted as the religion spreads to new areas. Missionaries often link their own social, cultural, economic, and political customs, however, with the universal, core religious beliefs. Frequently these then become one and the same. Islam around the world has a distinctly Arabic nature, due in no small part to the requirement that the Qur'an be read in Arabic. Buddhism reveals its roots in Indian philosophy and culture wherever it is practiced. Chinese Confucian and Daoist concepts are closely woven into the fabric of Son and Zen Buddhism in Korea and Japan. Western Enlightenment ideas about human rights, rational thought, and the scientific method accompany many Christian missionaries. While the central religious message is universal, cultural expressions such as wearing a certain style of clothing, having only one spouse, doing "manly" work, or eating in a certain manner are often required for one to be considered a good convert to the new faith. Because of this, missionaries, such as those Christian missionaries that accompanied European imperial expansion over the last five hundred years, are sometimes viewed as cultural imperialists.

One reason for this charge of cultural imperialism is that Christian missionaries, unlike the missionaries of any other religion, have more often been involved in activities that have gone far beyond simply teaching the gospel under a tree or building a church. Jesuits served as advisers to the Chinese emperor and Japanese shogun in the 1500s and 1600s. Franciscan, Dominican, and other Catholic missionaries owned slaves in the Americas, and both Protestant and

To make potential converts feel comfortable, two Protestant missionaries in China wear traditional Chinese clothing.

Catholic missionary societies owned vast plantations and lands abroad. Besides their ministry, and sometimes instead of their ministry, Christian missionaries were involved in myriad secular activities, including establishing schools and colleges, setting up hospitals and clinics, serving as doctors, nurses, translators, interpreters, government agents, merchants, and military advisers. This involvement in local economies, governments, and cultures had an immense impact on societies and peoples around the world. To cite just one example, many newly independent countries in the second half of the twentieth century, particularly in Africa, were led by men who had obtained their primary and often higher education in Christian missionary schools, which led them to be very "Westernized" in their thinking and attitudes.

Implicit in the charge of cultural imperialism is the idea that the missionary has employed some type of force, coercion, or deception on the convert

A Spanish mission in central Mexico.

to convince him to abandon traditional ways and accept new ones. It is true that at some time in its past, every missionizing religion has been advanced through force—Islam by conquest, Buddhism by zealous feudal warlords, Christianity through the Inquisition. Still, it is also true that each of these religions recognizes that forced conversion is a counterfeit conversion, and that converts must come to their new faith with a free and open heart. The Qur'an, for example, declares, "There is no compulsion (force) in religion" (2:256).

Conversion is a major topic of study in its own right and is too complex to discuss in any detail here. But, depending on the culture in which one lives, conversion to a new religion may require the abandonment of all or large parts of one's birth culture. In many societies religion and culture and daily life are all so closely linked together that it is impossible to change one without changing all. The missionary,

who believes absolutely in the correctness of his or her vision and the benefits, such as eternal salvation, to be gained from it, will argue that each individual should be free to hear the compelling and, it is hoped, convincing message. The problem arises when the missionary has the might of imperial military and economic forces behind him or her and can call on those forces whenever necessary. When European nations and the United States, for example, forced Japan to sign "Open Door" treaties in the mid-1800s, there was generally a clause in each treaty that allowed Christian missionaries to travel anywhere in this country and proselytize freely with no restrictions. Because of the perceived threat that missionaries pose to their traditional cultures and religion, many countries with a single state-supported religion have forbidden missionaries representing other beliefs to proselytize within their borders. Many of the predominantly Roman Catholic countries in South and Central America, for example, place restrictions on Protestant evangelical missionary activities, and Russia has placed similar restrictions on Protestants, whom they view as threatening the Russian Orthodox Church. In many Islamic countries all non-Islamic missionary activity is strictly forbidden, and conversion from Islam to another religion is punishable by death.

On the other hand, converts have often taken advantage of the missionary's connections to a wider world. For example, as more scholarly studies appear detailing Christian missionary activity during the age of European imperialism, it is clear that many nonbelievers converted less for spiritual reasons than for economic, political, or social ones. Missionaries provided chiefs with firearms, children with education, women with health care and freedom from patriarchal domination, poorer citizens with a perceived enhanced status through the opportunity to wear Western clothing, speak a Western language, and become a clerk or some other functionary in a colonial government. These self-serving motives for conversion meant that missionary successes were often quite tenuous, and there are numerous accounts of backsliders and even whole villages or chiefdoms reverting to traditional beliefs as the material or political advantages of becoming Christian changed. Missionary critics argue that even in those examples where local elites invited foreign missionaries to come and freely spread their message, there were always underlying economic or political motives that dictated this action rather than a deep spiritual commitment to the missionary's religion. It must also be said, however, that many missionaries of all faiths have been remarkable, altruistic people who truly cared for the people among whom they worked. Some fought against the harsh treatment or injustice inflicted upon local people by outside forces, such as colonial settlers, or even local governments. The priests and nuns who have been killed by dictatorships in Central America during the past thirty years represent but a few examples of this compassion and sacrifice.

No matter how or where they arrive, missionaries always meet some resistance and their chances for success often depend on whom they are able to reach most effectively. In many cases they begin with the people at the margins—women, children, people with physical or mental handicaps, outcasts, the poor and illiterate, widows. In these instances missionaries are tolerated at best, and sometimes martyred by the elites who feel their positions threatened. When missionaries directly challenge the power elites they may be viewed as political troublemakers and their converts as traitors. Rulers in these situations may take exceptionally harsh measures against both the missionaries and converts, such as the massacre of Christians at the beginning of the Edo period (1600/03–1868) in Japan. Only in those cases where a majority of the elites and common people accept the new religion are missionaries able to initiate revolutionary change in a society. Generally, it has also been the case that missionaries are more effective among peoples who do not practice other world religions. Christian missionaries, for example, have had relatively little success in converting Muslims or Hindus.

Missionizing Religions

Buddhism, Christianity, and Islam are the three principal missionary religions in world history. In the twentieth century it was also possible to speak of missionaries for the secular belief of communism. (Although communism and the missionaries who spread it meet many of the criteria listed above, this article will discuss only religious missionaries.) But other religions have had less impact or less sustained missionary activity than these three principal religions.

Although Judaism is one of the oldest continuous world religions, it has discouraged missionary work and even conversion for many centuries. Prior to the Jewish revolts against the Romans in 66–70 and 132–135 CE, there was extensive Jewish missionary activity among certain sects of Judaism to fulfill the prophecy in Habakkuk 2:14, "For the earth will be filled with the knowledge of the glory of the Lord, as the waters cover the sea." Following the second revolt, however, as many Jews entered the Diaspora, the focus shifted to maintaining a holy community awaiting

136 · RELIGION AND BELIEF SYSTEMS IN WORLD HISTORY

Statistics of Protestant Missions in China—December, 1888.

FROM THE CHINESE RECORDER.

	Name of Society	Date of Mission	Foreign Missionaries.			Total.	Native Ordained Ministers.	Unordained Native Helpers.	Communicants.	Pupils in Schools.	Contributions by Native Churches.
			Men.	Wives.	Single Women						
1	London Missionary Society...	1807	31	21	13	65	8	72	3,695	1,927	(?) 14,420.00
2	A. B. C. F. M.	1830	16	13	6	35	4	105	816	443	425.07
3	American Baptist, North	1834	11	9	10	30	6	37	1,340	244	1,077.00
4	American Protestant Episcopal	1835	10	8	3	21	17	3	496	1.614	568.18
5	American Presbyterian, North	1838	48	36	18	102	23	84	3,788	2,352	7,090.00
6	American Reformed (Dutch)	1842	7	6	2	15	6	16	844	163	2,870.03
7	British and Foreign Bible Society	1843	14	7	...	21	...	(?)114	...	...	...
8	Church Missionary Society	1844	28	17	5	50	11	81	2,832	2,041	3,469.20
9	English Baptist	1845	21	16	...	37	1	8	1,130	210	425.00
10	Methodist Episcopal, North	1847	32	31	17	80	43	91	3,903	1,288	4,490.91
11	Seventh Day Baptist...	1847	2	2	1	5	...	1	30	9	...
12	American Baptist, South	1847	7	6	7	20	7	18	776	292	687.70
13	Basel Mission...	1847	24	19	...	43	2	49	1,885	692	949.86
14	English Presbyterian	1847	24	16	10	50	8	89	3,428	575	5,435.10
15	Rhenish Mission	1847	4	2	...	6	1	4	154	37	50.00
16	Methodist Episcopal, South	1848	10	9	15	34	4	7	286	855	246.91
17	Berlin Founding Hospital	1850	1	1	4	6	...	1	27	80	...
18	Wesleyan Missionary Society	1852	25	12	6	43	2	33	975	552	403.00
19	Woman's Union Mission	1859	...	...	4	4	...	2	36	109	8.18
20	Methodist New Connexion	1860	7	4	1	12	...	36	1,232	180	101,00
21	Society Promotion Female Educ.	1864	...	...	7	7	...	...	...	...	...
22	United Presbyterian, Scotch	1865	7	5	1	13	...	14	773	67	(?) 150 00
23	China Inland Mission	1865	139	62	115	316	12	118	2,415	153	459.45
24	American Presbyterian, South	1867	10	6	3	19	...	5	82	300	92.00
25	United Methodist Free Church	1868	3	3	...	6	2	8	329	72	263.00
26	National Bible Society of Scotland	1868	4	2	...	6	...	(?)60	...	...	...
27	Irish Presbyterian	1869	3	3	...	6	...	12	68	...	...
28	Canadian Presbyterian	1871	5	4	1	10	2	50	2,650	318	491.80
29	Society Propagation of the Gospel	1874	(?)5	2	4	(?)11	...	...	...	...	...
30	American Bible Society	1876	7	4	...	11	...	33	...	...	...
31	Established Church of Scotland	1878	1	1	...	2	...	3	30	80	...
32	Berlin Mission	1882	4	4	1	9	3	21	500	70	...
33	Allem. Ev. Prot. Miss. Gesell.	1884	1	...	...	1	...	...	...	...	...
34	Bible Christians	1885	4	2	...	6	...	...	3	...	...
35	Foreign Christian Mission Society	1886	5	2	...	7	...	...	2	32	...
36	Soc. Prop. Christ. & Gen. Knowledge	1886	1	1	...	2	...	...	...	...	...
37	Society of Friends	1886	1	1	2	4	...	...	...	...	...
38	Am. S'dinavian Congregational	1887	2	...	...	2	...	...	...	...	...
39	Ch. of Eng. Zenana Miss. Society	1888	...	...	3	3	...	...	...	...	...
40	Independent Workers		2	...	1	3	...	3	(?) 30	(?) 62	...
	Total—December, 1888		526	337	260	1123	162	1,278	34,555	14,817	841,473.39
	Increase over Dec., 1887		37	17	39	93			2,295	1,140	$5,936.69

This table shows the extent of Protestant missionary activity of the 39 missionary societies and 1,123 missionaries active in China in 1888.

---

the messiah. Jewish missionary activity ceased and potential converts were even discouraged through an emphasis on strict observance of Torah (Jewish law), and by requiring male circumcision.

Some ancient religions, such as Zoroastrianism or the Egyptian cult of Isis and Osiris, claimed universal messages but were closely tied to specific sociopolitical contexts. They spread most commonly through migration, trade, war, and the conversion of neighboring peoples without the direction of any central mission authority. Many syncretic religions, such as Sun Myung Moon's Unification Church (the Moonies), the Sikhs, and the Baha'i faith have universal messages, do actively promote missionary activity, and seek converts, as do many of the myriad

independent, indigenous churches in Africa, such as the Kimbanguist Church in the Democratic Republic of the Congo.

One of the oldest and most populous religions in the world, Hinduism, with over 800 million practitioners, almost defies description because of its complexity. Because Hinduism had no founder, possesses no single creed, and looks to no single source of authority, it does not possess some of the key characteristics of a missionary religion. In the past, Hinduism essentially spread by the gradual adoption of Vedic sacred texts and practices across India and had no missionary tradition. Beginning in the nineteenth century, however, and continuing today, some "evangelical" Hindu sects, often organized around a particular guru, have actively sought converts through missionary activities. The most well-known of these are the Maharishi Mahesh Yogi's Transcendental Meditation movement and the Ramakrishna Mission, or Hare Krishnas.

Buddhist Missionaries

"Go forth O Monks, for the good of many, for the happiness of many, out of compassion for the world, for the welfare, the good and happiness of both gods and men. Let no two of you go in the same direction. Teach the Dhamma . . . Explain both in letter and in spirit the holy life, completely fulfilled and perfectly pure" (Vinaya, Mahavagga: I.II.I).

Buddhism was the first world missionary religion, crossing boundaries of race, ethnicity, language, culture, and politics. Having given his Great Commission, the historical Buddha (Siddhartha Gautama; c. 566–c. 486 BCE), living in northern India, sent his disciples in all directions to share his teachings, the dharma. There was to be no centrally organized missionary movement, but simply individual monks and teachers going their separate ways to propagate the Buddha's teachings. The Buddha showed the way by refusing to enter into Nirvana after becoming enlightened, but living on into his eighties to teach what he had discovered through meditation and contemplation.

While Buddhist missionaries may belong to different sects, they all share a central core of beliefs, particularly the Four Noble Truths and the Eightfold Path. They do not teach that the Buddha is a deity, nor recognize any supreme god or creator. They consider the Buddha's message universal, one truth having relevance for one mankind. As there is no concept of sin in the dharma, Buddhist missionaries do not offer salvation, but rather the overcoming of, and freedom from, ignorance. They also believe that no outside spiritual force or deity, including the Buddha, can confer enlightenment. After hearing the dharma teachings, each individual must experience and realize the truth for oneself. Buddhist missionaries are unique in not competing against missionaries

from other religions. They are never to use coercion or violence to gain converts, never to try to convert someone who is content in his or her own faith, never to speak disparagingly of other faiths. Intolerance, dogmatism, and religious fanaticism are decidedly non-Buddhist-like behaviors.

Following the Buddha's death, individual monks from the monastic community, the Sangha, traveled with their alms bowls and taught the dharma along caravan routes, such as the Silk Roads, thereby linking Buddhism's spread to the development of long-distance trade. Around 262 BCE the Mauryan ruler, Asoka, adopted Buddhist principles for his vast empire. Besides commissioning the first written dharma texts, he also sent out Buddhist missionaries (monks) across India and beyond. Indian Buddhist monks brought the dharma to China in 67 CE at the emperor's invitation. By the 500s Buddhism had spread to Nepal, Sri Lanka, Vietnam, Burma, Thailand, southern China, Indonesia, and Cambodia. Ch'an Buddhism began in China around 520, and spread from there to Korea. By the 1200s, Japanese Buddhists had developed their own version of Ch'an Buddhism known as Zen. Tibet received its first Indian Buddhist missionary, the Guru Rimpoche (Padmasambhava), in 817. Ironically, when northern India came under the political control of Turkish Muslims between the ninth and twelfth centuries, many Buddhist monks were killed and their universities/monasteries destroyed. By the 1500s, Buddhism had nearly died out in the Buddha's homeland.

After several centuries of relative stagnation, Buddhism began in the 1800s to spread to Europe and the Americas. Since World War II Buddhism has gained a wide following in the West. In the 1950s and 1960s dozens of Europeans and Americans traveled to Asia where they spent years studying throughout the Asian Buddhist world. Many of them have now returned and together with thousands of recently arrived Asian immigrants have established monasteries and Buddhist societies throughout Europe and the Americas. Asian Buddhist monks now regularly visit the West to teach the dharma. Some scholars now speak of American Buddhism, which is

A Protestant missionary in Africa in the late 1800s stands with indigenous Africans who are training to assist in the conversion of other Africans.

characterized by a unique blending of many different Buddhist practices.

Christian Missionaries

"Therefore go and make disciples of all nations, baptizing them in the name of the Father and of the Son and of the Holy Spirit, and teaching them to obey everything I have commanded you" (Matthew 28:19–20).

Matthew writes that after the Resurrection, Jesus appeared among his disciples and gave them his Great Commission. Like the Buddha, Jesus had already set a missionary example as he gathered followers, promising to make them "fishers of men" (Matthew 4:19). Following Jesus' death, his Jewish Christian followers, based in Jerusalem, spread his message to others in the surrounding Jewish community. Whether they were one of Jesus' original followers or new converts to his teachings, however, they remained Jews and were expected to keep the Hebrew law. It was Paul of Tarsus, recognized as the prototype and greatest of all Christian missionaries, who began to tell Jesus' story to the Gentiles (non-Jews), and he and others carried the gospel, or good news, across Anatolia (modern Turkey) and Greece to Rome. It was Paul who separated Christianity from the Hebrew law and its Jewish context, thereby giving it a universal appeal to people of all nations.

Although there have been nearly an infinite number of schisms among Christian believers since Jesus preached his gospel, there are still some core beliefs that a majority of Christian missionaries share. Some of these beliefs Christians adopted from Judaism, such as a belief in one God, in a messiah, or Christ, and in an afterlife. The central Christian belief is that through faith in Jesus' sacrificial death and resurrection, individuals are spiritually and physically saved from death, their sins are redeemed, and they will return to God in heaven. All Christian missionaries will also teach that God is a Trinity, a single supreme being in three persons, Father, Son, and Holy Spirit, and that Jesus is both fully human and fully God, two natures in one.

The missionaries who followed Paul carried the gospel across the Roman Empire. A critical turning point in Christian history came when Constantine made Christianity the religion of the Roman Empire in 312 CE. Over the next seven hundred years, missionaries evangelized large parts of Europe, Ireland, Anatolia (including the important city of Constantinople [now Istanbul]), and North Africa. Much of this missionary work was undertaken by monastic monks, such as the Nestorians and Cistercians.

The second millennium began with the Great Schism of 1054, which divided Christianity between the Roman Catholic Church in western Europe and the Orthodox Church in eastern Europe and Russia. Both branches now sent out missionaries. The European Reformation that began in the 1520s gave rise to numerous Protestant sects but conflicts with the Roman Catholic Church and constant fissures and schisms prevented them from sending out missionaries in any significant number. Meanwhile the Catholic Church dominated the missionary field, sending Dominicans, Franciscans, Jesuits, and others to the Americas, India, and Asia. Since Protestants entered the mission field in the late 1700s, Christian missionaries have encircled the globe, often accompanying Europe's imperial expansion.

While this discussion has focused on organized forms of Christian foreign missionary activity, it is also true that every Christian is expected to make public witness of his or her faith; in effect, to be a missionary. There are several statements attributed to Jesus in the New Testament that Christians believe call on them to personally spread the gospel. One such statement is found in Mark: "Go ye into all the world, and preach the gospel to every creature" (16:15). Thus, while Christian churches send missionaries abroad, members of their congregations serve the "home" mission.

Islamic Missionaries

"Invite (all) to the way of Your Lord with wisdom and beautiful preaching and argue with them in ways that are best and most gracious. For Your Lord knows the best, who have strayed away from His path" (Qur'an 16:125).

Islam is always described as a missionary religion, it has a universal message, and it has been one of the fastest-growing religions in world history. It now numbers well over a billion members worldwide. There has never been, however, a sustained and organized missionary effort in Islam to spread the message said to have been given by God to Muhammad (c. 570–632) and recorded in the Qur'an.

In the Qur'an there are many suras, or chapters, that can be interpreted as referring to missionary work. Like the earlier examples of the Buddha and Jesus, Muhammad was the first missionary for Islam. His missionary role is described clearly in the Qur'an: "O you prophet, we have sent you as a witness and a herald of good tidings, and a warner, and someone who invites people unto God by His permission, and

as an illuminating lamp" (33:45). But the Qur'an also relates that Muhammad is only the messenger, whose duty is simply to convey the message, not to convert his audience to Islam: "It is not required of you (O Muhammad), to set them on the right path but it is God who guides whom He wills" (2:272). Muhammad is to convey God's message "with wisdom and beautiful preaching," and by arguing "in ways that are best and most gracious." Through these and other verses Muslims believe that they too are obligated to share Allah's message with unbelievers. In Islam, this missionary work is know as dawah, and every believer is considered a missionary, whether through example or by proselytizing.

Although, as with Christianity and Buddhism, there are different branches of Islam, every Muslim would agree on certain fundamental beliefs. First among these would be the simple statement of faith: "There is no God but God, and Muhammad is his messenger." To convert to Islam, one need only recite this statement in front of witnesses. Actually, it is believed that every person is born pure and a Muslim, but some become corrupted and therefore each new Muslim is considered a "revert," having gone back to their original faith, rather than a convert. Muhammad is believed to be the last and greatest prophet of God, but not divine in any way. There will be a final judgment day and life after death in heaven or hell. A devout Muslim must also perform the Five Pillars, or duties, which include expressing the statement of faith, giving alms, praying five times a day, fasting during the month of Ramadan, and making a pilgrimage to Mecca at least once in one's lifetime.

Muhammad is said to have received his first revelations from God in 610 CE, and they continued until his death twenty-two years later. Muhammad's wife, Khadijah, was his first convert. By the time of his death Muhammad had acquired several hundred thousand followers and spread Islam across much of the Arabian Peninsula. Within a hundred years Islam was practiced across North Africa as far west as Morocco, north into southern Europe, and east to India.

While it is often argued that Islam spread by the sword (i.e., force), scholars have generally discounted this view. Rather, as Muslim armies conquered they also destroyed opposition. Islam has no clergy per se, only local prayer leaders, scholars, and holy men. Therefore Islam spread behind military conquest and through trade, following the caravan routes across North Africa and Asia, with merchants, travelers, holy men, and bureaucrats as well as soldiers carrying God's message. As they settled in new areas they established Islamic institutions, married locally, and over the decades converts appeared. Only in the past century, as Muslims have come under increasing pressure from Christian missionaries to convert, have Islamic associations, organizations, and missionary societies been formed to counter Christian efforts.

Outlook in the Twenty-First Century

Missionaries are not easily defined, as the discussion above and the examples from the three major religions illustrate. In reality, every member of every religion is a witness and example for his or her faith. Religions frequently acquire new members in ways that meet few of the conditions set out at the beginning of this essay. Islam has become the second largest religion in the world without, until very recently, any formal missionary effort. Buddhism is spread by simple monks who depend on the charity of lay believers to survive. Many religions carry out very active and passionate missionary work but their converts are few because their message does not seem to have universal appeal.

From the beginning, Christianity has combined both personal witness and intentional mission organization to spread the gospel. Over the past five hundred years Christian missionary efforts have been aided by Western colonialism and domination of technology. In 2004 there were more missionaries than ever before in world history. Christians alone have over 400,000 missionaries spreading the gospel and spend an estimated $11 billion on foreign missions. At the end of 2009 the Church of Latter-day Saints (Mormon Church) alone had over 50,000 missionaries serving in some 160 countries. Evangelical Christians have made it their goal to convert the entire world population to Christianity and provide "a church for every people."

And yet it appears that Islam is the fastest-growing religion today, having increased from around 400 million in 1960 to over 1.5 billion in 2009. A significant reason for this growth is the high birthrate in Asia and Southwest Asia. But Islam is also growing in the former Soviet Union, Europe, and the United States through both conversion and immigration. Buddhism is also gaining many adherents in Europe and the United States. India is experiencing a Hindu revival and many Native Americans, Africans, and other groups are recovering their traditional religions.

As the global village becomes more of a reality, the difference between home and foreign mission will lose all meaning. As transportation and communication become more accessible to the world's peoples, individuals will be able to choose their religious faith more easily than at any time in human history. A simple search on the World Wide Web reveals that in many ways, the Internet is becoming the missionary of the future. In the end, however, it will still be the single believer who brings others to his or her faith, as did the Buddha, Jesus, and Muhammad.

Roger B. BECK

Eastern Illinois University

See also Buddha; Jesus; Muhammad; Paul, Saint; Thomas Aquinas, Saint

Further Reading

Arnold, T. W. (1986). *The preaching of Islam: A history of the propagation of the Muslim faith*. Westminster, U.K.: Archibald Constable.

Baum, W., Winkler, D. W., & Winkler, D. (2003). *Apostolic church of the East: A history of the Nestorian Church*. New York: Routledge.

Beckerlegge, G. (2001). *Ramakrishna mission: The making of a modern Hindu movement*. Oxford, U.K.: Oxford University Press.

MISSIONARIES · 141

To convert somebody, go and take them by the hand and guide them. • **Saint Thomas Aquinas (1225–1274)**

Bernstein, R. (2002). *Ultimate journey: Retracing the path of an ancient Buddhist monk who crossed Asia in search of enlightenment.* New York: Vintage.

Bosch, D. J. (1991). *Transforming mission: Paradigm shifts in theology of mission.* Maryknoll, NY: Orbis.

Dickson, J. P. (2003). *Mission-commitment in ancient Judaism and in the Pauline communities.* Tubingen, Germany: J. C. B. Mohr.

Esposito, J. L. (2000). *The Oxford history of Islam.* Oxford, U.K.: Oxford University Press.

Esposito, J. L. (2004). *Islamic world: Past and present.* Oxford, U.K.: Oxford University Press.

Geraci, R. P., & Khordarkowsky, M. (2001). *Of religion and empire: Missions, conversion, and tolerance in tsarist Russia.* Ithaca, NY: Cornell University Press.

Goldstein, J. (2003). *One Dhama: The emerging Western Buddhism.* New York: HarperCollins.

Goodman, M. (1994). *Mission and conversion: Proselytizing in the religious history of the Roman empire.* Oxford, U.K.: Clarendon Press.

Holtrop, P. N., & McLeod, H. (Eds.). (2000). *Missions and missionaries.* Rochester, NY: Boydell, for the Ecclesiastical History Society.

Kedar, B. Z. (1984). *Crusade and mission: European approaches toward the Muslims.* Princeton, NJ: Princeton University Press.

MacMullen, R. (1984). *Christianizing the Roman empire (A.D. 100–400).* New Haven, CT: Yale University Press.

Matthews, S. (2001). *First converts: Rich pagan women and the rhetoric of mission in early Judaism and Christianity.* Palo Alto, CA: Stanford University Press.

Neill, S. (1987). *A history of Christian missions* (2nd ed.). New York: Penguin.

Poston, L. (1992). *Islamic da'wah in the West: Muslim missionary activity and the dynamics of conversion to Islam.* New York: Oxford University Press.

Rambo, L. R. (1993). *Understanding religious conversion.* New Haven, CT: Yale University Press.

Sanneh, L. (1992). *Translating the message: The missionary impact on culture.* Maryknoll, NY: Orbis Books.

Scott, J., & Griffiths, G. (Eds.). (2004). *Mixed messages: Materiality, textuality, missions.* New York: St. Martins Press.

Smith, H. (2001). *The world's religions: Our great wisdom traditions.* New York: HarperCollins.

Smith, H., & Novak, P. (2003). *Buddhism: A concise introduction.* New York: HarperCollins.

Stanley, B. (Ed.). (2001). *Christian missions and the Enlightenment.* Grand Rapids, MI: Eerdmans.

Tweed, T. A. (2002). *The American encounter with Buddhism, 1844–1912.* Chapel Hill: University of North Carolina Press.

Walls, A. F. (2002). *The missionary movement in Christian history: Studies in the transition of faith.* Maryknoll, NY: Orbis Books.

Moses
(c. 13th century BCE)
Hebrew prophet and leader

Moses, the Hebrew prophet and leader, figures prominently in biblical accounts of his people. Yahweh, the Hebrew God, charged Moses with freeing the Hebrews enslaved in Egypt and leading them to Canaan, the land promised to their ancestors. Moses also consulted Yahweh and instituted the Decalogue and Covenant Code, both of which would prove to be major elements in establishing the Israelites' culture and religious practices.

The prophet Moses, leader of the Hebrews and one of the Bible's most renowned figures, began his life in Egypt during a difficult time for his people. The reigning pharaoh, who some scholars suggest may have been Ramses II or Seti I, felt that the Hebrew populace had become too large and decreed that every Hebrew male child be killed at birth. Moses was born in the midst of this compulsory genocide, but with the aide of his sister, the pharaoh's daughter, and two defiant midwives, he survived. Three months after his birth, Moses' mother crafted a papyrus basket and plastered it with bitumen and pitch. She then carefully placed Moses and the basket in the Nile River; his sister stood at a distance to watch what would happen. The daughter of the pharaoh saw the floating container and had her maid bring it to her. After discovering the child, she took pity on him, and requested that a Hebrew woman come and serve as his nurse. Ironically, the woman chosen for this task was Moses's mother. Moreover, she was able to rear him in the household of the pharaoh who desired to kill him.

This special birth motif is a common theme in stories found throughout the Near East and in cultures around the world. The theme often introduces people, primarily men, who amazingly avoid death during their infancy or are born miraculously to mothers who are barren. Subsequently, the children become great leaders. One example of note from the neighboring Mesopotamian culture is the legend of Sargon. According to Akkadian writings, the mother of Sargon of Agade also made a basket sealed with pitch after the birth of her son. She placed the infant in the basket and let it sail down the Euphrates River. Akki, the drawer of water, discovered baby Sargon and reared

A drawing of Moses copied from the catacombs at the Basilica of St. Agnes outside Rome.

142

Let me tell you something that we Israelis have against Moses. He took us 40 years through the desert in order to bring us to the one spot in the Middle East that has no oil! • **Golda Meir (1898–1978)**

Sir Lawrence Alma-Tadema, *The Finding of Moses* (1904). Oil on canvas. Alma-Tadema was renowned for fanciful representations of classical antiquity. In this painting, which depicts a caravan carrying Moses in his papyrus basket from the Nile, the artist included archaeologically precise details and inscriptions.

him; the goddess Ishtar protected him, and Sargon became a successful king.

Although Moses did not become a king, he lived his youthful years in the home of the ruling pharaoh. Here Egyptian teachers educated him, and he learned the intricacies of Egyptian culture. However, the biblical writers explain that Moses was very much aware of his Hebrew ethnicity. For example, he murdered an Egyptian whom he saw beating a fellow Hebrew. But because someone witnessed his crime, Moses had to leave Egypt immediately in order to save his life.

Shortly after his departure, he encountered Yahweh, the Hebrew God, for the first time. He was now married to Zipporah, the daughter of Jethro, a Midianite priest. While walking his father-in-law's flock on Mt. Sinai, he witnessed a bush that burned without being consumed. Yahweh spoke to Moses from the bush and charged him to return to Egypt, liberate the Hebrews, and lead them to a land that had been promised to their ancestors.

With the assistance of his brother Aaron, Moses confronted the pharaoh regarding the release of the Hebrews. The process was taxing, as the pharaoh refused his numerous requests. Thus, the writers describe how Moses, with the hand of Yahweh, instituted ten plagues, some of which brought darkness upon the land, a cacophony of frogs, locusts, excruciating boils, and damaging hail. However, the tenth and final plague, the death of all of the Egyptians' firstborns, was the zenith of this battle of wills. This act, without question, reflects the Hebrew genocide that Moses narrowly escaped during his birth. There

Domenico Feti, *Moses before the Burning Bush* (1613–1614). Oil on canvas.

Domenico Beccafumi, *Moses and the Golden Calf* (1536–1537). Oil on wood. Duomo, Florence.

are continuing scholarly debates regarding the exodus from Egypt, the route(s) taken, and the famous parting of the sea, but most agree that the event would have happened at the Red Sea.

Once the Hebrews safely left Egypt, Moses and Aaron began their trek to the Promised Land. The journey led them through the wilderness for forty years. During this time, there were problems with apostasy, grumblings regarding the conditions during the journey, and disagreements among the leadership. Yet Moses consulted Yahweh and instituted the Decalogue and Covenant Code, both of which would prove to be major elements in establishing the Israelites' culture and religious practices. Sadly, the brothers were not permitted to enter the Promised Land. Nevertheless, Moses—as the prophet, the liberator, and the spiritual leader—is responsible for the Hebrew Exodus and the victorious trek to Canaan. There are no contemporary extra-biblical writings that reference Moses or the Exodus. But most scholars argue that the biblical sources are well constructed and that later authors would have been unable to create such an individual as Moses.

Theodore BURGH
University of North Carolina Wilmington

See also Judaism

Further Reading

Auerbach, E. (1975). *Moses* (R. A. Barclay & I. O. Lehman, Trans. and eds.). Detroit, MI: Wayne State University Press.

Childs, B. (1974). *The book of Exodus.* Philadelphia, PA: Westminster.

Coats, G. W. (1988). *Moses: Heroic man, man of God.* Sheffield, UK: JSOT Press.

Muhammad
(c. 570–632 CE)
PROPHET AND FOUNDER OF ISLAM

Muhammad is the founder of the religion of Islam. Born into the Quraysh clan in the city of Mecca, he belonged to a family of merchants. At the age of forty he had a vision that turned him to preaching the word of one true God, Allah. He fled from Mecca to Medina where he attracted many Muslim converts. His teachings are recorded in the Qur'an.

Muhammad (570–632 CE) was the Prophet of Islam, now the second largest religion in the world with a following of 1.5 billion people across different regions and races. He belonged to the Arab-celebrated tribe of Quraysh in the oasis town of Mecca, Saudi Arabia. His father died prior to his birth, so he was raised first by his grandfather, Abdul Muttalib, and then following his death by an uncle, Abu Talib. In his early youth, Muhammad adopted his family profession of business in which he prospered more by his personal morals than by the maneuvers of a merchant. He is known to have accompanied his uncle on trading trips to Syria, where he came into contact with Christians and Jews, His community bestowed upon him the honorific titles of *al-Ameen* (the trustworthy) and *al-Sadiq* (the truthful).

Muhammad later made the same journey in the service of a wealthy widow named Khadijah. Despite a fifteen-year disparity in their age, they were married not along after the trip and eventually had two sons and four daughters. It proved to be a long and successful marriage of twenty-six years, broken only by Khadijah's death. One of Muhammad's daughters, Fatimah, married his cousin, Ali, giving rise to the direct line of descendants from the Prophet. At the age of forty, Muhammad claimed that God (Allah in Arabic) had selected him as a prophet to call his people and the rest of humanity to the worship of this one true God who had also sent the prophets Abraham, Moses, and Christ with the same duty. Muhammad took upon himself the mission of reforming the Meccan society and religion. Messages that God revealed to Muhammad are contained in the Qur'an, the holy book of Islam.

Muhammad gained a few converts to his new religion, Islam ("submission [to God]"). But the powerful, rich Meccan elites, whose socioeconomic interests and political power he challenged, persecuted his followers. These elites were just about to kill him, too, when he moved to another oasis town, Medina (al-Medina in Arabic, "the City [of the Prophet]"). This important event, which came to be known as the Hijra (emigration) in the history of Islam, took place in 622 CE and marks the year 1 in the Islamic lunar calendar.

Muhammad worked to reconcile the warring tribes of Medina into peace and brotherhood. After gaining many more new converts (Muslims), he established the Ummah, a small community of people based solely on faith rather than on tribal, racial, or any socioeconomic relations. Along with preaching God's revelations in the Qur'an, Muhammad instructed his people through his own precepts and practices, called the hadith. The Qur'an and the hadith are two primary sources of Islamic sacred law (sharia). The law calls upon people to establish peace, socioeconomic justice, political enfranchisement, and respect for the human rights of women and minorities. The main thrust of the Qur'an and the hadith is to build an Islamic society on the basis of good conduct, brotherhood, kindness, sharing and caring, respect

Jabal al-Noor, or Mountain of Light, is the place where Muhammad used to pray and meditate.

for others, helping the poor, protecting the helpless, justice and equity for all, promoting virtue, and preventing evil. Muslims take Muhammad as a model of moral perfection.

Under Muhammad's guidance, the small Muslim community (Ummah) that he founded in 622 turned Medina into a city-state. Muhammad framed a signed contract between the Muslims and the Jews of Medina, the Charter of Medina, which is the first of its kind in world history. The Charter guaranteed protection of life and property and freedom of religion to the people of Medina and their allies in the region. The signatories of the charter promised to defend the city-state, to maintain peace and law and order, to submit to equity and justice in judicial and debt matters, to fulfill their obligations in protecting the defenseless, to stop mischief, murder and tyranny, to treat each other as equal partners in peace, and to guarantee religious freedom to all.

The peace and safety of the city-state of Medina under its charter and guidance of Muhammad attracted non-Muslims inside and outside its borders, and the number of Muslim converts increased. But Muhammad's old enemies in Mecca soon started intrigues with internal and external enemies of the new city-state that threatened Mecca's economic and political domination in Arabia. Skirmishes between the Muslims of Medina and the pagans of Mecca turned into the Battle of Badr in 624. Muhammad with a small band of 313 Muslim followers was outnumbered and outmatched by the 1,000-strong, well-equipped army of Mecca. But the superb war strategy of Muhammad and the courage of his followers defeated the Meccan army. Despite the guarantees in the charter, claims were made following each battle that Jews had sided with the enemies of Medina, resulting in expulsions from the city.

Muhammad said that he initiated his first war of defense (jihad, "making efforts [in the cause of Allah]") with the divine permission that God revealed to him (Qur'an XXII: 39–40). The permission God gave him was to fight against wrongfulness and oppression—not to grab the natural or national resources of an enemy. In his first jihad, Muhammad established

The ink of the scholar is more sacred than the blood of the martyr. • **Muhammad (c. 570–632 CE)**

rules of engagement. He prohibited the killing of women and children and of weak, peaceful, and innocent men. He prohibited the mutilation of dead enemy soldiers and the scorched-earth destruction of an enemy's water and food supplies. He forbade the mistreatment of prisoners of war. Poor prisoners could pay for their ransom by teaching Muslim children reading and writing, and by promising not to fight again. The Meccan pagans imposed two more ferocious battles upon the Muslims, but they failed to obliterate the city-state of Medina.

In 628, Muhammad offered the Treaty of al-Hudaybiya, which guaranteed mutual peace, security, and freedom, to his allies and to his bitter but defeated Meccan enemies. But Meccans soon started violating the treaty, and in 630 Muhammad marched on Mecca with a force of ten thousand Muslims to protect his allies. Before his march, he guaranteed peace and respect to all noncombatants. Mecca fell to his troops without a fight, but rather than slaughtering his enemies, he forgave and embraced them and let them keep their properties. The phenomenal peace of Muhammad turned enemies into friends and Muslims.

In his last Sermon of the Mount, shortly before his death in 632, Muhammad reemphasized the importance of kindness, of protecting the rights of women and slaves, of the strict prohibition of bloodshed, injustice, and usury, and of the significance of peace and brotherhood. Muhammad reminded his audience, "There is no superiority of Arabs over non-Arabs, and vice versa, nor is there any superiority of whites over blacks, and vice versa."

Karim KHAN
University of Hawaii, Leeward

See also Islam

Further Reading

Armstrong, K. (1992.). *Muhammad: A biography of the prophet.* San Francisco: Harper San Francisco.

Cook, M. (1983). *Muhammad.* New York: Oxford University Press.

Esposito, J. L. (1999). *The Oxford history of Islam.* New York: Oxford University Press.

Watt, W. M. (1953). *Muhammad at Mecca.* Oxford, U.K.: Clarendon Press.

Watt, W. M. (1956). *Muhammad at Medina.* Oxford, U,K.: Clarendon Press.

Watt, W. M. (1964). *Muhammad: Prophet and statesman.* London: Oxford University Press.

Mysticism

Humans can depart from normal states of consciousness in many different ways—by holding their breath, dancing together, taking drugs, or contemplation. What happens differs from case to case, but people often claim such experiences as a direct encounter of God or other supernatural spirits. Most religions made room for such mystic visionaries, and their lives often inspired new departures, especially when organized groups arose to pursue mystic visions together.

Mysticism is a type of religious experience claimed to involve a direct and personal experience of God, or of some eternal, spiritual element in the universe. Most of the major world religions have a significant mystical dimension to their faith. It is sometimes the case, however, that such mystical trends are not regarded as an orthodox feature of the religion. Although mystical experience differs somewhat from religion to religion, there appear to be features in common. Mystics typically subscribe to forms of spiritual discipline involving meditation or the repetition of the name of the divine. Such disciplines may often involve asceticism or withdrawal from the world. Mystics usually aspire to achieve a form of merging with God, or of spiritual salvation. The process of spiritual training undergone by mystics is often supervised by a spiritual adept or teacher. Within a particular religious tradition, the experiences associated with mysticism may be written in spiritual texts or transmitted orally. However, since the mystical experience is essentially individualistic and subjective, there may be difficulties in comparing the experience of one person with that of another.

It seems reasonable to suppose that people have, from very ancient times, attempted to gain a direct relationship with spiritual elements in the world around them. But documented traditions within the major faiths are much more recent. Hinduism has many traditions that may legitimately be described as mystical, most notably the practice of yoga. This mystical philosophy may be dated to the Upanishads of approximately 500–400 BCE and has been practiced in various forms until the present day. Yoga emphasizes the control of breathing as an aid to concentration and meditation. It is often accompanied by a renunciation of the world and by a tendency toward asceticism. The goal of yoga is that one should obtain union with Brahman, the spiritual force of the universe, and hence release from the cycle of rebirth. The use of yoga postures, or asanas, is but one element of yogic mysticism. In more recent times, celebrated practitioners of yoga include Ramakrishna (1836–1886) and Vivekananda (1863–1902).

Sikhism also espouses a form of mysticism whose goal is a direct experience of the divine. The principal approach is that of *nam japan*, or repetition of the name of God. This method, along with a meditation upon the nature of God, was the mystical approach advocated by the founder of Sikhism, Guru Nanak (1469–1539?). In another Indian religion, Jainism, there is an emphasis upon asceticism, and also meditation. Jainism was founded by Vardhamana (Mahavira), who lived from approximately 599–527 BCE. The ultimate goal of Jaina mysticism is *moksha*, or release from the cycle of birth and death.

Buddhism, founded by Siddhartha Gautama (c. 566–c. 486 BCE), subsequently known as the Buddha, is arguably a mystical religion, although it does not

For several hundred years mystics have been drawn to standing stones found throughout northern Europe, such as these in Avesbury, England.

incorporate any form of divine figure. The practice of Buddhism is derived from the enlightenment experience of the Buddha, achieved after a prolonged period of meditation. The express purpose of Buddhism is to enable human beings to eliminate their feelings of suffering, and the practice of meditation is one of the principal methods used to achieve this. The initial aim of meditation is to calm the fluctuations of the mind, and then to gain insight into the nature of existence. In this way the Buddhist comes to understand that the world is impermanent, and that through nonattachment to the world, one can begin to eliminate feelings of suffering. Eventually the Buddhist aspires to a state of supreme calmness and equanimity known as enlightenment. Buddhism spread from India to Southeast Asian countries such as Thailand and Cambodia, and north to Tibet, China, and Japan. The Buddhist tradition that developed in Japan became known as Zen, and one of its main exponents was Dogen (1200–1253). Zen has had an important influence on Japanese art and poetry, an example being the work of the poet Matsuo (Basho) Munefusa (1644–1694). Buddhism continues to influence Japanese cultural life to this day.

The Daoist tradition in China advocates a tranquil life, and one in which the aspirant seeks to live in tune

Religion is to mysticism what popularization is to science. • **Henri Bergson (1859–1941)**

Headquarters of Theosophical Society at Adyar, India. In 1875 Madame Blavatsky, a Russian mystic and spirit medium, founded the Theosophical Society in New York with her friend, Colonel Olcott. The organization was a boon to the spiritualism movement. Photo by Klaus Klostermaier.

with the natural world. The Daoist attempts to live in harmony with the Dao, or the creative energy that is present throughout the natural world. The *I Ching* is usually regarded as the principal text of Daoism, and was historically attributed to Laozi in approximately the sixth century BCE.

The mystical tradition in Islam is known as Sufism, a term that may be derived from *suf*, the Arabic for wool. This may refer to the tradition of Sufis wearing a cloak of rough wool. This very much reflects the ascetic tendency, which is an element in Sufism much as it is in other mystical traditions. The aim of Sufis is a direct experience of God. Sufis often traditionally associate themselves with a religious community, led by a sheikh or spiritual leader. Sufism continues to be an active tradition in the present day.

The approach to mysticism within Judaism is known as kabbalah, and it emphasizes a direct understanding of God as being the force behind the entire universe. Judaic mysticism utilizes meditation and contemplation, and encourages the aspirant to develop a sense of love toward humanity.

Within Christianity the history of mysticism is connected to some extent with that of monasticism, which evolved in Egypt during the third and fourth centuries CE. The early monastics led extremely simple lives, withdrawing from the world and devoting themselves to God. The monastic tradition was placed on an established basis by Saint Benedict (c. 480–547 CE). Noted Christian mystics include Saint John of the Cross (1542–1591), Saint Teresa of Ávila (1515–1582), and Jakob Böhme (1575–1624).

Mystics have generally attempted to seek the most direct spiritual experience of their particular religious tradition. In so doing, they have often been perceived as a threat by the religious orthodoxy. From time to time, mystics have given expression to subjective experience, and while this may have been contrary to established tradition, it has been a reminder of the attempt to seek direct understanding of the divine. To that extent, mysticism is still an important contemporary tradition, particularly for those who seek that form of religious experience.

Paul OLIVER
University of Huddersfield

See also Buddhism; Daoism; Jainism; Philosophy, Asian

Further Reading

Carmody, D. L., & Carmody, J. T. (1996). *Mysticism—Holiness east and west*. Oxford, U.K.: Oxford University Press.

Eliade, M. (1967). *From primitives to Zen*. London: Collins.

Katz, S. T. (Ed.). (2000). *Mysticism and sacred scripture*. Oxford, U.K.: Oxford University Press.

Merton, T. (1967). *Mystics and Zen masters*. New York: Farrar.

Otto, R. (1960). *Mysticism, east and west*. New York: Macmillan.

Stace, W. T. (1960). *Mysticism and philosophy*. Philadelphia: Lippincott.

Suzuki, D. T. (1957). *Mysticism, Christian and Buddhist*. New York: Harper.

Underhill, E. (1964). *Mystics of the church*. New York: Schocken.

Watts, A. W. (1971). *Behold the spirit: A study in the necessity of mystical religion*. New York: Pantheon.

Zaehner, R. C. (1957). *Mysticism, sacred and profane*. Oxford, U.K.: Oxford University Press.

Native American Religions

The term *religion* suggests that the sacred can be separated from ordinary life. Among Native American peoples the sacred, the appearance of the extraordinary, and the most meaningful values are intertwined with daily concerns. Thus the pursuit of sustenance, and the making of useful objects or political decisions, may be charged with the presence and power of that which moves the cosmos. The term *lifeway* indicates this close connection.

Such a complex topic as understanding historical consciousness in Native American religions begins with two major insights. First, the religions of the over one thousand indigenous societies of the American hemisphere involve concepts and practices that cannot be separated from the spheres of life in those societies termed economic, political, cosmological, and artistic. *Lifeway* is used here to indicate this seamless interweaving of the spiritual and the historical. Second, history can be recorded and transmitted in forms other than writing. There are, for example, the winter counts on bison hides among the North American Plains peoples, *quipu* or knot-tying of narratives among Andean peoples, and the accordion-style screen-fold picture books of preconquest Mexico. All of these historical expressions have oral myth-telling at their core.

Diversity of Native American Religions

The term "Native American" suggests homogeneous societies, but the native communities of North, Central, and South America are extremely diverse in their lifeways. For example, the archaeological record gives evidence of major cultural and civilizational developments in central Mexico associated with the pyramids at Teotihuacán (200–900 CE), Toltec sites (900–1000 CE), and the massive pyramidal structures built by Mayan peoples in Yucatan, Guatemala, and Belize (300–900 CE). Archaeological evidence in South America suggests that interactions of Amazonian cultures are as complex and old as those in the Andean highlands that led to the late Incan Empire. Moreover, while North and Central America were home to over five hundred native languages, South America has over eight hundred indigenous languages.

In the region of the current United States alone, the diversity of cultural-historical developments is ancient and impressive. An indigenous culture named Hopewell (200 BCE–400 CE), based on corn agriculture, piled soil to create burial and effigy mounds in the central Ohio River watershed. A cultural florescence called Mississippian (600–1400 CE) left temple mounds from the Gulf of Mexico up the Mississippi River to the current state of Wisconsin. Similarly, in the Southwest cultures now called Anasazi and Kayenta (400–1300 CE) built remarkable cliff and pueblo dwellings at many sites including Mesa Verde in Colorado, Chaco Canyon and Montezuma in New Mexico, and Keet Seel and Betatikin at the Navajo National Monument in Arizona. Finally, the pottery skills and irrigation canals for agriculture of the T'ohono ancestors sometimes named Mogollon and Hohokam (100–900 CE) are still used. The progeny of these ancestral archaeological cultures migrated into diverse settings, continued ancient visions, and developed distinct religious concerns.

152

An Iroquois pictograph from the nineteenth century describes a ceremony in which the Iroquois give thanks to the Great Spirit. Beliefs and practices of native lifeways vary in North, Central, and South America.

Religious Differences Among Native Americans

The North American Plains native peoples place a greater emphasis on individual visions and their relationships, in the symbolism of the circle, with the well-being of the community of life. The Northwest coast peoples celebrate a human community's privileges and obligations in a universe of giving subtly imaged as worlds within worlds symbolically imaged as boxes within boxes.

Southwest Puebloan peoples stress processes of nurturing rain and corn-growth in communitarian ethics and ritual cycles that connect with ancestral histories. Southeastern native peoples continue ancient ceremonies of the first corn of the season, the Green Corn, at which they light the new fire of the community as a cosmological act revivifying creation.

Northern sub-Artic and Artic peoples produced elaborate technologies (e.g., seal hunting, snowshoes, toboggan, igloo) developed for survival in that harsh cold climate as well as intense shamanistic healing practices. A variety of terms are used to refer to all of these peoples in an effort to suggest shared similarities, such as American Indian, First Peoples, and First Nations. The most appropriate terms that honor their differences are those used by the peoples themselves, for example, Anishinabe (Ojibway), Lakota (Sioux), Yup'ik (Eskimo), Muskogee (Creek), and Haudenosaunee (Iroquois).

Lifeway as the Context of Native American History

The term "religion" suggests that the sacred can be separated from ordinary or profane life. But among Native American peoples the sacred, the appearance of the extraordinary, and the most meaningful values of life are inextricably intertwined with the pragmatic concerns of daily existence.

Thus, the ordinary pursuit of sustenance, the making of useful objects, as well as political decision-making may be charged with the presence and power of that which moves the cosmos. The term "lifeway" indicates this close connection of the spiritual awareness of cosmological forces as the key to understanding the meaning of both individual lives and larger societies.

154 • RELIGION AND BELIEF SYSTEMS IN WORLD HISTORY

This drawing of an Inuit mask from Alaska depicts a supernatural being said to control the supply of game. The carved seals attached to the mask suggest that the wearer sought to obtain help for a good seal hunt.

From Denial to Ethnography

Early European studies of Native American societies from the late-fifteenth-century encounter period often reported that historical consciousness and religion did not exist among these peoples. This rejection of religion and systematic remembrance of the past among Native American peoples largely derived from the dominance of the Bible in European worldviews as the singular, literate revelation in which all of world history was revealed. Thus, when unknown peoples were encountered they were explained by locating them within the Bible.

Gradually, the significance of the encounters and the striking differences of native peoples caused Europeans to rethink their own identities and to reflect on their own historical past. The European Enlightenment and scientific worldview from the eighteenth century gave rise to ethnographic analyses of the societies and religious activities of distinct native peoples. Influenced by nineteenth- and early-twentieth-century anthropology, the historical studies of Native American societies from this period often presented a single informant's remembered culture as normative and timeless for that whole society. These idealized perspectives tended to freeze Native American lifeways as unchanging over time.

Ethnohistorical studies have critiqued these static interpretations by simply presenting the changing descriptions of native peoples within written Euro-American historical records themselves. These academic investigations are significant, but they are strikingly different from native modes of historical remembrance. In fact, many researchers manifest an ahistorical bias that does not allow them to understand the deep historical visions embedded in Native American lifeways. Some of these native modes of historicity are consciously articulated while others are more performative and symbolic. Often these native modes of remembering and transmitting the deeper meanings of their cultures resisted the historical impositions of dominant societies.

We walk in our moccasins upon the Earth / And beneath the sky / As we travel on life's path of beauty / We will live a good life and reach old age. • **Navajo Blessing**

History Among Native American Religions

From Native American perspectives the question "What ways of knowing history are embedded in Native American religions?" generates strikingly different responses. While not exhaustive, the following list includes some considerations for understanding the history of "Native American religions" from the standpoints of native communities and individuals:

1. Native American religions begin and end with living peoples who speak of the origins of the world and themselves as present realities. This historical consciousness is now both oral and literate, but in both instances it is told by native voice and not locked in library texts or museum holdings of mainstream societies.
2. Discussion of rituals, myths, sacred objects, songs, and seminal places and ideas all hold historical insight for native peoples. Unlike academic history that attempts to describe objectively events, religious objects, and narratives, native historical awareness often sees them as persons deserving respectful treatment, even avoidance if one is not qualified to approach or embrace them.
3. Native history typically makes connections that seem atemporal to Western academic perspectives, but that actually link past, present, and future like a "hypertext" in which past or future events stand in immediate relationship with the present with regard to meaning, causality, and consequence. This shape-shifting and multivocal character of native narratives is not simply a matter of style of literature but indicates ways of perceiving the world that are creatively different.
4. Place occupies a central role in native historical consciousness. In native understanding the sensual engagement with place is an act of cultivation that may bring an individual or group to realization of cosmological values embedded in the lifeway. Sacred places provide foundational insight into that

which gives identity to native peoples. This is unlike the passive, objective roles of the environment in Western historical thought, in which the subjective human constructs, manipulates, and imposes meaning on place.

Narratives as Present Realities

Regarding the first point in the list above: the ways in which native peoples present themselves in remembered form are the myths of origin and legends of historical events considered to have happened since humans arrived. The historicity of myths and legends is a major stumbling block for most Western historians. For example, the Tewa anthropologist Alphonse Ortiz, in recounting the San Juan Pueblo origins, gave a strikingly simple and direct account of his people, saying: "In the very beginning we were one people. Then we divided into Summer people and Winter people; in the end we came together again as we are today" (Ortiz 1969, 29). Understanding this complex mythological statement involves research into Tewa language, myth, social structure, political governance, and religious ecology. That is, the myth provides insight into the living social structures of San Juan Pueblo, and the myth provides formative insight into Puebloan understanding of who they are as a people from the origin time into their present homeland.

The Jemez Pueblo historian Joe Sando (1982, 2) observed that:

> If we accept Native North American oral history... then we can start with the ancient people who have been in North America for many thousands of years and still allow for European and Mediterranean colonists to strengthen or boost the developing culture. This appears to be what indigenous people have been saying in their oral history. But later Europeans with their "proof positive" and "show me" attitudes have prevailed, and remain largely unwilling to consider, much less confirm, native creation accounts.

Sando claims a literalist interpretation for myth based on the living presence of his people in their ancestral Pueblo homes. Acceptance of the historicity of myths is a major challenge for historians, but it also opens the possibility for "seeing with a native eye" the historical facts embedded in these stories (Capps 1976, 9).

The Oral Native Voice

The second point in the list draws attention to the need for native voice in reconstructing Native American religious history. Deep authenticity and fragility of native voice are found in the oral narratives that transmit the creation stories, legends, and tales of the people. Actual native voice, layering of stories within stories, and the immediacy and intimacy of oral narratives are crucial correctives to a view of native history that abhors subjective interpretation, ambiguity of outcome, and experiential voice as authoritative.

When oral stories are labeled myths it accentuates their sacred, revelatory character, but that term may also situate the stories as timeless, unchanging, and permanently past. When native peoples narrate stories of origins they may or may not be evaluated according to their conformity to traditional versions. Often narrations are accompanied by rituals that emphasize the living, present character of the beings, places, and events named. Thus, among a number of native nations there are animal-addressing, place-naming, ethic-declaiming narratives that accompany major rituals. These should not be seen as either simply describing past events or as objectively categorizing land, animals, or laws.

For example, the Midewiwin ceremony of the Anishinabe peoples of the Great Lakes region transmitted narratives of these tribes' origin-migration. Named geographical locations not only indicate where the ceremony had been performed but they are also honored as significant stopping places of sacred, spirit beings (Manitou). In effect the ceremony of Midewiwin validated the migration and formation of this Great Lakes people by appealing to the ancient spiritual animal masters. Midewiwin has been described as an "extinguished" ceremony in some academic works, but native practitioners have reasserted the contemporary survival and relevance of this ceremonial complex. While not all Anishinabe religiosity can be collapsed into Midewiwin, the revitalization of this ceremony in the contemporary period accentuates an emphasis in native religious understanding that formative cosmological experiences endure into the present and identify living people as much as ancestors, according to the author Wub-e-ke-niew (1995) in *We Have the Right to Exist.*

Cosmological Narrative and Song

The third point draws attention to the interactions of rituals, myths, sacred objects, songs, and seminal places and ideas as having the status of "persons" in Native American religions. While this complex of relations is differently expressed among particular peoples, one striking example comes from the Gitskan peoples of central British Columbia.

> Each Gitksan house is the proud heir and owner of an *adáox.* This is a body of orally transmitted songs and stories that act as the house's sacred archives and as its living, millennia-long memory of important events of the past. This irreplaceable verbal repository of knowledge consists in part of sacred songs believed to have arisen *literally from the breaths of the ancestors.* Far more than musical representations of history, these songs serve as vital time-traversing vehicles. They can transport members across the immense reaches of space and time into the dim mythic past of Gitskan creation *by the very quality of their music and the emotions they convey....*
>
> Taken together, these sacred possessions—the stories, the crests, the songs—provide a solid foundation for each Gitskan house and for the larger clan of which it is a part. According to living Gitskan elders, each house's holdings confirm its ancient *title to its territory and the legitimacy of its authority over it.*
>
> In fact, so vital is the relationship between each house and the lands allotted to it for fishing, hunting, and food-gathering that the *daxgyet,* or spirit power, of each house and the land that sustains it are one. (Wa and Delgam 1987, 7, 26)

The historical testimony of this complex of songs and rituals connects architecture and traditional environmental knowledge. Gitskan elders voice their concerns in these religious performances for the cosmological and historical continuity of community vitality.

The Linkage of Past, Present, and Future

Regarding the fourth point, namely, the simultaneity of memory in Native American religions, the Pawnee/Otoe author Anna Lee Walters (1992, 77) wrote that she:

> discovered two principal sequences of tribal history. The first starts at the beginning and works its way toward the present. The second starts with the present and works its way back to the beginning. Although there may be discussions on the history of the people moving to a particular place, for example—isolated events—often these historical notes seem to be just that until they are pinned down in this large framework.

Interpreting these dynamics of native historicity may necessitate abandoning chronological, linear, interpretive-building emphases on personalities, events, or social and economic forces. In the time-linkage narratives of Native American lifeways the primary focus is more typically on seminal realities of place, action, and spiritual presence. Rather than accept ideas or mental constructs as primary, the mutual participation of humans and the beings of the Earth opens a way toward understanding the wisdom of history.

A striking illustration of this complex linkage is the tobacco symbolism found throughout the American hemisphere. In one particularized expression of tobacco ceremonialism the shaman-healers of the Warao peoples of the Orinoco Delta in Venezuela describe the history of human consciousness as beginning in the House of Tobacco Smoke. When a Warao shaman applies tobacco smoke to a patient or a victim, he breathes a cosmological force that simultaneously reaches back to primordial origins, heals in the present, and establishes ethical responsibilities and orientations into the future. For the Warao

wisdom-keepers tobacco symbolism is a linkage to an archaic shamanistic substratum that still extends throughout the American hemisphere, according to Wilbert in *Mystic Endowment* (1993).

Place and Historical Consciousness

Finally, a widespread cultural activity among Native Americans that provides exceptional insight into their historical consciousness is sensing place. Native sensing of place is a daily, lifeway engagement with the local landscape as a means of cultivation of self and community. Ordinary lifeway interactions with local places are charged with stories that transmit ethical teachings, community identities, and cosmological presences.

The felt authority of the past in a particular place is communicated with humor and poignancy by the Western Apache, whose understanding of place is likened to drinking deeply of the ancestral wisdom that resides there. Such wisdom cannot be taught by rote but is awakened by engaging place deeply with all of the senses, with one's body. This is a historical consciousness that acknowledges informative ideas rising up from soil, that filters stories linked to places through one's own emotions, and that searches visually and intellectually for a whole understanding. After hearing a story of an Apache ancestor who fooled Coyote by enticing him to look up at her in a tree, Keith Basso describes how an Apache wisdom teacher, Dudley Patterson, affirmed his deep yearning to know the historical presence in places, saying:

> "Our Ancestors did that!" Dudley exclaims with undisguised glee. "We all do that, even the women and children. We all look up to see her with her legs slightly apart. These places are really very good! Now you've drunk from one! Now you can work on your mind."...As vibrantly felt as it is vividly imagined, sense of place asserts itself at varying levels of mental and emotional intensity. Whether it is lived in memory or experienced on the spot, the strength of its impact is commensurate with the richness of its contents, with the range and diversity of symbolic

associations that swim within its reach and move it on its course. (Basso 1996, 143, 145)

Thus, Native American lifeways provide multiple ways of thinking about history, namely, in terms of the precontact history of Native American societies, the history of the encounter with European cultures, and the modes of historical consciousness embedded within Native American religions themselves.

John A. GRIM
Yale University

See also Shamanism

Further Reading

Asatchaq. (1992). *The things that were said of them: Shaman stories and oral histories of the Tikigaq.* Berkeley: University of California Press.

Basso, K. (1996). *Wisdom sits in places: Landscape and language among the Western Apache.* Albuquerque: University of New Mexico Press.

Capps, W. (1976). *Seeing with a native eye: Essays on Native American religion.* New York: Harper Forum Books.

Hill, J. D. (1988). *Rethinking history and myth: Indigenous South American perspectives on the past.* Urbana: University of Illinois Press.

Hoxie, F. E. (1988). *Indians in American history.* Arlington Heights, IL: Harlan Davidson.

Mihesuah, D. A. (1998). *Native and academics: Researching and writing about American Indians.* Lincoln: University of Nebraska Press.

Nabokov, P. (2002). *A forest of time: American Indian ways of history.* Cambridge, U.K.: Cambridge University Press.

Ortiz, A. (1969). *The Tewa world: Space, time, being, and becoming in a Pueblo society.* Chicago: University of Chicago Press.

Sando, J. S. (1982). *Nee Hemish: A history of Jemez Pueblo.* Albuquerque: University of New Mexico Press.

Thornton, R. (1998). *Studying native America: Problems and prospects.* Madison: University of Wisconsin Press.

Wa, G., & Delgam, U. (1987). *The spirit of the land: The opening statement of the Gitskan and Wets'uwetén hereditary chiefs in the Supreme Court of British Columbia.* Gabrola, BC: Reflections.

Walters, A. L. (1992). *Talking Indian: Reflections on survival and writing.* Ithaca, NY: Firebrand Books.

Wilbert, J. (1993). *Mystic endowment: Religious ethnography of the Warao Indians.* Cambridge, MA: Harvard University Center for the Study of World Religions.

Wub-e-ke-niew. (1995). *We have the right to exist: A translation of "Aboriginal indigenous thought," the first book ever published from an Ahnishinahbaeotjiway perspective.* New York: Black Thistle Press.

Paul, Saint
(10–67 CE?)
EARLY CHRISTIAN THEOLOGIAN

More than any other single person, Saint Paul transformed Christianity from a Jewish sect into a world religion. His missionary travels founded churches across Anatolia and Greece; letters to his converts defined doctrine and settled quarrels; and above all, he persuaded Peter and the other apostles in Jerusalem to abandon the Jewish law as a guide to Christian life.

Although he considered himself a Jew throughout his life, Saint Paul is recognized today as the first distinctly Christian theologian. Paul was the first follower of Jesus to insist on the inclusion of Gentiles, or non-Jews, into the family of God. He also was the first to insist upon the importance of Jewish Scripture for the earliest followers of Jesus, and his insistence indirectly helped to form the two-part Christian Bible, which includes the Hebrew Scriptures and the New Testament. His seven authentic letters (Romans, 1–2 Corinthians, Galatians, Philippians, 1 Thessalonians, and Philemon) are the earliest New Testament writings and thus the earliest Christian documents available. These letters are indispensable for any study of the relationship between Jews and Gentiles in the first-century church or any examination of first-century church controversies, doctrines, and practices. In the history of Christianity, Paul's letter to the Romans facilitated Saint Augustine's conversion in the fourth century and Augustine's development of the doctrine of salvation by grace in the fifth century; it buttressed Martin Luther's insistence on salvation by grace through faith alone in the sixteenth century and anchored Karl Barth's work in the neo-Orthodox movement of the twentieth century.

Born a Jew in Tarsus in the early first century CE, Paul persecuted followers of Jesus early in his life. After seeing a vision of the resurrected Jesus, Paul became a follower himself and worked as a missionary between 35 and 60 CE, traveling throughout the ancient Near East and the Mediterranean and establishing churches. The dissonance between Paul's earlier life as a practicing Jew and his new life as a follower of Jesus was not lost on those around him, and Paul had to spend a great deal of time defending his right to be an apostle for Jesus, or a preacher called to spread the gospel (Galatians, 1–2 Corinthians). Paul appears to have been executed as a martyr during the reign (54–68 CE) of the Roman emperor Nero.

Paul's churches consisted mostly of Gentiles, and Paul argued vigorously that Gentiles did not have to adhere to Jewish traditions in order to be considered followers of Jesus. Instead, Jesus' message was available to anyone who believed in his life, death, and resurrection, regardless of ethnicity (Galatians, Romans). Paul also gave instruction regarding the significance of Christian doctrines such as the resurrection and the second coming of Jesus (1–2 Corinthians, 1 Thessalonians). Paul's discussion of the Eucharist, or the Lord's Supper, in 1 Corinthians and the hymn about the Incarnation (the belief that Jesus is both human and divine) in Philippians 2 are the first descriptions of these doctrines. Furthermore, because Paul wrote to specific congregations, he had much to say about social ethics in each of his letters. For example, the status of women in the early church is mentioned in 1 Corinthians, and Philemon may address slavery, although no scholarly consensus exists regarding the exact purpose of the letter.

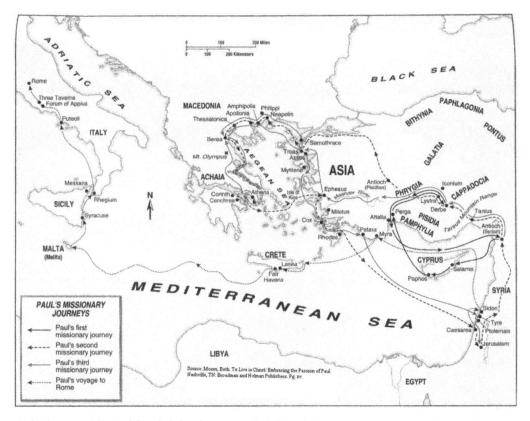

On his journeys Saint Paul founded churches across Anatolia and Greece.

Paul's legacy remains controversial. While some scholars credit him for the establishment of Christian theology, others accuse him of establishing Christian anti-Judaism because of his occasionally polemical critiques of Jewish practices and his claim that only faith in Jesus, and not adherence to Jewish tradition, makes one righteous before God. His opinions about women and slaves also have been criticized for their apparent support of first-century ideals, which kept both groups in a socially subservient position to freemen. Whether one considers him worthy to be a saint or denounces him as the ringleader of Christian anti-Jewish sentiment and an advocate for social oppression, Paul left his permanent and unmistakable mark on the New Testament and consequently on all forms of Christianity, past and present.

Stacy DAVIS
University of Notre Dame

See also Jesus

Further Reading

Dahl, N. A. (1977). *Studies in Paul: Theology for the early Christian mission*. Minneapolis, MN: Augsburg.

Dunn, J. D. G. (1998). *The theology of Paul the apostle*. Grand Rapids, MI: Eerdmans.

Hawthorne, G. F., & Martin, R. P. (Eds.). (1993). *Dictionary of Paul and his letters*. Downers Grove, IL: InterVarsity.

Roetzel, C. J. (1998). *The letters of Paul: Conversations in context* (4th ed). Louisville, KY: Westminster John Knox.

Sanders, E. P. (1983). *Paul, the law, and the Jewish people*. Philadelphia, PA: Fortress.

Stowers, S. K. (1994) *A rereading of Romans: Justice, Jews, and Gentiles*. New Haven, CT: Yale University Press.

Pentecostalism

Pentecostals, who interpret the Bible literally and believe in the imminent return of Christ, are distinguished from other Fundamentalists or Evangelicals by greater exuberance in their religious services. Pentecostals emphasize prophecy, interpretation of tongues, healing, and exorcism of demons. The movement has spread from its roots in the United States to the Caribbean, Latin America, sub-Saharan Africa, Southeast Asia, South Korea, Britain, and Eastern Europe.

Pentecostalism emerged as a distinct movement following the Civil War. It was a radical extension of the Holiness movement that sought to revitalize the Wesleyan doctrine of perfection in various mainstream U.S. denominations, particularly the Methodists. But speaking in tongues (glossolalia), a significant factor in of Pentacostalism, appears to have existed off and on for millennia. Despite a diversity of beliefs among them, Pentecostals generally emphasize (1) the baptism of the Holy Spirit manifested by speaking in tongues; (2) the imminent return of Jesus Christ; and (3) the significance of speaking in tongues as an evangelical mechanism. Although Pentecostals take a literal interpretation of the Bible and stress a puritanical morality, they are distinguished from other Fundamentalists or Evangelicals, such as Southern Baptists and the Churches of Christ, by greater exuberance in their religious services. Pentecostals also emphasize prophecy, interpretation of tongues, healing, and exorcism of demons. At the ideological level, Holiness and Pentecostal sects emphasize the notion of "sanctification." As opposed to the relatively subdued tone of Holiness services, Pentecostalism emphasizes inspirational outbursts of ecstasy such as shouting, gesticulating, twitching, fainting, rolling on the floor, and especially speaking in tongues or glossolalia. Some Pentecostal sects in southern Appalachia and the Ozark Mountains even handle poisonous serpents.

Pentecostalism Develops in the United States

Early sites of the Pentecostal movement included a center in western North Carolina and eastern Tennessee connected with A. J. Tomlinson and the Church of God; a center in Topeka, Kansas, associated with Reverend Charles Parham; and the interracial Asuza Street Revival of 1906–1909 in Los Angeles. Parham left the Methodist Episcopal Church to establish Bethel Healing Home in Topeka, Kansas, in 1898. He had been inspired by the healing ministry of J. A. Dowie of Zion City, Illinois, and visited Holiness and healing ministries from Chicago to New York to Georgia in 1900. In late 1900, Parham established the Bethel Bible College in Topeka. Some of his students began to speak in tongues in early 1901 after investigating the doctrine of the "baptism of the Spirit." Parham closed his school and instructed his students to spread the Pentecostal message. He opened another Bible college in Houston in 1905 and recruited William Seymour, an African American Holiness preacher, who went on to provide the impetus for the famous revival at the Asuza Street Mission. Particularly poor and lower-class people from not only many parts of the United States but also other countries attended the revival. Seymour spread the Pentecostal gospel to both whites and blacks in the Southeast. After

This picture of the U.S. missionary George T. Candlin, who participated in the 1893 Chicago Exposition's World Parliament of Religions (an antecedent of the Pentecostal movement), was accompanied by the caption "This is Pentecost, and behind it is the conversion of the world."

attending the revival with two compatriots in early 1907, Charles H. Mason, one of the two founders of the Church of God in Christ (COGIC), transformed the Holiness sect into a Pentecostal group. His cofounder, C. P. Jones, rejected Pentecostalism and formed the Church of Christ (Holiness) U.S.A. By the early 1910s, the Pentecostal movement had attracted converts in much of the United States, Canada, and northern Mexico with estimates ranging from 50,000 to 100,000 followers.

The initial interracial character of the Pentecostal movement began to break down in the years following the Asuza Street Revival. In 1914, COGIC-ordained white ministers formed the Assemblies of God. Whereas the COGIC, headquartered in Memphis, Tennessee, today constitutes the largest predominantly black Pentecostal group in the world, the Assemblies of God has evolved, with its present headquarters in Springfield, Missouri, into the largest Pentecostal group in the world. Several years later, Canadian-born Aimee Semple McPherson broke away from the Assemblies to establish her congregation in Los Angeles, which was incorporated in 1927 as the International Church of the Foursquare Gospel. Some Pentecostals, particularly those associated with the Pentecostal Assemblies of the World and the United Pentecostal Church International, emphasized the oneness of God and baptism in the name of Jesus, rather than in the name of the Father, Son, and Holy Ghost. By the end of the twentieth century several hundred Pentecostal sects, many of them African American, had emerged in the United States alone. Both African American and European American Pentecostalism have had a rich history of colorful and even flamboyant evangelists. In the 1940s, Oral Roberts, a Pentecostal Holiness Church evangelist, created a healing and radio ministry based in Tulsa, Oklahoma. "Sweet Daddy" Grace, the founder of the United House of Prayer for All People, functioned as one of the "gods of the black metropolis." Kathryn Kuhlman, a white Presbyterian, and Bishop Ida Robinson, an African American and the founder of the Mt. Sinai Holy Church of America, testified to the ability of women to rise to positions of leadership in the Pentecostal movement, despite the efforts of males to assume dominance. Pentecostal sects also have tended to attract a higher percentage of women than have mainstream denominations.

The Charismatic Movement Develops

While Pentecostalism proper has catered largely to lower-middle- or working-class people, neo-Pentecostalism, or the charismatic movement, has tended on the whole to cater to more affluent people, ranging from the lower-middle class to the upper-middle class. The charismatic movement first spread among some members of mainstream Protestant churches (e.g., Episcopalians, Lutherans, and Presbyterians) in the 1950s and among Roman

Catholics in the 1960s. Demos Shakarian established the Full Gospel Business Men in 1952, and David J. du Plessis, a South African–born Assemblies of God pastor in Connecticut, established connections with mainstream churches by joining the World Council of Churches in 1954 and attending the Vatican II conference as the sole Pentecostal observer. Although the Assemblies of God excommunicated him for these actions in 1962, du Pleissis served as an important catalyst in sparking the charismatic movement in mainstream churches. The charismatic movement also received an infusion of energy in the form of the Jesus People movement, a young people's revival that began in California. Jim Bakker, an Assemblies of God minister, and Jimmy Swaggart, also an Assemblies of God minister, joined Oral Roberts as highly visible and influential charismatic televangelists.

The Pentecostal movement within Catholicism began in the spring of 1967 at Duquesne University in Pittsburgh, but later spread to North Dame University and Michigan State University. Although members of the Catholic Pentecostal movement initially called themselves "Pentecostal Catholics" or "Catholic Pentecostals," they later referred to themselves as "Catholic charismatics" for class reasons (McGuire 1982, 4).

Global Diffusion of Pentecostalism

Pentecostalism has spread from its roots in the United States to many other parts of the world, including the Caribbean, Latin America, sub-Saharan Africa, Southeast Asia, South Korea, Britain, and even Eastern Europe. David J. Barrett and Todd M. Johnson (cited in Wacker 2001), renowned statisticians of Christianity, maintain that by 2000 there were 525 million Pentecostals/charismatics (27 percent of the Christian population in the world), which to that date made Pentecostalism the single largest Christian category after Catholicism. Large independent Pentecostal congregations sprang up in large numbers in Latin America and America, particularly during the 1980s and 1990s. Massive conversion to Protestantism, particularly of a Pentecostal variety, has

occurred in Brazil, where various estimates indicate that Protestant churchgoers outnumber Catholic ones on any given Sunday. Many members of Protestant mainstream congregations in Brazil have left in order to establish Pentecostal congregations. Although North Americans introduced Pentecostalism into Latin America, by and large Latinos are now responsible for diffusion of the movement. As in the United States, South African Pentecostalism emerged at the beginning of the twentieth century as a racially integrated movement that attracted blacks and poor Afrikaners and quickly became racially fragmented, in the view of Allan H. Anderson in "Dangerous Memories for South African Pentecostal." (1999). The efforts of various North Americans and Europeans resulted in the formation of the South African District of the Assemblies of God. Many black Pentecostals opted to affiliate themselves with a wide array of African independent sects in South Africa. Some Pentecostals around the globe are interconnected through the Pentecostal World Fellowship, but apparently most are not affiliated with this body.

Interpretations of Pentecostalism

A number of sociologist and religious scholars have written about Pentacostalism as it is now practiced around the world. Robert Mapes Anderson, in *Vision of the Disinherited* (1979), provides perhaps the most insightful analysis of European American Pentecostalism, noting that it serves several functions, none of which seriously challenges the larger society or significantly alters the position of Pentecostals within it. Pentecostalism, he asserts, (1) constitutes a cathartic mechanism for marginalized people; (2) provides career opportunities for its leaders; (3) serves as a "safety valve" for dissatisfaction within mainstream churches; (4) facilitates the migration process from the countryside to the city; (5) instills in its members passivity, industriousness, and thrift; and (6) develops a compliant working class. While the same could be argued historically for African American Pentecostalism as well, an increasing number of black Pentecostal congregations have become more politically and socially engaged due to the impact of the civil rights and black power movements on a third generation of black Pentecostal ministers. Pentecostal Institutional Temple, COGIC's mother church (located about a mile east of downtown Memphis), played an instrumental role in the establishment of the Ministers and Christians League, an organization that spearheaded a drive that doubled the number of black registered voters in Memphis. Black Pentecostals have won seats on city councils and in state legislatures and have been appointed to minor cabinet positions in the executive branch of the federal government.

Meredith McGuire views the search for empowerment as central to the Catholic charismatic movement. She asserts that even relatively affluent and conservative people in U.S. society "sense that change has 'robbed' them of the power to control the future, to effect their wills on their environment, to know what to expect and to act accordingly" (McGuire 1982, 176). Thomas J. Csordas, in *The Sacred Self*, asserts that the perception of divine presence often instills in Catholic charismatics a sense of security that enables them to overcome memories of traumatic events.

Various scholars have examined the role that Pentecostalism plays in Latin America and other developing and underdeveloped countries. For the most part, Pentecostalism in Brazil and elsewhere in Latin America caters to the poor. Despite the fact that Christian-based communities inspired by liberation theology provided Catholicism with a new lease on life in Latin America, Pentecostalism has proven to be a fierce competitor because of its ability to tap into deeply felt emotional needs and to promise its adherents upward social mobility. Based upon an ethnographic study of Pentecostals in Belem, Brazil, R. Andrew Chestnut, in *Born Again in Brazil*, reports that the great majority of his subjects converted to Pentecostalism during or shortly following a serious sickness. In a similar vein, Thomas R. Lancaster in *Thanks for God and the Revolution* (1988) found that Pentecostal churches in Nicaragua recruit most of their members from the lowest echelon of the poor, many of whom are alcoholics or sick or elderly.

Despite their traditional political fatalism, Pentecostals have also become politically active in Latin America, although they have generally favored conservative candidates such as Rios Montt in Guatemala, a former Pentecostal Sunday School teacher, and Alberto Fujimori in Peru. Indeed, General Augusto Pinochet provided support to Chile's largest Protestant sect, the Pentecostal Church, according to David Stoll in *Is Latin America Turning Protestant?* Some Brazilian Pentecostals have supported left-wing candidates and parties, such as Luiz Inacio Lula da Silva and the Workers' Party. Nevertheless, Chestnut argues that Brazilian Pentecostalism generally "reinforces the political status quo by engaging in the clientelistic politics that predominate in the republic" (1997, 146). South African Pentecostalism for the most part maintained its distance from the antiapartheid movement, although some of the younger black Pentecostals expressed opposition to the regime. In the case of South Korea, Jung asserts that Pentecostalism assumed an explicitly anti-Communist orientation and "produced an ahistorical, apolitical and otherworld-centered form of faith" (1999, 151) that served to support the country's capitalist class. Conversely, as Stoll observes, Pentecostal pastors and congregations "tend to retain considerable autonomy in their dealings with state and society" (1990, 319).

An Increasingly Diverse Movement

Pentecostalism, like other religious traditions, is not a monolithic entity. As this essay has indicated, it exhibits tremendous diversity within specific countries, such as the United States or Brazil, and from country to country. At any rate, in the course of a little more than one hundred years, it has become a significant force politically, economically, and culturally. Furthermore, particularly in its charismatic form, it no longer is simply the religion of the downtrodden and disinherited. As a consequence, an increasing number of historians, theologians, sociologists, anthropologists, and other scholars, both Pentecostal and non-Pentecostal, have deemed it a topic to warrant serious consideration with the context of the world-system.

The sociologist David Martin views Pentecostalism, on the one hand, as the Christian equivalent of Islamic fundamentalism in the sense that it constitutes a cultural revolution responding to changes in the large global economy, while, on the other hand, unlike the latter, not offering an overarching political agenda. As a consequence, Pentecostalism, perhaps like Christianity as a whole, may be utilized to support existing sociopolitical and socioeconomic arrangements or to challenge them.

Hans A. BAER
University of Melbourne

See also Missionaries; Religious Fundamentalism

Further Reading

Anderson, A. H. (1999). Dangerous memories for South African Pentecostals. In A. H. Anderson & W. J. Hollenweger (Eds.), *Pentecostals after a century: Global perspectives on a movement in transition* (pp. 89–107). Sheffield, U.K.: Sheffield Academic Press.

Anderson, R. M. (1979). *Vision of the disinherited: The making of American Pentecostalism.* New York: Oxford University Press.

Baer, H. A., & Singer, M. (2002). *African American religion: Varieties of protest and accommodation* (2d ed.). Knoxville: University of Tennessee Press.

Blumenhofer, E. L., Spittler, R. P., & Wacker, G. A. (Eds.). (1999). *Pentecostal currents in American Protestantism.* Urbana: University of Illinois Press.

Chestnut, R. A. (1997). *Born again in Brazil: The Pentecostal boom and the pathogens of poverty.* New Brunswick, NJ: Rutgers University Press.

Csordas, T. J. (1994). *The sacred self: A cultural phenonomenology of charismatic healing.* Berkeley: University of California Press.

Harrell, D. E. (1975). *All things are popular: The healing and charismatic revivals in modern America.* Bloomington: Indiana University Press.

Hollenweger, W. J. (1997). *Pentecostalism: Origins and developments worldwide.* Peabody, MA: Hendrickson.

Jung, L. H. (1999). Minjung and Pentecostal movements in Korea. In A. H. Anderson & W. J. Hollenweger (Eds.), *Pentecostals after a century: Global perspectives on a movement in transition* (pp. 138–160). Sheffield, U.K.: Sheffield Academic Press.

Lancaster, R. N. (1988). *Thanks for God and the revolution: Popular religion and class consciousness in the new Nicaragua.* New York: Columbia University Press.

Mariz, C. L. (1994). *Coping with poverty: Pentecostals and Christian base communities in Brazil.* Philadelphia: Temple University Press.

Martin, D. (2002). *Pentecostalism: The world their parish.* Oxford, U.K.: Blackwell.

McGuire, M. (1982). *Pentecostal Catholics: Power, charisma, and order in a religious movement.* Philadelphia: Temple University Press.

Sanders, C. J. (1996). *Saints in exile: The Holiness-Pentecostal experience in African American religion and culture.* New York: Oxford University Press.

Stoll, D. (1990). *Is Latin America turning Protestant? The politics of evangelical growth.* Berkeley: University of California Press.

Synan, V. (1997). *The Holiness-Pentecostal tradition: Charismatic movements in the twentieth century.* Grand Rapids, MI: William B. Eerdmans Publishing.

Wacker, G. (2001). *Heaven below: Early Pentecostals and American culture.* Cambridge, MA: Harvard University Press.

Pilgrimage

The word *pilgrimage* is derived from the Latin words *per* (meaning "through") and *ager* (meaning "field" or "land"). People usually think of pilgrimage as involving a journey—made either alone or in a group—to and from a sacred site. Pilgrims often perform rituals not only at the sacred site itself, but also at the beginning and end of the journey. In addition, pilgrims may visit other holy places during the course of the journey.

Since ancient times people have been engaged in pilgrimage, either alone or in groups, leaving their homes to journey to a sacred place. Motivations for pilgrimage can include a desire for divine healing, penance for a wrong committed, thanks for a prayer answered, fulfillment of a religious injunction, or some combination of these motivations. The fact that pilgrimage occurs, in some form, in so many societies makes studying this phenomenon fascinating but difficult.

Pilgrimage in the Classical World

No single word in Greek or Latin specifically described travel to a holy destination, but festivals brought together people from scattered settlements both to celebrate the gods and to engage in trade. The numerous shrines of the Hellenic (Greek) world illustrated a great variety of possible reasons to travel. The frieze (an architectural ornament in the form of sculptured, horizontal band) of the famous Parthenon in Athens commemorates the Great Panathenaea, an event celebrated every four years and aimed at achieving a union of all Athenians. Epidauros provided a place for the god Apollo and his son Asklepios to cure the sick. Delphi delivered prophecies through the medium of a priestess. At Olympia the festival of Zeus was celebrated with sporting competitions every four years—an event echoed in the contemporary games, which have taken on global significance in their revived form. Wealthier people in particular had the resources to travel, and pilgrimage also provided one of the few opportunities for women to travel outside their home cities. Roman patterns of pilgrimage were often modeled on Hellenic precedents, with numerous gods celebrated in shrines of greater or lesser size, but with few written doctrines or rules being drawn upon.

Pilgrimage in the World Religions

Pilgrimage is performed in all of the great religions and is usually—unlike its position in the classical world—provided with a justification and model in sacred texts. The degree to which pilgrimage is seen as obligatory varies. Islam is the most prescriptive faith. Every Muslim is required to perform the hajj (pilgrimage to the holy city of Mecca in Saudi Arabia) at least once unless prevented by illness or lack of economic resources. The binding nature of the hajj is combined with other features that distinguish it from other activities. Only Muslims are allowed to enter the holy city; the timing of the pilgrimage is fixed at certain days within the twelfth month of the Muslim year; and pilgrims, dressed in two sheets of unsown cloth or plain dresses, must perform a predetermined sequence of ritual actions, including walking seven times around the Kaaba, the cube-shaped stone building in the court of the Great Mosque.

Hindu pilgrims enter the Shri Ranganath Temple in Vrindavan, India. Photo by Klaus Klostermaier.

Just as the practices of the hajj developed out of earlier traditions already extant in the Arabian Peninsula of the seventh century CE, so Islam emerged within a wider sacred landscape already occupied by Judeo-Christian religious assumptions and influences. The Prophet Muhammad (c. 570–c. 632 CE) regarded Jerusalem as sacred, and the seventh-century Dome of the Rock—even today an object of Muslim pilgrimage—was constructed on the site of the former Jewish Temple and resting place of the Ark of the Covenant in Jerusalem. The hajj had some parallels with the *haggim* of Judaism, the ancient pilgrimage feasts involving the convergence of the Israelites on Jerusalem. (The Hebrew term *hag* implies the actions of turning around and dancing.) But such feasts also expressed specific aspects of Jewish history. The oldest feast, Passover, celebrated deliverance from servitude in Egypt. Tabernacles involved the construction of temporary shelters and commemorated the forty years spent by the Jews in the wilderness. Shavuot (Weeks) was a harvest festival that also marked the giving of the Ten Commandments to Moses on Mount Sinai. These gatherings therefore provided occasions for pilgrimage while also recalling different forms of movement: escape from slavery, wandering in the desert before locating the Promised Land, or ascending a mountain. They are still celebrated by members of a faith whose identity remains rooted in the experience of dispersal, the so-called Diaspora (the settling of scattered colonies of Jews outside Palestine after the Babylonian exile). Even today, two thousand years after the final destruction of the Temple but with the State of Israel restored, Passover is an occasion when many Jews proclaim: "Next year in Jerusalem!"

Christianity echoes Islam and Judaism in its reverence for Jerusalem, both in relation to scripture and in relation to pilgrimage. The landscape of the Holy Land and the holy city have provided potent reminders of Jesus' life as well as of the location of his future return (just as in Islam Paradise will be transferred to Jerusalem during the Last Days). The early centuries of the church brought the quick emergence of a pious tradition of traveling. During the fourth century CE Helena (c. 255–327 CE), the mother of the Roman emperor Constantine (c. 274–337 CE), toured the Holy Land, adapting the model of traditional Roman imperial progress through a province for her own spiritual as well as political purposes. As the Christian empire developed so did the pilgrimage routes of often highly ascetic travelers, who expected to see the biblical narrative played out in the places visited. A growing monastic tradition was also evident in Palestine and neighboring lands. But with the decline in Muslim tolerance of Christian visitors to Jerusalem from the tenth century onward, European sites became increasingly prominent pilgrimage locations. Rome housed the tombs of St. Peter and St. Paul, and other shrines, such as Santiago de Compostela in northwest Spain, were viewed as symbols of Christian military opposition to Islam, celebrating St. James in his role as a warrior, armed with both a sword and a cross. Some sites even replicated the sacred landscape of the Holy Land, such as Walsingham in Norfolk—known as "England's Nazareth" because it claimed to have an exact copy of the holy house that Jesus had inhabited as a boy.

The qualities of the landscape have been central to Judeo-Christian pilgrimage traditions, but also—and perhaps especially—to those of south Asia. The Hindu term *tirtha-yatra* means broadly "journey to river fords," illustrating a devotion to flowing water evident since Vedic (relating to the Hindu sacred

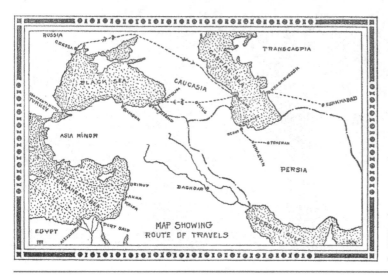

The 1908 travel route of pilgrim Charles Mason Remey, a teacher and defender of the Baha'i Faith.

writings) times (from c. 1500 BCE), and pilgrimage practices often involve taking a purifying dip, as well as visiting holy figures or gaining sight of a deity contained within an image. The *Mahabharata* (c. 300 BCE), a Vedic epic, contains sections describing and noting the religious merit to be gained from visiting numerous *tirtha*s (sacred places). Such merit is said to apply to people of all classes and castes and usually involves a temporary renunciation—akin in some ways to Christian asceticism—that rejects bodily comforts and pleasure. As one scholar of Hindu pilgrimage puts it, "The returning pilgrim should be thinner and poorer" (Gold 1988, 263). Other important features of the Hindu pilgrimage landscape include hilltops, caves, and forests, creating a complex sacred geography that encompasses the whole of India. Furthermore, with the economic migration of Hindu populations into the West, features of the sacred Indian landscape have been translated into new parts of the world, so that, for instance, the convergence of two rivers in Ohio has been compared by some Hindus with the confluence of the sacred Indian rivers: the Ganges, Yamuna, and Sarasvati.

On the Indian subcontinent the religions of Jainism and Sikhism maintain pilgrimage traditions that have some similarities with Hindu practices. According to Buddhist tradition, among the last words of Buddha (c. 563–c. 483 BCE) were instructions to his followers to visit places marking the most significant events of his life. People soon added numerous holy spots to this biographical landscape, within and beyond India. Just as the emperor Constantine reinforced his imperial power by placing pilgrimage churches in the Holy Land, so the emperor Ashoka—the first Buddhist pilgrim of whom we know—used imperial patronage during the third century BCE to create a Buddhist landscape of pilgrimage by improving roads and resting places for travelers. As the religion itself spread, new pilgrimage sites emerged in China, Tibet, and Japan.

Similarities and Differences

Both in the past and in the present pilgrimage practices across the world's religions have appeared to exhibit some striking similarities. Circumambulation of shrines and other sacred objects is evident not only in Islam but also in Hinduism and Buddhism, for instance. Pilgrims also commonly take some material evidence of their journey back home—perhaps a vial of holy water, an image, or a token. However, we should not assume that actions that look similar from the outside have the same meaning to participants from different cultures and religions. Furthermore, pilgrimages have tended to contain within them—even to foster—conflicts between pilgrims supposedly united by the same religion or between ordinary pilgrims and shrine authorities. Thus, the famous Catholic site of Lourdes, situated on one

Life is a pilgrimage. The wise man does not rest by the roadside inns. He marches direct to the illimitable domain of eternal bliss, his ultimate destination. • **Swami Sivananda (1887–1963)**

of the main medieval pilgrimage roads of southern France and commemorating the visions of the Virgin Mary granted to a young girl during the nineteenth century, is enormously popular in the present, attracting millions of visitors a year. Such popularity inevitably creates tensions over the varied motivations of the pious, for instance, between the desire for miraculous healing expressed by the sick who visit the site and the general emphasis on spiritual rather than physical benefits that is promoted by the clergy.

The religious and often political (and even economic) power contained in many pilgrimage sites has often led to acute, even destructive, conflicts. Jerusalem is not the only site of competition between faiths. The pilgrimage center of Ayodhya in Uttar Pradesh, India, remains a site of troubled relations between Hindus and Muslims, resulting not only in violence but also in rivalrous construction and destruction of sacred buildings. Elsewhere in India, the Golden Temple at Amritsar, holiest of shrines for Sikhs, became the center of conflict between religious separatists and the Indian government, leading in 1984 to the storming of the temple by the army and the killing of many people, including pilgrims.

Pilgrimages have also been attacked from within their religious traditions, with critics often denying the value of physical travel or challenging the idea that the divine can be particularly located in a single spot on Earth. The tenth-century Sufi (Muslim mystic) authority Abu Sa'id enjoined his followers not to undertake the hajj on the grounds that they should concentrate on cultivating mystical experiences instead. Within Hinduism some writers have argued that pilgrimage implies too much attachment to the material world. A key aspect of the Protestant Reformation was the iconoclasm that denied the spiritual value of the statues and relics in numerous shrines and that attacked the economic corruption in both the guardianship of sacred sites and the selling of "indulgences"—remissions of punishments for sin that the Catholic Church granted in return for pious acts such as pilgrimage.

Pilgrimage in the Future

Despite some predictions that the world is becoming more secular, pilgrimage remains a flourishing institution. Although it has always been combined with other activities, pilgrimage is increasingly being associated with tourism, so that sacred travel is often undertaken alongside other forms of leisure, and pilgrimage sites have become accustomed to hosting both pilgrims and tourists at the same time. As more people can more easily travel throughout their own countries or even across the globe, pilgrimage seems likely to become an ever more visible part of life in the twenty-first century.

Simon M. COLEMAN

Centre for the Study of Religion, University of Toronto

See also Buddhism; Hinduism; Islam; Jainism; Judaism; Missionaries; Muhammad; Protestantism; Roman Catholicism

Further Reading

Bajc, V., Coleman, S., & Eade, J. (Eds.). (2007 November). Special issue: (Dis)placing the centre: Pilgrimage in a mobile world. *Mobilities 2*(3).

Bhardwaj, S. M. (1973). *Hindu places of pilgrimage in India (A study in cultural geography)*. Berkeley and Los Angeles: University of California Press.

Coleman, S. M., & Elsner, J. (1995). *Pilgrimage past and present in the world religions*. Cambridge, MA: Harvard University Press.

Coleman, S. M., & Eade, J. (Eds.). (2004). *Reframing pilgrimage: Cultures in motion*. London: Routledge.

Dillon, M. (1997). *Pilgrims and pilgrimage in ancient Greece*. London: Routledge.

Dubisch, J. (1995). *In a different place: Pilgrimage, gender, and politics at a Greek island shrine*. Princeton, NJ: Princeton University Press.

Eade, J., & Sallnow, M. (Eds.). (1991). *Contesting the sacred: The anthropology of Christian pilgrimage*. London: Routledge.

Eickelman, D. F., & Piscatori, J. (Eds.). (1990). *Muslim travellers: Pilgrimage, migration, and the religious imagination*. London: Routledge.

Elad, A. (1999). *Medieval Jerusalem and Islamic worship: Holy places, ceremonies, pilgrimage.* New York: E. J. Brill.

Gold, A. (1988). *Fruitful journeys: The ways of Rajasthani pilgrims.* Berkeley and Los Angeles: University of California Press.

Howard, D. R. (1980). *Writers and pilgrims: Medieval pilgrimage narratives and their posterity.* Berkeley and Los Angeles: University of California Press.

Hummel, R., & Hummel, T. (1995). *Patterns of the sacred: English Protestant and Russian Orthodox pilgrims of the nineteenth century.* London: Scorpion Cavendish.

Hunt, E. D. (1982). *Holy Land pilgrimage in the later Roman Empire AD 312–460.* Oxford, U.K.: Clarendon.

Kunin, S. (1998). *God's place in the world: Sacred space and sacred place in Judaism.* London: Cassell.

Morinis, E. A. (1984). *Pilgrimage in the Hindu tradition: A case study of west Bengal.* Delhi, India: Oxford University Press.

Morris, C., & Roberts, P. (Eds.). (2002). *Pilgrimage: The English experience from Becket to Bunyan.* Cambridge, UK: Cambridge University Press.

Nolan, M. L., & Nolan, S. (1989). *Christian pilgrimage in modern western Europe.* Chapel Hill: University of North Carolina Press.

Ousterhout, R. (Ed.). (1990). *The blessings of pilgrimage.* Urbana: University of Illinois Press.

Peters, F. E. (1994). *The hajj: The Muslim pilgrimage to Mecca and the holy places.* Princeton, NJ: Princeton University Press.

Reader, I., & Walter, T. (Eds.). *Pilgrimage in popular culture.* London: Macmillan.

Swatos, W. H., & Tomasi, L. (Eds.). (2002). *From medieval pilgrimage to religious tourism: The social and cultural economics of piety.* Westport, CT: Praeger.

Turner, V., & Turner, E. (1978). *Image and pilgrimage in Christian culture: Anthropological perspectives.* New York: Columbia University Press.

Protestantism

Protestantism, which thrives in numerous denominations and usually adapts to the cultures of the congregants to whom it has spread since the sixteenth century, uses the Bible as its authority and stresses the grace of God. Religious demographers estimate the number of Protestant Christians worldwide to increase from 370 million in the early twenty-first century to half a billion by 2025.

Protestantism represents a form of Christianity that spread in five hundred years from northwest Europe to every continent. This global version of the faith derives from a cluster of movements within Western or Catholic Christianity in the early sixteenth century and thrives in the form of thousands of independent church bodies. Rejecting the authority of the pope, Protestants almost universally profess that the Bible—that is, the Hebrew Scriptures and the New Testament—is the authoritative source and norm of their teaching. Through the centuries, Protestantism quite naturally took on the culture of whatever new environments its churches spread to. Thus Lutherans in Namibia differ in many respects from those in Norway, yet both stress the grace of God and are critical of any teaching that they associate with the historic Catholic teaching that insisted on human endeavors to impress and please God.

Global Protestantism Today

Early in the twenty-first century, religious demographers estimate that about 370 million people are Protestant. Often associated with Protestantism but insisting on its Catholic character is Anglicanism, the heritage of the Church of England, which numbers 82 million adherents; a third group, informally labeled Independents, numbers 415 million. Taken together, after 2000 these non-Roman Catholic varieties of Christianity, all of which derived from the sixteenth-century Reformation, have over 800 million followers. (By comparison, there are an estimated 101 million Roman Catholics and 217 million Eastern Orthodox adherents.) Demographers estimate that by 2025 the Protestant numbers will grow from 370 million to almost half a billion, a sign that Protestantism is not confined to the period of early prosperity from the sixteenth through the nineteenth century, but faces a prosperous yet at the same time an ambiguous future. While these are necessarily imprecise numbers, the totals suggest the enormous historical importance of this movement.

The momentum of Protestantism, however, has dramatically shifted. While much of its base remains in northwest Europe, the point of its origin, the membership there is often nominal. In some Scandinavian nations, for instance, over 90 percent of the population will be listed as Protestant because most children are baptized by the Lutherans, yet church participation is very low. Meanwhile, in sub-Saharan Africa, where several thousand new members are added every twenty-four hours, Protestants, especially in forms called "Pentecostal" or "charismatic," as they expand, are known for their vital and even exuberant patterns of worship and are among the chief deliverers of health care and works of mercy.

Protestant Origins in Western Europe

While Protestantism did not receive its name until 1529, historians of Protestantism characteristically

172 · RELIGION AND BELIEF SYSTEMS IN WORLD HISTORY

date its rise from sporadic pioneering reform movements in England under John Wycliffe (1320–1384), William Tyndale (1494?–1536), and others. They and their followers combined efforts to translate the Bible into English and then to use biblical teachings, as they interpreted them, to criticize the Catholic Church. The Czech reformer Jon Hus (1372–1415), a critic of Catholic practices who died for his faith, endeavored to break the hold of the hierarchy and to teach lay people to base their views of divine grace on the Bible.

While the English reformers and the Hussites were put out of the Catholic Church or put to death, many other reform movements which tested the Roman church of the day, denouncing it as legalistic, corrupt, and inefficient as a deliverer of the message of divine grace, remained within the Church. Typical among this group were humanists like Desiderius Erasmus (1467?–1536) of the Netherlands, a man who satirized the papacy and monasticism with a wit and savagery unmatched by most of his Protestant-leaning contemporaries. However, Erasmus and other humanists in the universities of England and throughout the Holy Roman Empire on the continent could not envision carrying their reform to the point of a break with the papacy.

Breaks that led to permanent breaches began to occur in the second decade of the sixteenth century. Most visible and best-remembered among them were the university-based reforms at Wittenberg in Saxony. A cluster of monks and professors led by Martin Luther (1483–1546) set out to attack the Church's modes of dealing with people who sought salvation and attempted to live a moral life. Luther and his followers saw the Papacy as repressive, self-centered, and corrupt, and declared their intent to recast Church teachings from within Catholicism. However, they became so upsetting to both the Church and the Holy Roman Empire that Rome took action—usually, as in the case of Luther, it excommunicated them as heretics. Many other critics left voluntarily.

The map of early Protestantism indicates that a great number and variety of sites developed quickly. In England, a controversy between the Pope and King Henry VIII led to a sundering of ties and the birth of the Anglican Church. In Switzerland, reformers such as Huldreich Zwingli (1484–1531) and John Calvin (1509–1564) complemented or competed with Luther and the Germans and with Scandinavian leaders, while more radical reformers spread through Switzerland and the Lowlands. By mid-century essential changes in allegiances had occurred and Protestantism had reached its early geographical limits. However, Mediterranean Catholics on the Iberian Peninsula, in France, and in the Italian states were unmoved, as were Eastern Europeans, whose Catholic churches abutted Orthodox churches in Russia, Poland, and Greece.

The Inner and Outer Expressions

The early Protestants, who acquired their name almost accidentally from the act of some princes who "protested" imperial and Catholic action at the Diet of Speyer in 1529, were more frequently referred to with a more congenial and positive term, *evangelical*. Although five centuries later that name appears to characterize only conservative Protestantism, in the beginning it simply implied that those who professed it were devoted to the *evangel*, the message of the New Testament gospels. They were not to be confined by Roman Catholic Church law and did not define themselves as legalistic followers of Jesus and the church. Instead, they professed to take the risk of governing the church and inspiring individual members' lives with the message of grace as mediated only by the Christian gospels and voiced in the acts of preaching and prayer.

The inner expression of Protestantism arose from the way some Christians gave expression to this evangel, how they worshiped and lived. The outer expression refers to the ways in which Protestants in various societies and cultures

PROTESTANT REGIONS of EUROPE c. 1600

related to governments and economic and social powers.

The Gospel and the Inner Life of Protestants

Once the hold of the papacy and the Catholic hierarchy was tested and broken, the people called Protestant set to work to give voice and form to personal and church life in ways that would distance them from Rome and yet keep them within the Christian tradition, a tradition that they were soon to claim as belonging more rightfully to them than to the members of what they considered a corrupt Catholic church. Many Protestant leaders, especially the Anglicans and the Lutherans, continued to think of themselves as representing a kind of Catholicism without a pope, and they affirmed all that they could from the life of the existing Church. Yet their criticism of its forms was often searching, radical, and even savage. In fact, for many, the pope became not a faulty follower of Christ but the Antichrist.

Although they were unwilling to be defined only negatively vis-à-vis the Roman hierarchy and church or canon law, Protestants had difficulty defining themselves positively. The genus had to include everyone from Anabaptists, ancestors to latter-day Mennonites and radical Baptists, to church bodies that worshiped in very formal ways, including the use of incense and what radicals considered reintroducing the trappings that belonged in Rome, not in evangelicalism. The genus also had to include Protestants who supported the religious establishment, who did not sever the ties between religion and regime, separate "church and state," or cease taxing the whole citizenry for church support. At the same time, in the same cluster, were Protestants—again, the Anabaptists and Baptists led the way—who wanted religious life in their churches to be independent of political organizations and leadership; they advocated very simple forms of worship that demonstrated their distance from Rome.

Authority and Grace

Despite these diversities and the outlooks and actions of many charismatic reformers who started independent movements, some broadly defined motifs can be used to characterize most Protestants. First, most of them did and still do give highest priority to the canonical scriptures, which they share with Catholics. Most Protestants, however, want to downgrade Catholic affirmations of church tradition and papal interpretations of the Bible. They may affirm that the Christian faith had been expressed through the ages wherever Catholics were baptized or where they observed the Lord's Supper ("the Mass") as a second sacrament, where the gospel of Jesus Christ was read, and where it served as the basis of preaching and teaching to summon people to faith and the living of a godly life. The Protestant rejection of so much tradition and its refusal to turn to other authority, led Protestants to put a major, sometimes unique, stress on divine revelation in Scripture (on the interpretation of which the various groups disagreed with each other). One frequent statement of this motif was the authority of *sola scriptura* (scripture alone).

Second, while Protestants differed from each other in interpreting the scripture, most found in the writings of Paul and classic teachers such as Augustine an accent on divine grace. In this case, the distinctive elements were *sola gratia* (grace alone) and *sola fide* (faith alone)—people were saved from sin and from eternal punishment by the graceful and generous action of God, especially through the death and resurrection of Jesus Christ, in whom they had faith. Catholics, of course, also acknowledged divine initiatives, but in the eyes of Protestants their emphasis on the need to please God through personal merit or works made them subject to Rome, which stipulated exactly how they should acquire merits and which works were beneficial to those who would be saved.

Continuing to baptize and to celebrate the Lord's Supper or Holy Communion, the sacred meal that memorialized Jesus and, most said, was a means of imparting grace among believers, the majority of evangelical Protestants simplified worship. Preaching, singing hymns, and saying prayers became the main features.

Authority and Public Life

Protestants, whose early breakthroughs were often connected with particular nationalist or territorial movements and strivings by political rulers, knew that they had to find ways to promote civil life and instill obedience among populations. Few were ready to go so far as to repudiate existing earthly authority, be it that of emperors, monarchs, princes, or

magistrates. Indeed, many of the latter converted to Protestantism and gave protective cover to reformers who were allied with them and who promoted their cause. By 1555 at the Peace of Augsburg, all but the radical reformist Protestant leaders had signed on to a concept that they took for granted: *cuius region, eius religio* (whoever determined the government of a region stipulated what religion should be favored or have a monopoly).

That halfway stage of reform led many Protestant leaders to adopt a servile attitude to their government, and many clergy became lower-grade civil servants. Dependent upon the government for funds, they were often uncritical of rulers, and Protestant radicals charged that they were replacing the tyranny of the pope with the tyranny of princes. Yet from the beginning, early Protestant witnesses to the value of conscience and of relative autonomy in respect to spiritual choices produced a widespread restlessness that by the middle of the seventeenth century had led to edicts and settlements of toleration in England and elsewhere.

A century later, these protesting impulses and liberated consciences served many Protestants as they teamed up with political thinkers, revolutionaries, and statesmen, to draw a line of distinction between the sphere of religion and the civil authorities—to use the terms of American constitutionalist James Madison—or the separation of church and state, Thomas Jefferson's term. Such distinguishing and separation became marks of Protestant life in the United States after 1787, and were important instruments in determining Protestant church life when its missionaries founded churches in Asia and Africa, where no form of Christianity became more than a small minority presence.

Not all the external life of Protestant Christians had to do with government and politics. There was also an accent on personal ethics, based on the gospel in ideal circumstances, though many evangelical churches developed laws and nurtured legalistic ethics. As religion and regimes became more independent of each other, the ethic of "faith made active in love" inspired Protestants during and after the eighteenth century to invent many forms of voluntary associational life. Their churches formed groups where leaders and followers could promote charity and reform. The legacy of these inventions in the late eighteenth century, especially in Anglo-America, is evident wherever the Protestants took their efforts to convert people, even on continents where Protestants were never more than a minority presence.

Protestant Phases of Development

The first generations of Protestantism were what sociologist Emile Durkheim called "effervescences," bubblings-up, hard-to-discipline eruptions, usually marked by the language and life of an outstanding leader. By the second generation such movements, in order to sustain themselves and give an accounting of their ways, saw the rise of definers. Thus in the Church of England, Richard Hooker (1554–1600) brought legal expertise to the drafting of the *Lawes of Ecclesiastical Polity*. John Calvin, arriving on the scene slightly later on the scene of reform than Luther or Zwingli, was himself a principled systematic theologian and defined the Calvinist or Reformed wing of Protestantism with his *Institutes of the Christian Religion*. Martin Luther, a man of contradictions who favored paradoxical language, gave place to university systematicians in the seventeenth century, giants of dogmatic expression like Johann Gerhard. The impulse among the second-generation leaders was to reintroduce more legalistic norms and in some cases to adopt the scholastic approach to faith which their predecessors had criticized. This meant that they offered philosophical defenses of the verbal inspiration of the Bible or reasoned apologies for the existence of God and the workings of grace.

Such defining legalism and scholasticism, especially where Protestants were linked with and dependent upon civil authorities, could follow a predictable means toward an unsurprising end. That is, they often appeared to degenerate into desiccated or fossilized forms, inert, incapable of keeping the evangelical spark alive. Such kinds of settlement bred restlessness. Thus, in a third long generation or short century of

Protestant life, inspired leaders and movements from within devoted themselves anew to the inner life of the individual prayerful soul, the piety of believers, and the reform of worship. These eighteenth and early nineteenth century movements, concurrently in the *reveil* in French-speaking lands, the *Glaubenserweckung* among German speakers, and the "awakening," "revivalist" or "pietist" movements in the British Isles and the American colonies or young United States, brought forth fresh accents.

Now the concentration was on the personal experience of God acting through the Holy Spirit to lead individuals from indifference or apathy to fervent faith. The converts, once "awakened" or "revived," were to turn to their reprobate or spiritually lifeless and wicked neighbors and convert them. Then they were to form small groups, often within the established church, as was the case with Jonathan Edwards or George Whitefield, the towering figures in colonial America at mid-century, or with John Wesley, who eventually moved out of the Church of England to form Methodism. In general, these awakened movements matched and fed the democratic spirit of the times and empowered lay people to engage in works of reform and missionary endeavor.

In the nineteenth century, the age of colonialism, such awakened Protestants, moved by the sense that they were advancing the millennium (for Christ's return to Earth) or promoting human progress through conversion and reform, boarded ships from the British Isles, western European nations, and the United States, and took their gospel to the Middle East, Asia, and the Pacific Island world, sometimes but with less success in Catholic Latin America, and finally to Africa. Most of these evangelical missionary movements date from the 1790s in England and after the 1810s in the United States.

Gifted college graduates, ambitious entrepreneurs, and sacrifice-minded men and women accompanied their message of salvation with efforts to educate heal and then provide physical benefits for the populations they reached. It is easy to connect their moves with colonial and imperial impulses, but without the entrepreneurs and conquerors they could probably

176 · RELIGION AND BELIEF SYSTEMS IN WORLD HISTORY

Wherever the battle rages, there the loyalty of the soldier is proved and to be steady on all the battlefield besides is mere flight and disgrace if he flinches at that one point. • **Martin Luther (1483–1546)**

not have moved as efficiently as they did. Yet they paid a high price, because anti-colonialism eventually made it necessary for them to distance themselves from many of the Euro-American missionary endeavors—in sub-Saharan Africa, for example. They developed what they thought of as autochthonous Protestant churches—that is, churches rooted in the cultural soil of their new country.

At the beginning of the twentieth century, a new expression of Protestantism called Pentecostalism broke forth. Pentecostals claimed that their charismatic form of Christianity was as old as the biblical prophets and the New Testament. They believed they were reviving gifts of early Christianity, which had long fallen into disuse. They "spoke in tongues," for example; they prophesied and claimed miraculous healings. Pentecostalism quickly became a dominant form among Protestant late-arrivals in Latin America and sub-Saharan Africa. Some demographers claimed that over 570 million Protestants, Anglicans, Independents, and sometimes even Roman Catholics were Pentecostal. Having become the dominant form in the emerging world, Pentecostalism seemed ready to become the most prominent form of global Protestantism as the European churches declined in numbers and significance.

One Millennium Ends, Another Begins

Through centuries, Protestantism developed many schools of theology, not least impressively in the twentieth century, long after many cultural observers had expected such fresh flowerings in a secular world. These schools reflected the dominant philosophies of the day, as their ancestral versions had done during periods characterized, for example, by idealism and the Enlightenment. In the same way existentialism, language analysis, phenomenology, and other philosophies inspired Protestant thinkers, usually in university settings, to rework biblical and historic evangelical motifs to meet new challenges. These included coming to terms with whatever industrialization, urbanism, globalization, and humanistic

crises brought to people's lives. Far from fading, as it seemed to be doing in its own heartland, Protestantism in the early twenty-first century represents a confusing, explosive, adaptive force in secular and religiously pluralistic settings. Hard-line reactive Protestant fundamentalists resist adaptations, but their leaders manifest an ability to engage in invention on the ever-changing front of Protestantism.

Martin E. MARTY

University of Chicago, Emeritus

See also Missionaries; Pentecostalism; Religious Fundamentalism

Further Reading

Ahlstrom, S. (Ed.). (1967). *Theology in America: The major voices.* New York: Bobbs-Merrill.

Barth, K. (1972). *Protestant theology in the nineteenth century: Its background and history.* London: SCM Press.

Bergendoff, C. (1967). *The Church of the Lutheran Reformation: A historical survey of Lutheranism.* St. Louis, MO: Concordia.

Bossy, J. (1985). *Christianity in the West, 1400–1700.* Oxford, U.K.: Oxford University Press.

Bouyer, L. (2001). *The spirit and forms of Protestantism.* San Francisco, CA: Sceptre.

Brauer, J. C. (1965). *Protestantism in America.* Philadelphia: Westminster.

Brown, R. M. (1961). *The spirit of Protestantism.* New York: Oxford University Press.

Cragg, G. R. (1960). *The Church in the age of reason.* Grand Rapids: MI: Eerdmans.

Curtis, C. J. (1970). *Contemporary Protestant thought.* New York: Bruce.

Dillenberger, J., & Welch, C. (1954). *Protestant Christianity interpreted through its development.* New York: Scribner's.

Drummond, A. L. (1951). *German Protestantism since Luther.* London: Epworth.

Flew, R. N., & Davies, R. E. (Eds.). (1950). *The Catholicity of Protestantism.* London: Lutterworth.

Forell, G. (1960). *The Protestant spirit.* Englewood Cliffs, NJ: Prentice-Hall.

Greengrass, M. (1987). *The French Reformation.* London: Blackwell.

Groh, J. E. (1982). *Nineteenth century German Protestantism: The church as a social model.* Washington, DC: University Press of America.

Halverson, M., & Cohen, A. A. (Eds.). (1958). *A handbook of Christian theology: Definition essays on concepts and movements of thought in contemporary Protestantism.* New York: Meridian.

Hastings, A. (1976). *African Christianity.* London: Continuum.

Hastings, A. (1991). *A history of English Christianity 1920–1990.* Philadelphia: Trinity Press.

Heim, K. (1963). *The nature of Protestantism.* Philadelphia: Fortress.

Heron, A. (1980). *A century of Protestant theology.* Philadelphia: Fortress.

Kerr, H. T. (1950). *Positive Protestantism.* Philadelphia: Westminster.

Léonard, E. (1966, 1967). *A history of Protestantism* (Vols. 1–2). London: Nelson.

Marty, M. E. (1972). *Protestantism.* New York: Holt.

Nichols, J. H. (1947). *Primer for Protestants.* New York: Association Press.

Pauck, W. (1950). *The heritage of the Reformation.* Boston: Beacon.

Rupp, G. (1986). *Religion in England, 1688–1791.* Oxford, U.K.: Oxford University Press.

Tillich, P. (1951). *The Protestant era.* Chicago: University of Chicago Press.

Troeltsch, E. (1966). *Protestantism and progress: A historical study of the relation of Protestantism to the modern world.* Boston: Beacon.

Von Rohr, J. (1969). *Profile of Protestantism.* Belmont, CA: Dickenson.

Weber, M. (1958). *The Protestant ethic and the spirit of capitalism.* New York: Scribner's. (Original work published 1904)

Welch, C. (1972, 1983). *Protestant thought in the nineteenth century* (Vols. 1–2). New Haven, CT: Yale University Press.

Whale, J. S. (1955). *The Protestant tradition.* Cambridge, U.K.: Cambridge University Press.

Williams, G. H. (1961). *The radical Reformation.* Philadelphia: Westminster.

Worrall, B. G. (1988). *The making of the modern church: Christianity in England since 1800.* London: SPCK.

Religion and Government

Religion has traditionally served as a source of authority, law, and moral norms for society, even in predominantly secular societies. Through most of the world's history, religious traditions have had formal ties with governments and have been seen as an important source of legitimacy of rulers.

Religion and government have often existed in complementary roles throughout world history—with religion lending authority to a government, and government legitimizing a leader's rule. Various societies throughout history have practiced toleration or acceptance of minority faiths, although only rarely based on principled beliefs in religious freedom. Modern ideas of rights to religious freedom and secular governmental systems are based in a variety of sources, but draw great strength from the Western church-state tradition and the Enlightenment.

Religion: Source of Law, Authority, and Moral Values

Throughout world history, religious traditions and beliefs have been a direct and indirect source of law and authority. The Babylonian Code of Hammurabi, for example, begins with a reference to the gods Anu and Bel, who called Hammurabi (reigned 1792–1750 BCE) to "bring about the rule of righteousness in the land." The Jewish Law of Moses not only codified religious belief, but also set forth an extensive and elaborate legal system that governed all areas of social life. In more recent times, the Bible formed the basis for laws in the early American colonies and was used to resolve issues as far-ranging as procedural rules, property law, criminal law, and, in general, the ideal of the rule of law. Even in modern secular societies, religion is still regularly used as the source for moral values and arguments for reform. For example, Reverend Martin Luther King Jr. (1929–1968) and Mohandas Gandhi (1869–1948) drew extensively on the Christian and Hindu traditions in their calls for social change, and similar religious beliefs have informed debates on the abolition of slavery, care for the poor, abortion, marriage, and other social and economic issues.

Traditional Religious–Governmental Ties

In the ancient world, religion was traditionally intertwined with ruling hierarchies, through either theocracies or divinely ordained rulers. In the Chinese Confucian tradition, for example, emperors were believed to have the Mandate of Heaven, sanction from a divine power that justified a ruler's actions as long as it was beneficial to those he ruled. Roman emperors claimed to be descended from the gods or to be gods themselves, as did Egyptian pharaohs. The Japanese emperor served as the head of the Shinto tradition. In the caste systems of the Vedic and Hindu traditions in India, the priests were traditionally the highest castes. Roman Catholic popes ordained the Holy Roman Emperors and Protestant kings claimed a divine right to rule. From the time of Byzantium, Orthodox countries were marked by caesaropapism, a system in which the head of state has authority over the church. Ties such as these conferred legitimacy on the rulers and gave religion an important

God is on everyone's side ... and in the last analysis, he is on the side with plenty of money and large armies. • **Jean Anouilh (1910–1987)**

The remains of a large kiva at Pueblo Bonito, New Mexico, suggest that the structures within the kiva were used for community meetings as well as for religious ceremonies.

role in ensuring the community's stability, unity, and compliance with law. For example, a strong, unified religious tradition was seen as playing an important role in ensuring the binding power of oaths and contracts. The close association of a religious tradition with the ruling hierarchy was usually also associated with political privileges for the favored religion and limitations or bans on the practice of minority religions.

Experiences of Religious Tolerance

Despite the tendency for governments with strong religious ties to limit protections to a favored religion, some rulers throughout history have accommodated and tolerated minority religious traditions, although this tolerance was not always principled and was often limited by the perceived needs of the sovereign. In many cases, tolerance served as a practical way to handle a multiethnic, multireligious empire. For example, the Persian Empire from Cyrus II (reigned 559–530 BCE) to Darius I (reigned 522–486 BCE) employed a policy of religious toleration and support for minority groups, allowing the Jews to rebuild the temple in Jerusalem and returning images of Babylonian gods to their sanctuaries in Babylon. The Mongol Empire created by Chingghis (Genghis) Khan (c. 1162–1227 BCE) practiced toleration of Buddhists, Christians, Confucians, Daoists, and Muslims, and the Qing dynasty in China (1644–1911/12) maintained a general policy of religious toleration toward Jews, Muslims, and Christian missionaries until antiforeign and anti-Christian sentiments led to the expulsion of foreign missionaries from China in 1720. The Muslim Ottoman Turks developed a "millet" system in which other "religions of the book," that is, Christianity and Judaism, could be practiced and had some self-rule, albeit with significant discrimination. The Peace of Westphalia (1648) at the end of the European Thirty Years' War established limited religious tolerance in which believers had time to leave their country and move to one that supported their religious beliefs.

Principled Conceptions of Religious Freedom

In contrast to tolerance or acceptance of religious minorities by the grace of the sovereign, rulers and governments have only occasionally developed a principled basis for protecting the beliefs of others. In most cases, this basis itself has come from the religious beliefs of the ruler. For example, Asoka, the last major emperor in the Mauryan dynasty of India (reigned c. 265–238 or c. 273–232 BCE), adopted Buddhism and then promoted religious tolerance through his "Rock Edicts" based on the Buddhist idea of dharma. Anabaptist preacher Balthasar Hubmaier (1485–1528 CE) argued against the coercion of heretics or nonbelievers and wrote a defense of religious freedom based on the Bible. Roger Williams (c. 1603–1683 CE), the founder of the American colony of Rhode Island, wrote passionately in support of religious freedom and the separation of church and state, both based on his understanding of the Bible. Despite his own strong religious convictions, he opened the colony of Rhode Island to people of all faiths, where they were welcome to freely practice their beliefs. During the Second Vatican Council, the Roman Catholic Church adopted a policy statement, *Dignitatis humanae* (1965), which endorsed religious freedom and the independence of church and state based on religious reasons such as human dignity.

While some thinkers and religious leaders in some traditions still struggle with a principled basis for religious tolerance, modern scholars from all major religious traditions have identified resources within their own traditions that could support a principled belief in religious freedom. Drawing on worldwide legal, philosophical, and religious beliefs, the Universal Declaration of Human Rights, adopted by the United Nations in 1948, supports the right to "freedom of thought, conscience and religion," which includes "freedom to change his religion and belief and freedom, either alone or in community with others and in public or private, to manifest his religion or belief in teaching, practice, worship, and observance." (Stahnke and Martin 1998, 59).

Much of the contemporary strength of the concept of religious freedom as a human right and the role of a secular state, however, comes from the Western tradition. The growth of Christianity in the originally pagan Roman Empire led to a system of "two kingdoms," where both the emperor and church leaders exerted power over the faithful. The competition for power between the Roman Catholic Church and the Holy Roman Empire escalated in the middle ages under Pope Gregory VII (c. 1020–1085), who forbade the appointment of bishops by kings in 1078. This controversy, referred to as the Investiture Contest, strengthened the power of the church vis-à-vis the state. This contest for power, together with Western Christian notions of an independent duty to obey one's conscience and natural rights, laid the groundwork for modern conceptions of a limited government and individual rights to religious freedom. Enlightenment scholars, such as John Locke in his famous *Letters on Toleration*, also advocated religious freedom and argued for the limited competence of governments in the field of religion, based on both philosophical and pragmatic reasons. The search for religious freedom was an important factor in the founding of the American colonies and was first embodied in a written constitution in the First Amendment to the U.S. Constitution. While religious freedom has since been enshrined in many national and international legal norms, many governments still significantly limit religious freedom.

Although most modern governments are primarily secular in nature, religion still plays an important role in government and society. For example, religious traditions still often serve as a source of reform and law. Religion traditions and emblems still provide important ceremonial and spiritual influences

RELIGION AND GOVERNMENT · 181

*Religion is regarded by the common people as true, by the wise as false,
and by rulers as useful.* • **Seneca the Younger (4 BCE–65 CE)**

in most countries. Unlike the United States, most governments still have formal, institutional ties, often including subsidies and other forms of state cooperation. Religious buildings, social services, or workers may be supported by the state and may serve as a resource in times of national crisis or on public holidays. Even in more separationist governmental systems, such as the United States and France, religious leaders often serve as chaplains in the military, prisons, and hospitals. While individual countries may have particular historical or cultural ties with a single religious tradition, most governments with cooperationist or accommodationist systems allow multiple religions to obtain government benefits and cooperate with the state. Despite the wide variety of current structures of the relationship between religion and governments and the many remaining challenges to religious freedom, a range of accommodationist and cooperationist systems throughout the world still preserve religious freedom.

Elizabeth A. SEWELL
Brigham Young University

See also Religion and War; Religious Freedom

Further Reading

Berman, H. J. (1985). *Law and revolution.* Cambridge, MA: Harvard University Press.

Berman, H. J. (2004). *Law and revolution, II: The impact of the Protestant reformations on the Western legal tradition.* Cambridge, MA: Belknap Press.

Evans, M. D. (1997). *Religious liberty and international law in Europe.* Cambridge, U.K.: Cambridge University Press.

Janis, M. W., & Evans, C. (Eds.). (1999). *Religion and international law.* The Hague, The Netherlands: Martinus Nijhoff.

Laurensen, J. C. (Ed.). (1999). *Religious toleration: "The variety of rites" from Cyrus to Defoe.* New York: St. Martin's.

Lindholm, T., Durham, W. C., Jr., & Tahzib-Lie, B. G. (Eds.). (2004). *Facilitating freedom of religion or belief: A deskbook.* Norwell, MA: Kluwer.

Mullan, D. G. (Ed.). (1998). *Religious pluralism in the West.* Malden, MA: Blackwell.

Reynolds, N. B., & Durham, W. C., Jr. (1996). *Religious liberty in Western thought.* Grand Rapids, MI: Eerdmans.

Stahnke, T., & Martin, J. P. (1998). *Religion and human rights: Basic documents.* New York: Columbia University Center for the Study of Human Rights.

Van der Vyver, J., & Witte, J., Jr. (1996). *Religious human rights in global perspective: Legal perspectives.* The Hague, The Netherlands: Martinus Nijhoff.

Witte, J., Jr., and van der Vyver, J. (1996). *Religious human rights in global perspective: Religious perspectives.* The Hague, The Netherlands: Martinus Nijhoff.

Wood, J. E., Jr. (Ed.). (1989). *Readings on church and state.* Waco, TX: J. M. Dawson Institute of Church-State Studies at Baylor University.

Religion and War

War and religion are universal historical phenomena, occurring in nearly all places and all time periods. It should not be surprising, then, to find that the two have a long, complex, and varied historical relationship—one which is sometimes antagonistic, at other times mutually supportive, and often deeply ambivalent.

Warrior gods played a central role in the pantheons of many early religions as civilizations struggled to subdue the cosmos and, often, their neighbors. The war god Indra ranks among the most prominent Vedic divinities; the warrior god Marduk is the hero of the Babylonian creation epic, Enuma Elish; the war gods Ares and Mars, respectively, populate a host of Greek and Roman myths; and the war god Thor wages battle in ancient Norse mythology. War and religion, for better or worse, have gone hand in hand throughout history.

In many ancient civilizations—including Indo-Aryan, Greek, Egyptian, Babylonian, Hittite, Roman, Aztec, Crow, Norse, and Celtic—war was considered a fact of life and heroes were divinized. Religious epics emerged surrounding the exploits of human (if at times legendary) war heroes such as Arjuna (Hindu), Achilles (Greek), Arthur (Celtic), and Siegfried (Norse). Being a warrior was socially prestigious in cultures such as Indian (where the warrior class, the Kshatriya, ranked high in the Hindu caste system), Crow (where the warrior's raiding activities provided him with access to valued economic goods, most particularly horses), and ancient Babylonian (where male warriors were often rewarded with the society's most desirable female partners). Even great spiritual leaders could, at times, take up the sword and lead armies (for example, Joshua in Judaism and Muhammad in Islam).

But even in cultures that valued war and warriors, the religious attitude toward them was often one of ambivalence. In the Hindu caste system, the priest (*Brahman*) ranked above the warrior. Holy men enjoyed a similarly elevated social standing in Crow and Babylonian cultures. In Greek mythology, war was as often seen as the source of tragedy as it was of glory. According to the anthropologist C. Scott Littleton, "The role of the warrior...was steeped in paradoxes. He was at once at the apex of the social order and a potential threat to that order. Indeed, the contradiction here, which is reflected throughout Indo-European religious beliefs, is inherent in the profession of arms: it involves a social institution dedicated to the destruction of society" (Littleton 1987, 345).

The histories of many of the major world religious traditions evidence a continuing struggle to come to grips with this paradox. In the process, the phenomenon of war has come to play a major role in defining, distinguishing and, at times, dividing particular religions, while the phenomenon of religion has come to give meaning and inspiration to war.

Judaism: Debating the Warrior Ethic

Judaism was founded in the ancient Middle East where warfare was the norm. The earliest Jewish texts, which probably stem from the mid-to-late second millennium BCE, reflect this violent reality. In Genesis, Yahweh (the ancient Hebrew term for god) is said to have told Abraham: "Know this for certain, that your descendants will be aliens living in a land

Hans Memling, *The Archangel Michael* (c. 1479). Oil on wood. As the "field commander" of God's Army, Michael figures prominently in the book of Revelation fighting against Satan. Wallace Collection, London.

that is not theirs; they will be slaves, and will be held in oppression there for four hundred years. But I will punish that nation" (Genesis 15:13–24). Yahweh promises the Jews the lands of "the Kenites, Kenizzites, Kadmonites, Hittites, Perizzites, Rephaim, Amorites, Cannanites, Gigrashites, Hivites, and Jebusites" (Genesis 15:19–21). Much of early Jewish history consists of the ensuing, often exceedingly bloody, battles between the Jews and these various peoples. The book of Joshua in the Hebrew Bible records the story of the conquest of Canaan in which, at God's bidding, the Israelites burn entire enemy cities to the ground, slaughtering all inhabitants—men, women, and children alike. As the biblical scholar Millard Lind writes, "Yahweh is a God of war.... Violent political power is thus a central issue in Israel's experience of Yahweh" (Lind 1980, 24).

Yet existing side-by-side with these violent episodes is a deep-seated Jewish reluctance to embrace the warrior life. Speaking of Abraham, Moses, and other seminal figures in the history of Judaism, the nineteenth century German scholar Julius Wellhausen writes, "It is remarkable that the heroes of Israel...show so little taste for war" (Lind 1980, 34). The Jewish hero of the Exodus account, Moses, does not, with a warrior might, destroy the Egyptian army as it pursues the Jews; Yahweh drowns the army with Moses as a bystander. Powerful Jewish kings like David and Solomon are as often chided for hubris as lauded for their might. While Jewish history speaks of nationhood, land, and national destiny, its prophets more often speak of peace: "They shall beat their swords into mattocks and their spears into pruning-knives; nation shall not lift sword against nation nor ever again be trained for war" (Isaiah 2:4).

These two rival attitudes toward war emerge repeatedly in Jewish history. The Maccabean revolt in the middle of the second century BCE pitted Jewish rebels against their Greek oppressors. When the Greeks, led by Antiochus Epiphanes, attempted to stamp out Judaism by forbidding all Jewish practices and desecrating the temple in Jerusalem, the Jews, led by the Maccabaeus family, rebelled, eventually recapturing Jerusalem and reconsecrating the temple (an event celebrated in the Jewish holiday Hanukkah). While the rebellion was doubtlessly violent in nature—some scholars see it as an early instance of successful guerilla warfare—a number of Jewish historians emphasize the fact that it was a group of nonviolent Jerusalem Jews who brought the ultimate victory. By peaceably withdrawing into the wilderness in response to the Greek actions and taking their tax "dollars" with them, these Jews, it is argued, forced the Greeks to relent and to accept Jewish worship practices in Jerusalem. Jewish scholars also point to the fact that the passage from Zechariah that is traditionally read on the Sabbath of Hannukah declares: "Not by might and not by power but by my spirit, saith the Lord of the Hosts" (Ferguson 1978, 86).

The ambivalence in Judaism concerning participation in warfare and the use of violence continues to this day in the emotional and often divisive Jewish debate over the proper response by the state of Israel to challenges posed by Palestinians and their fight for statehood.

Christianity: Pacifism, Crusades, and Just Wars

The religious ambivalence toward warfare is perhaps nowhere more graphically evidenced than in the history of Christianity, as adherents of the religion have, at different times (and sometimes simultaneously), embraced pacifism, "holy" crusades, and "just" wars (that is, a war limited by strict moral principles).

For the first three centuries following the crucifixion of Christ (c. 30 CE), the Christian church was almost exclusively nonviolent. Founding its actions upon the teachings of Jesus to love the enemy and Jesus' refusal to take up arms in order to fight the Romans or even to prevent his own arrest and execution, the early church opposed killing and warfare. Whereas the Roman gods were seen as advocates of the Roman people in their battles against foreign foes, the influential Christian Bishop Clement of Alexandria (d. c. 215) writes in the second century, "Divinity now pervades all humankind equally...deifying humanity" (Pagels 1988, 39).

Christianity's minority status within the powerful Roman Empire—until 312 CE, Christians constituted no more than 10 percent of the population of the Empire and were periodically subjected to savage persecution at the hands of the state—provided an additional (and, some scholars say, more practical and hence decisive) reason for the Christian rejection of war. As the religious scholar Elaine Pagels (1988, 39) writes: "Christians had discovered a terrible secret: the powers behind the Roman magistrates are not gods...but demons, active evil forces bent upon corrupting and destroying human beings." The state meant death to Christians. As such, Christian complicity in the state, and in the institution of war, was largely rejected and pacifism was embraced. A minority of Christians—including members of most monastic orders, as well as denominations such as the Mennonites—continue to this day to reject all wars.

In 312, Constantine (c. 280–337 CE) became the first Christian leader of the Roman Empire and quickly legalized the practice of Christianity. In 381, Emperor Theodosius (c. 346–395 CE) made Christianity the state religion of the Empire, forbidding the worship of the Roman gods entirely. As Christians for the first time began to ascend to positions of political power, the religion began to consider anew the question of bearing arms. Aurelius Augustine (354–430 CE), the Catholic bishop of the city of Hippo in North Africa who is later canonized as St. Augustine, produced one of the most influential works in the history of Christianity, *City of God*, in which he argued that the state was an instrument provided by a loving God to help keep human sinfulness in check until Christ's return.

While a kingdom of true and eternal peace will ultimately be established by God, in the interim "the natural order which seeks the peace of mankind ordains that the monarch should have the power of undertaking war if he thinks it advisable, and that the soldiers should perform their military duties in behalf of the peace and safety of the community" (Christopher 1994, 40). Augustine defines "just wars" as those which "avenge injuries...punish wrongs...or restore what has been unjustly taken" (Christopher

1994, 40). Augustine himself would come to advocate Christians participating as both soldiers and military commanders in wars to fend off the attackers of the Roman Empire, even though he acknowledged that grave injustices would inevitably be committed.

The notion of war as an instrument of the Christian God would reach its logical, if bloody, conclusion in the crusades. The crusades were a series of Christian military expeditions prompted by papal declarations and aimed, at least initially, at the recovery of the Holy Land from Muslim control. Initiated by Pope Urban II (c. 1035–1099) at the Council of Clermont in 1095 and extending for several centuries, the crusades promised participants the remission of their sins if they took up the cross and defended the faith. (The Latin word for cross, *crux*, is the root of the word "crusade.") Tens of thousands of European Christians answered the call. Eventually this "defense" of the faith included attacks not only upon Muslims but upon all alleged enemies of the church, including European Jews and Christian heretics, with perhaps hundreds of thousands of people being brutally slaughtered in the name of Christ. One crusader reports, "Wonderful sights: piles of heads, hands, and feet. It was a just and splendid judgment of God that this place should be filled with the blood of unbelievers" (Baran 1998, 1).

With the end of the crusades, placed variously by scholars between the fourteenth and sixteenth centuries, came the rise of the Christian just-war tradition. Over the course of several centuries, so-called Scholastic authors such as Francisco Suarez (1548–1617) and Hugo Grotius (1583–1645) built upon the foundation established by Augustine and Thomas Aquinas (1225–1274) to develop a set of moral principles which, while allowing Christian warfare, attempted to place strict limits on its conduct—limits which presumably would prevent the barbaric excesses of the crusades. These principles, which would eventually serve as an important impetus for the founding of international law, consist of the *jus ad bellum*— rules which establish the circumstances under which Christians may enter war—and the *jus in bello*—rules covering the ethical conduct of war once it has been initiated. Central to the *jus in bello*, for instance, is the principle of discrimination, which holds that Christians may kill even noncombatants as long as the deaths are unintentional: "The death of the innocent must not besought for its own sake, but it is an incidental consequence; hence it is not considered as voluntarily inflicted but simply allowed..." (Suarez 1944, 847–848).

In the twenty-first century, although Christians continue to debate various historical attitudes toward warfare, the just-war perspective has come to gain the support of the vast majority of individual Christians and Christian institutions, with *jus ad bellum* criteria such as "just cause" and "last resort" emerging as central aspects of public debate on initiating war.

Islam: War and Tolerance

Islam is often depicted as a religion that not only allows for but embraces warfare. In reality, the history of the religion is complex and surprisingly pluralistic with regard to issues of violence.

The Qur'an at times is clear in its support of the institution of war: "Warfare is ordained for you, though it is hateful to you; but it may happen that you hate a thing which is good for you, and it may happen that you love a thing which is bad for you" (Qur'an 2:216). Such passages combine in Islam with an important historical fact about the prophet Muhammad (571–632 CE): "Muhammad, it will be recalled, was not only a prophet and a teacher, like the founders of other religions; he was also the head of a polity and a community, a ruler and a soldier. Hence his struggle involved the state and its armed forces" (Lewis 1990, 49). In one of the most famous episodes in the founding of Islam, Muhammad flees his native city of Mecca in 622 CE, ridiculed and threatened by the town leaders for his religious teachings. Eight years later, he returns as a conqueror, leading an army of ten thousand into Mecca and converting the city in the process. As John Kelsay (1993, 45), a professor of religion at Florida State University, writes, "At least with respect to the example of Muhammad, then, it was possible to speak of the use of lethal force which

186 · RELIGION AND BELIEF SYSTEMS IN WORLD HISTORY

There will be peace on Earth when there is peace among the world religions.
• Hans Küng (b. 1928)

was right, in the sense of divinely sanctioned —even divinely commanded."

The Abbasid caliphate during the classical period of Islamic civilization (c. 750–1258 CE) established an imperial state based in Baghdad and, employing the principles of divinely sanctioned war, ruled an empire extending from Egypt to Spain. During the Christian crusades, Muslim forces enjoyed a series of decisive victories over the crusaders, keeping much of the Middle East in Muslim control. Thus, although pacifism is found in some forms of Sufism (Islamic mysticism), mainstream Islam historically accepts warfare as a God-given instrument.

This does not mean, though, that war is accepted in Islam as a normal and acceptable condition. Far more of the Qur'an speaks of peace than of war: "The good deed and the evil deed are not alike. Repel the evil deed with one that is better. Then lo! He between whom and thee there was enmity will become a bosom friend" (41:34). Even the concept most often associated with the Islamic support of violence, jihad, literally translates from the Arabic as "striving" and not, as it is often translated, as "holy war." In traditional Islamic thought, the "greater jihad" represents the striving of Muslims to overcome their own tendencies toward selfishness, hatred, and hubris; it does not mandate the slaughtering of infidels. Muhammad's triumphant return to Mecca is recast accordingly in some Islamic historical sources. In 630 CE, when Muhammad enters the city with his huge army, he asks the Meccan nobles who had threatened his life eight years earlier, "What am I to do with you?" Their leader, Abu Sufyan, replies: "The best." With that, Muhammad frees all his rivals, in the process converting them to Islam by his generosity. In this strain of Islam, Muhammad rules by justice not fear, war is never initiated by Muslims, but fought defensively and reluctantly, and tolerance is among the highest values.

This moderate vision of Islam has guided much of the religion historically. When the Moors (a Spanish term for Muslim) crossed the Mediterranean to Gibraltar in 711 CE and conquered Spain, they ushered in a seven-hundred-year-long period not of oppression but of cultural flourishing, as Muslim art, architecture,

and ideas were peaceably integrated with those of the indigenous culture. The longest continually existing Christian community in the world exists not in Greece, Italy, or England; it is a Coptic Christian community in Egypt, a land dominated by Islam since 700 CE.

Islam's history with regard to war is thus more varied than many popular contemporary depictions in the West would suggest.

Hinduism: From Kshatriya to Ahimsa

War would seem to hold an unquestioned position of acceptance in Hinduism. The structure of the caste system suggests as much, with the Kshatriya (warrior) constituting one of the four main social classes. While classical Hinduism traditionally holds that all of creation is infused with a spark of the divine and killing is thus not to be taken lightly, the warrior's dharma (duty) to fight is consistently judged to outweigh this consideration. The *Mahabharata*, one of the greatest epic poems in all of world religious literature, examines the dilemma faced by the Kshatriya and concludes: "Since those evil actions belong to the duties of your profession, the penalty of evil karma will not attach to you" (Ferguson 1978, 29). In fact, the entire *Mahabharata* tells the tale of a great multigenerational war between members of the Bharata clan. In its most beloved segment, the *Bhagavad Gita*, the warrior Arjuna debates whether to fulfill his dharma to fight or his dharma to protect life, since the two seem to be incompatible; he is told by Krishna, an avatar of the great god Vishnu, quite directly: "Fight, O Bharata!"

Not surprisingly, then, war is common in the history of Hinduism. Candragupta and his son Samudragupta, two soldier-monarchs and unapologetic conquerors, established the Gupta Empire (320–484 CE), often viewed as the golden age of Hinduism. In the early eleventh century, when the Muslim Mahmud of Ghazna (971–1030 CE) invaded India, Hindus fought fiercely to defend the temple with, according to some accounts, fifty thousand men dying in a single battle. The Rajputs—calling themselves the "sword arm of Hindustan" and the protectors of the Brahmans —emerged in the ninth century and have fought foreign challengers to Hinduism ever since.

There is a counterstrain in Hinduism, though, found in the Upanishads and other sacred texts. In the Chandogya Upanishad, ahimsa (nonharmfulness or nonviolence) is seen as a foundational Hindu value, equal in importance to austerity, almsgiving, uprightness, and trustfulness. Mohandas Gandhi (1869–1948), the great spiritual and political leader of twentieth-century India, was the most influential advocate of ahimsa. In his teachings, Gandhi attempted to explain classical Hindu works that had for centuries been seen to support the warrior life as in fact embodiments of the principle of nonviolence. The *Mahabharata*, Gandhi argues, ends by depicting not the glory but the futility of war; Krishna in the *Bhagavad Gita* tells Arjuna to fight, but only as a means of illustrating to Arjuna the essential incompatibility of violent acts and the spiritual obligation to remain unattached to the "fruits of action." Gandhi emerges with an approach to combating evil, which is both grounded in Hinduism and entirely nonviolent. As he writes, "I seek to blunt the edge of the tyrant's sword, not by putting up against it a sharper-edged weapon, but by disappointing his expectation that I would be offering physical resistance" (Ferguson 1978, 38).

Hence, while Hinduism traditionally preserves a privileged place for the warrior, in recent decades a revisionist interpretation of Hinduism, founded on the rejection of war and violence suggested by Gandhi and others, has become highly influential.

Buddhism: From No Harm to the Warrior Ethic

Buddhism may well be the major religious tradition that has most consistently rejected warfare, but the history of even this religion is far from uniform.

The first of the Five Precepts of Buddhism, incumbent on monks and laity alike, is to not take life nor be a party to its taking. This prohibition applies equally to war, murder, and the killing of animals for food or ritual sacrifice. According to the *Dhammapada*, "Everyone is afraid of violence; everyone likes life. If one compares oneself with others one would never take life or be involved in the taking of life" (Ferguson 1978, 47). The Buddha, Siddhartha Gautama (c. 566–c. 486 BCE), preached and lived by a code that mandated the causing of no harm, and he attracted many adherents to pacifism, both in his lifetime and beyond. The Maurya emperor Asoka (c. 270–232 BCE) was a military imperialist who, upon converting to Buddhism, established a welfare state, prohibiting all killing. The pervasive effect of the Buddha's teachings with respect to pacifism can be seen in the harsh words of Yuan Tchen (779–831 CE), who chastises Buddhists for using their religion as an excuse for shirking military duty.

Yet the historical Buddha, born into the Hindu Kshatriya caste, is also regularly depicted as employing martial analogies, even after his awakening to Buddha status. *The Sutra of 42 Sections* records: "A man practicing the Way is like a lone man in combat against ten thousand.... [S]ome retreat; some reach battle and die; some are victorious and return to their kingdoms triumphantly" (Sharf 1996, 45). The *Suttanipata* draws a distinction between accidental and intentional killing and, like the principle of discrimination in Christianity, condemns only the latter. In fact, all major strains of Buddhism, including both Theravada and Mahayana, contain important historical instances of support for war. In China during the Tang dynasty (618–907 CE), Buddhist monks were accorded military honors for their actions and, in 619, five thousand of them led a violent uprising that resulted in one monk proclaiming himself emperor with the title of "Mahayana." In Korea, kings historically recruited thousands of Buddhist monks into the military—to fight the Mongols in the fourteenth century, the Japanese in the sixteenth, and the Manchus in the seventeenth.

After Zen Buddhism was introduced to Japan in 1192, it became the religion of the soldiered aristocracy and contributed to the emergence of the Bushido ideal, the way of the Samurai warrior. In the 1930s and 1940s, a series of Zen masters in Japan used the Zen notion that truth lies beyond reason (and that there are thus no absolute moral principles) to excuse and even to support military aggression on behalf of Japanese imperialism, with Daiun Sogaku Harada Roshi (1870–1961) declaring, "The unity of Zen and war... extends to the farthest reaches of the holy war now underway" (Baran 1998, 1).

Thus, Buddhism, like Christianity, begins historically with a rejection of war and comes, over the course of centuries, to accept and even embrace warfare as an aspect of religious duty.

The Relationship Considered

Does war shape religion or does religion shape war? As the above examples indicate, the answer is almost surely both. Religious beliefs are often adopted and adapted to support political enterprises of various sorts, and warfare is a prominent instance of the political use of religion. But historically, religions have also used warfare as an instrument for their own advance, initiating wars or prompting others to do so on their behalf. While war remains an accepted part of the mainstream components of all the leading world religious traditions, it continues to raise the question pondered by ancient religions: is war the instrument of society's preservation or the source of its destruction?

Timothy M. RENICK
Georgia State University

See also Religion and Government; Religious Freedom

Further Reading

Augustine. (1984). *City of God*. New York: Penguin Books.

Baran, J. (1998). Zen holy war? *Tricycle, 27,* 53–56.

Christopher, P. (1994). *The ethics of war and peace: An introduction to legal and moral issues*. Englewood Cliffs, NJ: Prentice Hall.

Duncan, R. (Ed.). (1951). *Selected writings of Mahatma Gandhi*. Boston: Beacon Press.

Ferguson, J. (1978). *War and peace in the world's religions*. New York: Oxford University Press.

Good, R. M. (1985). The just war in ancient Israel. *Journal of Biblical Literature, 104*(3), 385–400.

Johnson, J. (1981). *Just war tradition and the restraint of war*. Princeton, NJ: Princeton University Press.

Kelsay, J. (1993). *Islam and war: A study in comparative ethics*. Louisville, KY: Westminster/John Knox Press.

King, W. L. (1993). *Zen and the way of the sword: Arming the Samurai psyche*. New York: Oxford University Press.

Lewis, B. (1990, September). The roots of Muslim rage. *Atlantic Monthly, 266*(3), 47–60.

Littleton, C. S. (1987). War and warriors: Indo-European beliefs and practices. In M. Eliade (Ed.), *The encyclopedia of religion* (15, pp. 344–349). New York: Macmillan Library Reference.

Lind, M. (1980). *Yahweh is a warrior: The theology of warfare in ancient Israel*. Scottdale, PA: Herald Press.

Kulke, H. (1993). *Kings and cults: State formation and legitimation in India and Southeast Asia*. New Delhi, India: Manohar.

Narasimhan, C. V. (1965). *The Mahabharata: An English version based on selected verses*. New York: Columbia University Press.

National Conference of Catholic Bishops. (1983). The challenge of peace: God's promise and our response (the pastoral letter on war and peace). In J. Elshtain (Ed.), *Just war theory* (pp. 77–168). New York: New York University Press.

Olivelle, P. (1996). *The Upanishads*. Oxford, U.K.: Oxford University Press.

Pagels, E. (1988). *Adam, Eve, and the serpent*. New York: Vintage Books.

Pearse, M. (2007). *The gods of war: Is religion the primary cause of violent conflict?* Downers Grove, IL: Inter-Varsity Press.

Popovski, V. Reichberg, G. M. & Turner, N. (Eds.). (2009). *World religions and norms of war*. Tokyo: United Nations University Press.

Riley-Smith, J. (Ed.). (1995). *The Oxford illustrated history of the Crusades*. New York: Oxford University Press.

Sharf, R. (Ed.). (1996). The scripture in forty-two sections. In D. S. Lopez Jr. (Ed.), *Religions in China in practice* (pp. 360–371). Princeton, NJ: Princeton University Press.

Strong, J. S. (1983). *The legend of King Asoka*. Princeton, NJ: Princeton University Press.

Suarez, F. (1944). *Selections from three works of Francisco Suarez*. Oxford, U.K.: Clarendon Press.

Victoria, B. (1997). *Zen at war*. New York: Waetherhill.

Religious Freedom

Religious freedom did not emerge in world history as a widely accepted idea until the modern era. Governments generally mandated religious belief on the assumption that a common religion is essential to social stability. This assumption has not died easily, and still prevails in some areas of the world. Nevertheless, religious freedom has now become an almost universally accepted norm, backed by international law and the constitutions of most nations.

Religious freedom can be defined as the liberty, guaranteed by a state authority to its people, to believe (in matters concerning religion) that which is dictated by conscience, including no belief at all. The concept is relatively new in world history because governments since the earliest times adopted religions as a means of fostering stable and unified societies.

Ancient Societies

In ancient societies there was no differentiation between the religious and the secular. All of life was religious, and state authority generally assumed the role of moral agent and mandated religious belief to further its own ends. Ancient Mesopotamia, Egypt, and Greece were polytheistic cultures in which civil authorities were also considered either priests or gods themselves, and the religious life of subjects was closely regulated. As popular new religions emerged, state machinery frequently adopted these religions as a basis of unity for society. Thus Hinduism in India, Buddhism in Thailand, Shintoism in Japan, Confucianism and Daoism in China, Judaism in Israel, and Islam in the Middle East all influenced law and public policy and still retain today a status as formal or semiformal state religions. In these settings, freedom and religion have not been natural allies. The brave heretic who has pursued religious ideas outside those of official sanctions has frequently been persecuted or even executed.

The Union of Church and State in Medieval Europe

This pattern of persecuting heretics persisted in the early Roman Empire. Under emperors such as Nero, Trajan, Decius, Valerian, and Diocletian, Christians were sometimes executed for violating the mandatory worship requirements of the empire. But Christianity continued to grow, and by the fourth century claimed as much as 10 percent of the Roman population. The persecutions against the Christians ended, however, only when Constantine became the first emperor to become a Christian. He was instrumental in the passage of the Edict of Milan in 313, a document of landmark proportions in the history of religious freedom. It provided "that liberty of worship shall not be denied to any, but that the mind and will of every individual shall be free to manage divine affairs according to his own choice" (Pfeffer 1967, 13). The edict elevated Christianity to a status equal to that of other religions in the empire, although within a decade Constantine altered laws to give legal preference to Christianity. The Roman state built great Christian edifices, instituted Christian holidays, granted exemptions from taxation to Christian clergy, and persecuted adherents of "heathen" religions. The persecuted had become the persecutor. In 380, under Emperor Theodosius,

In an act of defiance, John Endicott, a follower of Roger Williams and passionate supporter of religious freedom in colonial New England, cuts the cross from the King's banner.

Christianity was officially enshrined as the state religion of the empire.

The Christian state became the model for all of Europe during the Middle Ages. The Orthodox Church became the established religion over much of the Eastern Roman Empire, including Greece and Russia; Catholicism prevailed in the West. The goal of the church–state partnership was the glory of God and the salvation of man. Any impediments to this goal were dealt with harshly. Thus by the thirteenth century, Western authorities devised a formal Inquisition by which heretics would be systematically sought out and, if deemed beyond rehabilitation, executed. Between 1231, when the Inquisition was formally instituted by Pope Gregory IX, until 1834, when the Spanish Inquisition was finally abolished, tens of thousands of heretics were burned at the stake because their faith did not match the officially approved Christian doctrines. Religious freedom, obviously, was not part of the medieval vocabulary.

Occasionally there emerged, however, from within the Christian Church, voices in behalf of religious freedom. Tertullian, Justin Martyr, Hilary of Poitiers, Chrysostom, and Augustine, among others, pleaded the cause of toleration and condemned punishment of heresy. In the early third century, for example, the lawyer-cleric Tertullian wrote, "it is a fundamental human right, a privilege of nature, that every man should worship according to his own convictions. One man's religion neither helps nor harms another man" (Pfeffer 1967, 15). In the late fourth century, Augustine similarly defended toleration of unorthodox religious views. Later, however, when members of the Donatist sect engaged in acts of civil disobedience, he apparently changed his view and opined that compulsion was benevolent, "for what is a worse killer of the soul than freedom to err" (Pfeffer 1967, 16). Due to the weighty influence of the brilliant Augustine, one scholar had articulated what has become an accepted estimation of him. Because of Augustine, he wrote, "the Medieval Church was intolerant, was the source and author of persecution, justified and defended the most violent measures which could be taken against those who differed from it" (Pfeffer 1967, 16). Some have said that Augustine's views became the "charter for the Inquisition."

The Crusades

Equally out of step with the spirit of religious freedom were the crusades of the eleventh, twelfth, and thirteenth centuries. The purpose of the seven crusades, initiated by Pope Urban II in 1095, was to recapture the Holy Land that had been lost to the Muslims and to extend the rule of Christianity in the "land of Christ." The motto of the crusades became "Kill the infidels." In carrying out the slaughter of tens of thousands of Muslims, the crusaders availed themselves of the opportunity to root out Jewish and Orthodox infidels as well. The popular Peter of Cluny asked, "Why wait for the infidels in the Holy Land? We have infidels here—the Jews" (Wood 1966, 9). It

A plaque mounted on the wall of a Protestant church in Provence, France, recounts the Protestant fight for religious rights in this mainly Roman Catholic region.

has been estimated that in the First Crusade alone thousands of Jews across Europe were massacred. Pope Innocent III, perhaps the greatest exemplar of militant Christianity, launched the Fourth Crusade in 1202. While en route to the Holy Land, his army of twenty thousand crusaders sacked and destroyed the great Orthodox city of Constantinople, slaughtering thousands of citizens, burning much of the city, and destroying more of the city's great religious treasures than were lost when the Turks later bludgeoned and captured the city in 1453.

Religious Intolerance during the Reformation

The Roman Catholic Inquisition of the fifteenth and sixteenth centuries unleashed fresh attacks against a rising number of Protestants. Protestants in turn persecuted Catholics as well as competing Protestants. Contrary to popular belief, the Protestant Reformation did not usher in a new era of religious freedom. In fact, the rise of Protestantism witnessed a fresh outbreak of religious intolerance. Protestants were vigorous in winning converts from Catholicism, but they were often as vicious in their persecution of Catholic and Protestant heretics as Catholics had been against them. The leading lights of the Reformation, Martin Luther and John Calvin, were never reluctant to exterminate their own adversaries. Luther frequently recommended to the Duke of Saxony the execution of Catholic, Jewish, and Anabaptist heretics. Calvin himself prescribed the execution of numerous heretics, including the Unitarian Michael Servetus at Geneva in 1553. Calvin's contemporary and Protestant scholar Sebastian Costello probably had it right when he wrote of Calvin, "If Calvin ever wrote anything in favor of religious liberty, it was a typographical error" (Wood 1966, 11).

The spread of new religious ideas across Europe during the Reformation led to a series of religious wars that was finally curtailed only by the Peace of Westphalia settlement of 1648. By then, it was apparent to many that religious tolerance was essential, lest everyone in Europe die of heresy. A healthy spirit of tolerance appeared in many dissenting groups, most notably the Socinians, Anabaptists, Diggers, Quakers, Politiques, and Baptists. These groups, all of whom experienced acute degrees of religious intolerance, were far apart on theological matters but united in their advocacy of religious freedom.

The growth of religious tolerance was not merely a matter of expediency, however. Seminal thinkers such as Hugo Grotius, Henry Parker, Thomas Hobbes, John Locke, Jean-Jacques Rousseau, Sidney Algernon, John Milton, Erasmus, Voltaire, Thomas More, and Dirck Coornhert all protested the mania of the times—"hereticide"—and took up their pens to propose new political and theological bases for religious freedom. Locke in particular was instrumental in proposing the notion of the secular state, which removed jurisdiction over religious matters from civil authority, thereby protecting each

This drawing depicts the massacre of Mormons at their camp at Haughn's Mill, Illinois, in 1838. The Mormons were subjected to nearly seventy years of government-backed oppression in the 1800s.

individual from state-mandated religious conformity. He articulated a theory of natural rights that placed fundamental rights of life, liberty (including religious freedom), and property beyond the reach of government.

Religious Freedom in America and Elsewhere

These ideas took root as nowhere else in America. Roger Williams, who founded the colony of Rhode Island, fought an ideological war against theocratic traditionalists in Puritan New England. Williams set up a secular state and welcomed to his colony settlers of every religious persuasion, requiring only that they conform to standards of good citizenship. His policies led Puritans and others to refer to Rhode Island as "that sewer," but his ideas eventually found their way into the U.S. Constitution in the late eighteenth century.

The new Constitution and its Bill of Rights guaranteed religious freedom and ensured it with an establishment clause that prevents government from establishing any religion or even from preferring some religions over others. The United States was the first nation in human history to formally adopt the principle of the separation of church and state as a fundamental element of its public philosophy. It was a noble experiment in the founding era and remains so today. The experiment was undertaken by the framers in the hope that it would enable America to escape the persecutions and religious wars that had characterized the Christian West for almost two millennia. Due to the success of this formula in America, other nations have since adopted the idea of church-state separation as a guarantor of religious freedom, and today, approximately one-half of the nations of the world make formal guarantees of church-state separation in their constitutions.

Internationalization of Religious Freedom

The twentieth century witnessed unprecedented progress toward the internationalization of religious freedom. Of the three major international documents that universalized the principle of religious freedom in the twentieth century, by far the most central is the Universal Declaration of Human Rights, passed by the United Nations in 1948. This landmark document declares that "Everyone has the right to freedom of thought, conscience and religion; this right includes freedom to change his religion or belief, and freedom, either alone or in community with others and in public or private, to manifest his religion or belief in teaching, practice, worship and observance" (Claude and Weston 1992, 421).

The declaration embraces modernity's political principle that one of human government's main roles is to protect people's religious choices, not to mandate religious conformity. It took centuries, even millennia, of religious wars and government-perpetrated religious persecution for the majority of modern nation-states to come to this position, but the principle is now widely accepted, especially in the West, and its near universal recognition in the 1948 declaration is undoubtedly a human milestone.

Whereas the declaration imposed a *moral* obligation upon all signatory nations, later documents went further in creating a *legal* obligation to comply with its broad principles. The International Covenant on Civil and Political Rights (1966), ratified already by approximately 150 nations, prohibits religious discrimination "without distinction of any kind, such as race, colour, sex, language, political or other opinion, national or social origin, property, birth or other status" (Claude and Weston 1992, 432). Moreover, the 1966 covenant provides a broad definition of religion that encompasses both theistic and nontheistic religions as well as rare and virtually unknown faiths. The covenant is especially important because its provisions are mandatory for the states that have ratified it.

Finally, the United Nations Declaration on the Elimination of All Forms of Intolerance and of Discrimination Based on Religious Belief, enacted in 1981, is a fundamentally important document protecting religious rights. The declaration includes the most comprehensive list of rights to freedom of thought, conscience, and religion enumerated in any international instrument.

Human civilization has achieved much over the last three thousand years in making religious freedom a fundamental human right. Much remains to be done, however, to make religious freedom a reality for all peoples of the world. There is no more important project to be undertaken by the human community now and in the future.

Derek H. DAVIS
University of Mary Hardin-Baylor

See also Religion and Government; Religion and War

Further Reading

Bainton, R. (1951). *The travail of religious liberty.* New York: Harper & Brothers.

Bates, M. S. (1945). *Religious liberty: An inquiry.* New York: International Missionary Council.

Boyle, K., & Sheen, J. (Eds.). (1997). *Freedom of religion and belief.* New York: Routledge.

Claude, R. P., & Weston, B. H. (1992). *Human rights in the world community* (2nd ed.). Philadelphia: University of Pennsylvania Press.

Doerries, H. (1960). *Constantine and religious liberty* (R. H. Bainton, Trans.). New Haven, CT: Yale University Press.

Fergeson, M. L. (1966). *The church-state problem and the American principle of separation.* Waco, TX: Baylor University Press.

Gavin, F. (1938). *Seven centuries of the problem of church and state.* Princeton, NJ: Princeton University Press.

Kamen, H. (1967). *The rise of toleration.* New York: McGraw Hill.

Kramnick, I., & Moore, L. R. (1996). *The godless Constitution: The case against religious correctness.* New York: Norton.

McNeil, J. (Ed.). (1950). *John Calvin on God and political duty.* New York: Liberal Arts Press.

Oakley, F. (1979). *The Western church in the later Middle Ages.* Ithaca, NY: Cornell University Press.

Pfeffer, L. (1967). *Church, state, and freedom* (2nd ed.). Boston: Beacon Press.

Skinner, Q. (1978). *The foundations of modern political thought.* New York: Cambridge University Press.

Solt, L. F. (1990). *Church and state in early modern England 1509–1640.* New York: Oxford University Press.

Stokes, A. P. (1950). *Church and state in the United States: Historical development and contemporary problems of religious freedom under the Constitution.* New York: Harper & Brothers.

Tierney, B. (1982). *Religion, law, and the growth of constitutional thought, 1150–1650.* Cambridge: Cambridge University Press.

Tracy, J. D. (Ed.). (1986). *Luther and the modern state in Germany.* Kirksville, MO: Sixteenth Century Journal Publishers.

Treece, H. (1994). *The Crusades.* New York: Barnes & Noble Books.

Wardman, A. (1982). *Religion and statecraft among the Romans.* Baltimore: Johns Hopkins University Press.

Wood, J. E., Jr. (1966). Religion and freedom. *Journal of Church and State, 8*(1), 5–13.

Wood, J. E., Jr., Thompson, E. B., & Miller, R. T. (1958). *Church and state in scripture, history, and constitutional law.* Waco, TX: Baylor University Press.

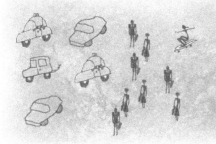

Religious Fundamentalism

Lexicographers in the 1920s narrowly defined fundamentalism to describe movements in American Protestant denominations that were devoted to biblical literalism. The term has been widely applied in a broader sense (often contentiously) to other religious movements or sects worldwide. Some scholars see the term as stigmatizing or unfairly lumping groups together, while others recognize its value as a "genus" that can foster comparative analyses among groups it comprises.

Religious fundamentalism, often confused with conservatism or traditionalism, is a name for a movement in any religion that retrieves "fundamental" elements of that religion and projects them into new formulations in reaction to challenges from modernity, however that is defined. This reaction may lead to protective withdrawal by groups in some cases, at least in early stages. In practice, however, leaders of such movements attract followers to engage in militant action against whatever it is they regard as a profanation or whatever stands in the way of their battles for their God. Since fundamentalisms appear in Protestant Christianity, Judaism, Hinduism, and Islam, they can be seen as both local and global assaults on both secular and settled religious orders, be they conservative or liberal.

Problems with the Word "Fundamentalism"

Scholars agree that the first use of the term occurred in American Protestantism early in the twentieth century. Some question, therefore, whether the word might fairly, and without causing confusion, be used to characterize forces in other religions. On the side of the critics are factors such as these: it seems unfair and perhaps imperial to borrow from an American domestic movement a term to impose on other religious movements that draw on vastly different sources. Second, the term is often seen as pejorative, stigmatizing. In addition to that, it does not always have a cognate term in the languages identified with other religions. Fourth, it may license comparisons that unfairly lump together disparate movements that lose their identity when so classified.

Over against these, defenders of the usage recognize that the term is simply established, in textbooks and media, in statecraft and scholarship, and argue that efforts are better aimed at clarifying the term than trying to abolish it. In addition, they point out that similar categories of words travel from language to language, situation to situation. Words like colonialism, revolution, conservatism, nationalism, and others are all "born" somewhere in the West and travel to other settings and languages. Third, fundamentalism is a genus, and scholars or communicators can clarify issues by pointing to species: the Islamic fundamentalism of the Wahhabi movement might have formal congruence with the Jewish fundamentalism of Gush Emunim or a party of Protestants in Northern Ireland, but the content of their claims differs vastly. Finally, no other term has come forward to foster comparative analysis. Thus "Islamist" works only for Islamic movements. And comparisons are valuable, since only by isolating them do certain features stand out.

Features of the Fundamentalist Movements

The word "fundamentalism," in religious contexts at least, is not to be found in any dictionaries published before the 1920s. When Baptist Protestants in the United States during intradenominational struggles in the early 1920s coined it, and when Presbyterians took it up, lexicographers had to take note of it and defined it as a Protestant movement devoted to biblical literalism. What they may not have noticed is that in the same decades such movements were developing in India in what have become major political parties, or in Egypt under the Muslim Brotherhood, from which fundamentalisms spread to Saudi Arabia, Iran, and the larger Islamic world.

World historians have it as their mission to account for the long record of movements, and ask about the distant origins of fundamentalism. But students of the movements will find that they rose as reactions to modernity, again "however defined." Definitions may, for instance, take into account critical assaults on sacred canons, such as the Bible or the Qur'an. When conservatives perceive these as assaults from within their religious camp, they feel they must react and respond. Thus Muslim fundamentalists from the 1920s to the 1990s almost always directed their fire to what they perceived, not always inaccurately, to be corrupt and repressive but only nominally Muslim governments. American Protestant fundamentalists did not have the old enemy of Protestantism, Catholicism, as an object of attack so much as rival groups that were religiously "closer to home." They attacked their fellow Presbyterians or Baptists for treason to their own cause. The critical movements that inspired the responses developed just before the twentieth century or early in it, so one could not have located and defined fundamentalism without this modern assault.

Just as often, the reactive response may be against perceived threats to one's domain. Thus "Westerners" as "infidels" were seen to be subverting Iran in the 1970s, thus evoking purifying countermovements by the followers of the Shi'a Ayatollah Khomeini.

Fundamentalists in the United States felt called to oppose liberal Protestants allied with secular humanists and others who were critical of cherished practices such as issuing prayers in public schools while these critics provided theological justifications for disapproving moral expressions, for example, the legalizing of abortions. In Israel, if there seemed to be even a trace of conciliation by peace-seeking governmental administrations, movements like Gush Emunim (Bloc of the Faithful) organized, demonstrated, and built not-yet-approved settlements on the West Bank.

To pursue their aggressive missions in the name of God, fundamentalist movements must build at least figurative boundaries around their movements. They may not keep outsiders or compromisers at a physical distance, as sectarians were able to do before the rise of mass media, mass higher education, and global commerce. But they can develop their own media of communication, their own separatist institutions, their own sets of stigmas with which to label the moderates or other deviators. In media especially, their difference from conservatives or traditionalists is most apparent: they embrace the very modern instruments of communication—tapes, videos, radios, films, the Internet—that were agents of assaults against them. They fight modernity with modern technology.

Their spiritual weapons need ammunition. They all find it in shared sacred texts, usually from centuries before, from times that they perceive to have been perfect or that offered prototypes for living in a perfected world. From these they select the elements that will most help them fight off modernity; these become "the fundamentals." They need strategies, which can range all the way from attempts at boycotting or demonstrating, from efforts at amending constitutions to revolution and warfare—and, in the end, in some cases, terrorism in the name of God. With these self-confident moves, which they experience or claim to be God-guided, they are certain about where history is going, however long it takes.

Fundamentalisms have to be efficient; what are called "free riders" and others who are only half-committed are unwelcome. Participants have to be ready for total sacrifice of self. So they will pursue most zealously the group members they perceive as compromisers, people who should know better but who are too ready to barter too much away. Thus an American Protestant fundamentalist chronicler named the evangelist Billy Graham the most dangerous American of the last century—because, he claimed, Graham knew better than to appear on platforms with others who do not share all details of fundamentalist faith.

Finally, fundamentalists need all-or-nothing ideologies. Scholars speak of these as "Manichaean," after a dualistic religious movement: dark opposes light, with no shadows between them; it is God versus Satan, Christ versus Antichrist, Allah versus the infidels. There is no room for ambiguity or compromise in the minds of individuals or in the approach of the group as a whole.

Still problematic to the student of world history is the claim that since the movements developed in reaction to modernity, including the experience of religious pluralism and the often accompanying tendency to relativize "truth," is it not true that many religious movements had to fight off their own "modernities" long ago? Thus New England Puritans abhorred the very idea of "innovation," and promoted the old ways. If this is the case, would not one have to begin the story of any modern religious fundamentalism by looking at precedents and antecedents through history? Thus Hindus and Muslims have had to fight off modernisms in many generations. Protestant fundamentalists bear some resemblances to Anabaptist or sectarian movements of the sixteenth and seventeenth centuries. So what is new?

The Place of Fundamentalisms

American Protestant fundamentalism, for one instance, fights its battles in the context of a republic where political means are accessible. Resorting to violence is extremely rare. Exceptions such as the bombing of abortion clinics by radical fundamentalists are criticized by mainstream fundamentalists, who find their movements set back by such violence. They may express resentment against a modern world that they believe is depriving them of their rightful place. After that, their energies go into political organization, attempting to persuade voters, to gain power with holders of office, to employ mass media to make their case.

In the United States it is hard to remain a "pure" fundamentalist. To gain anything in a republic a movement must enter into coalitions, make alliances, swallow some principle for a common cause. Or one may turn to more moderate movements that are religiously satisfying in respect to message though less attractive in their cultural roles. Fundamentalists have been in the public eye since the Scopes trial, a battle over evolution in public schools in 1925. Many people on all sides have been nettled, unsettled, angered, frightened lest their cause be defeated, but they have not had to fear guns.

In Israel one of the very rare fundamentalist movements was Gush Emunim. It was a very modern force, organized under charismatic rabbis who agitated in America and in Israel especially against Israeli leaders who even entertained the idea of coming to terms with the Palestinians. Many in this "Bloc of the Faithful" were offspring of barely observant Jews who in their new turn "went all the way" into and beyond Orthodoxy. Members make claims that they are relying on ancient sacred texts in which the land of Israel was given, with stipulated and precise boundaries, to the people of Israel, the Jews. They find support from and kinship with American Protestant fundamentalists and their slightly more moderate kin who read biblical passages "fundamentalistically" in order to certify and sustain their support of Israel.

In India, the Rashtriya Swayamsevak Sangh (RSS) organized what many Hindus call a cultural, not a religious institution. Maharashtrian Brahmans developed it within Hinduism and it became a base for militant opposition to equally militant Muslims. The two hard-line groups fought over sites that were holy to both. The RSS is an ideology of the Hindu nation. Keshav Baliram Hedgewar, founder of the movement, now a party, wanted to purge India of non-Hindu influences. It is highly organized in order to stimulate emotional response to Hindu appeals and to stand off the Muslims. Many Indians welcome talk of a Hindu nation, but memories of the assassination of Mohandas Gandhi by RSS people makes them uneasy. And the RSS did teach people to use Western instruments, including weaponry. The RSS literature suggests a sense of embattledness, but the leaders have taught ordinary members to take out their rage on Muslims, who crowd what they think of as uniquely Hindu holy places.

The Muslim Brotherhood was founded in Egypt under the leadership of Hasan al-Banna' (1906–1949), a moralist who was repulsed by moral and spiritual corruption in Egypt and wanted to use the resources of Islam to counter it. The Brotherhood organized schools and hospitals, and became a very vocal critic of semisecular or nominally Muslim governments there. Most influential in the Brotherhood was Sayyid Qutb (1906–1966), a former secularist who turned to be a zealous Sunni Muslim leader. He abhorred what he saw in the United States, which looked corrupt, sensual, immoral, and godless. Qutb was executed by the Egyptian government for his subversion, but his version of Wahhabi Islam thrived, especially in Saudi Arabia. It is out of this tradition that the al-Qaeda movement emerged.

Best known to the West has been the Iranian revolution of 1979. It serves as a model of how fundamentalist movements make their way. The United States–backed Shah of Iran presided over a corrupt regime. As population grew and needed resources were not available to all but the upper classes, resentment developed among young urban males. So did aspiration and hope. After the shah fell, the exiled Ayatollah Khomeini came back from Paris to reoccupy the land that his followers felt had been immorally taken over from them. Soon the shah had to flee, the Khomeini faction grew in power and threat, the United States retreated, and a new pattern of militant, revolutionary unrest followed. Whether they are called fundamentalist or not, movements like the RSS and the Muslim Brotherhood illustrate how the forces develop.

They begin as conservative or traditionalist complexes. They are oppressed (not all fundamentalists are literally poor, though many are desperately so). Their enemy is seen as a corrupt betrayer of the tradition they believe is theirs. No matter what the world thinks, they must act. Allah will bless them now or, more likely, in eternity. And they will have made a contribution to purifying and ennobling an often corrupt and repressive regime. Something similar goes on in fundamentalist movements elsewhere, and in different religions.

As for the future, militant fundamentalisms are likely to continue to create upheavals of a sort unanticipated at the end of the Cold War. They resort to terrorism or destabilize regimes. At the same time, others run their course and settle for somewhat moderated expressions. In almost every major religious complex—Christian, Muslim, Jewish, Hindu, and the like—nonviolent fundamentalists will seek to make their way through efforts to convert others, to out-vote them, or to influence public policy through means and toward ends that they find satisfying. And "modernism" in its many forms, including with its manifestations of pluralism and relativism will remain the enemy.

Martin E. MARTY
University of Chicago, Emeritus

See also Manichaeism; Pentecostalism

Further Reading

Armstrong, K. (2000). *The battle for God.* New York: Knopf.

Antoun, R. T., & Hegland, M. E. (Eds.). (1987). *Religious resurgence: Contemporary cases in Islam, Christianity, and Judaism.* Syracuse, NY: Syracuse University Press.

Bjorkman, J. W. (Ed.). (1986). *Fundamentalism, revivalists, and violence in South Asia.* Riverdale, MD: Riverdale Company.

Caplan, L. (Ed.). (1984). *Studies in religious fundamentalism.* Albany: State University of New York Press.

Dollar, G. W. (1973). *A history of fundamentalism in America.* Greenville, SC: Bob Jones University Press.

Falwell, J. (Ed.). (1981). *The fundamentalist phenomenon: The resurgence of conservative Christianity.* New York: Doubleday.

Hodgson, M. (1979). *The venture of Islam: Conscience and history in a world civilization.* Chicago: University of Chicago Press.

Juergensmeyer, M. (2000). *Terror in the mind of God: The global rise of religious violence.* Berkeley: University of California Press.

Kepel, G. (1994). *The revenge of God.* Oxford, U.K.: Blackwell.

Lawrence, B. B. (1989). *Defenders of God: The fundamentalist revolt against the modern age.* San Francisco: Harper & Row.

Lustig, I. S. (1989). *For the land and the Lord: Jewish fundamentalism in Israeli.* New York: Council on Foreign Relations.

Marsden, G. M. (1980). *Fundamentalism and American culture: The shaping of twentieth-century evangelicalism, 1870–1925.* New York: Oxford University Press.

Marty, M. E., & Appleby, R. S. (Eds.). (1991). *Fundamentalisms observed.* Chicago: University of Chicago Press.

Marty, M. E., & Appleby, R. S. (Eds.). (1993). *Fundamentalisms and society.* Chicago: University of Chicago Press.

Marty, M. E., & Appleby, R. S. (Eds.). (1993). *Fundamentalisms and the state.* Chicago: University of Chicago Press.

Marty, M. E., & Appleby, R. S. (Eds.). (1994). *Accounting for fundamentalisms.* Chicago: University of Chicago Press.

Marty, M. E., & Appleby, R. S. (Eds.). (1995). *Fundamentalisms comprehended.* Chicago: University of Chicago Press.

Piscatori, J. P. (1991). *Islamic fundamentalisms and the Gulf crisis.* Chicago: Fundamentalism Project, American Academy of Arts and Sciences.

Sandeen, E. (1970). *The roots of fundamentalism.* Chicago: University of Chicago Press.

Sivan, E. (1985) *Radical Islam: Medieval theology and modern politics.* New Haven, CT: Yale University Press.

Sprinzak, E. (1986). *Gush Emunim: The politics of Zionist fundamentalism in Israel.* New York: American Jewish Committee.

Watt, W. M. (1988). *Islamic fundamentalism and modernity.* London: Routledge.

Religious Syncretism

Syncretism is the attempt to reconcile disparate—and sometimes opposed—beliefs and practices. It represents a blending of schools of thought and is often associated with establishing analogies between two or more discrete and/or formerly separate traditions. Most studies of syncretism focus on the blending of religion and myths from different cultures.

Syncretism, in its attempt to reconcile disparate beliefs and practices, can be seen from positive and negative perspectives. Viewed positively, syncretism seeks underlying unity in what appears to be multiplicity and diversity. It is common in many aspects of society and culture, including language, literature, music, the arts, technology, politics, social organization and kinship, and economics. Robert D. Baird asserted that the term syncretism contributes little to our understanding of world religions since what it seeks to describe is nearly universal. He suggested that the term "syncretism" should be replaced by the term "synthesis." Other scholars—most notably the anthropologist Richard Werbner—have suggested that anthropologists restrict their use of the term to the study of religions. Werbner has since rescinded his position. Still other social scientists—notably Peter Beyer and Jonathan Friedman—have suggested that the term syncretism may prove extremely useful for understanding many aspects of culture and society, including social organization, material culture, and processes of localization and globalization.

Viewed negatively, syncretism is a contentious concept that has undergone many transformations. To religious leaders, syncretism often implies impurity and/or contamination and is associated with—but is not identical to—"eclecticism." It is unlikely that any contemporary scholar or theologian would argue that processes of syncretism do not exist. Disagreements center on the word itself and on the history of its applications.

Classical Greek and Roman Concepts of Syncretism

The Ancient Greek prefix *syn-* means "with" and the word *krasis* means "mixture." Thus, the term *synkrasis* meant "a mixture or compound." The Greek words *synkretismos* and *synkretizein* do not appear in classical literature until the time of Plutarch (c. 46–after 119 CE). Plutarch utilized a political meaning of the term in an essay entitled "On Brotherly Love" (*Peri philadelphias*), which appeared as a chapter in his *Moralia*. In searching for the origin for the word "syncretism," Plutarch claimed to have found an example of syncretism in the Cretans who reconciled their differences and came together in an alliance whenever they were faced with an external threat. He labeled this coming together as "their so-called syncretism." Plutarch's use of the term later gave rise to negative connotations—many of which were never intended by Plutarch. For Plutarch, syncretism was not only a testament to political expediency, but also had potential to foster sociability and brotherly love. On the other hand, he also saw it as the root of insincerity and impurity. It became synonymous with a lack of authenticity. Passages from Plutarch's *Moralia* attest that the term "syncretism" was known in the first century CE. Unfortunately, there are few other examples of the term's use during this period.

The bell-towers of this Roman Catholic Church at Acoma Pueblo, New Mexico, combine features of Christian and Native American architecture.

Although the word "syncretism" was not in common use among the ancient Greeks and Romans, the practice of syncretism seems to have been very common. It was central to both Greek and Roman political culture as well as Roman and Greek religions. In many respects, the commingling of religions was a direct result of Roman conquest, slavery, and forced migration. Franz Cumont (1956, 4), a historian of religion, speculated, "Who can tell what influence chambermaids from Antioch and Memphis gained over the minds of their mistresses?"

During the time of Alexander the Great (Alexander of Macedon 356–323 BCE), Hellenistic culture was itself a mixture, having blended Persian, Anatolian, Egyptian, and later Etruscan-Roman elements into an overall Hellenic framework. It is apparent that the syncretic gods of the Hellenistic period enjoyed wide favor among the Romans. Serpis, Isis, and Mithras were the most prominent among these deities. The goddess Cybele—as she was worshipped in Rome—was also highly syncretic.

In addition, pagan elements were incorporated into first-century Christianity. But—as with all religious syncretisms—not everyone agrees on the specifics. There are numerous and acrimonious debates with respect to "who, what, when, where, and why." While a majority of classicists and New Testament scholars agree that syncretism has occurred within Christianity and is likely to continue, specific examples often give rise to heated debates.

The Romans—who saw themselves as the heirs to Greek civilization—identified Greek deities with members of the Etruscan and Roman pantheons. Interestingly, they accepted the Greek and Etruscan gods but rarely copied Greek or Etruscan rituals. Vague attempts to establish equivalencies between Roman, Greek, and Etruscan deities were seldom contested. But putative correspondences vary; for example, Jupiter was seen as a better equivalent for Zeus than the huntress Diana was an equivalent for Artemis. Classicists argued that Ares was not a good match for Mars. The Anatolian goddess Cybele—who was imported to Rome from her cult center at Pessinus—was identified as Magna Mater and given a matronly image that had been developed earlier in Hellenistic Pergamum. The Egyptian god Amun was borrowed from a Hellenized "Zeus/Ammon" after Alexander the Great's quest for Amun's oracle at Siwa. The Greek god Dionysus was imported into Rome as Bacchus, and the Anatolian Sabazios was transformed into the Roman deity Sabazius. Given these precedents, the Romans would have recognized few barriers to the worship of Isis or Mithras. Likewise, when the Romans first encountered the Celts and Teutonic peoples, they commingled these northern gods with their own gods, creating, among others, "Apollo Sucellos" (Apollo the Good Smiter) and "Mars Thingsus" (Mars of the War Assembly). As Charles Stewart and Rosalind Shaw have emphasized, attempts to explain syncretism by reference to perceived equivalencies and/or correspondences are often flawed. Equivalencies, they asserted, must be recognized by actors—and even when such

202 · RELIGION AND BELIEF SYSTEMS IN WORLD HISTORY

No difference there is between a temple and a mosque, nor between the Hindu worship or the Muslim prayer: for men are the same all over, though they appear not the same. • **Guru Gobind Singh (1666–1708)**

equivalencies are recognized, they do not have to be accepted.

Such identifications and equivalencies may stem from a Hellenic practice of identifying deities of disparate mythological traditions with their own. When proto-Greeks—whose language would later become classical Greek—first arrived in the Pelonnesus over two thousand years ago they encountered localized nymphs and divinities already associated with important geographical features such as mountains, groves, caves, and springs—each of these geographical features had its own locally venerated deities.

Syncretism from the Renaissance to the Present

The term "syncretism" fell into disuse from the time of Plutarch to the time of the Renaissance. It was reborn with Erasmus (1466?–1536) and his reading of Plutarch. Erasmus modified the term "syncretism" in his *Adagia* (Adages)—first published in 1517—with reference to the coherence of dissenters despite their myriad philosophical and theological differences. Syncretism, for Erasmus, represented agreement among peoples with seemingly different beliefs and ideals. In a letter to Melanchthon dated 22 April 1519, Erasmus specifically referenced the Cretans (borrowing from Plutarch) as an example of the adage "Concord is a mighty rampart." Nearly a century later, in 1615, David Pareus of Heidelberg urged Christians to adopt what he called "pious syncretism" in opposition to the Antichrist, but few seventeenth-century Protestants seriously considered compromises that might bring about the ultimate reconciliation of Protestantism and the Roman Catholic Church. In the seventeenth century, Calixtus (1586–1656) sought to reconcile the various Protestant denominations with each other. He was ridiculed by Calovius (Abraham Calov, 1612–1686) for being an advocate of "syncretism."

Nonpejorative connotations of the term "syncretism" began again in the eighteenth century with the publication of Dennis Diderot's *Encyclopedie,* which contained entries on "Eclecticisme" and "Syncrétistes, Hénotiques, ou Conciliateurs." Although Diderot published two separate entries, he equated syncretism with eclecticism and portrayed syncretism as the concordance of eclectic sources.

Throughout the nineteenth century, overt syncretism in folk beliefs was seen as a strong indication of the cultural acceptance of an alien and/or earlier tradition. Nevertheless, it was also recognized that "foreign" cults may survive or infiltrate other religions without an official, authorized syncretism. By the end of the nineteenth century, identities were no longer predicated on the existence of continuous and immutable cultures, and the concept of syncretism came to the forefront largely because it blurred local distinctions—a characteristic that made it useful for rulers of multicultural populations. At the same time, the rejection of syncretism, that is, antisyncretism in the name of purity and/or orthodoxy, helped to generate and legitimize a strongly felt desire for cultural unity. Contemporary celebrations of Christmas, Easter, and Halloween offer many telling examples of syncretism in practice. This is not a new phenomenon. The ancient Romans adopted pagan Yule traditions that eventually made it into Christmas celebrations (Christmas trees, Yule logs, and the like), and Roman Catholics in Central and South America have integrated a large number of elements that are taken from indigenous Latin American and North American religious traditions. It is of interest that religious leaders who oppose syncretism almost always express their opposition in terms of personal piety.

A number of so-called new religious movements like Reverend Moon's Unification Church or L. Ron Hubbard's Church of Scientology have openly embraced syncretism, while others—Christian fundamentalism and Islam are perhaps the most dramatic examples—have rejected syncretism as a devaluing of precious, genuine religious and cultural truths and distinctions. Examples of intense syncretism can be found in Romanticism and in various other "new religions" like mysticism, occultism, theosophy, paganism, and New Age. In the fine arts, the eclectic aspects in postmodernism are abundantly apparent.

Generally, the term "syncretism" has been positively regarded by social scientists. Yet Stewart and Shaw report that there is growing uneasiness with the term among anthropologists who have been influenced by postmodernism. Other anthropologists have devoted their attentions to showing that syncretism is not inevitable. It is possible, they contend, for two groups to live in close proximity and largely ignore each another. For this reason, scholars find it both necessary and informative to examine syncretism with respect to relations of power. In *Syncretism and the Commerce of Symbols,* Goren Aijmer dramatically shifted the direction of research by asking, "Under what specific conditions do people in any one group pay attention to the cultural symbols of another group?" (1995, 27). Often, it seems that syncretism has been most intense whenever inequality between cultures has been the most pronounced. Equally important, war, conquest, colonialism, trade, migration, and intermarriage bring syncretism to the forefront. Race, gender, age, and social class are also factors. Scholars must examine the relationships between global and localized syncretisms. Are two or more religions influencing one another equally or is one dominating the rest? How does syncretism relate to issues of entrepreneurship and to theories of modernization?

In anthropology, the term "syncretism" is most closely associated with Melville J. Herskovits, who is best known for his research on the survival of African cultural traits among blacks in the Americas. Herskovits advocated an appreciation of what he called "syncretized Africanisms" and focused on various types of "acculturation" in order to address more general issues of culture contact. Again, there is need to recognize that acculturation (and syncretism) is not inevitable, and that all major world religions and cultures seem to be of composite origin.

Marked evidence of syncretism has been identified in New World religions such as Brazilian Candomble, Haitian vodun, and Cuban Santeria. These religions analogized various Yoruba and other African gods and selected Roman Catholic saints. Some Candomble leaders have incorporated the spirits of American aboriginal leaders like Sitting Bull and Black Hawk into their rituals. The most syncretic New World religion is perhaps Brazilian Umbanda, which combines African deities with a form of French spiritism attributed to Alan Kardec (1804–1869). In Brazil, French spiritism is also known as *Kardecism* or *Kardecismo*. Umbanda also incorporates local aboriginal spirits, African and Hindu deities, and North American aboriginal leaders.

Roger Bastide's influential study *The African Religions of Brazil* attempted to account for syncretism by stressing historical processes like conquest and migration. He traced the various ways in which African, European, and aboriginal religions have come together in what he termed an "interpenetration" of civilizations. Rather than offering a psychological explanation, Bastide's sociological approach focused on groups of people who were differentiated by sex, social class, and age. By contrast, Stephen D. Glazier's research on of the Spiritual Baptists in Trinidad focused on individual Baptist leaders and their practice of borrowing rituals from a variety of religious traditions but keeping these borrowed rituals separate in time and space. According to Glazier, one outcome of this process is a religion that is marked not so much by syncretism as by juxtaposition.

In South Africa, studies of syncretism have focused on independent churches. The earliest studies of African Independent Churches (AICs) were conducted by Christian missionaries, and the term syncretism was used in derogatory ways. Contemporary anthropologists—most notably J. Y. D. Peel—argued effectively that syncretism was not central to independent churches in South Africa because these churches represented reinterpretations of Christianity but never encouraged a mixture of Christianity and tribal elements.

It should be emphasized that authenticity and originality are not always dependent on the alleged purity and uniqueness of religions and vice versa, and that many so-called "original" religions—like the religions of Australian aborigines—are actually the result of a unique syncretism that has not occurred elsewhere. It is difficult to separate religion from the rest of culture. Scholars studying syncretism cannot specify their field of study in advance and must be sensitive to the ways in which people negotiate and redefine the boundaries

204 · RELIGION AND BELIEF SYSTEMS IN WORLD HISTORY

of their ideas and practices. For example, since Vatican II the Roman Catholic Church has implemented a concerted program of "inculturation" whereby local communities were encouraged to apprehend the Christian message "on their own terms." Is this, too, a type of syncretism? Shaw and Stewart pointed out that global religions—like Christianity, Hinduism, Buddhism, and Islam—have been able to effectively "standardize" their responses to syncretism. They suggested, for example, that antisyncretism within Islam can be seen as a standardized response to global capitalism, labor migration, and travel—not least of which is participation in the hajj. Shaw and Stewart also underscored the need to examine problems of agency, especially when agency is ascribed to religious traditions without reference to religious specialists. A difficulty is that when one ascribes agency to a religion, religions are portrayed as having their own dispositions like "free-flowing rivers." Such is seldom the case.

At times, syncretism is largely intentional, while at other times it is largely unintentional. Whatever the case, there are always unexpected consequences. Syncretism sometimes proceeds from misinterpretations and radical misunderstandings; for example, Christian missionaries working among the Ewe in Ghana identified one Ewe deity, Mawu, as the Christian God and labeled all other Ewe deities as "devils." An unintended consequence of this labeling was that the Ewe devoted a seemingly disproportionate amount of ritual time to honoring their "devils."

It is imperative for scholars to chart the increasingly complex interconnections between syncretism, social change, and resistance. Stewart and Shaw concluded their study of syncretism by suggesting that the term be recast as the politics of religious synthesis. A major focus, they postulated, should be on antisyncretism and the antagonisms shown by agents who are largely concerned with the defense of religious boundaries.

Stephen D. GLAZIER

University of Nebraska, Lincoln

See also African-American and Caribbean Religions

Further Reading

Aijmer, G. (Ed.). (1995). *Syncretism and the commerce of symbols.* Goteborg, Sweden: Institute for Advanced Studies in Social Anthropology.

Baird, R. D. (1971). *Category formation in the history of religions.* The Hague, The Netherlands: Mouton.

Bastide, R. (1978). *The African religions of Brazil: Toward a sociology of the interpenetration of civilizations.* Baltimore: Johns Hopkins University Press.

Beyer, P. (1994). *Religion and globalization.* New York: Sage.

Clifford, J. (1988). *The predicament of culture.* Cambridge, MA: Harvard University Press.

Cumont, F. (1956). *Oriental religions in Roman paganism.* New York: Dover.

Droogers, A. (1989). Syncretism: The problem of definition, the definition of the problem. In J. D. Gort, H. M. Vroom, et al. (Eds.), *Dialogue and syncretism: An interdisciplinary approach* (pp. 7–25). Grand Rapids, MI: Eerdmans.

Friedman, J. (1995). *Cultural identity and global process.* London: Sage.

Glazier, S. D. (1985). Syncretism and separation: Ritual change in an Afro-Caribbean faith. *Journal of American Folklore, 98*(387), 49–62.

Greenfield, S., & Droogers, A. (Eds.). (2001). *Reinventing religions: Syncretism and transformation in Africa and the Americas.* New York: Rowman & Littlefield.

Herskovits, M. J. (1947). *Cultural dynamics.* New York: Alfred A. Knopf.

Lawson, E. T. (2003). Agency and religious agency in cognitive perspective. In S. D. Glazier & C. A. Flowerday (Eds.), *Selected readings in the anthropology of religion: Theoretical and methodological essays* (pp. 99–106). Westport, CT: Praeger.

Peel, J. Y. D. (1968). Syncretism and religious change. *Comparative Studies in Society and History, 10,* 121–141.

Stewart, C., & Shaw, R. (Eds.). (1994). *Syncretism/anti-syncretism: The politics of religious synthesis.* New York: Routledge.

Werbner, R. (1994). Afterword. In C. Stewart & R. Shaw (Eds.), *Syncretism/anti-syncretism: The politics of religious synthesis* (pp. 212–215). New York & London: Routledge.

Roman Catholicism

Roman Catholicism traces its origins to Jesus Christ of Nazareth (born between 6 BCE and 6 CE and died between 28 CE and 30 CE) and regards the bishop of Rome (the pope, as the successor of Peter) as the visible head of the church. Roman Catholics worship Jesus as the Son of God and the Second Person of the Blessed Trinity. The religion had a profound effect on the development of Western civilization.

Found today in some 235 countries, the Roman Catholic Church is the largest of the Christian churches, with a world population of about 1.147 billion (as of 2007), or 17 percent of the world's population. The largest number of adherents is found in Brazil, Mexico, Philippines, the United States, and Italy. (In the United States Roman Catholics comprise 22 percent of the population and constitute the largest religious body.) This article is concerned only with the Roman (or Latin) branch and is divided into four sections: basic teachings, major historical developments, contemporary trends and problems, and Roman Catholicism in the non-European world.

Basic Teachings

The teachings of Roman Catholicism rest upon Scripture (revelation as found in the Old Testament and New Testament), tradition, and the magisterium, the teaching authority of the church. Tradition has enabled the church to adapt to new realities. It is closely linked to Scripture, and the interpretation of both is considered the prerogative of the magisterium. The expression of the revealed truth in Scripture may take diverse forms, such as history, prophecy, parable, and allegory. A literal interpretation is not required. Throughout the Christian era, reformulation and adaptation have been characteristic of Roman Catholicism in moral teachings, liturgy, and societal roles. The process has involved change and continuity, conflict and consensus.

The distinctive marks of Roman Catholicism are unity, holiness, catholicity, and apostolicity. Unity means that each individual transcends all cultures and classes; holiness signifies that the church is intrinsically sacred despite the sins of its members, either individually or as a body; catholicity is the universality of the church; and apostolicity denotes faith, ministry, and the sacraments in communion with Rome. The Roman Catholic Church recognizes elements of itself in other Christian churches, and it does not require that a state be Catholic or that it enjoy any privileged status. It accepts the principle of religious freedom, and it holds that salvation is possible for all who act in good faith, according to their consciences.

There is a definite hierarchy in the Roman Catholic Church. As the successor of the apostle Peter, the supreme ruler is the pope. Elected by the College of Cardinals since the Middle Ages, the pope resides in Vatican City, a minute but sovereign state in the center of Rome. The other bishops are also seen as the direct successors of the apostles, and most reside in geographical and organizational units known as dioceses. The pope and the bishops are joined together in a collegial body, but collegiality does not lessen the papal primacy or affect papal infallibility in matters of faith and morals.

Just as the pope has primacy over the bishops, the bishops have the final authority in their respective dioceses. After ascertaining their orthodoxy, a bishop

In the eleventh century Pope Gregory VII brought about major changes in the church by eliminating the laity's role in choosing bishops.

ordains priests and deacons, who become his assistants. Priests must be male, and since the fourth century, enter upon a lifetime of celibacy. Deacons, also male, may be married. Most priests reside in ecclesiastical units called parishes. In addition to bishops, priests, and deacons there are monks and nuns who are members of religious orders and normally take vows of poverty, chastity, and obedience.

The "People of God" includes not only the clergy and the religious but the laity as well. Married or single, engaged in secular professions or occupations, lay persons are said to share in the mission of the church. As lay apostles, they assist bishops and priests in the conduct of church affairs, but they cannot act independently or in opposition to their religious superiors. Despite some softening by Vatican II (1962–1965) and more lay participation, the church remains an authoritarian, hierarchical structure.

As defined by the Council of Trent (1545–1563), the vehicles of divine grace that enable a Catholic to attain salvation are the seven sacraments: baptism, penance, the Eucharist, confirmation, matrimony, Holy Orders, and anointing of the sick. Only those who have received Holy Orders are authorized to administer all seven sacraments. Other basic teachings of Roman Catholicism are the Trinity (the presence of three Persons in one God: the Father, the Son, and the Holy Spirit), the immortality of the soul, the resurrection of the dead, justification by faith and good works, an afterlife of reward or punishment, and special veneration of the Virgin Mary as the Mother of God. There is also veneration of the saints, but Catholics are directed not to pay an exaggerated attention to the saints.

The expression of Roman Catholicism takes the form of the liturgy, the rites and ceremonies of the church. The most important act of worship is the Mass, which is composed of the Liturgy of the Word (readings from Scripture) and the Liturgy of the Eucharist (Holy Communion). Like other aspects of Roman Catholicism, the liturgy, especially the Mass, has been adapted to regional environments, and the uniqueness of each culture is respected. Since Vatican II the vernacular has been used extensively, and although Gregorian chant is considered proper to the Roman liturgy, other forms of music are permitted.

Major Historical Developments

The beginning of the Roman Catholic community, as of other Christian bodies, is dated from the appearance of Jesus Christ to the apostle Peter after his crucifixion, burial, and resurrection. The apostles, like Jesus, were Jewish, as were the first Christians. What distinguished these early Christians from other Jews was their conviction that Jesus was the Messiah, that he had been resurrected from the dead. After the martyrdom of the Deacon Stephen, about 33 CE, these Christians, who had maintained close ties with the Temple, scattered and preached the Gospel wherever they settled. With Paul (died c. 67 CE), Christianity came out of its Jewish mold, and Paul's missionary labors in the Mediterranean world made it the religion of the Gentiles.

Christianity spread rapidly in the Roman Empire. Women, especially widows and unmarried women, were active in the evangelization of pagan areas. Whether as preachers, deaconesses disbursing charity, or leaders of groups studying devotional literature, these women made their mark on the early church. Their influence, however, was short-lived; by the third century their activities had been curtailed, and they were gradually excluded from any clerical function. The patristic writings disparaged women. Saint Augustine of Hippo considered women innately inferior to men and saw them as symbols of carnality and original sin.

Another important development of Christian antiquity was the emergence of the concept of the primacy of Rome. Although Jesus had conferred preeminence on Peter among the apostles, he did not directly establish a papacy in Rome. Peter was almost certainly martyred in Rome, and thus Rome became a sacred place, a new Jerusalem for early Christians. The prestige of the bishopric of Rome because of its association with Peter was enhanced by the fact that Rome was the political and cultural center of the vast Roman Empire. In an age of heresies such as Arianism, Montanism, and Pelagianism, the bishop of Rome was frequently called upon to condemn unorthodox teachings and mediate jurisdictional disputes.

The first pope to claim primacy for Rome was Damascus (366–384 CE) at a council in 382 CE. Leo I (440–461 CE) made the formulation of the doctrine, which stated that the pope had the plenitude of power over the universal church. Papal authority was subsequently augmented by papal missionaries who evangelized new kingdoms. It was also strengthened by the secession of Eastern Orthodoxy, first in the ninth century and then in 1054 in a final and permanent break.

To the concept of the primacy of Rome was added that of the primacy of the pope over secular rulers as well. Thus in the eleventh century Pope Gregory VII

(1073–1085) and his successors ended the control of feudal lords and kings over the selection of bishops and abbots, but in the process, brought about major changes in Roman Catholicism. Secular and sacred domains were sharply delineated, and the role of the laity in the selection of bishops, which dated back to Christian antiquity, was completely eliminated. Absolute papal monarchy over the whole of Christendom reached its apogee under Innocent III (1198–1216) and Boniface VIII (1294–1303). In his quarrel with John of England, Innocent III claimed that temporal authority depended on spiritual authority. Boniface VIII went even further, maintaining in *Unam Sanctam* (1303) that every human being had to be subject to the pope in order to be saved.

Despite the extravagance of papal statements, Roman Catholicism contributed much to the development and achievements of Western civilization. The concepts of popular sovereignty and limited government were part of Catholic political thinking, and canon law, which was applicable whenever a sacrament or a cleric was involved, was the most humane and equitable law of the times. In education, first the monastic schools and then the cathedral schools and the universities made formal schooling more accessible than ever before, though men, and especially those destined for a clerical life, were the principal beneficiaries. However, until the High Middle Ages, talented women in female monastic establishments received a high level of education and made contributions to theology, philosophy, and literature.

Gothic art and architecture, the magnificent works of Dante and Chaucer, and liturgical art, music, and drama all owed their inspiration to Roman Catholicism. In the universities the scholasticism of Thomas Aquinas (1225–1275) provided a systemization of Catholic theology and philosophy that was to last well into the twentieth century. Members of religious orders, such as the Benedictines, Franciscans, and Dominicans, provided social services and medical assistance.

Marring these achievements were coercion in religious matters through the Inquisition, established by Boniface VIII, and the persecution of Jews. The cruelty of the medieval Inquisition, which could employ torture to obtain confessions of guilt and could sentence those convicted of heresy to death by burning at the stake, varied considerably, depending on times and places. Wherever and whenever it existed it was a dreaded institution. As for anti-Semitism, ever since the beginning of the Christian era, Jews had encountered hostility when living among Christians, because they were considered guilty of deicide, of rejection of the Messiah.

As commerce and trade entered the medieval world, and as the proportion of Jews to Christians in these areas, especially money lending, increased, so did aggression against Jews. Jews were accused of avarice and economic exploitation, as well as of more serious charges, such as child murder and alliance with Satan. The worst of the persecutions took place during the Black Death of 1348/49, when Jews from Spain to Poland were accused of having deliberately caused the plague. In vain did the Avignon Pope, Clement VI (1342–1352), denounce this persecution, pointing out that the plague was striking Christian and Jewish communities indiscriminately and offering Jews a haven in Avignon.

The most traumatic event in the history of Roman Catholicism was the Protestant Reformation, which made the Roman Catholic Church a distinct and separate entity in the Christian world. By the beginning of modern times, the Renaissance, the scandal of the Great Western Schism ([1378–1417], when there were two or three who claimed to be Pope), the notorious immorality in the church from top to bottom, and the prevalence of superstitious practices produced skepticism among intellectuals, anticlericalism among the common people, and fodder for nationalistic rulers. The indulgence controversy following Luther's posting of the Ninety-Five Theses united all who had reason to oppose the papacy, and by the end of the century Lutheranism, Anglicanism, and Calvinism had cost the church the allegiance of half of Europe.

The Council of Trent (1545–1563) was convoked to deal with this crisis. Adopting a very rigid, defensive position, the Council defined the sacraments, especially those that had been questioned by the Protestant reformers, and upheld traditional teachings regarding papal primacy, the hierarchical structure of the church, justification, the nature of the Mass, clerical celibacy, and both tradition and Scripture as the deposit of faith. Latin was retained as the mandatory language of the Roman Church. The legacy of Trent was a very conservative Roman Catholicism.

During the scientific revolution of the seventeenth century, members of the curia opposed the heliocentric theory proposed by Galileo and brought about his condemnation (to be reversed by Pope John Paul II in the 1980s). During the Enlightenment in the eighteenth century a climate of opinion that endorsed religious freedom, the power of reason, the possibility of a heavenly city on Earth, and a natural religion ran counter to the tenets of Catholicism. The era of the French Revolution and Napoleon (1789–1815) inaugurated a period when secular nationalism became the new religion. Almost all modern trends and movements were declared anathema by Pope Pius IX (1846–1878) in the *Syllabus of Errors* (1864). This pontiff convened the First Vatican Council (1869–1870), which formally defined the doctrine of papal infallibility in matters of faith and morals, much to the consternation of many Catholic theologians, ecclesiastics, and lay persons of the period.

Early in the twentieth century, Pope Pius X (1903–1914) railed against "Modernism," excommunicated "Modernists," and suppressed liberal Catholic theologians and historians. His successor, Benedict XV (1914–1922), ended the hunt for "Modernists." He also permitted Italian Catholics full participation in politics, something that had been forbidden by previous popes because Italy had been unified at the expense of the Papal States. During the era of totalitarianism, Roman Catholicism came under attack by Italian Fascism, Nazism, and Communism.

World War II broke out during the reign of Pope Pius XII (1939–1958), a controversial figure. As the war developed and Nazi atrocities, especially against Jews, became known, he was expected to speak out on behalf of Jews. For reasons that became the subject of heated debate after the war in both Catholic and non-Catholic circles, he alluded to the genocide of

A peaceful man does more good than a learned one. • **Pope John XXIII (1881–1963)**

Jews only in general, not specific, terms, even while providing Jews with money and refuge in the religious houses of Rome.

Contemporary Trends and Problems

With Pope John XXIII (1958–1963), Roman Catholicism embarked upon uncharted waters. A compassionate and approachable man, John XXIII's most momentous act was the convocation of a general council, known as Vatican II (1962–1965). In his inaugural address to the three thousand bishops and theologians drawn from all over the world, he declared that the "Church could and should adapt to the needs of the world." His message was one of *aggiornamento*. During the four sessions held between October 1962 and December 1965, every aspect of Roman Catholicism was explored, with a view to creating more openness and flexibility.

The Decree on the Church, instead of identifying the Roman Catholic Church with the Church of Christ, stated that the Church of Christ "subsisted" in the Roman Catholic Church. Papal infallibility was to some extent weakened by the introduction of the concept of collegiality—that is, the pope and bishops shared responsibility for the church. Even more revolutionary were the decrees on religious freedom, Jews, and relations with the other Christian churches. The Decree on Religious Liberty stated that every person "has a right to religious liberty." The Decree on Other Religions asserted that Christ's passion (the suffering culminating in the Crucifixion) could not be "blamed on all Jews then living, without distinction, nor upon the Jews of today." It deplored "the hatred, persecutions, and displays of anti-Semitism directed against Jews at any time and from any source." The Decree on Ecumenism called for dialogue with the Protestant churches to achieve agreement on theological differences. In this decree, the focus is not on a "return" to the Catholic Church, but on the spirit of Christ at work in the churches and communities beyond the visible borders of the Roman Catholic Church.

The air of optimism that pervaded Vatican II soon dissipated in the post-Vatican years. The dialogue with Protestant churches made little progress with respect to such issues as papal primacy and infallibility, the nature of ordination, the relationship between Scripture and tradition, the nature of the Eucharist (a memorial service or transubstantiation) and the role of Mary in the Divine Plan. The "silence" of Pope Pius XII regarding the Holocaust was an irritant in many Jewish circles, despite the repeated apologies by Pope John Paul II (1978–2005) for the sins of the church against Jews.

Within the Roman Catholic Church there was increasing polarization, some Catholics believing that Vatican II had gone too far and others countering that it had not gone far enough. The positions of Pope John Paul II were generally conservative. Traditional morality in such matters as divorce, premarital sex, contraception, abortion, homosexuality, euthanasia, and genetic engineering was affirmed. The role of women in the church and clerical celibacy occasioned fierce controversy.

In the 1980s and 1990s, as traditional religious orders declined and the number of priests declined dramatically, women assumed liturgical and administrative positions in the church, serving as chaplains, seminary professors, and spiritual directors. Inevitably the question of the ordination of women came up. In an effort to end the discussion, John Paul II in *Ordinatio Sacerdotatis* unequivocally stated that the church did not have the authority to ordain women.

A revival of the issue of clerical celibacy was provoked by the priest sex scandal that rocked the Roman Catholic Church, especially its American branch. It became evident at the turn of the century that for decades bishops had moved priests who sexually abused children from one parish to another in an effort to avoid scandal. In 2002 the Vatican and the American hierarchy adopted stringent measures to purge the clerical ranks of offenders and to ensure the protection of children, but the extent of priest sexual abuse raised the question of clerical celibacy as the possible cause of such offenses. But the Vatican denied a link between celibacy and pedophilia and/or homosexuality, and reaffirmed the validity of a ban on marriage for priests. The priest sex scandal, no longer confined mostly to the United States, resurfaced on Vatican soil some five years after the German-born Cardinal Joseph Ratzinger was elected as Pope Benedict XVI on 19 April 2005. Amid a papacy already beset with controversies that had offended Muslims, Jews, Anglicans, and many Roman Catholics, Benedict XVI and his direct subordinates were accused in early 2010 of neglecting to alert civilian authorities or discipline priests involved in sexual abuse when he was archbishop in Germany.

As the twenty-first century unfolded, discord and polarization seemed to foretell a new crisis for the church, paralleling that of the Reformation era. Yet most Catholics refused to abandon the church and sought instead a new identity, respectful of the past but adapted to the needs of society.

Roman Catholicism in the Non-European World

Until the sixteenth century Roman Catholicism was co-extensive only with western and central Europe. During the Age of Discovery, religious orders, always the church's pioneers in evangelization, reached out to the far corners of the world. The first missionaries to the Americas, Africa, and Asia were the Franciscans and Jesuits, soon joined by Augustinians, Dominicans, Carmelites and others. As early as 1622 the papacy set up the Sacred Congregation for the Propagation of the Faith. In the nineteenth century the older orders were augmented with new ones, such as the Missionaries of Africa and the Missionaries of the Divine Word, orders formed specifically for work in the non-Western world. Consciously or unconsciously, these missionaries were conduits for the expansion of important elements of the Western world.

Catholicism achieved its greatest success in Latin America (Spanish and Portuguese America). From its earliest settlements in the Americas, the Spanish crown had a papal mandate to Christianize the lands it colonized. Beginning in 1573 Spain established *la mision*, whereby the native Indians were placed under the direct care of missionaries, protected by Spanish troops. Most missions flourished, notably the Jesuit Reductions of Paraguay and the Franciscan missions of California and the U.S. Southwest. The native peoples adopted not only the religion of the Spanish but also their language, culture, and occupations. As a result, native culture was all but obliterated, and inhumane treatment of the Indians occurred, despite government regulations to the contrary and the strong defense of the Indians vocalized by such missionaries as the Franciscan Junipero Serra and the Jesuit Pedro Claver.

Spanish rule ended early in the nineteenth century, but the church and especially the hierarchy retained its dominant role in society. As the masses gradually became estranged from the church because of its wealth, anticlerical legislation was enacted in many of the Latin American states. The church-state quarrels ended in separation of church and state, although restrictive legislation if not persecution persisted in many countries, notably Mexico.

Catholicism had to contend with internal dissension as well as external hostility. From the 1960s to the end of the century, liberation theology divided the church. According to this theology the church's primary obligation was to improve the socioeconomic status of the masses. Liberation theology encountered the opposition of both Latin American and Vatican prelates, who contended that it was too sympathetic to Marxist models and that its base communities ("the popular church") were anti-institutional.

The history of Catholicism in Brazil, originally a Portuguese possession, does not differ radically from that of Catholicism in Spanish America, although the Brazilian brand of Catholicism had a greater admixture of ancient heathen elements. From the first Portuguese settlements in the sixteenth century, Franciscans and Jesuits preached the Gospel, at the same time building churches and establishing schools and charitable institutions. Catholicism prospered especially between 1680 and 1750. Decline followed when the anticlerical ministry of the Marquis of Pombal expelled the religious orders. The missionaries were readmitted in the nineteenth century, but the

emergence of an independent Brazil and the subsequent disestablishment of the church under the Republican constitution of 1889 prevented attempts to recoup previous losses. In the twentieth century recurring economic crises and military governments further hampered advances in the Catholic Church. Liberation theology was embraced by many churchmen as a way to end the socioeconomic injustices that plagued Brazilian society, but, as elsewhere, this theology had to be jettisoned. In the early years of the twenty-first century, some 75 percent of Brazilians continued to call themselves Roman Catholics, giving Brazil the largest Catholic population in the world. Latin America as a whole had the largest block of Roman Catholics in the world: 473 million. The monopoly held by the church in this part of the world, however, has been threatened by the inroads of Protestantism, especially evangelical Protestantism from the United States, as well as urbanization, consumerism, and globalization.

In North America, New France (Canada) became Catholic owing in large measure to the zeal of the Franciscans and Jesuits who accompanied the French colonizers and established a real bond with the natives. When France surrendered Canada to England in 1763, it was with the assurance that the rights of the Roman Catholics would be protected. The church continued to flourish; by 2000, about 45 percent of the population was Roman Catholic.

In the United States Roman Catholicism was first introduced by the Spanish missionaries in the areas controlled by Spain, such as California in the West and Florida in the East. In English colonial America Catholicism grew from a small group of English Catholics who settled in Maryland in 1634. The American Catholic Church was strongly committed to separation of church and state. Annual episcopal conferences dealt with problems peculiar to the American environment, such as the assimilation of immigrants, trusteeism, and the threat presented by nativism. Lay Catholic generosity and the labors of religious orders, especially female orders, contributed to the success of the church. By 2000 it was the largest religious body in the United States.

Roman Catholicism can be said to have achieved only moderate success in Africa. North Africa was solidly Muslim when the Europeans first sought settlements in Africa. Missionary activity in central and southern Africa was initiated by the Portuguese in the sixteenth century. The advent of the slave trade and intertribal warfare were serious obstacles to the evangelization of the Portuguese outposts. By the mid-nineteenth century, as European imperialistic rivalry heated up, most of the natives who had been converted had reverted to paganism. Another wave of evangelization began with the White Fathers in the last quarter of the nineteenth century. Large areas of the Congos (French and Belgian) were converted, as well Uganda. Military coups, tribal warfare, in which Catholics of one tribe slaughtered Catholics of another tribe, and Cold War politics all had devastating results for Catholic churches. Vatican II was a mixed blessing for the African churches. On the one hand it led to a hierarchy that was almost entirely African and it also provided Mass in the vernacular, with the addition of traditional singing and dancing. On the other, the prelates who replaced the Europeans tended to be more conservative, and the downplaying of sacramentals, such as medals and holy water, eliminated a previous point of contact with traditional religions. By the beginning of the twenty-first century, Catholics comprised about 16 percent of the total African population. These Catholics were to be found mostly in Angola, the Democratic Republic of the Congo (former Belgian Congo), the Republic of the Congo (former French Congo) and Uganda. Noteworthy in the history of African Catholicism is the general lack of acculturation as well as deviation from Roman Catholic norms in various areas, such as priestly celibacy, monogamy, and mixed marriages.

In Asia the greatest success of Roman Catholicism was achieved in the Philippines, where Catholicism was introduced by Governor Miguel de Legazpi and the Augustinians in 1565. Through the friars (Augustinians, Franciscans, and Dominicans) and the Jesuits, Spanish culture was easily transplanted to the Philippines, encountering resistance only in the southern islands, where Islam had been established since the fourteenth century. The Spanish missionaries taught the natives better agricultural and horticultural techniques, introduced arts and crafts, and strongly influence architecture. Respectful of Philippine traditions, they produced some excellent studies of Philippine history and culture. No attempt was made to suppress Tagalog, one of the major languages of the islands. Despite difficult times brought on by decades of foreign occupation (American and Japanese), dire poverty, and terrorist organizations, Catholicism was the religion of 83 percent of the population as of 2008.

Little headway was made by Roman Catholicism in the rest of Asia: Roman Catholics numbered less than 3 percent of the total Asian population as the twenty-first century opened. The main reason for the failure of Roman Catholicism to make inroads in countries such as China, Japan, and India was that missionaries encountered ancient and proud civilizations that made the missionaries seem culturally inferior as well as possible political threats. A contributory factor was the failure of papal authorities to allow the missionaries sufficient flexibility in dealing with Asian religions until it was too late.

A survey of Roman Catholicism in the non-European worlds indicates that it was very successful in Latin America, moderately successful in Africa, and except in the Philippines, a failure in Asia. The degree of implantation of Western culture varies with time and place.

Elisa A. CARRILLO
Marymount College of Fordham University

See also Augustine, Saint; Missionaries; Paul, Saint; Religion and War

Further Reading

Abbott, W. (1966). *Documents of Vatican II.* New York: America Press.

Ben-Sasson, H. H. (1976). *A history of the Jewish people.* Cambridge, MA: Harvard University Press.

Bokenkotter, T. (2004). *A concise history of the Catholic church.* New York: Doubleday.

Brown, R. (1994). *Introduction to New Testament Christology.* New York: Paulist Press.

Catholic University of America (Eds.). (2003). *New Catholic encyclopedia.* Farmington Hills, MI: Gale Press.

Duffy, E. (1997). *Saints and sinners, a history of the popes.* New Haven: Yale University Press.

Dulles, A. (1988). *The reshaping of Catholicism.* New York: Harper and Row.

Encyclopedia Britannica Almanac. (2004). Chicago: Encyclopedia Britannica Press.

Himes, M. (2004). *The Catholic Church in the 21st century.* Liguori, MO: Liguori Press.

McNamara, J. (1996). *Sisters in arms.* Cambridge, MA: Harvard University Press.

Reuther, R. (1974). *Religion and sexism.* New York: Simon and Schuster.

Shamanism

Shamanism is an ideology and a set of techniques or rituals that deal with communication among spirits. Shamanistic practices are attached to a system of beliefs, and therefore they are always considered in the context of the religion or society in which they are found. The shaman, the person who performs the rituals, often serves as a healer, diviner, clairvoyant, or a possessor of magic or spiritual power.

Shamanism is a distinctive complex of social roles, psychospiritual activities, and religio-ecological ideation embodied in the person of a ritual specialist, called a shaman. The term *shaman* comes from the Siberian Tungus (Evenk) word *aman* via Russian sources. Shamanism has been intensely studied in Eurasia and the Americas, and extends from the Saami (Lapps) of Finland to the Yamana (Yaghan) of Tierra del Fuego at the southern tip of South America. Scholars have also identified shamanism in Aboriginal Australia, Southeast Asia, and Oceania and more sparsely in Africa, where spirit possession and spirit mediumship seem to be more prevalent.

There are many different approaches to the study of shamanism, including anthropology, archaeology, comparative religion, ethnomedicine, history, linguistics, prehistory, psychology, and folklore studies.

History and Distribution

Some scholars claim shamanism displays an ancient heritage discernible in the cave paintings of Paleolithic (foraging) era and hunting cultures found in southern France and northern Spain. For example, the upper Paleolithic Les Trois Frères cave (c. 14,000 BCE) contains the *Sorcerer of Les Trois Frères*, a famous black-painted figure overlooking a gallery of engraved game animals, and interpreted to be a master of animals, a shaman.

Siberia is the locus classicus of shamanism and there is considerable variation from the northwestern Saami (Lapp) shamanism, known only through historical sources first written down in 1180 CE, through to the Turkic Central Asian language group (e.g., Yakut [Sakha], Tuvins, and Khakass), the Mongolian languages (e.g., Mongolian and Buryat), the Tungusic group (e.g., Evenki [Tungus], Even, Manchu), the Paleo-Asiatic (e.g., Chukchi and Koryak) group, and the Eskimo-Aleut group. Shamanism is also found in southern Eurasia in Nepal and India, and throughout Southeast Asia. The Northern and Southern Aslian shamanism of Peninsular Malaysia (Bateg, Temoq, Semelai, and Semaq Bri) is remarkably similar to forms found throughout Siberia. Polynesian mythology also amply attests to shamanic themes and cosmological images.

The distribution of shamanism throughout the Americas also suggests not only great antiquity but also Eurasian origins. Shamanism was brought in several waves to the Americas by hunting peoples who crossed the Bering land bridge between Siberia and Alaska. In the far south of Chilean Patagonia artifacts dating between 11,000 and 8000 BCE have been excavated by archaeologists at Fell's Cave. Here too we find shamanism, extinguished by the genocidal wars of the late nineteenth and early twentieth century, among guanaco hunting Ona (Selk'nam) and the marine hunting and littoral foraging Yamana (Yaghan). Farther north in central Chile we find Mapuche shamanism displaying an almost Siberian

Having attracted the disease-spirit into the spirit boat, the Temoq shaman Pak Loong bin Gudam prepares to send the disease-spirit back to its celestial home.

character. Although there is no evidence of cultural continuity between the original settlers circa 10,000 BCE and historically known cultures in this region, the pervasiveness of shamanism throughout the cultures of North and South America certainly indicates a very early introduction. Perhaps the penultimate migration into North America is revealed by linguistic evidence linking the Yeniseian family of languages spoken today only by the Ket of central Siberia with the Na-Dene languages of North America, two culture areas steeped in shamanism. This recent finding further deepens our understanding of the circumpolar or circumboreal cultural continuum long recognized by scholars.

Shamans and the Shamanic Complex

The shaman is a visionary, healer, singer and poet, ecstatic soul traveler, psychopomp (capable of escorting the soul of the deceased to the domain of the dead), a mediator between his or her social group and the spirit world, a diviner, and a sacrificer. Shamans are specialists in the life and fate of the soul, the travails of their own soul during initiation, and their patient's afflicted soul in a ritual healing performance. These features constitute a complex that frequently lies at the psychospiritual core of a society, and can thus be identified as the religion of many Siberian and circumpolar peoples, as well as the religion of peninsular Malaysia's Temoq, Semelai, and Semaq Bri Orang Asli ("aboriginal") cultures. However, in many other cultures shamanism is just one dimension of a more inclusive religious worldview and in this instance may be more appropriately identified as a belief subsystem as among the Mapuche of Chile and the Uzbeks of Central Asia.

The shaman is a person who is able to break through the planes of ordinary day-to-day life by acquiring a deep and profound knowledge of the supramundane world. Shamanism has been defined as a "technique of ecstasy" involving the magical flight of the shaman's soul to the sky or to the underworld (Eliade 1964, 4ff.). The shaman is empowered to enter into this world through the acquisition of visionary capabilities, most usually during initiation. These powers are renewed and strengthened with every ritual performance directed toward healing, divination, sacrifice, and various other rites important to the welfare of the group. The powers are embodied in the shaman's cosmographic experience and in the control of familiar and guardian spirits who provide knowledge and direction, and protect the shaman's highly labile and vulnerable soul during a visionary rite. The shaman's altered state of consciousness ranges from intense ecstasy as with some Siberian shamans, to quiet reverie as the Malaysian Temoq shaman contemplates the overpowering beauty of the visionary world. At the age of nine the Lakota holy man Black Elk, during an episode of acute illness, gained his visionary powers by ascending into the cloud-mountain abode of the powerful Grandfathers, who he realized were the "Powers of the World," the powers of the four directions, the heavens, and the earth below.

Shamanic séances are almost always performed at night, and in many shamanistic societies nighttime is not the absence of daylight, but a qualitatively different type of reality. In almost all societies the shaman is a nocturnal being, a specialist in the existential realities that emerge after nightfall. For the Temoq even seasonality is suspended at night, and the identities that differentiate the diurnal mundane world transform into another dimension at sunset.

Initiation into the shamanic vocation takes many forms throughout the world. In some Siberian societies, the shaman involuntarily experiences a frightening dismemberment by demons or evil spirits. The shaman's reconstitution into a new, spiritually reborn body empowers the shaman to perform supernormal feats. The death and resurrection theme also occurs in the Americas. In contrast, the Temoq shaman knows he is chosen when he has a waking daylight encounter with the spirit of a beautiful young woman dressed in red. The Temoq mountain journey shaman is then initiated by a master shaman who, during a nighttime ritual performance, places a *cermin*, a "visionary mirror", into the unawakened third eye of the initiand, thus giving the new shaman's soul the power to see and visit all the cosmic regions necessary for healing, and for maintaining the fertility and fecundity of the tropical rain forest.

Throughout tropical South America tobacco intoxication and hallucinogens, such as the *Banisteriopsis caapi* plant (ayahuasca), are used to engender visionary experiences. Although only introduced several centuries ago, tobacco is also used by Siberians and some Temoq shamans to induce an altered state of consciousness. The induction of ecstatic trance states by ingesting hallucinogenic mushrooms is also widespread in Siberia.

A ritual assistant daubs a rubber tiger figure, the spirit of which will accompany a Temoq shaman to the edge of world.

Drumming is used throughout Eurasia and in many cultures of the Americas to embrace the suprasensible world of the spirits. In Temoq shamanism intense drumming over several hours, as the author has experienced, induces a soporific state of consciousness, a drowsy state experienced by ritual participants as the temporary loss of their astral body as it travels with the shaman's celestial entourage.

The raison d'être of nearly all shamans is healing. The shaman uses his or her visionary powers to either search out the location of a lost soul or to extract disease-spirits from the body of the afflicted. The retrieval of a lost soul implies that either the shaman or the shaman's spirit allies journey out into the upper or lower worlds. Although the shaman's expertise is at the center of the therapeutic field, healing is almost always a communal event and often an intense social drama.

Shamans are preeminently singers and poets. Whether ecstatic cries of a Siberian Sakha shaman, the long spirit-journey epics of Malaysian Semaq Bri, Semelai, and Temoq shamans, or the low murmuring of Yamana shamans in Tierra del Fuego, almost all shamans vocally express their experience through singing. In some societies such as the Temoq and the Siona of South America, the song is the primary expression of the shaman's power. Indeed, for the Temoq, the term "song" is a misnomer, for only powerless shamans sing "songs," while powerful shamans give fresh and clear voice to visionary experience. The Temoq shaman's singing is replete with the calls of animal and bird familiar and guardian spirits. A beautiful example is the Tuvan shaman's song in *Shu-De*.

The Shamanic Worldview

Shamanic activity is couched within a cosmological structure that facilitates the movement of the shaman's soul or spirit from the middle world of human society and the natural world to the upper and lower worlds inhabited by ancestors, guardian and familiar spirits, deities, animal masters, the land of the dead, and frequently the soul of a patient. A multi-tiered world, often three-tiered, is integrated by an axis mundi—a vertical structure lying at the center of the world and imaged as a tree, a mountain, a pillar, a rainbow, or even a river that flows from the upper world, through the middle world of day-to-day life, to the lower world of the dead as with the hunting and reindeer-herding Evenki of the Siberian taiga.

In a ritual performance the shamanic cosmos is symbolically represented in the structure and function of the shaman's venue and in the shaman's costume and musical instrument, such as a drum or rattle. This ritual microcosmos, projected to the "center of the world," embodies core symbolic forms that,

variously empowered, enable the shaman to engage spirits and supernatural beings and visit the far-off places necessary for the success of the ritual.

> The shaman's costume itself constitutes a religious hierophany and cosmography; it discloses not only a sacred presence but also cosmic symbols and meta-psychic itineraries. Properly studied, it reveals the system of shamanism as clearly as do the shamanic myths and techniques. (Eliade 1964, 145)

The Evenki (Tungus) shaman's *kamlanye* performance demonstrates the relation between their shamanic worldview and the structure of the ritual venue. The tepee-shaped tent is either a modified domestic tent or one specially constructed by clan kinsmen several days before the performance. The ordinary tent is used for rites directed at finding lost reindeer or foretelling the future and as a preparatory venue for major rites where the shaman fasts, smokes heavily, and encourages visionary dreams.

Major *kamlanye* performances were held for guiding the soul of a dead person to the underworld, for feeding ancestral souls, and for the expulsion of disease-spirits. The ritual tent, containing a larch sapling positioned next to the hearth and emerging through the smoke hole, is surrounded by a small fenced-off enclosure containing platforms and carvings representing the structure of the world and designed to assist the journey of the shaman's animal-double spirit—his *khargu*—to the lower world. From inside the tent the east-facing shaman sees a double row of wooden knives and bear spears, and wooden images of salmon and pike familiar and guardian spirits. The shaman's drum (made of larch wood) and drumstick are often imaged as the canoe and paddle by which the shaman travels the shamanistic clan river. In front of the tent entrance is the *darpe*, a gallery of fresh larch saplings with roots skyward, and carved shamanic figures representing the upper world. To the west of the tent the *onang* structure, representing the lower world of the dead, constructed from dead fallen timbers, displays carved larch trees with roots facing downward. In the upper world larch trees grow downward from the soil of the sky vault, whereas they grow upward in the lower world. The larch tree protruding through the smoke vent signifies the world tree integrating the three levels or planes of existence. During a performance the shaman's spirit climbs the cosmic larch tree in his ascent to the upper world.

Similarly, while singing and drumming a Chilean Mapuche *machi* or shaman climbs her *rewe*, a large pole often displaying carvings of her familiar spirits, during a *machitan* or healing rite. Aboriginal shamans in central Australia climb a pole to signify ascent, and in Malaysia the Temoq shaman, traveling the rainbow shadow snake, signifies his ascent by dancing over the patient with a model of the world tree bedecked with miniature birds and fruit. The vision of Black Elk the Lakota shaman also strongly embodied the image of a life-giving world tree intimately connected to the welfare of his people.

Shamanism Today

Siberian shamans were persecuted and imprisoned and thousands died during the Soviet era. Since the establishment of the Russian Federation shamanism has shown a remarkable resurgence along with re-emergent ethnicities in such places as Tuva. A clinic has been opened by shamans in Kyzyl, the capital of the Tuvan Republic, south Russia, where shamanism and Buddhism amicably coexist. Folk groups travel with shamanically inspired repertoires to international venues, and many documentaries have been made on shamanism over the past few years. Native American shamans travel to Mongolia to deepen their calling under the tutelage of Mongolian shamans. In other places shamanism is under pressure not only from missionary activities, but also from globalization, which is seriously threatening the languages and cultures of minority peoples.

In the West, shamanism has captured the imagination of many, and this new form, called neoshamanism, attempts to selectively integrate aspects of indigenous shamanism with a range of concerns from New Age spirituality to transpersonal psychology. Neoshamanism aspires to go beyond modernity by grounding identity within a more inclusive spiritual,

psychological, and ecological vision of personal, social, and planetary well-being.

Peter F. LAIRD

Independent scholar, Farmingdale, New York

See also Animism

Further Reading

Anisimov, A. F. (1963). The shaman's tent of the evenks and the origin of the shamanistic rite. In H. N. Michael (Ed.), *Studies in Siberian shamanism.* Toronto: University of Toronto Press.

Balzer, M. M. (Ed.). (1990). *Shamanism: Soviet studies of traditional religion in Siberia and Central Asia.* New York & London: M. E. Sharpe.

Blacker, C. (1975). *The catalpa bow: A study of shamanistic practices in Japan.* London: George Allen & Unwin.

Dioszegi, V., & Hoppal, M. (1996). *Shamanism in Siberia* (Bibliotheca Shamanistica 2). Budapest, Hungary: Akademiai Kiado.

Eliade, M. (1964). *Shamanism: Archaic techniques of ecstasy* (Bollingen Series 76). Princeton, NJ: Princeton University Press.

Faron, L. C. (1968). *The Mapuche Indians of Chile.* New York: Holt, Rinehart & Winston.

Grim, J. A. (1983). *The Shaman: Patterns of Siberian and Ojibway healing.* Norman: University of Oklahoma Press.

Halifax, J. (1979). *Shamanic voices: A survey of visionary narratives.* New York: E. P. Dutton.

Halifax, J. (1982). *Shaman: The wounded healer.* London: Thames & Hudson.

Harner, M. (1982). *The way of the shaman: A guide to power and healing.* New York: Bantam Books.

Hultkrantz, A. (1992). *Shamanic healing and ritual drama: Health and medicine in native North American religious traditions.* New York: Crossroad.

Kendall, L. (1985). *Shamans, housewives, and other restless spirits: Women in Korean ritual life.* Honolulu: University of Hawaii Press.

Langdon, E. J. M., & Baer, G. (Eds.). (1992). *Portals of power: Shamanism in South America.* Albuquerque: University of New Mexico Press.

Mumford, S. R. (1989). *Himalayan dialogue: Tibetan lamas and Gurung shamans in Nepal.* Madison: University of Wisconsin Press.

Narby, J., & Huxley, F. (Eds.). (2001). *Shamans through time: 500 years on the path to knowledge*. London: Thames & Hudson.

Neihardt, J. G. (1972). *Black Elk speaks: Being the life story of a holy man of the Oglala Sioux*. New York: Pocket Books. (Original work published 1932)

Nowak, M., & Durrant, S. (1977). *The tale of the Nisan shamaness: A Manchu folk epic*. Seattle: University of Washington Press.

Ruhlen, M. (1998). The origin of the Na-Dene. *Proceedings of the National Academy of Sciences USA, 95,* 13994–13996.

Salchak, B. (1994). Kham (Shaman Ritual). In *Shu-De: Voices from the distant steppe*. Compact Disk No. 2339-2. New York: New World Records Ltd.

Seaman, G., & Day, J. S. (Eds.). (1994). *Ancient traditions: Shamanism in Central Asia and the Americas*. Niwot: University Press of Colorado.

Thomas, N., & Humphrey, C. (Eds.). (1996). *Shamanism, history, and the state*. Ann Arbor: University of Michigan Press.

Van Deusen, K. (2004). *Singing story, healing drum*. Montreal: McGill–Queen's University Press.

Waley, A. (1973). *The nine songs: A study of shamanism in ancient China*. San Francisco: City Lights Books.

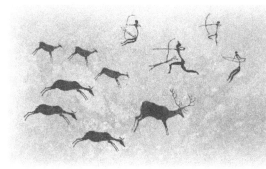

Shinto

The practices of Shinto in Japan developed over centuries, perhaps beginning as early as the fourth century BCE, and became distinctive as influences from Buddhism and Chinese religions spread eastward. A characteristic feature of Shinto, which still pervades contemporary Japanese culture, is *kami*, beings that dwell in heaven or reside on Earth as sacred forces within nature.

Shinto is the name for the religious beliefs and practices that are believed to have developed in Japan prior to the importation of foreign religious traditions from the Asian continent, beginning in the sixth century CE. With rare historical exceptions, the Japanese have not attempted to propagate Shinto outside of Japan, believing that it was the foundation of their cultural heritage and identity. One might conclude that the impact of Shinto in world history has been minor, but this is not the case. Shinto deeply influenced Japan's interactions with other cultures. Moreover, it continues to serve as a major religious and cultural institution in contemporary Japan.

Shinto in the Premodern Period

It is difficult to say with any certainty when Shinto began. Shinto had no founder and no scriptural tradition. Rather, the elements of what eventually became identified as Shinto developed over a period of centuries, perhaps from the fourth century BCE to the sixth century CE. During this period, ritual specialists worshipped spirits called *kami*; Shinto, in fact, literally means the "Way of the *kami*." While "spirit" is one generally accepted English equivalent for *kami*, the concept of the *kami* defies any simple translation. One eighteenth-century scholar of Shinto offered this explanation:

> I do not yet understand the meaning of the term kami. Speaking in general, however, it may be said that kami signifies, in the first place, the deities of heaven and earth that appear in the ancient records and also the spirits of the shrines where they are worshipped . . . It also includes such objects as birds, beasts, trees, plants, seas, mountains, and so forth. In ancient usage, anything whatsover which was outside the ordinary, which possessed superior power, or which was awe-inspiring was called kami. (Motoori Norinaga, quoted in Tsunoda 1958, 21)

Until the seventh century CE, there was no coherent state in Japan. Instead, various clans controlled their own territories. Historians believe that one of these clan leaders managed to convince other powerful clans of his ability to communicate with the *kami*. Over the course of the fifth and sixth centuries, the hereditary leader of this clan formed alliances with other clans, and Japan's first state, known as Yamato, was born. The leader of the dominant clan became the sovereign of this state and the "emperor" of Japan. That clan's connection with the *kami* meant that Shinto was linked with the new ruling family. Three of the most important Shinto shrines, for example, house the regalia that symbolize imperial rule. The Grand Shrines at Ise, which have been rebuilt every twenty or twenty-one years since the seventh century, are especially important as the primary site for the reverence of the *kami* Amaterasu, the deity of the sun and divine ancestor of the imperial family. It is at the Ise shrines that certain Shinto rituals connected with

Two Shinto good-luck charms. Photo by Mark McNally.

the imperial family, such as the enthronement of a new emperor, are usually conducted.

The institutional and doctrinal character of Shinto during this early period lacked coherence. Its rituals and practices were confined mostly to the social and political elites of the clans; the rest of Japanese society had their own forms of worship, which were only absorbed into Shinto in the nineteenth and twentieth centuries. Shinto became more clearly defined in contradistinction to Buddhism, which arrived in Japan in 538. Korean monks from the state of Paekche brought copies of Buddhist sutras with them to Japan, and many of these monks took up residence in Japan as teachers. Unlike Shinto, Buddhism had a founder, scriptural texts, and an exegetical tradition. Japanese elites were fascinated with Buddhism, which far surpassed Shinto in the sophistication of its teachings and practices. The "magic" of Buddhism, as evidenced by some Buddhist monks' knowledge of medical herbs and healing, also seemed superior to the magic of Shinto. During the sixth century, a rivalry developed between the adherents of Buddhism and Shinto priests, and it was during this period that Shinto began to develop a true institutional identity.

Although Shinto never lost its close association with the imperial court, Buddhism was very nearly given the status of a state religion in 745 CE by Emperor Shomu (701–756; reigned 715–749). In addition, Buddhism began to appeal more to the general populace during the eleventh century, as less esoteric, more faith-based schools of Buddhism were introduced. For the most part, Shinto leaders ignored commoner worshippers.

Ryobu Shinto

During Japan's classical and medieval periods (seventh through sixteenth centuries), there were two important developments in Shinto. The first was the emergence, beginning in the ninth century, of an esoteric strain called Ryobu Shinto, a syncretization of esoteric Buddhism and Shinto that equated particular Shinto deities with particular Buddhist deities. In this effort, the Shinto deities were viewed as incarnations of Buddhist gods, so that the latter took precedence over the former. In Ryobu Shinto, Shinto's doctrinal void was filled with Buddhist teachings. Ryobu Shinto was a dominant presence in the world of doctrinal Shinto until the fifteenth century.

A Shinto shrine in Japan. Deep connections to the Japanese imperial institution survive to this day, helping Shinto to preserve its authority and majesty. Photo by Mark McNally.

Yoshida Shinto

A Shinto priest, Yoshida Kanetomo (1435–1511), was dissatisfied with Ryobu Shinto because of its theological emphasis on Buddhism. He reversed Ryobu Shinto's syncretistic hierarchy and introduced Neo-Confucian values and teachings into Shinto. The result was called Yoshida Shinto. Although there were other Buddhist-Shinto blendings prior to the seventeenth century, Yoshida Shinto gradually became associated with the imperial court and Yoshida priests became the court's ritual specialists.

Shinto and Modern Japan

During the early modern period, roughly 1600 to 1870, scholars and intellectuals who wanted to purge Shinto of all foreign influences created a new field of Shinto scholarship. These nativist scholars (Japanese: *kokugakusha*) argued that Shinto must be purified of its long-standing ties to Buddhism, since the latter was a foreign creed. Yoshida Shinto's emphasis on Neo-Confucianism was similarly problematic because Neo-Confucianism was an intellectual import from China. The nativists believed that their mission was to eliminate foreign doctrinal contaminants from Shinto and to replace them with authentically Japanese teachings and values. They argued that these teachings could be found after a careful and thorough examination of Japan's classical literature, especially works composed in the period from the eighth to thirteenth centuries. According to the nativists, once Shinto was properly purified, it could become the basis for asserting a truly unique Japanese culture, which they believed was the only way to rectify the problems of their society. At the same time, the nativists of the early modern period believed that Shinto's lack of articulated teachings was one of its unique and valuable features. There was no need to govern the behavior of the Japanese people, they argued, because they were already blessed by the *kami* with the internal capacity to self-regulate. Another aspect of Shinto that the nativists called attention to, and that continues to be important in contemporary Shinto, is Shinto's the reverence for nature. Scenes of natural beauty, such as mountains, rock formations, and waterfalls, are believed to harbor their own *kami*. To commemorate the presence of the *kami*, a small shrine is erected, symbolized by a *torii*, a gate-like structure composed of two support beams and a crossbeam.

In 1868, when samurai political domination came to an end and the emperor was, in theory, restored to actual power, Shinto was given renewed cultural and political power. Shinto priests advocated that the new government be modeled on the one that had existed before the advent of warrior rule in 1192. Although the effort to resurrect the imperial government of the classical period was abandoned in favor of the creation of a government similar to those of the European powers, the services of Shinto priests were retained by government officials in the movement to establish a state religion. Japanese intellectuals argued that the material and technological successes of the Europeans were rooted, in part, in the strength of their religious values. The Japanese, they believed, needed to identify their own values and foreground them if they were to transform Japan into a strong nation like those of the West. After much debate, chiefly with the Buddhists, the Shinto priests succeeded in the creation and adoption of State Shinto. Thus, Shinto had an instrumental part in the emergence of Japan's modern state.

During the 1930s and 1940s, supporters of State Shinto were vocal supporters of the view that it was Japan's destiny to dominate the rest of Asia. When the tide turned against Japan in World War II, "special attack brigades" were formed, the most famous of which were the suicide pilots who flew their planes into enemy ships. Since the hope was that these pilots could reverse Japan's military decline, the Japanese called them the *kamikaze*, the "wind of the *kami*" in a deliberate invocation of a typhoon that had arrived, apparently in answer to the prayers of Shinto priests, and destroyed the boats of an invading Mongol army in the thirteenth century. Just as the *kami* had saved Japan from the Mongols, it was hoped that they would save it from the Allies.

In the postwar period, one shrine has generated controversy beyond Japan's borders. Yasukuni Shrine in Tokyo was originally built at the end of the nineteenth century to commemorate the souls of those who had fought on behalf of the imperial court in the overthrow of the samurai government in 1868. Later, it became the site for the veneration of soldiers and sailors who had died in subsequent wars, such as the Sino-Japanese War (1894–1895), the Russo-Japanese War (1904–1905), and World War I. In the postwar period, the ranks of those who had died in World War II were included in that number. Government leaders, including the prime minister, have paid official visits to the shrine. This has sparked outrage in both North and South Korea and in the People's Republic of China over what the populations in those countries feel is a show of respect for the dead of an unjust and

Small shrines to commemorate the presence of a *kami* are symbolized by a *torii*, a gate-like structure composed of two support beams and a crossbeam.
Photo by Mark McNally.

aggressive war, and a sign that Japanese claims of remorse for the war are not genuine.

Contemporary Shinto

The leaders of the postwar Allied Occupation of Japan (1945–1952) insisted that the Japanese abolish State Shinto. Although the imperial institution was allowed to endure, Shinto itself settled into two major forms. The first, a successor to State Shinto, is a set of practices surrounding the emperor and the imperial court, but purged of prewar ideology. The other developed out of traditions not directly associated with the imperial court. These were the benign practices performed by many Japanese people as a way to mark important events, such as the milestone years of childhood, the coming of age for young adults, and especially weddings.

Shinto manifests itself in the lives of ordinary people in other ways as well. Purification rituals are a common occurrence in contemporary Japan. Metaphors of purity and defilement are central to Shinto. Many Japanese will hire Shinto priests to purify people, places, and objects by driving out evil spirits. A building site is normally cleansed after construction and before it is open to the public. In order to invoke the protection of the *kami*, many Japanese purchase talismans (*omamori*) from shrines for such things as academic success and successful conceptions. On the eve of their high school or university entrance exams, students compose notes inscribed with their wishes for academic success and tie them to tree branches at Shinto shrines. Throughout the year, in all parts of Japan, people participate in festivals that are usually organized around local Shinto shrines.

It is perhaps not inaccurate to characterize Shinto as a religion of practitioners but not believers. While there are some worshippers who observe Shinto exclusively, most Japanese people observe both Buddhist and Shinto practices, exhibiting what some Japanese scholars describe as a kind of psychological "cohabitation." For example, it is not uncommon for families to make offerings in their home at both

a Shinto "*kami* shelf" (*kamidana*) and at a Buddhist altar (*butsudan*). The latter is especially important for the veneration of ancestors and recently deceased family members.

Shinto and World History

Although Shinto is not generally considered to be one of the world's great religions, it has had an impact on world history. It has had its moments of infamy, serving as the pretext for war and invasion. During the 1570s, the war leader Toyotomi Hideyoshi (1536–1598) rose to become the most powerful samurai in Japan, earning the title of imperial regent. In a letter to the Portuguese viceroy in Goa, he cited Japan's special place in the world by invoking Shinto: "Ours is the land of the Gods [*kami*], and God is mind. This God is spoken of by Buddhism in India, Confucianism in China, and Shinto in Japan. To know Shinto is to know Buddhism as well as Confucianism" (quoted in Tsunoda 1958, 317). Hideyoshi made it clear that his rule was with the consent of the *kami* and the emperor, who himself was viewed as a living *kami*. Empowered with the sanction of Shinto, Hideyoshi ordered the invasion of Korea in 1592, with the eventual goal of subjugating China. Hideyoshi's death put an end to his plans for conquest, but not before Japanese forces had wreaked considerable havoc in Korea. In Japan, however, he was deified and subsequently worshipped as a Shinto *kami*.

As mentioned earlier, Shinto was also invoked in Japan's rise to militarism and imperialism in the 1930s. The unique "Japanese soul" (Yamato damashii) bespoke innate Japanese superiority and fostered an attitude of contempt for other, lesser peoples.

But Shinto was also instrumental in the emergence of the modern state in a more positive sense, supporting a sense of place and a sense of community. Shinto's deep connections to the Japanese imperial institution survive to this day, helping it to preserve its authority and majesty. Even without a coherent doctrinal tradition, Shinto has functioned as the foundation of Japan's cultural identity for more than a millennium.

Mark McNALLY
University of Hawaii

Further Reading

Akio, A., & Shigemichi, T. (Eds.). (1972). *Kinsei Shinto-ron zenki Kokugaku* [Early modern Shinto discourse and early nativism]. Tokyo: Iwanami Shoten.

Breen, J. (1991). "Shinto and Christianity: The dynamics of the encounter in bakumatsu Japan". *Transactions of the Asiatic Society of Japan (Fourth Series), 6*(6), 49–60.

Breen, J., & Teeuwen, M. (Eds.). (2000). *Shinto in history: Ways of the kami.* Honolulu: University of Hawaii Press.

Devine, R. (1981). Hirata Atsutane and Christian sources. *Monumenta Nipponica, 36*(1), 37–54.

Earhart, H. B. (1982). *Japanese religion: Unity and diversity.* Belmont, CA: Wadsworth Publishing Company.

Fujitani, T. (1996). *Splendid monarchy: Power and pageantry in modern Japan.* Berkeley and Los Angeles: University of California Press.

Hardacre, H. (1989). *Shinto and the state, 1868–1988.* Princeton, NJ: Princeton University Press.

Harootunian, H. D. (1988). *Things seen and unseen: Discourse and ideology in Tokugawa nativism.* Chicago: University of Chicago Press.

Maruyama Masao. (1961). *Nihon no shisô* [Japanese thought]. Tokyo: Iwanami Shoten.

Maruyama Masao. (1974). *Studies in the intellectual history of Tokugawa Japan* (M. Hane, Trans.). Princeton, NJ: Princeton University Press.

Matsumoto Sannosuke. (1972). *Kokugaku seiji shisô no kenkyû* [Studies in the political thought of nativism]. Tokyo: Miraisha.

Motoori Norinaga. (1997). *Kojiki-den, Book One* (A. Wehmeyer, Trans.). Ithaca, NY: East Asia Program, Cornell University.

Nelson, J. (1996). *A year in the life of a Shinto shrine.* Seattle: University of Washington Press.

Nelson, J. (2000). *Enduring identities: The guise of Shinto in contemporary Japan.* Honolulu: University of Hawaii Press.

Nosco, P. (1990). *Remembering paradise: Nativism and nostalgia in eighteenth-century Japan.* Cambridge, MA: Council on East Asian Studies, Harvard University.

Ono Sokyo. (1962). *Shinto: The kami way.* Rutland, VT: Tuttle.

Ooms, H. (1985). *Tokugawa ideology: Early constructs, 1570–1680.* Princeton, NJ: Princeton University Press.

Shinto jiten [Shinto encyclopedia]. (1999). Tokyo: Kobundo.

Teeuwen, M. (1996). *Watarai Shinto: An intellectual history of the outer shrine in Ise.* Leiden, The Netherlands: Research School, CNWS.

Tsunoda, R., de Bary, W. T., & Keene, D. (Eds.). (1958). *Sources of Japanese tradition* (Vol. 1). New York: Columbia University Press.

Sikhism

Sikhism is an eclectic faith combining the teachings of Hinduism and other traditions first laid down by its founder, Guru Nanak (1469–1539?), in the Punjab region of India. Sikhs have migrated to many parts of the world and set up large communities; they stress respect for other faiths, emphasize a sense of social duty, and give great importance to the equality of all human beings.

Sikhism is a religion that developed in the Punjab area of the Indian subcontinent in the fifteenth century CE. The founder of the religion was Guru Nanak, who was born in 1469 CE in Talwandi. Guru Nanak was originally a Hindu, but drew upon a range of religious influences in creating his distinctive spiritual message. In his early years he earned his living by keeping financial records, but was attracted to the religious life, and made a series of journeys to religious sites that were significant to both Muslims and Hindus. It seems that he traveled to Varanasi (Benares), to the very south of India, and also to Mecca. After this long period of pilgrimage, Guru Nanak moved to the village of Kartarpur in the Punjab where he gathered around himself a community of disciples. Toward the end of his life, Guru Nanak selected a man named Lehna to be his successor. From then onward, Lehna became known as Guru Angad.

In his teachings Guru Nanak laid the religious foundations of Sikhism, but his spiritual successors amplified the teachings. After Guru Angad there were eight other Sikh gurus, culminating in Guru Gobind Singh, who died in 1708 CE. The teachings of some of the Sikh gurus, along with those of several Hindu and Muslim teachers, were ultimately gathered together into the definitive scripture, the *Guru Granth Sahib*. The names and dates of the ten Sikh gurus are: Guru Nanak (1469–1539?); Guru Angad (1504–1552); Guru Amar Das (1479–1574); Guru Ram Das (1534–1581); Guru Arjun (1563–1606); Guru Hargobind (1595–1644); Guru Har Rai (1630–1661); Guru Hari Krishen (1656–1664); Guru Tegh Bahadur (1621?–1675); Guru Gobind Singh (1666–1708). It was decided by Guru Gobind Singh that he would be the last person who was guru, and that from then onward, the scripture of the Sikhs, the *Guru Granth Sahib*, would become the guru.

Religious Beliefs

Sikhism is a monotheistic religion that lays emphasis upon the relationship of the individual with God. The Sikh scripture emphasizes the influence of God in creating an ethical unity or the Punjabi *hukam* in the universe. The goal of human beings should be to try to live according to this ethical principle, while at the same time not being egoistic or focused on the self. If the individual tries diligently to adhere to this way of life, then with the grace of God, it is possible to attain salvation. Sikhs may also use a form of meditation involving the repetition of the name of God, to assist in achieving salvation. The state of salvation is sometimes described by the Punjabi term *sahaj*, which indicates the merging of the individual with the divine.

In a Sikh community, worship is normally focused upon a *gurdwara*. This is a place of communal worship, in which is kept a copy of the *Guru Granth Sahib*. This scripture is regarded with great reverence by the Sikhs, as it is considered to be one of the principal

A Sikh family crosses a bridge over the Thames. Founded in India, Sikhism is now a world religion, with Sikhs living in many nations.

ways in which God reveals his teachings to humanity. The holy book is kept on a pedestal at one end of a large prayer room, in which when services are being held, men sit on one side and women on the other. Worship at the *gurdwara* may consist of readings from the *Guru Granth Sahib*, the singing of hymns accompanied by music, and also spiritual talks.

After the worship, there is often a communal meal or *langar*. This social custom was instituted by the Sikh gurus to emphasize the equality of all people. In the India of the time, there were a number of prohibitions about food that related to the caste which a person occupied. The Sikh gurus felt that these were inappropriate, and the *langar* was developed to stress the absence of social divisions among Sikhs. Guru Nanak was opposed to extravagant forms of religious ritual, and this is reflected in the relative simplicity of Sikh worship. Sikhism does not particularly attempt to convert people to its faith. While Sikhs are very proud of their own religion, they also show respect for other faiths.

Historical Development

Sikhism developed at a period of conflict in northern India, exacerbated by the geographical position of the Punjab on the natural invasion route from the north into India. The historical period covered by the Sikh gurus saw intermittent conflict between the developing Sikh community and the Muslim invaders of India. The Sikhs felt, to some extent, the need to defend their community militarily in order to survive. But relations with the Mughal Empire were at times very friendly. Guru Amar Das, for example, was a contemporary of the Mughal emperor Akbar (ruled 1556–1605 CE), and it seems likely that the two men did in fact meet, under very amicable circumstances. Guru Arjan, on the other hand, possibly because of political conflict, alienated the emperor Jahangir (ruled 1605–1627) and was subsequently executed. The emperor Aurangzeb (ruled 1659–1707) instituted a period of stricter observance of Islamic views. There was conflict with the Sikhs, and the ninth guru, Tegh Bahadur, was ultimately executed. His son, Guru Gobind Singh, became leader of the Sikh community, and introduced changes that were to have long-term consequences for Sikhs. Besides establishing the Sikh scripture as Guru, he instituted the *khalsa*, or community of people who had been formally accepted as Sikhs. Members of the *khalsa* tend to be recognized by five characteristics: they do not cut their hair; they wear a comb to keep it in order; and they wear a sword, a steel bangle on the wrist, and a pair of shorts beneath their outer garment. These customs have given Sikhs a sense of coherence as a community.

When all efforts to restore peace prove / useless and no words avail, / Lawful is the flash of steel, / It is right to draw the sword. • **Guru Gobind Singh (1666–1708)**

Influence of Sikhism

Although there was some continuing conflict between Sikhs and Muslims, the Sikh community managed to sustain its sense of identity. In recent times, Sikhs have migrated to many parts of the world and set up large and successful communities, for example in Canada and in London. Sikhism has emphasized a number of principles that are of value to the world faith community. It has stressed a respect for other faiths; it has emphasized a sense of social duty, and given great importance to the equality of all human beings.

Paul OLIVER
University of Huddersfield

Further Reading

Cole, W. O., & Sambhi, P. S. (1978). *The Sikhs: Their religious beliefs and practices.* London: Routledge & Kegan Paul.

Gill, D. (2003). *World religions.* London: HarperCollins.

Jain, N. K. (1979). *Sikh religion and philosophy.* New Delhi, India: Sterling.

McLeod, W. H. (1968). *Guru Nanak and the Sikh religion.* Oxford, U.K.: Oxford University Press.

McLeod, W. H. (1997). *Sikhism.* London: Penguin.

Sambhi, P. S. (1989). *Sikhism.* Cheltenham, U.K.: Stanley Thornes.

Singh, H. (1985). *Heritage of the Sikhs.* Delhi, India: Manohar.

Singh, T. (1964). *Sikhism: Its ideals and institutions.* Calcutta (Kolkata): Orient Longmans.

Talib, G. S. (1999). *An introduction to Sri Guru Granth Sahib.* Patiala, India: Panjabi University.

Thomas Aquinas, Saint
(c. 1225–1274)
ITALIAN PHILOSOPHER AND THEOLOGIAN

Saint Thomas Aquinas represents the culmination of philosophical and theological achievement during the European Middle Ages, and his influence on subsequent generations of Western philosophers and Christian theologians has been profound.

The Italian philosopher and theologian Saint Thomas Aquinas (c. 1225–1274) proved a powerful and influential advocate of the philosophy of the Greek philosopher Aristotle. He was the author of what remains the most comprehensive effort at reconciling reason and religious faith ever attempted by a Catholic thinker.

The son of Count Landulf of Aquino, Thomas was a member of the south Italian nobility. Born at Roccasecca, between Rome and Naples, he received his preliminary education at the nearby monastery of Monte Cassino. In 1239 Thomas's parents sent him to the University of Naples, where he first engaged in intensive study of Aristotle under the scholar Peter of Ireland. During his years at Naples, Thomas made two important decisions: to devote the rest of his life to philosophy and theology and to become a Dominican friar. The two decisions were related because Dominicans were already among the leading scholars of the day. When Thomas became a friar in 1244 he received permission to leave Naples for Paris to study under the renowned Dominican philosopher and scientist Albert the Great (c. 1195–1280).

This move was opposed by his family, who intended for him to become a bishop or the abbot of a prominent monastery. Abducted by his family as he was traveling northward through Italy, he was held captive at Roccasecca for a year before being allowed to proceed on his chosen path.

Thomas studied under Albert the Great at both Paris and Cologne, Germany, where Albert relocated in 1248 to establish a Dominican *studium generale*, a college for study of the liberal arts. Thomas served as one of his assistants, giving introductory lectures on biblical interpretation. In 1252, his academic apprenticeship completed, Thomas returned to Paris to take up the position of lecturer on the Bible and the *Sentences* of the Italian theologian Peter Lombard (c. 1095–1161), the core textbook of the theology curriculum. He also began to publish his own work and in 1256 was appointed to the position of master of theology, the highest title attainable in the academic hierarchy.

In 1259 Thomas traveled to Italy and remained through 1268, lecturing at Dominican convents and colleges in Naples, Orvieto, and Rome. He frequently attended the papal court, providing his services as preacher and liturgist. He returned to Paris at the height of his reputation but soon found himself embroiled in a major controversy over the proper relationship of philosophy and theology.

Thomas's first major book, a commentary on Lombard's *Sentences*, contains more than two thousand references to the works of Aristotle. Already in his early days as a teacher he had defined his intellectual project: to establish the proper relationship between philosophy and theology. In this pursuit he made use of not only the works of Christian theologians and ancient Greek and Roman thinkers, but also the works of Muslim and Jewish philosophers such as Ibn Sina (980–1037), Ibn Rushd (1126–1198), and

THOMAS AQUINAS, SAINT · 229

The highest manifestation of life consists in this: that a being governs its own actions. A thing which is always subject to the direction of another is somewhat of a dead thing. • **Saint Thomas Aquinas (1225–1274)**

Vittore Carpaccio, *St. Thomas of Aquinas in Glory between St. Mark and St. Louis of Toulouse* (1507). Tempera on canvas. Staatsgalerie, Germany.

Ibn Gabirol (1021–1058). Thomas argued that both philosophy and faith are necessary to a true pursuit of theology because logical argumentation leads to a more precise and complete knowledge of religious belief. Thomas further held that, even without faith in Christian revelation, the human mind can use rational analysis of observations made through the five senses to attain an incomplete but still extensive understanding of the being of God and the nature of the rational laws governing the created universe.

While Thomas was in Italy, a group of scholars in Paris called the "Averroists" (followers of Ibn Rushd) were promulgating the position that the truths of philosophy and the truths of religion are equally true, but separate and distinct, because philosophical knowledge derives from rational analysis of human experience alone, whereas theological knowledge derives exclusively from divine revelation. The bishop of Paris, Stephen Tempier, condemned the position of the Averroists in 1270. Conservative critics associated Thomas with the Averroists because of his devotion to Aristotle, and he had to expend much energy in his final years to carefully distinguish his position from theirs.

In 1272 the Dominicans sent Thomas to Naples to set up a new *studium generale*, but at this point his health began to weaken. He died at the Cistercian monastery of Fossanova while on his way from Naples to Lyons to attend a church council summoned by the pope.

The principal writings of Thomas Aquinas include the *Disputed Questions* (1256–1272); the *Summa contra gentiles* (1259–1265), which provides a detailed defense of the philosophical validity of the Christian faith; and the *Summa theologiae* (begun in 1268 but unfinished at Thomas's death), which comprehensively synthesizes Thomas's rational investigation and logical demonstration of Catholic doctrine. When Tempier condemned the Averroists a second time in 1277, he explicitly included condemnations of several teachings from these works. However, Thomas had many posthumous supporters, including Albert the Great and the Italian poet Dante, who assigned him a privileged place in paradise. Pope John XXII had Thomas canonized in 1323. During the sixteenth century Thomas's *Summa theologiae* replaced Peter

Lombard's *Sentences* as the standard textbook in the theology curriculum of European universities, where his work remained influential well into the 1600s. Thomism has enjoyed a revival since the late nineteenth century, thanks in part to a papal bull (decree) of 1879 encouraging study of Thomas's work, and his brilliant and rigorous application of Aristotelian arguments retains considerable interest for twenty-first-century philosophers.

Scott C. WELLS
California State University, Los Angeles

See also Roman Catholicism

Further Reading

Chenu, M. D. (1964). *Toward understanding Saint Thomas.* Chicago: H. Regnery.

Dyson, R. W. (2002). *Aquinas: Political writings.* Cambridge, U.K.: Cambridge University Press.

Kretzmann, N., & Stump, E. (1993). *The Cambridge companion to Aquinas.* Cambridge, U.K.: Cambridge University Press.

McInerny, R. (1998). *Thomas Aquinas: Selected writings.* London: Penguin Books.

Persson, P. E. (1970). *Sacra doctrina: Reason and revelation in Aquinas.* Philadelphia: Fortress Press.

Rosemann, P. (1999). *Understanding scholastic thought with Foucault.* New York: St. Martin's Press.

Tugwell, S. (1988). *Albert and Thomas: Selected writings.* New York: Paulist Press.

Zionism

Zionism is a movement to establish a homeland for Jews who have been scattered throughout Europe. The word Zion refers to the land promised to the Jews by God in the Bible, but the activity of Zionism is almost exclusively political, rather than religious, because of Jews' understanding that the land is not to be inhabited until the coming of their Messiah.

The need for a Jewish homeland began in 70 CE with the destruction of the second Temple of Jerusalem by the Romans. Since that time Jews have lived as a minority group in many countries. Despite the diversity of cultural settings and political regimes during the centuries, they have been able to maintain their ethnic, religious, and linguistic characteristics. Because of their strong nationalistic identity, they have been subjected to prejudice—known as "anti-Semitism"—and even persecution in many of the countries to which they have migrated. As a result, the primary aim of Zionists has been to find a homeland (preferably in the Jewish ancestral home of Palestine) where they can gain political independence, develop Hebrew as the spoken language, and provide a community for Jews who have been dispersed for centuries.

Writers during the nineteenth century spread Zionist ideas throughout Europe. Moses Hess wrote two works outlining the return of Jews to Palestine, Rome and Jerusalem (1862) and Plan for the Colonization of the Holy Land (1867). Leo Pinsker wrote in his pamphlet Auto-Emancipation (1882) that "The Jews are not a living nation; they are everywhere aliens; therefore they are despised . . . The proper and only remedy would be the creation of a Jewish nationality . . . a home of their own."

Theodor Herzl (1860–1904), an Austrian journalist, moved to the forefront of the movement with the organization of the first Zionist Congress at Basel, Switzerland, in 1897. Delegates at the congress called for a publicly recognized Jewish home in Palestine. During the remainder of his life Herzl negotiated with world leaders to gain support for the Zionist movement. In 1903 the British government offered a large tract of land in Uganda, East Africa, for a Jewish homeland. Herzl promoted this idea to the Zionist Congress in 1903 as a "temporary haven" for Jews. Delegates at the congress strongly opposed the idea and remained committed to Palestine as the only sanctuary for Jews scattered throughout the world. Herzl died in 1904, but his contributions to the movement earned him the title of the "Father of Modern Zionism."

Between 1881 and 1903 the first modern migration of Jews to Palestine established a small but influential presence. The first group of settlers was known as "Chovevei Zion" (Lovers of Zion). Numbering just thirteen men and one woman, the group landed at Jaffa on 7 July 1882. Many others followed during the first aliyah (going up) to Israel. In 1904 the second aliyah brought a new wave of immigrants to Palestine, mostly Russian Jews, including such influential leaders of the nation of Israel as David Ben-Gurion and Izhak Ben-Zvi. By the beginning of World War I about ninety thousand Jews were living in Palestine.

Diplomacy

Zionists pursued their political agenda for a Jewish state in Palestine through diplomatic means with Great Britain and the other Allied powers (Russia, France, England, Italy, and the United States). The

British tried to gain support in the Palestinian region from both Jews and Arabs. Because Palestine was under the political control of the Ottoman Turks, who joined Germany to oppose the Allied powers, the postwar division of Palestine by the victorious Allied forces was complicated by secret and ambiguous agreements made during the war among the British and Arabs and Jews.

Correspondence between Arab leader Sherif Hussein and the British high commissioner in Egypt, Sir Henry McMahon, expressed British support for an independent Arab state in Palestine. At the same time as these negotiations, the Sykes-Picot Agreement divided the region into mandate territories that would be under the influence or direct control of the British and French governments. The Sykes-Picot Agreement of 1916 contained provisions that contradicted the Hussein-McMahon correspondence.

Meanwhile, Chaim Weizman, a Russian-born chemist and president of the World Zionist Organization, made contacts with many British leaders to gain sympathy for the Zionist cause. David Lloyd George, prime minister of Great Britain, viewed Palestine as the biblical home of the Jews. Also, British foreign secretary Arthur Balfour was supportive of the Zionist viewpoint and hoped that a Jewish homeland in Palestine would enable the British to have an influential presence in the region. On 2 November 1917, the Balfour Declaration expressed Britain's public support for the establishment of a Jewish home in Palestine.

As a mandate territory under British control, Palestine was defined geographically for the first time in modern history. The League of Nations ratified the Palestine mandate territory in 1922. The preamble of the mandate included the Balfour Declaration, thus promoting the Zionist ideal of a Jewish state in Palestine to the status of international law.

Under British rule immigration by Jews to Palestine continued. Political and economic competition between Arabs and Jews escalated during the 1920s. Tension between the two groups climaxed in August 1929 during a Jewish religious fast when riots broke out in Jerusalem. More than sixty Jews and Arabs were killed. The British declared martial law in the region and sent an investigative commission to conduct hearings and issue a report. The report, known as the "Passfield White Paper," stated that the riots had been caused by Arab fears of Jewish domination. The white paper called for a suspension of Jewish immigration until a policy could be created. The protest from Zionists and Jewish immigrants was so strong that the white paper was repealed the next year.

The rise of the German Nazi leader Adolph Hitler in 1933 resulted in a new wave of anti-Semitism in Europe and a large migration of Jews to Palestine. By 1936, 30 percent of the population in Palestine was Jewish. Arabs reacted violently to the migration because they feared that they would become the minority group. Arabs pleaded with the British for their support.

In 1939 the British sought to resolve the Arab–Jewish problem by limiting the Jewish population in Palestine to one-third of the total population. Furthermore, the British declared that Palestine would become an independent state within ten years. Many Zionists saw this declaration as unacceptable because the state would be under Arab majority control, and the movement to establish a Jewish homeland would end. Many Palestinian Jews demanded an immediate uprising against the British. But the most prominent Zionist group, led by David Ben-Gurion, opposed an uprising. Instead, Jews undertook active resistance to the restrictions on Jewish immigration.

During World War II Zionists supported the Allies (France, England, China, Russia, and the United States) against Germany. Zionist leaders did not become aware of the Holocaust and the German plan to annihilate the Jewish people until 1942. The war in Europe and the Holocaust made it essential for Zionists to enlist support from the United States for a Jewish state in Palestine. Prior to World War II the United States had been neutral on the issue and saw the Palestine region as the responsibility of the British government. At the Biltmore Conference of the World Zionist Organization in 1942, Zionist leaders unanimously called for the immediate establishment of a Jewish commonwealth in Palestine and sought to pressure the United States into supporting their agenda. However, both British and U.S. governments opposed the Zionist plan because they wanted to maintain close ties with Arab neighbors who controlled vital oil deposits.

U.N. Resolution 181

At the end of World War II the British government sought an end to the mounting violence between Jews and Arabs in Palestine. Unable to mediate a settlement, the British unceremoniously turned the problem over to the United Nations in 1947. After much deliberation the United Nations on 29 November 1947 passed Resolution 181, which proposed partition of Palestine into separate Arab and Jewish states, with Jerusalem under permanent trusteeship. This resolution guaranteed a Jewish homeland. The Arabs immediately opposed the partition with violence. British troops hastily left the region in May 1948, refusing to enforce the U.N. resolution, and Zionists proclaimed the creation of the state of Israel. The first Arab–Israeli war erupted on 15 May 1948, with Arab armies from Egypt, Lebanon, Syria, and Iraq invading Israel. After a series of ceasefires and armistice agreements, Israel won its independence, and the Zionist dream was a reality.

Since the establishment of Israel as a state, Zionism has continued, offering a homeland to Jews who embrace Israel as theirs. Formalized support also continues as Zionists create economic and political programs that support their cause and as they continue to remind Israel that their definition as a state also delineates their culture and history as Jews. The most activist sects of the Zionist movement have viewed the military successes of Israel in the 1948 War of Independence and the Six-Day War of 1967 as divine miracles and a foreshadowing of the coming of the biblical Messiah. Thus, some Zionists view the retaining of the biblical land of Israel as a "holy war" against Palestinian nationalist ideologies and Islamic religious movements. Furthermore, they believe that the existence of Palestinian settlements in the West Bank and Gaza Strip has prevented Jews from being able to claim complete or at least peaceful success in their goal of a homeland. More moderate Zionists have maintained a purely political agenda to continue to secure a homeland for Jews and maintain a cultural identity, trying to live in peace with their neighbors. However, some countries outside of the Middle East strongly believe that Zionism has refined itself from what had begun as a political agenda to an agenda driven by religious ideology.

To gain influence with the Arab community, Russia influenced the United Nations to draft Resolution 3379 on 10 November 1975, condemning Zionism as a form of racism and racial discrimination. The United States and its Western allies, who saw the resolution as a condemnation of the nation of Israel, bitterly contested the resolution. In 1991 the resolution was repealed amid efforts to allow the United Nations to play a role in the ongoing Middle East peace talks.

Zionism continues to play a major role in the Middle East peace talks as recent terrorist attacks have led to a call for more national unity in Israel in the spirit of the early days of the movement. Zionist rhetoric is used by both Jews and Arabs to describe the tense political situation in the region. The key to the future of Zionism is the connection between its religious identity and its desire for a homeland.

Mark McCALLON

Abilene Christian University

See also Judaism

Further Reading

Bickerton, I. J., & Klausner, C. L. (1998). *A concise history of the Arab-Israeli conflict* (3rd ed.). Upper Saddle River, NJ: Prentice Hall.

Cohen, R. (2009). *Israel is real: An obsessive quest to understand the Jewish nation and its history.* New York: Farrar, Straus, and Giroux.

Halpern, B., & Reinharz, J. (1998). *Zionism and the creation of a new society.* New York: Oxford University Press.

Hertzberg, A. (Ed.). (1959). *The Zionist idea: A historical analysis and reader.* Garden City, NY: Doubleday & Herzl Press.

Levin, N. G., Jr. (Ed.). (1974). *The Zionist movement in Palestine and world politics, 1880–1918.* Lexington, MA: D. C. Heath.

Radosh, A., & Radosh, R. (2009). *A safe haven: Harry S. Truman and the founding of Israel.* New York: Harper.

Zoroastrianism

Zoroaster was a Persian prophet who taught that rival gods—one good, one evil—struggled for control of the world. He called on his followers to support the good and promised them eternal life after the fiery end of the world. Today about two hundred thousand Zoroastrians remain in Iran, India, and North America. Zoroastrian dualism survives in concepts of hell and the devil as formulated in the Christian and Muslim religions.

Zoroastrianism is the ancient religion of the Iranian people. The prophet of this religion is Zarathushtra (Greek form Zoroaster), who lived approximately 1000 BCE in eastern Persia. The religion of the Iranians was closely related to that of the Indians who had immigrated to the Indus region. The Indo-Iranian religion was polytheistic and included two groups of deities, the Ahuras and the Daivas. Zoroaster reformed the old Indo-Iranian religion and made one group of these deities the beneficent ones (Ahuras), and another maleficent (Daivas). Among the Ahuras, one named Ahura Mazda (Wise Lord) was made supreme and the creator of the world and all that is good. Ahura Mazda was aided by a group of deities who act as his aspects or his archangels. While they were not a fixed number during the time of the prophet, they include Khshathra (Dominion); Haurvatat (Health); Spenta Armaiti (Devotion); Ameretat (Immortality); Vohu Manah (Good Thought); Asha (Truth/Order); and Spenta Mainyu (Holy Spirit).

Ahura Mazda is opposed by a host of fallen deities, the Daivas, who remained supreme in the Indic religion. For of each of Ahura Mazda archangels a deadly and maleficent demon was created to bring death and destruction to the world. These Daivas are headed by Angra Mainyu (Ahriman), which can be translated as Evil Spirit. It is the Daivas who attempt to destabilize the universal order (arta) and are in constant battle with the Ahuras. According to Zoroaster's own words, people have the freedom of will to choose with a clear mind between the two sides, but if one chooses to be on the side of the Daivas and Angra Mainyu, he or she will suffer at the time of renovation (end of time) and will be placed in the Zoroastrian hell, which is dark and full of stench. But if one chooses on the side of Ahura Mazda, he or she will be prosperous and at the end of time will remain in the house of songs and best existence, that is, heaven. This is the first time in history that we find these concepts set forth, which later influenced Abrahamic religions when the Achaemenid Persian Empire ruled over Asia and the eastern Mediterranean.

The prophecies of Zoroaster are contained in seventeen hymns known as the Gathas of Zoroaster, which are part of a greater collection of hymns written down in the Sasanian period in the sixth century CE, known as the Avesta. The Avesta is multilayered and parts of it can be dated to different periods of Persian history. When Zoroaster passed away, his community composed a series of seven hymns known as Yasna Haptanhaiti, which is a further blessing of the Ahuras and solidification of Zoroastrian beliefs. By the time of the Achaemenid Persian Empire, the old Ahuras and some of the Indo-Iranian deities who were not the focus of Zoroaster's devotion made their appearance in the Zoroastrian religion. A number of deities such as Anahita, Mithra, Verethragna, Sraosha, and Tishtarya are worshiped and mentioned

Let us be such as help the life of the future. • **Zoroaster (c. 1000 BCE)**

in the part of the Avesta known as the Yashts. These Yashts are hymns to various deities who are invoked for specific purposes and have various functions and associations. For example, Anahita is associated with water and fertility, Mithra with oaths and later the sun, and Verethragna with offensive victory. The section of the Avesta that mainly deals with law of purity and pollution as well as early myths of the Iranian people is known as Widewdad (antidemonic law).

The priests who memorized these sacred words and were responsible for the compilation of all the hymns are known as the Magi. They appear to have been a Median tribe (according to Herodotus) who were specialists in religion and served from the time of the Achaemenid period onward. One of the ceremonies of the Magi was the Haoma ceremony, in which the Magus mixed plant juice with milk and drank it in order to gain power and have visions. Fire is the other sacred element, which the Magi respected and before which they sang hymns. Hence, the place where the sacred fire burned and the place where the Magi worshiped was known as the fire-temple.

By the Sasanian Persian Empire in the third century CE, the hymns that were memorized were collected and those that were deemed unfit were forsaken. The Sasanian state became allied with the Zoroastrian Magi and a Zoroastrian Empire was born. The Avesta was codified and written down in a specific script. With the Arab Muslim conquest of Persia in the seventh century CE, the number of Zoroastrians began to dwindle. The Zoroastrians became a minority in the Muslim Empire and while some remained in Persia, many left for India. Today about two hundred thousand Zoroastrians remain in the world, mainly in Iran, India, and North America. Because of the low birth rate and the fact that Zoroastrianism is not a proselytizing religion, the number of followers of this religion is dwindling.

> In the Zoroastrian pantheon Ahura Mazda (Wise Lord) is the supreme deity and the beneficent creator of the world.

Touraj DARYAEE
University of California, Irvine

Further Reading

Boyce, M. (1984). *Textual sources for the study of Zoroastrianism.* Chicago: University of Chicago Press.

Kellens, J. (2000). *Essays on Zarathustra and Zoroastrianism* (P. O. Skjaervo, Trans. & Ed.). Costa Mesa, CA: Mazda Publishers.

Malandra, W. W. (1983). *An introduction to ancient Iranian religion: Readings from the Avesta and the Achaemenid Inscriptions.* Minneapolis: University of Minnesota Press.

Index

Notes: 1) Names, terms, and page-number ranges in **bold** denote chapter entries.

A

Abbasid caliphate, 91–92
　religion and war, 186
Abduh, Mohammad, 93
Abraham, 10–12, 182
　See also **Islam; Judaism**
Abu'l Fazl, 79
Abu Sufyan, 186
Afghanistan (2009 statistics),
　Bamiyan Buddhas, 40
　Islam in, 95
Africa,
　Kanem-Bornu, 22
　religions. *See* **African religions**
　See also **African American and Caribbean religions**
African American and Caribbean religions, 13–20
　African religions in the New World, 13–14
　African religions in the United States, 17–18
　Caribbean religions, 15–17
　music of, 19
African Americans, music, 19
African Independent Churches, 203
African Methodist Episcopal Church, 19
African Methodist Episcopal Zion Church, 18
African religions, 21–25
　Catholicism, 210, 211
　Christianity, 15, 22, 23
　Islam, 15, 22–23
　Mormonism, 115, 117
　possession cults, 24
　secret societies, 21
　supreme deity, 21–22
　See also **African American and Caribbean religions**
Akan, 14
Akbar, 79

al-Afghani, Jamal al-Din, 94
al-Ala Mawdudi, Abu, 95
al-Banna, Hasan, 95
Alchemy, 71, 74
Ali Muhammad (Islamic reformer), 93
Allah, 5
　See also **Islam**
Allen, Richard, 18
al-Nasir, Gamal Abd, 95
al-Qadir, Abd, 93
al-Qaeda, 95, 131, 198
al-Shafi'i, Abu 'Abd Allah, 92, 95
al-Wahhab, Muhammad ibn Abd, 94
American Muslim Mission, 18
Anabaptists, 180
Ancestor worship, Chinese, 46
Anglicanism, 171
Angola, slave trade, 13
Animism, 26–27
　See also **Shamanism**
Anti-Semitism, Nazism and, 232
Apophatic theology, 56–57
Aquinas, Thomas. *See* **Thomas Aquinas, Saint**
Arab caliphates, 186
　See also **Muhammad**
Art—Native North American. *See* **Native American religions**
Ashante (Ghana), 22
Asia, religions in, 212
　Mormonism, 117
　See also **Buddhism; Chinese traditional religions; Confucianism; Daoism; Hinduism; Islam; Missionaries**
Assyrian Church of the East, 53
Atatürk, Mustafa Kemal, 95
Athens, 2
Atonement (Christian orthodoxy), 57–58
Augustine, Saint, 28–30, 57, 159, 183–185, 190, 207
　See also **Roman Catholicism**
Ayurvedic medicine, 87
Aztec Empire, religions, 2

237

B

Bab, the, 31–33
Babylon, 4
Bahá'i, 31–34
Baha'u'llah (Baha' Allah), 31–34
Baird, Robert D., 200
Bakker, Jim, 163
Balfour, Arthur, 232
Balfour Declaration, 232
Baptist religion, 16, 17–18, 195
Barbarism, 11
Barrett, David J., 163
Bastide, Rober, 203
Benedict XV, Pope, 208
Ben-Gurion, David, 231
Ben-Zvi, Izhak, 231
Beyer, Peter, 200
Bhagavad Gita, 83, 86
Bible, 6
    Native American religions and, 153
Big bang theory, 69
Bligh, Captain William, 170
Bodhidharma, 42
Boniface VIII, Pope, 207
Bori cult, 24
Brazil,
    religions, 202, 203, 204, 212
    slavery, slave trade, and forced labor, 13
British Empire,
    in Palestine, 231–232
    slave trade, 36
Bubonic plague (Black Death), 208
Buckle, Henry Thomas, 172
Buddha, 35–36, 187
    See also **Buddhism**
Buddhism, 3, 5, **37–45,** 50–51, 220
    basic beliefs, 37–43
    change and, 44
    China, 41–44, 62
    Chinese traditional religion and, 46–52
    Confucianism and, 62
    Daoism and, 71, 75, 72
    India, growth in, 38–39, 180
    in Japan, 41–42
    Mahayana, 3, 5, 39
    missionaries and, 136, 137–138
    pilgrimage and, 167–169
    sacred law, 119
    Silk Roads and spread of, 39–40

    spread of, map, 42
    Theravada, 39
    Vajrayana (Tantric), 39
    warfare, 187–188
    in West, 43–44
    Zen (Chan), 43–44
    See also **Buddha**
Byzantine Empire,
    caesaropapism, 178
    end of, 35
Byzantine rite. *See* **Christian orthodoxy**

C

Caesaropapism, 178
Calendars, Christian orthodox, 55
Calixtus, 202
Calvin, John, 172, 175, 191
Cambodia, religions, 39
Canada, religions, 6, 211, 227 (*See also* **Native American religions**)
Candlin, George T., 162
Candomble religion, 203
Canon law, 121, 207
Caribbean region. *See* **African American and Caribbean religions**
Caste system (India), 84–86, 178, 182, 186
    See also **Mahavira**
Catholicism, Roman. *See* **Roman Catholicism**
Charisma, religious, 127
Charismatic movement, 162
Chiang Kai-shek, 111
Chile, 213
China,
    household rituals, 46–47
    Japanese invasion, 75
    religions, 209 (*See also* **Buddhism; Chinese traditional religions; Confucianism; Daoism; Missionaries**)
    Russia/Soviet Union, relations with, 46
Chinese traditional religion, 46–52
    Buddhism, 50–51
    Daoism, 48–49
    household rituals, 46–47
    public rituals, 47–48
    Supreme Deity, 48–49
    Syncretism, 51
    See also **Buddhism; Confucianism; Daoism**
Christ. *See* **Jesus**
Christian orthodoxy, 53–58
    apophatic theology, 56–57
    atonement, 57–58
    Eastern and Oriental Orthodox churches, 53

Notes: 1) Names, terms, and page-number ranges in **bold** denote chapter entries.

INDEX · 239

Christian orthodoxy *(continued)*
    Grace versus Free Will, 58
    Great Schism, 54–55
    liturgical theology, 55–56
    moral theology, 58
    mystical theology, 56
    Original Sin, 57
    science and religion, 58
    Soteriology, 58
    spiritual theology, 58
    theological authority, 53
    Trinity, 57
    See also **Roman Catholicism**
Christianity, 2–4
    in Africa (*See* **African religions**)
    creation myth, 65
    Daoism and, 75
    ecumenicim, 78–80
    as mass movement, 8
    mysticism and, 148–151
    Christian orthodoxy, 53–58
    pacifism and just wars, 184–185
    Paul, Saint, 120, 159–160, 207
    pilgrimage and, 166–169
    sacred law, 121
    slavery and, 15, 17
    in twenty-first century, 7
    See also **Roman Catholicism; Missionaries;**
        Protestantism
Church of England, 171
Church-state law. *See* **Law, sacred**
Church year, 55
Circumcision, 104
Citizenship, Catholic Church, role of, 207
Coffee, 13
Colonialism, League of Nations mandates, 232
Communism and socialism, religion and, 7
Confucianism, 60–64
    Chinese traditional religion and, 46, 49
    Daoism and, 71, 72, 74
    development of, 74
    early, 60
    ecumenicism, 78
    modern, 63
    Neo-Confucianism, 62–63, 221
    state, 61–62
Confucius, 60–61
Congo [Kongo], Democratic Republic of, 13
Congo [Kongo] Free State (Belgian Congo), 211
Constantine the Great, 184
Constantinople

    Council of, 78
    crusades, 190
    Ottoman conquest, 5
Copernicus, Nicolas, harassment of, 7
Coptic Church, 23, 186
Cosmology, Native American religions and, 156–157
Council of Chalcedon, 54
Council of Constantinople, 54
Council of Ephesus, 54
Council of Nicea, 78
Council of Trent, 206, 208
Creation myths, 65–70
    Native American, 155–156
Crusades, the, 190
    Christian theory of just war, 184–185
Cuba,
    Afro-Cuban music, 19
    Santeria religion, 15, 16, 17, 203
    slave trade, 13, 14
Cumont, Franz, 201
Cyrus II, 179

D

Damascus (pope), 207
Dao (the Way). *See* **Daoism**
Daodejing (Tao-te Ching—The Way and the Power),
    112–114
Daoism, 3, 48–49, 62, **71–77**, 112–114
    basic concepts, 72
    Chinese popular religion and, 46, 49–50
    Chinese syncretism and, 72
    development of, 74–75
    mysticism and, 148
    spread/influence of, 75–76
    See also **Laozi**
Darius I, king of Persia, 179
Das, Guru Amar, 226
De Gaulle, Charles, 90
Diderot, Denis, 202
Divine right of monarchs, 48, 178
Dogon (Mali), 22
    creation myth, 66–68
Dominican Republic, 14
Dong Zhongshu, 61–62
Dowie, J. A., 161
Dreaming and animism, 26

E

Eastern and Oriental Orthodox churches. *See* **Christian**
    orthodoxy
Eastern Orthodox Church, 53, 190

240 · RELIGION AND BELIEF SYSTEMS IN WORLD HISTORY

Eastern Orthodox Church *(continued)*
  caesaropapism, 178
  ecumenicism, 78–81
  Great Schism from Roman Catholic Church, 4, 78,
    207
  See also **Christian orthodoxy**
Ecumenicism, 78–81
  See also **Religious freedom; Religious
    synchronicity**
Edict of Milan, 189
Education. *See* **Missionaries**
Edwards, Jonathan, 175
Egypt, 5
  religions, 178–179
Eisai, Myozen, 43
Empire. *See* **Religion and government**
Engines of history, animism, importance of. *See* **Animism**
Enlightenment, the, 7
  religion and government/politics, 180
Erasmus, Desiderius, 172, 202
Ethiopia,
  Haile Selassie, 16
  religions, 23
Europe,
  Catholic Church, 205
  religions, 5, 7, 115, 116
Evangelical, defined, 172

F
Farrakhan, Louis, 18
Fascism, 7
Festivals,
  Hindu, 84
  See also **Pilgrimage**
First Council of Constantinople, 54
First Council of Nicaea, 53
Flute Society, Hopi, 154
Foraging societies, animism, 26
Freedom. *See* **Religious freedom**
French Congo, 211
French Empire, new empire, 104–111
Friedman, Jonathan, 200
Fulani, 23

G
Galileo Galilei, 7
  Catholic Church and, 208
Gandhi, Mohandas, 178
  assassination, 198

Jainism and, 99
Gaozu, Han, 61
Gautama, Siddhartha. *See* **Buddha**
Genesis, 10–11, 65, 182
Germany, religions, 5–6
Ghana, religions in, 23
Ghost Dance movement, 130
Glazier, Stephen D., 203
Gospel music, 19
Government, theocracies, 178
Grace versus Free Will (Christian orthodoxy), 58
Graham, Billy, 197
Great Schism, 54–55
  See also **Christian orthodoxy**
Great Western Schism, 208
Greece, ancient,
  religions, 1
  syncretism, concept of, 200–202
Greek Orthodox churches, 57
  See also **Christian orthodoxy**
Gregory IX (pope), 190
Gregory VII (pope), 180
  See also **Roman Catholicism**
Grenada, 16
Griaule, Marcel, 66–68
Grotius, Hugo, 185
Guanyin, 50
Gush Emunim, 195, 196, 197
Gutenberg, Johannes, 6

H
Haile Selassie, 16
Haiti, Vodun religion, 15, 16, 17, 18, 203
Hajj, 166
Hammurabi, Code of, 107, 178
Han dynasty,
  Laozi, 112–114
  religions, 61–62
  state Confucianism, 61–62
Han Wendi, 62
Han Wudi, 62, 74–75
  See also **Confucianism**
Hausa states, 24
Hawaii, missionaries in, 134
Hebrew Bible, 10–11
Hebrew language, 231
Hebrew people, 2–3
  See also **Judaism**
Hedgewar, Keshav Baliram, 197
Hegel, Georg Wilhelm Friedrich, Daoism, opinion of, 75
Heidegger, Martin, 76

Notes: 1) Names, terms, and page-number ranges in **bold** denote
chapter entries.

INDEX · 241

Henry the Navigator, 62
Herskovits, Melville J., 203
Herzl, Theodor, 231
Hess, Moses, 231
Hinduism, 3, 7, **82–89,** 178–179
  development of, 37
  education, 86
  fundamentalism, 195
  government and, 84–86
  medicine and, 87
  origins, 82–83
  philosophy and, 87
  rituals, 84–85
  sacred areas, 83–84
  societal hierarchy, 84–85
  tradition, transmission of, 86
  warfare and, 186–187
  world history and, 88
Hispaniola, 14
Hitler, Adolf, 232
  as secular messiah, 128
Holocaust. *See* **Judaism**
Hooker, Richard, 175
Hsuan-tsang, 40
Hsü Shen, 46
Hubmaier, Balthasar, 180
Human rights, 180
Hus, Jan, 979, 172
Hussein, Sherif, 232

I

I Ching (Classic of Changes). *See* **Confucianism**
Ibn Rushd (Averroes), 228–229
Ibn Sina, 228
Ibo, 22
India,
  independence, 86–87
  religions, 5, 38–39, 40, 180, 198 (*See also*
    Hinduism; Jainism)
Innocent III (pope), 191
Inquisition (Holy Office), 134, 190–191, 207–208
Iran,
  Islam in, 93–95
  religious fundamentalism, 195–198
  Zoroastrianism, 234–235
Iraq, Islam in, 94–96
Islam, 4, **90–97**
  in Africa (*See* **African religions**)
  African Americans and, 13
  caliphs, era of, 91–92
  development of, 92–96

ecumenicism, 78
  as a growing movement (21st c.), 7–8
  missionaries and, 139–140
  modern era, challenges of, 93–96
  mysticism (Sufism) and, 150
  pilgrimages, 166–167, 169
  Ramadan, 139
  See also **Muhammad; Pilgrimage**
Islamic law, 120
  See also **Islam; Muhammad**
Islamic world,
  facism and fundamentalism, 195–198
  slavery in, 15
Israel, 231–233

J

Jade Emperor, 48–49
Jainism, 98–100, 148, 168
  See also **Mahavira**
Jamaica, slave trade, 13
Japan, 41–43
  Daoism in, 75
  religions, 3, 39, 63, 188, 189, 212 (*See also* **Shinto**)
Japanese Empire,
  missionaries in, 133, 134, 135, 137
  See also **Shinto**
Jaspers, Karl, 3
Jazz, 19
Jefferson, Thomas, government, form of, 174
Jesus, 4, **101–103**
  millennial movements and, 128, 130
  pilgrimage and, 167
  Protestantism and, 174
  Roman Catholicism and, 205–206
  on war, 184
  See also **Christian orthodoxy; Paul, Saint;
    Pentecostalism**
Jews. *See* **Judaism**
Jia Yi, 62
Jihad, 90, 95
  Hausa states, and, 186
Johnson, Todd M., 163
John the Baptist, 102
John XXIII (pope), 209
Jones, C. P, 162
Judaism, 3–5, **104–111**
  Babylonia captivity, 4
  covenant, 106–107
  diaspora, 4
  duties of, 107
  election (doctrine of), 105–106

242 · RELIGION AND BELIEF SYSTEMS IN WORLD HISTORY

Judaism *(continued)*
    fundamentalism, 195–197
    from Israelites to Jews, 107–108
    missionaries and, 135–136
    modern period, 110–111
    mysticism and, 150
    origins, impact of, 104–105
    pilgrimage and, 166–169
    rabbis and, 109–110
    sacred law, 119
    warrior ethic, debating, 182–183
    Zionism, 231–233
    See also **Abraham; Moses; Zionism**
Jung, Karl, 76

K
Kafka, Franz, 76
Kalabari, 14
Kamikaze attacks, 222
Kanem-Bornu, 22
Kapleau, Philip, 44
Kataphatic theology, 56
Khomeini, Ayatollah Ruhollah, 196, 198
Kigen, Dogen, 43
King, Martin Luther, Jr., 178
Kinship, 21
Kongo, 13, 14
Kongo [Congo], Democratic Republic of the, 13, 211
Kongo [Congo] Free State (Belgian Congo), 211
Korea, 39
    religions, 39, 63, 75
Kuhlman, Kathryn, 162
Kushan Empire, Buddhism, 39

L
Lantern Pagoda, 73
Lao Dan. *See* **Laozi**
Laozi, 71–74, **112–114,** 150
    See also **Confucianism; Daoism**
Latin America, religions, 112, 119
Latter-Day Saints, 115–118
    See also **Religious freedom**
Law, sacred, 119–121
    See also **Christian orthodoxy; Judaism; Religion and government**
League of Nations, 232
Letters and correspondence. *See* **Missionaries**
Li Bai, 113
Liberia (Africa), 21

Lind, Millard, 183
Liturgical theology (orthodox Christian), 55–56
Liturgy, Roman Catholic, 206
Lloyd George, David, 232
Lu Jia, 61
Luther, Martin, 6
    Ninety-Five Theses, posting of, 208
    religious freedom and, 191
    See also **Protestantism**

M
Madison, James, 174
Magisterium, Roman Catholic, 206
Mahavira, 98, **122–123**
    See also **Jainism**
Mahayana Buddhism, 50 (*See also* **Buddhism**)
Mahmud II, Ottoman sultan, 93
Mali,
    religions in, 22
    slave trade, 13
Mandate of Heaven, 178
Manichaeism, 124–126
Mao Zedong, secularism and Maoism, 7
Maori, 130–131
Mason, Charles H., 162
McMahon, Henry, 232
Mecca, 90–91
    See also **Muhammad; Pilgrimage**
Medicine, Ayurvedic, 87
Mencius, 61
    See also **Confucianism**
Mennonites, 173
Methodism, 17
Millennialism, 127–131
Ming dynasty, and Daoism, 75
Missionaries, 132–141
    Buddhist, 137–138
    in China, 179
    colonialism and, 135
    as cultural imperialism, 133–134
    ecumenicism and, 78–81
    Islamic world, 135, 139–140
    Mormon (Latter-Day Saints), 116
    outlook for, 140
    See also **Buddha; Jesus; Muhammad; Paul, Saint; Thomas Aquinas, Saint**
Modernity, ecumenicism in, 78
Mohammad Mirza 'Ali (Bab, the), 31
Mongol Empire, religions, 40, 179
Monotheism, 10–11, 105, 104
    See also **Islam; Judaism**

Notes: 1) Names, terms, and page-number ranges in **bold** denote chapter entries.

INDEX · 243

Moral theology, 58
Mormon Church, 115
Moses, 142–144, 183
    See also **Judaism**
Muhammad, 2, 5, 145–147
    as ruler and soldier, 185–186
    See also **Islam**
Muhammad, Elijah, 18
Muhammad, Wallace D., 18
Muslim Brotherhood, 196–198
Myanmar (Burma), 82
    religions, 39
Mystical theology (in Christian orthodoxy), 56
Mysticism, 148–151
    See also **Buddhism; Daoism; Jainism**

N
Nanak, Guru, 148, 225–226
Nasir, Gamal Abd al-, 95
Nation of Islam, 18
Nationalism—overview, Catholic Church and, 208
Native American religions, 152–158
    differences in, 153–154
    diversity of, 152
    historical consciousness, 158
    history, 153–155
    linkages, 157–158
    narratives, 155–156
    See also **Shamanism**
Nazi Germany, 6, 232
    Catholic Church, role of, 208–209
Nehru, Jawaharlal, 86
Neo-Confucianism, 62–63, 221
Nepal, Buddha, birth of, 35
Nestorian Christianity, 53
New Age, 24, 202
New Testament, 4, 205
    Abraham in, 10–11
New Year festivals, Chinese, 49, 73
New York City, African American and Caribbean religions
    in, 16–18
Nicaea, Council of, 78
Nicene-Constantinopolitan Creed, 54
Ninety-Five Theses, 208
Nonviolence, 98
    See also **Mahavira**
North America, shamanism in, 213

O
Old Testament, 57
    See also **Judaism**
Open Door treaties, Japan, 134

Oriental Orthodox Churches, 53
Original Sin, 57
Orthodox Christianity. *See* **Christian orthodoxy**
Orthodox Church. *See* **Christian orthodoxy**
Orthodoxy. *See* **Christian orthodoxy**
Ottoman Empire, religions, 5, 179–181

P
Pacifism, 184, 187
Paleolithic (foraging) era,
    animism, 26
    shamanism, 213
Palestine, 3, 4
    Zionism, 231–233
Parham, Charles, 161
Parthenon, 2, 166
Paul, Saint, 207, 209, 121, **159–160**
    See also **Jesus**
Peel, J. Y. D., 203
Pentateuch, 119
Pentecostalism, 7, 161–165
    See also **Missionaries; Religious fundamentalism**
Persian Empire,
    Baha'i religion, founding of, 31
    religious tolerance, 179
    See also **Zoroastrianism**
Peter, Saint, 205, 206, 207
Peter of Cluny, 190
Phenomenology, 176
Philippines, religions, 82, 205, 211–212
Philokalia, 58
Philosophy, Hinduism and, 82–89
Philosophy, Asian. *See* **Confucianism; Buddha;**
        Buddhism; Daoism; Hinduism; Jainism
Photian Schism, 54
Pilgrimage, 166–170
    to Mecca, 90
    See also **Buddhism; Hinduism; Islam; Jainism;**
        Judaism; Missionaries; Muhammad;
        Protestantism; Roman Catholicism
Pinsker, Leo, 231
Pius IX (pope), 208
Pius X (pope), 208
Pius XII (pope), 208–209
Plutarch, 200
Poland, 208
Political thought. *See* **Laozi**
Polygamy, 116
Popes, 178
    early history of, 207
    infallibility of, 208, 209
    role in Catholic Church of, 205

244 · AFRICA IN WORLD HISTORY

Poro society (Liberia), 21
Protestant Reformation, 208
   religious intolerance during, 191–192
Protestantism, 103, **171–177**, 191
   African Americans and, 17–18
   Catholic Church and, 209, 211
   ecumenicism, 78–79
   fundamentalism, 195
   Pentecostalism, 161–165, 7
   See also **Missionaries; Religious fundamentalism**
Puerto Rico, 13

Q

Qin dynasty, 61, 113
Qing dynasty, religions, 75, 179
Qur'an, 5, 90, 92, 145
   Abraham, 10–12
   Islamic law, 145
   war, 185
Qutb, Sayyid, 198

R

Rabbinic Judaism, 109
Rastafarianism, 15–17, 18
Religion. *See* **Religion and government; Religion and war; Religion—overview; Religious freedom; Religious fundamentalism; Religious syncretism;** *individual religions*
Religion and government, 178–181
   Shinto, 219–223
   war and. *See* **Islam**
   See also **Religious freedom**
Religion and war, 178, **182–188**
   See also **Religion and government; Religious freedom**
Religion—overview, 1–9
   contemporary world, functions of religion in, 7–8
   divided Christendom, 4–5
   Islam, rise of, 4–5
   Latter-day Saints, 115–117
   religious expansion and division, 5–6
   religious survival and revival, 7
   renaissance, enlightenment, and secularism, 6–7
   See also **African American and Caribbean religion; African religions; Bahá'í; Buddhism; Christian orthodoxy; Daoism; Hinduism; Islam; Judaism; Pentecostalism; Protestantism; Religion and government; Religion and war; Religious fundamentalism; Roman Catholicism; Shinto**

Religious freedom, 189–194
   internationalization of, 189
   medieval church, union of church and state in, 189
   Mormonism, 117
   reformation, intolerance during, 191–192
   in United States, 192
   See also **Religion and government; Religion and war**
Religious fundamentalism, 195–199
   al-Qaeda, 95, 131, 198
   See also **Manichaeism; Pentecostalism**
Religious syncretism, 200–204
   African American and Caribbean religions, 16
   Chinese traditional religion, 46, 51
   Daoism, 72
   Shinto, 220
Renaissance, and religion, 6–7
Revolution—Haiti, 13
Revolution—Iran, 198
Ricci, Matteo, 75
   See also **Missionaries**
Roberts, Oral, 162
Roman Catholicism, 205–212
   in Africa (*See* **African religions**)
   African-Americans and, 19
   basic teachings, 205–206
   contemporary trends/problems, 205, 209
   ecumenicism, 78–80
   education of children, 207
   major historical developments, 180, 205–206 (*See also* **Christian orthodoxy**)
   non-European, 212
   in twenty-first century, 7
   See also **Augustine, Saint; Missionaries; Paul, Saint; Pilgrimage; Religion and war**
Roman Empire,
   Catholic Church and, 209
   religions, 3–4, 178–179, 180
   secularism, 6
   syncretism, concept of, 200–202
Romanticism, 202
Rublev, Andrei, 57
Russian Soviet Empire, Palestine and, 233
Russo-Japanese Wars, 222

S

Sacraments, Roman Catholic, 206
Sacred law. *See* **Law, sacred**
Saint Vincent Island, 16
St. Augustine of Hippo. *See* **Augustine, Saint**
Sanctified churches, 18, 19

INDEX · 245

Sande society (Liberia), 21
Sangh, Rashtriya Swayamsevak, 197
Santeria, Cuban, 15, 16, 17, 203
Sargon, 142
Sasanian Empire. *See* **Manichaeism; Zoroastrianism**
Scandinavia, early religion, 182
Second Coming, the, 127, 131
Second Council of Constantinople, 54
Second Council of Nicaea, 54
Secret societies, African, 21
Secularism, 6–7
Senegal, 13
September 11, 2001, terrorist attacks, 131
Servetus, Michael, 191
Shakarian, Demos, 163
Shamanism, 213–218
  See also **Animism**
Shang dynasty, 48
Shi'a Muslims, 91, 92
Shinto, 219–224
Sho⁻mu, Emperor, 220
Siberia, 213
Siddhartha Gautama. *See* **Buddha**
Sikhism, 149–150, 168, **225–227**
Silk Roads, Buddhism, spread of, 39–40
Sima Qian, 112
Singh, Guru Gobind, 225, 226
Sino-Japanese Wars, 222
Sioux. *See* **Native American religions**
Slave trades,
  Caribbean region. *See* **African American and Caribbean religions**
  religion, role of, 13–15, 17
Smith, Joseph, Jr., 117
Song dynasty, religions, 43, 48, 62
Songhai, 22
Soteriology, 58
South Africa,
  nonviolence in, 99
  religions, 203
Southern Baptist Convention, 18
Spanish Empire, Catholicism and, 210
Spiritual Baptists, 16, 17, 18, 203
Spiritual Churches, 19
Spiritual theology, 58
Spirituality. *See* **Animism; Creation myths; Mysticism**
Sri Lanka (Ceylon), 5
  religions, 39
State Shinto. *See* **Shinto**
Stonehenge, 2
Stupas, Buddhist, 40

Suarez, Francisco, 184
Sudan, religions, 21–22
Sufism, 93
Sui dynasty, 62
Sunni Muslims, 91
Supreme being (deity),
  in African religions, 21–22
  in Chinese traditional religion, 48–49
Suzuki, D. T., 43
Suzuki, Shunryu, 43
Swaggart, Jimmy, 163
Sykes-Picot Agreement, 231
Syncretism. *See* **Religious syncretism**
Syria, 5

T
Taiwan, religions, 46, 75
Tang dynasty, religion and, 39, 62
Terrorism. *See* **Religion and war**
Textiles, jacquard, 230
Thailand, religions, 39
Theocracies, 178–179
Theodosius I, 189–190
Theological authority, 53
Third Council of Constantinople, 54
Thomas Aquinas, Saint, 185, 207, **228–230**
  See also **Roman Catholicism**
Tiriki, 22
Tokugawa shogunate, 135
Tolstoy, Leo, 75
Tomlinson, A.J., 161
Torah, 107–108, 119
Tourism. *See* **Pilgrimage**
Trade, Islam's expansion and, 91–92
Travel guides. *See* **Pilgrimage**
Treaty of Westphalia, religious tolerance, 180
Treblinka (concentration camp), 191
Trinidad and Tobago,
  slave trade, 13
  Spiritual Baptist religion, 16
Trinity, Holy (Christian orthodoxy), 57
Turkey, Islam in, 95
Tyndale, William, 172

U
Uganda, 211
'Umar ibn al-Khattab. *See* **Islam**
Umayyad caliphate, 91
Umbanda religion, 203
Ummah, 145, 146
United Nations, Israel, founding of, 232–233

246 · RELIGION AND BELIEF SYSTEMS IN WORLD HISTORY

United States of America
   Israel and, 233
   Pentecostalism in, 162–163
   religions, 43, 205, 211, 180–182, 192–198
   slavery and slave trade, 13, 14, 17
Universal Declaration of Human Rights, 180, 193
Universe, origins of. *See* **Creation myths**
Universities. *See* **Missionaries; Thomas Aquinas, Saint**
Untouchables, 85
Urban II (pope), 184, 190
   See also **Roman Catholicism**

V

Vatican II Council, 206, 209, 211
Vedas and vedic culture, 82–84
   creation myth, 67–69
Venezuela, 16
Verger, Pierre, 14
Victoria (queen of Great Britain), 34
Vivekananda, Swami, 148
Vodun, Haitian, 15, 16, 17, 18, 203

W

Wagadu Empire. *See* **African religions**
War and peace—overview. *See* **Religion and war**
Warfare, religion and. *See* **Religion and war**
Weizman, Chaim, 232
Wendi, Han, 62
Werbner, Richard, 200
Williams, Roger, 180
Women, Catholic Church and, 208, 209
World Council of Churches, 79
World history, oral history, 156
World history, writing of. *See* **Creation myths**
World Missionary Conference, 79
World War II,
   Catholic Church, role of, 208
   Shinto, role of, 221–222
Wycliffe, John, 172

X

X, Malcolm, 18
Xuanzang, 40
Xunzi, 61

Y

Yahweh, 143, 182
Yasakuni Shrine, 221–222
Yin and yang, 72, 75
Yoga, 148–149
Yoruba (Nigeria), 13, 14, 16, 19, 21, 22
Yoshida Shinto, 221
Young, Brigham, 116

Z

Zaire, 13
Zen Buddhism. *See* **Buddhism**
Zhen Zong, 48
Zhou dynasty, 48
Zhuangzi (philosopher and eponymous text), 71, 73, 74
Zionism, 231–233
   See also **Judaism**
Zoroastrianism, 124–125, **234–235**
Zwingli, Huldreich, 172

Editorial Board and Staff

Editors

David Christian, *Macquarie University, Sydney*
William H McNeill, *University of Chicago, Emeritus*
Jerry H. Bentley, *University of Hawaii, Manoa*
Ralph C. Croizier, *University of Victoria*
J. R. McNeill, *Georgetown University*
Heidi Roupp, *World History Center*
Judith P. Zinsser, *Miami University*

Associate Editor

Brett Bowden, *University of Western Sydney*

Advisory Board

Ross E. Dunn, *San Diego State University*
Ryba Epstein, *Rich East High School*
Brian Fagan, *University of California, Santa Barbara*
Daniel R. Headrick, *Roosevelt University, Emeritus*
Kailai Huang, *Massachusetts College of Liberal Arts*
Marnie Hughes-Warrington, *Macquarie University*
Tom Laichas, *Crossroads School*
Craig Lockard, *University of Wisconsin, Green Bay*
Pamela McVay, *Ursuline College*
Carl Nightingale, *University of Wisconsin, Milwaukee*
Patrick O'Brien, *London School of Economics*
Hugh Page Jr., *University of Notre Dame*
Paul Philip, *Lancaster High School*
Mrinalini Sinha, *Pennsylvania State University*
Peer Vries, *Leiden University*

Publisher

Karen Christensen

Senior Staff Editor

Mary Bagg

Editorial Staff

Kathy Brock
Rachel Christensen
Hillary Cox
David Gagne
Barbara Resch
Ashley Winseck
Chris Yurko

Design and Photo Research

Anna Myers

Cover Art

Cave-art illustration: Lisa Clark

Front cover images, left-to-right:

1. Guercino, *Abraham Casting Out Hagar and Ishmael* (1657). Pinacoteca di Brera, Milan.
2. A Shi'a Shrine in Capetown, South Africa. Photo by Frank Salamone.
3. Sculptural representation of the Buddha, from the Gandharan region of northern Pakistan (first century CE). Musée Guimet, Paris.

Back cover images, left-to-right:

1. Ganesh, also called the Remover of Obstacles, is one of the best-known Hindu gods.
2. Mosaic design from the Dome of the Rock.
3. Tomb of the Bab, Mount Carmel, Israel. Photo by Tom Habibi.

Author Credits

Religion and Belief Systems in World History—Introduction
by **Martin E. Marty**
University of Chicago, Emeritus

Abraham
by **Reuven Firestone**
Hebrew Union College

Animism
by **David Christian**
Macquarie University, Sydney

Augustine, Saint
by **Elisa A. Carrillo**
Marymount College of Fordham University

Bahá'í
by **Stephen N. Lambden**
Ohio University

Buddha
by **Leo Lefebure**
Fordham University

Buddhism
by **Phillip Whigham**
Georgetown University

Christian Orthodoxy
Allyne L. Smith Jr.
St. Joseph Center

Creation Myths
David Christian
Macquarie University, Sydney
Ewha Womans University, Seoul

Chinese Traditional Religion
by **Michael C. Lazich**
Buffalo State College

Confucianism
Daniel W. Y. Kwok
University of Hawaii

Daoism
by Maritere Lopez
California State University, Fresno

Ecumenicism
by Adam K. Webb
Princeton University

Hinduism
by Klaus K. Klostermaier
University of Manitoba

Islam
by John O. Voll
Georgetown University

Jainism
by Christopher Key Chapple
Loyola Marymount University

Jesus
by Bill Leadbetter
Edith Cowan University

Judaism
by Reuven Firestone
Hebrew Union College

Laozi
by Lily Hwa
University of St. Thomas, Minnesota

Latter-Day Saints
by Elizabeth A. Sewell
Brigham Young University

Law, Sacred
by Douglas Palmer
Emory University

Mahavira
by Tara Sethia
California State Polytechnic University

Manichaeism
by Timothy M. Renick
Georgia State University

Millennialism
by Catherine Wessinger
Loyola University

Missionaries
by Roger B. Beck
Eastern Illinois University

Moses
by Theodore Burgh
University of North Carolina Wilmington

Muhammad
by Karim Khan
University of Hawaii, Leeward

Mysticism
by Paul Oliver
University of Huddersfield

Native American Religions
by John A. Grim
Yale University

Paul, Saint
by Stacy Davis
University of Notre Dame

Pentecostalism
by Hans A. Baer
University of Melbourne

Pilgrimage
by Simon M. Coleman
Centre for the Study of Religion, University of Toronto

Protestantism
by Martin E. Marty
University of Chicago, Emeritus

Religion and Government
by Elizabeth A. Sewell
Brigham Young University

Religion and War
by Timothy M. Renick
Georgia State University

Religious Freedom
by Derek H. Davis
University of Mary Hardin-Baylor

Religious Fundamentalism
by Martin E. Marty
University of Chicago, Emeritus

Religious Syncretism
by Stephen D. Glazier
University of Nebraska, Lincoln

Roman Catholicism
by Elisa A. Carillo
Marymount College of Fordham University

Shamanism
by Peter F. Laird
Independent scholar, Farmingdale, New York

Shinto
by Mark McNally
University of Hawaii

Sikhism
by Paul Oliver
University of Huddersfield

Thomas Aquinas, Saint
by Scott C. Wells
California State University, Los Angeles

Zionism
by Mark McCallon
Abilene Christian University

Zoroastrianism
by ouraj Daryaee
University of California, Irvine

This **BERKSHIRE** *Essentials* book was distilled from the

Berkshire Encyclopedia of World History 2ND EDITION

AWARDS
Library Journal Best Reference Source
Booklist Editor's Choice
Choice Outstanding Academic Title

William H. McNeill

Jerry H. Bentley, David Christian,

Ralph C. Croizier, J. R. McNeill,

Heidi Roupp, and Judith P. Zinsser

Editors

Brett Bowden

Associate Editor

This landmark work has grown from 5 to 6 volumes and includes over 100 new articles on environmental history, world art, global communications, and information technology, as well as updates on events such as earthquakes and the global economic crisis. Hundreds of new illustrations enhance visual appeal, while updated Further Reading sections guide readers toward continued study.

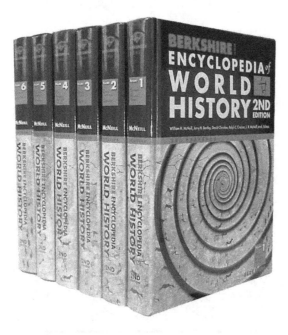

CHOICE

"Challenging traditional encyclopedias that offer the standard who, what, when, and where, the second edition of the *Berkshire Encyclopedia of World History* continues to focus on cultural comparisons and interactions using broad themes. The second edition offers much more material on such distinctive and interdisciplinary entries. Groups of entries, such as the nine on trading patterns and the nine on revolutions, allow for easy comparisons between cultures. The big, traditional encyclopedias lack much of the unique content offered in this work, and do not focus on the historical significance of topics such as sweet potatoes and trees or discuss emerging trends such as "big history" and trade cycles. **Summing Up:** Highly recommended. Lower-division undergraduates and above; general readers."

6 VOLUMES • 978-1-933782-65-2
Price: US$875 • 3,152 pages • 8½ × 11"

Booklist

"One of the great strengths of this unique resource is that although it is accessible to novices and younger users, it is still useful to more advanced researchers and scholars. It succeeds in tying specific and local histories to larger patterns and movements. Overall, this magnificent set provides an interconnected and holistic perspective on human history and is recommended for most libraries."

Award-winning supplementary materials

"This World of Ours" series

"I became an avid student of David Christian by watching his course, *Big History*, on DVD, so I am very happy to see his enlightening presentation of the world's history captured in these essays. I hope it will introduce a wider audience to this gifted scientist and teacher."
—Bill Gates

"It is hard to imagine that such a short book can cover such a vast span of time and space. *This Is China: The First 5,000 Years* will help teachers, students, and general readers alike, as they seek for a preliminary guide to the contexts and complexities of Chinese culture."
—Jonathan Spence, *Yale University*

"I only wish I had had *This Is China* available during my 15 years of teaching Chinese at the college level. A tremendous resource for both Chinese language students and teachers."
—Scott McGinnis, *Defense Language Institute, Washington DC*

Berkshire's series of very short books on very big topics in world history are designed to help teachers and students get the big picture on big, challenging aspects of history and culture. The books, written by well-known scholars, include illustrations, discussion questions, "thought experiments," and suggestions for further readings. Digital versions are also available.

MULTIPLE COPIES DISCOUNTS

2–10 copies, **10% off**

11–20 copies, **20% off**

21–30 copies, **30% off**

Order two or more copies of any title or combination of titles in the "This World of Ours" series for a multiple copies discount (when shipped to the same address). Orders for *This Fleeting World*, *This Is China*, and *This Is Islam* will ship immediately. Orders that include *This Is Africa*, *This Good Earth*, or *This Sporting World*, will ship upon publication.

This Fleeting World

A Short History of Humanity

David Christian, *Macquarie University, Sydney*

Available now : 978-1-933782-04-1
http://bit.ly/thisfleetingworld

This Is China

The First 5,000 Years

Editors: Haiwang Yuan, *Western Kentucky University Libraries*, Ronald G. Knapp, Margot E. Landman, Gregory Veeck

Available Now : 978-1-933782-20-1
http://bit.ly/thisischina

This Is Islam

From Muhammad and the Community of Believers to Islam in the Global Community

Jamal J. Elias, *University of Pennsylvannia*

This is Islam offers readers an introduction to one of the world's major religions, its philosophies, and how it affects the world today. Geared to those unfamiliar with the religion and its rituals and customs—and written in clear and simple terms by one of the United States' leading scholars of religion—this volume explains Islamic law, major figures and sects, and the role of mysticism.

Available Now : 978-1-933782-81-2
http://bit.ly/thisisislam

FORTHCOMING

This Good Earth
978-1-933782-86-7

This Sporting World
978-1-933782-91-1

This Is Africa
978-1-933782-93-5

This Is America
978-1-933782-95-9

EACH: $14.95 : 6 x 9" : 152 pages : Paperback : Hardcover and Digital editions also available

CPSIA information can be obtained
at www.ICGtesting.com
Printed in the USA
BVHW082300300519
549623BV00007B/62/P